W9-ATY-582

Give Her This Day

A DAYBOOK OF
WOMEN'S WORDS

July 14, 1992

To Nancy Gaffney
with my best wishes
Lois Stiles Edgerly

Give Her This Day

A DAYBOOK OF WOMEN'S WORDS

Edited and Compiled by
Lois Stiles Edgerly

Tilbury House, Publishers
GARDINER, MAINE

Tilbury House, Publishers
The Boston Building
132 Water Street
Gardiner, Maine 04345

Copyright © 1990 by Lois Stiles Edgerly
All Rights Reserved.
THIRD PRINTING.

Cover and text designed on Crummett Mountain by Edith Allard
Keyboarding by Cheryl Moloney, Perfection Typing, Weymouth, Massachusetts
Copyediting by Nessa Burns Reifsnyder and Janice Brackett
Layout by Nina Medina, Basil Hill Graphics, Coopers Mills, Maine
Imagesetting by High Resolutions, Inc., Camden, Maine
Covers and jackets printed by Western Maine Graphics, Norway, Maine
Text printed and bound by Thomson-Shore, Inc., Dexter, Michigan

Grateful acknowledgment is made to the following publishers and journals for permission to reprint this material:

Boston Herald, obituary dated April 14, 1941. Reprinted with permission of the *Boston Herald*.

Kansas Historical Quarterly, Vol. 37, Autumn 1971, No. 3, entitled "Roughing it on Her Kansas Claim: The Diary of Annie Bright, 1870-1871." Reprinted by permission of Kansas state Historical Society.

Pioneering in Arizona: The Reminiscences of Emerson Oliver Stratton & Edith Stratton Kitt (Tuscon: Arizona Pioneers' Historical Society, 1964), pp. 111-112. Reprinted by permission of Arizona Historical Society.

Covered Wagon Women, Diaries & Letters from the Western Trails, 1840-1890, edited by Kenneth L. Holmes and David C. Duniway, Glendale, CA, 1986. Reprinted by permission of The Arthur H. Clark Company.

Covered Wagon Women—Volume I and Volume VIII, compiled and edited by Kenneth Holmes, Glendale, CA, 1983, 1984. Reprinted by permission of The Arthur H. Clark Company.

Second Sowing: The Life of Mary Aloysia Hardy. New York: Sheed and Ward, 1942. Reprinted by permission of Sister Margaret Williams.

Diary of a Union Lady, by Harold Earl Hammond. Copyright 1962. Reprinted by permission of Harper & Row, Publishers, Inc.

The Diary of Mary Atkins: A Sabbatical in the Eighteen Sixties; Mills College, published in 1937. Reprinted by permission of The Eucalyptus Press.

Twentieth Century Pioneering—Our Frontier Days Experience at Riverton, Wyoming, by Mary Julia (Moore) Allyn, 1956. Reprinted by permission of Frank R. Allyn.

Boston Public Library Quarterly, January, 1958. Courtesy of the Trustees of the Boston Public Library.

Mary Florence Denton and Doshisha, published by the Doshisha University Press in 1955 and written by Frances Clapp. Reprinted by permission of Doshisha Archives.

Letters of Elizabeth Palmer Peabody: American Renaissance Woman, Copyright 1984 by Bruce A. Ronda. Reprinted by permission of University Press of New England.

Heart Throbs of the West, Volume IX, compiled by Kate B. Carter. Copyright 1948. Reprinted by permission of Daughters of Utah Pioneers.

An Interrupted Night, by Isabella Alden. Copyright 1929 by Isabella Alden. Reprinted by permission of Harper & Row, Publishers, Inc.

Clothespins and Calendars, Recollections of the Past, written by Eunice K. Halfmann, 1985. Reprinted by permission of Phoenix Publishing.

A Frontier Lady, Recollections of the Gold Rush and Early California. Copyright 1932. Reprinted by permission of Yale University Press.

Ladies Now and Then, by Beatrice Fairfax. Copyright 1944, 1972, by the author. Reprinted by permission of Curtis Brown, Ltd.

Library of Congress Cataloging-in-Publication Data

Give her this day : a daybook of women's words / edited, with
biographic and bibliographic notes by Lois Stiles Edgerly.
     p.   cm.
     Includes bibliographical references and index.
ISBN 0-937966-35-5 : $29.95 — ISBN 0-937966-36-3 (pbk.) : $15.95
1. Women—United States—History—19th century—Sources.
2. Women—United States—Biography. I. Edgerly, Lois Stiles, 1929- .
HQ1410.G58 1990   90-44745
305.4'0973—dc20   CIP

Contents

to my mother

Acknowledgments

First and foremost I want to thank the most important person in my life, my dear husband Will, for his unfailing encouragement and faith in what I was doing through all the years of research. His enthusiasm for the material I was collecting became infectious, and often it kept me from being discouraged.

My son Len and my daughter Stephanie have both contributed helpful ideas and moral support far beyond the call of duty to one's mother.

The loving participation of my granddaughters, Sarah and Roo, will always be a special memory for me.

Without the help of my wonderful friend, Lynne Spiegel, with the biographical sketches, it could have taken me another ten years to finish. She does everything well and can make anything happen.

My research assistant, Jennifer Pulver, could easily have been Sherlock Holmes' Watson. She helped me gather material from far and wide. The happy and amusing memories I have of us working together are a delight.

Through long months, Cheryl Moloney typed and retyped the manuscript and kept track of names and dates on her computer discs with the flair of a magician.

Margaret Dines kept me from chaos. Her organizational genius and patience with my dismal lack of organization made the impossible happen.

Mary Elizabeth Taft untiringly worked on the problems of missing dates and mixed-up photographs.

Anna Marshall Shields, Matti Vargas, Que Nguyen, Gillian Pendergrast and Susan Murphy assisted me in library searches.

Many of my friends helped me with their thoughtful ideas and encouragement. I am especially grateful to Mason Hammond, Jean Dalrymple, Susan Riecken, Laura Shapiro, Carl Scovel, Sonia Landes, Bill Crout,

John Betlyon, Anna Ashton, Donna and Richard Curtin, Mie Abe, Mary Martin, Helen Pierce, Jane Bell, Jane Scovell, Eve Fishbein, Joanna Scott, Dorothy Fairweather, Ellen Whalen, Martha Dryer, Celia Hubbard, Be Be Nixon, Rick Reed, Pam Leary, Genevieve Betlyon, Pauline Cooke, David Phillips, Elizabeth Altman, Louise Borke, Peggy Biggs, Doris Clements and Michael Djordjevich.

I have been truly blessed to have such a supportive editor as Mark Melnicove. Since the afternoon he first saw part of the manuscript over tea at my kitchen table, he has shared my vision and enthusiasm for this collection.

Lois Stiles Edgerly
August, 1990
Cambridge, Massachusetts

Foreword

Lois Edgerly assembled much of this book in a tiny, windowed carrel on the sixth floor of Widener Library at Harvard. It's quiet up there, except for the clack of typewriters or the softer thump of a word processor's keyboard; sometimes a pair of graduate students will chatter in whispers, but for the most part the only disturbances come from the long, dark shelves of books. They're dusty and somnolent in the heavy air, but they have a beseeching quality that can make you restless in a hard wooden chair. If you wander through the library in search of a particular volume, you're likely to take another from the shelf too, and then another, running a hand across pages clumped together from disuse or soft and shredding from age. Sometimes a bit of paper will crumble away as you lift it. At Widener you're allowed to check books out for an indefinite period if they remain in your carrel, so it's possible to keep your favorites with you day after long day, while you work. Once they're in your carrel, they become as reassuring as a trail of bread crumbs that promises to lead you back to your starting place. With your books in front of you, you will never be quite so lost as you fear.

Give Her This Day beautifully evokes its origins in libraries, manuscript collections and historical societies. Each voice exerts a special claim on us and each demands to be heard, though in some cases the demand is so modestly pitched it's likely that nobody but Lois Edgerly would ever have paid attention to it. "I learned to spin the summer after I was twelve," wrote Mary Phenix in a volume of memoirs she produced, when she was 70, at the request of her son. "That summer I spun enough yarn for a large carpet." Back in 1838, when this achievement took place, her accomplishment would have been both a family marvel and the measure of her useful femininity. Small wonder she remembered it for more than half a century. Lizzie Neblett wouldn't have dreamed of making public her joy and relief that a long labor and delivery had passed successfully, though she did hasten to write to her soldier husband: "The mountain of anxiety and dread has been removed, the time of exquisite suffering has been passed, and I this morning lie on a bed of ease, a free unshackled woman once more." This fragment from her 1863 letter tells us as much about the pain and exhilaration of childbirth as any of the tracts, poems and films that have ever tried to capture that experience.

All these bits from recorded lives take us home, back to our starting places. They do so with special immediacy because in most cases the writers are reflecting on a subject so personal it wasn't even classed as history until very recently. For the most part American history has been an account of men and wars, with an occasional nod to exemplary wives if they happened to be married to presidents. The great biographical dictionary *Notable American Women*, published in four volumes beginning in 1971, marked a turning point in the meaning of the word "history," because this new scholarship wrote women into the record for good. Even more dramatically, the arrival of such works as Jean Strouse's *Alice James* (1980) and Susan Strasser's *Never Done: A History of American Housework* (1982) expanded the record to include days and lives that had never before been considered worthy of comment, much less study and research. But more so than political machinations or battlefield victories, these lives explain the substance of the past.

Some of the women whose writings are excerpted here show up in *Notable American Women*; many others will have no memorial but this. Helen Hamilton Gardener, a turn-of-the-century writer and feminist, gave more thought to posterity than most: she agreed to will her brain to Cornell College, so that the school might have an opportunity to examine the brain of a thinking and productive female. A few enjoyed at least a touch of fame—Florence Nicholson Coates was voted poet laureate of Pennsylvania a few years before her death in 1926—but descended to obscurity almost immediately. Perhaps Mattie Truman's 1884 letter to her longtime friend Nan tells us most, in its way: here is a plainspoken description of respectable hell. Genteel women who preferred or were condemned to spinster-hood had few choices in life, and one that at least offered independence was teaching. Mattie travelled from one school to another in her native Missouri, boarding with local families. "I haven't even a comb, glass or table in my room and have to wash with the family," she moaned to her friend. "I just detest school teaching. I am nine miles from Lamar and will only get my mail about once in two weeks. . . . If I ever do get home I'll stay there. . . ." She never did, maybe because life at home for a spinster often meant living with relatives—not quite a servant, not quite a charity case, but something of both, and forever a symbol of failure. Mattie longed to marry but had no luck; she died at forty. Her nephew Harry Truman became president; even so, her own dreary life would have been forgotten had not a nephew of her friend Nan donated Mattie's letters to the Truman Library in Independence, Missouri. Mattie's sisters, thousands of them, had no such bloodline to immortality. Her lament—"Oh goodness if you could only see me you would pity me, of all the places I ever saw, this bangs the bobtail"—must stand for theirs.

More moving than a novel and more accurate than the daily paper, each of these fragments begs us to remember that the past was once real life, and that it happened in kitchens and porches and back bedrooms. *Give Her This Day* includes women who fought for their rights in the usual ways, but it was not their politics that won them a place here; rather, it was the truth of the heart as Lois Edgerly learned to read it. A book may bear "singular witness," wrote Louise Guiney, a poet of Romantic inclination, in 1907. "It is not a game of mere inferences. . . . [T]he page. . .stands up and blurts out 'I am true.'" How fortunate for these women that Lois Edgerly was there to hear them; and what a pleasure for us to listen in on their conversations with her.

Laura Shapiro

JANUARY

Maggie Cline

1897

... He led me into the President's room. President McKinley and his wife were alone and playing cribbage. I hesitated for a moment, as I know how annoyed I am when a person breaks in on a game of forty-five for ale at my own home. But Mr. McKinley was all smiles and gave me new confidence. He threw down his cards and stepped towards me.

"Maggie Cline, the Irish Queen. Well, I'm mighty glad to meet you. Permit me to introduce Mrs. McKinley." The President put out his hand, and I said: "If you don't mind, give me both hands." He said, "certainly," and we shook hands. "Maybe you don't know," said I, "why I asked for both hands." He laughed and said "No." "Well, to tell you the truth, when I get back to New York I'll charge my friends $10 apiece to shake the only pair of hands that shook both hands of the President." The President laughed, as did Mrs. McKinley.

... Mrs. McKinley showed much interest in my theatrical work, and asked me very many questions. She is an awfully sweet little woman.

It possibly never occurred to many people that the President and his wife resemble one another very much. I was struck with this fact. Then, too, they are the most companionable couple I ever met. They seem to be greatly devoted to one another.

Maggie Cline, vaudeville singer, was born January 1, 1857, in Haverhill, Massachusetts. She began working in a shoe factory when she was twelve, but became determined that such work was not to be her lot in life and at sixteen ran away to Boston. She joined the "March of the Amazons" at the Howard Theatre for $3 per week.

By the 1880's Maggie had become known as the "Irish Queen" and was popular in vaudeville houses along the eastern seaboard. At that time there were no power amplifiers, so a strong voice was important. Maggie's voice was legendary; it was said that when she sang in Boston "you could hear her in South Boston," and the headline of her obituary in the *Boston Globe* proclaimed, "Maggie Cline could roar like two hundred

Vaudeville Queen meets a President

Maggie's writing is from an article she wrote for the August 8, 1897, Sunday edition of The World. *Maggie liked publicity and often wrote amusing newspaper accounts about herself and her activities.*

men." Her singing was described as "vocalism made visible" and she told jokes as well as sang during her boisterous performances. Her most famous number was "Throw 'Em Down McCloskey" for which she paid the writer $5 and according to her estimate sang over 75,000 times.

Martha Carey Thomas

A young man's blunder

1906

My conversion to woman suffrage, like my mother's, took place one day in Baltimore in 1875, when a young man from Philadelphia was calling on me—we called them beaux in those days—and I took him into what was then called the back parlor to say good-night to my mother. She asked him a question about some matter connected with the approaching presidential election, and he replied, in the blundering outspokenness of youth, that he never discussed politics with women, because as everyone knew, they were not allowed to vote because their opinion on such subjects was of no serious importance. Although we were frequently thrown together in our social circle, from that day until the day of his death a few years ago I never spoke to him. But after all, his crime was only that of putting into brutal words what most men, and strange to say most women, seem to think.

Martha Carey Thomas, educator and feminist, was born January 2, 1857, in Baltimore, Maryland, to a prominent Quaker family. Minnie, as she was nicknamed, suffered bad burns in a kitchen fire at age seven that left her with a painful limp. It was during her recovery period that she discovered her lifelong passion for reading. Her father, a physician and trustee at John Hopkins University, was opposed to advanced education for women. In spite of his views, Minnie, with the help of her mother, persuaded him to allow her to enter Cornell University. At college she left "Minnie" behind in favor of her middle name, "Carey." After receiving a B.A. in 1877, she left for Europe to study and later became the first foreign woman to obtain a Ph.D. from the University of Zurich.

Carey's writing is from an address she gave to the National Suffrage Association in 1906.

When Bryn Mawr College was being established in 1880, Carey applied to the trustees (among whom were her father

---

Give Her This Day

and other relatives) for the position of president. They elected James E. Rhoads instead, but appointed her dean as well as an English professor. Carey was not very interested in teaching and much preferred to be an administrator. Nine years after the college opened, President Rhoads retired and Carey was elected president, a position she held for twenty-eight years.

In 1935, when she was seventy-nine, Carey spoke one last time at the fiftieth anniversary of Bryn Mawr College. She died a month later in Philadelphia. Her ashes are in the cloisters of the college library.

Lucretia Coffin Mott

May 28, 1875

. . . When in England, in 1840, I saw one of the Egyptian idols in the British Museum. Some one of our company said, "Well, they don't admit that they worship such ugly images as this; they look through and beyond this to one great Supreme Power." "They were scarcely more idolatrous," I answered, "than our Quaker friends when they read their Bible with such reverence last evening." They brought it out with great solemnity, and laid it on the lap of the one who was to read it, and he bowed before it, and then opened it and read it in what we Friends call the preaching tone. The passages read were those that had no particular bearing upon the lives and conduct of those then present, nor upon the special occasion which had brought us together; but it was "the Bible" and "Scripture," and a chapter of it must be read in order, and in a solemn tone. I said to the friend who was pointing out this idol to me in the Museum, that the worship of that image was like the worship of the Bible as we had observed it the evening before. To me *that* was the worship of an idol.

*T*he Bible as an idol

Lucretia Coffin Mott was born January 3, 1793, on the island of Nantucket, Massachusetts. Her Quaker upbringing taught her that men and women were created equal.

When Lucretia was thirteen she went to Quaker boarding school in New York State. Two years later she became an assistant teacher at the school. She found that female teachers were paid less than half of what men teachers received and this inequity started her interest in the women's rights movement.

Lucretia's writing is from a talk she gave to the Free Religious Association in Boston on May 28, 1875. It is included in the book Life and Letters of James and Lucretia Mott, *edited by their granddaughter and published in 1884.*

The Coffin family moved from New York to Philadelphia in 1809. James Mott, another teacher at the boarding school, had fallen in love with Lucretia and followed her to New York. Two years later they were married and remained together for fifty-seven happy years. James shared his wife's beliefs and was devoted to her. He supported her reform work by accompanying her on her speaking engagements. His presence gave her a respectability which other feminist leaders lacked.

Helen Kendrick Johnson

*T*ime of change

1909

The settlement of the great West, the opening of professions and trades to woman consequent upon the loss of more than a half million of the nation's most stalwart men . . . have tended to place man and woman, but especially woman, where something like a new heaven and a new earth are in the distant vision.

. . . To this change the Suffragists call attention, and say, "This is, in great part, our work."

. . . I believe the principles on which the claim to suffrage is founded are those that turn individuals and nations backward and not forward.

Helen Louise Kendrick Johnson, author and anti-suffragist, was born January 4, 1844, in Hamilton, New York.

Her earliest publications were several children's books known collectively as the "Roddy books." The series was very popular. In 1878 she wrote *Tears for Little Ones* after the death of her first two children. Writing the book helped her with her own grieving, but she also hoped it would help other parents in similar situations.

Helen became involved with the woman suffrage movement and was editor of the *American Woman's Journal* from 1894-1896. She later changed her mind about suffrage and became an outspoken anti-suffragist. In 1909 she wrote *Woman and The Republic*, in which she derided all of the suffragists' arguments. She concluded that women did not need the vote and was often harshly attacked by suffragists for this unpopular view.

Helen's writing is from her book, Woman and The Republic *(1909).*

Matilda Sissieretta Jones

December, 1932

Dear Sister:

I sincerely trust that your mother, yourself and all the folks are well and getting along during these hard times. With it all God has been mighty good to us. He has spared us to live to see another Christmas so near. We have everything to be thankful for.

I am feeling fine, thanks to the Lord, and I shall continue to thank Him and pray and trust Him until I am called. Give my love to your mother and do write and tell me how she is and Arthur also.

Love to all,

Cousin Sis

Matilda Sissieretta Joyner Jones, dramatic soprano, was born January 5, 1869, in Portsmouth, Virginia. Her father, a former slave, was a Baptist minister. The family left the South when Sissieretta was seven, when Reverend Joyner accepted a ministry in Providence, Rhode Island.

Sissieretta sang in her father's church and took voice lessons at the Providence Academy of Music. At fourteen she married David R. Jones, who claimed to be alternately a hotel bellman and a newspaper dealer when in fact he was a gambler and a reprobate. They had no children and she divorced him in 1898.

In 1896 Sissieretta became the leader of the Black Patti Troubadours, a unique touring group of black comedians, acrobats, dancers and singers. Sissieretta had long been referred to as "the black Patti," a reference to famous soprano Adelina Patti [February 10]. She disliked the comparison, but her managers and the press used it freely until she accepted it as the title of her ensemble. The Black Patti Troubadours performed successfully to primarily white audiences from 1896 to 1916. By 1916 the public's interest in such a spectacle had waned, and Sissieretta retired to her home in Providence.

Hard times

Sissieretta's letter is to her cousin Mrs. Melvina Newsome. Mrs. Newsome gave the letter to the Journal and Guide, *published in Norfolk, Virginia, and it was included in the memorial article the paper printed after Sissieretta's death.*

Mary Martha Truman

A teacher's laments

Lamar, Missouri
September 16, 1884
My Dear Nan,

I am going to write and tell you some of my troubles. I have commenced teaching again. I took the school and had a very nice place to board and the woman had to get sick and she is going to have a young one to boot so I had to leave and get a new boarding place. Oh goodness if you could only see me you would pity me, of all the places I ever saw, this bangs the bob tail. I could cry for the whole five months. I almost wish I'd get sick so that I could quit. I am in the hottest hole you ever stuck your head into. The perspiration is just running in streams. I haven't even a comb, glass or table in my room and have to wash with the family. I just *detest* school teaching. I am nine miles from Lamar and will only get my mail about once in two weeks. Oh! I am so homesick. I would rather wash for a living than teach and board at such a place. If I ever do get home I'll stay there. . . .

Write me a long letter and let me know what folks are doing in civilization. . . .

Yours in sorrow, Mattie

Mary Martha (Mattie) Truman was born January 6, 1860, in Platte County, Missouri. Despite the fact that she was President Harry S. Truman's aunt, there is little biographical information available outside of her letters to a school friend and a diary.

Mattie's letters are to Miss Nan Bentley, her college roommate at Stephens College in Columbia, Missouri. They graduated and went their separate ways in 1881; the letters cover the period 1882 to 1891.

There are two recurring themes in Mattie's letters: bad weather and lost love. Although there are many letters, it seems as if it was raining each time she wrote. In one letter she is despondent at not being able to attend church due to the rain and mud. In another she writes "the rain is just pouring down and the wind is blowing furious. . . . I think I'll migrate to some more genial clime, where there isn't [sic] any cyclones."

Mattie's letter is one of fifty-three that were donated to the Harry S. Truman Library in Independence, Missouri by Mr. J. R. Bentley. Mr. Bentley is the nephew of Miss Nan Bentley, to whom the letters were written.

Give Her This Day

Mattie spent her life teaching in various towns in Missouri and never married, despite frequent mention of love and her hopes to be married in letters to Nan. In a letter of 1882 she laments that everyone around her is getting married. In 1884 she is heartbroken because her widower/friend has deserted her for a music teacher.

Mattie died at the age of forty and is buried in Independence, Missouri.

Louise Guiney

1907

Now and then, in portraits of persons unknown to us, we catch a certain impression, or, rather, conviction of reality.

. . . The same very singular witness is often borne by a book. It is not a game of mere inferences: the book's secret, rather, is fired at us like a pistol shot. We see as inerrably as the Recording Angel into the author's interior. The metaphysical data are so direct and authentic that the page, like the picture, stands up and blurts out '*I am true.*' A trained reviewer, if he be worth his salt, must often, perhaps even almost always, be able to tell how much heart's blood went into his author's ink.

Louise Imogen Guiney, poet and literary scholar, was born January 7, 1861, in Roxbury, Massachusetts. She idolized her flamboyant father. He dabbled in politics as Massachusetts' first prominent Irish-Catholic Republican, but never advanced very far. He died when Louise was sixteen, ending her formal education. She was left with very little money and remained poor all her life.

Louise wrote poems and essays which were published in magazines and local papers. She always felt that she belonged in another era and identified most with the Romantics, such as Lamb, Keats and Shelley. She led the Boston movement that encouraged a revival of Romantic works and was responsible for the erection of an American memorial to Keats in England.

In 1901 Louise moved to England, where she delighted in "the velvety feel of the Past under foot, like the moss of the forest floor to a barefooted child." She stayed in England the remainder of her life and is buried at Oxford.

A book reveals its author

Louise's writing is from a 1907 article entitled "Literary Spying" that she wrote for Catholic World *magazine.*

Emily Balch

*W*omen for peace

1916

When I sailed on the *Noordam*, in April [1915], with the forty-two other American delegates to the International Congress of Women at The Hague, it looked doubtful to me, as it did to many others, how valuable the meeting could be made. . . .

A very curious thing has been the attitude of the majority of the press representatives who were present. Most of them apparently had been sent to get an amusing story of an international peace gathering of women—"base and silly" enough to try to meet in war time—breaking up in quarrel. Day by day they went away with faces long with disappointment. "Nothing doing to-day, but something worthwhile may happen to-morrow." In England the Congress was reported to be managed in the interest of Germany; in Germany the delegates were threatened with social boycott for attending a pro-British meeting; and in many countries the meetings were reported to have been either practically unattended or to have closed in a row. Nothing could be further from the truth than all these stories.

What stands out most strongly among all my impressions of those thrilling and strained days at The Hague is the sense of the wonder of the beautiful spirit of the brave, self-controlled women who dared ridicule and every sort of difficulty to express a passionate human sympathy, not inconsistent with patriotism, but transcending it.

Emily Greene Balch, sociologist and Nobel Laureate, was born January 8, 1867, in Jamaica Plain, Massachusetts.

After graduating from Bryn Mawr in 1889, she left immediately to study in Europe, where she became interested in the new science of sociology. Upon her return she taught sociology and economics at Wellesley College.

In 1915 Emily's great interest in pacifism led her to be one of forty-two American delegates among fifteen-hundred world delegates to the International Congress of Women at The Hague. When Emily tried to return to Wellesley in 1917 after a two-year sabbatical, she found that the Board of

Emily's writing is from Women at The Hague: The International Congress of Women and its Results by Three Delegates to the Congress from the United States: Jane Addams, Emily G. Balch and Alice Hamilton, *published in 1916.*

Trustees would not reappoint her, thus ending her teaching career.

In 1919 Emily was elected secretary-treasurer of the newly formed Women's International League for Peace and Freedom. In 1946 she became one of two American women ever to receive the Nobel Peace Prize.

Carrie Chapman Catt

1928

I became a feminist when I was six years old. . . . The day is deeply impressed upon my memory. The warm sun was shining brilliantly through the windows of a little school house in Ripon, Wisconsin, where I was born. The sweet smell of a bouquet of lilacs on the teacher's desk filled the room and marked the date as spring. . . .

We boys and girls . . . were now taking another lesson in the multiplication table and were standing in a straight row with our little toes strictly lined on a crack in the floor, when suddenly, with a whirring clickety-clack, a little girl's hoopskirt settled in a ring around tiny feet. Every boy snickered. The teacher, being a woman of discretion, gathered up the little girl, hoopskirt and all, in her arms, and carried her off to the woodshed. Restored to convention, she brought her back and set her down with toes on the crack. Her little cheeks were burning, her eyes down cast, and tears were flowing down her face. Again every boy, good and bad, snickered and every little girl blushed.

. . . There was no girl in that school who did not know that our common sex was being maligned by the teasing male, and most of us felt a spirit of resentment rising in our young bosoms. School over, I seized the hand of the child who had experienced the disaster and ran (no child walks) flauntingly before the boy of the most offensive snicker and made a face at him. I never forgot the hot indignation I felt nor the sense of triumph when I gave him the most terrible grimace I could invent. Thus I became a champion; I had defended my sex!

A born leader

Carrie's writing is from an article, "Why I Have Found Life Worth Living," in the March 29, 1928, edition of Christian Century Magazine.

Carrie Chapman Catt, suffragist and peace leader, was born January 9, 1859, in Ripon, Wisconsin. Seven years later the family moved to the frontier prairieland of northern Iowa. She graduated from high school in three years, but her father refused to allow her to attend college, so she earned the money herself by teaching, washing dishes and working in a library. After graduation she became principal of the Mason City (Iowa) High School and two years later was promoted to superintendent of schools—a highly unusual position for a woman at that time.

Carrie married Leo Chapman, owner and editor of the *Mason City Republican*, in 1885, and became the assistant editor. He died of typhoid fever a year later.

Carrie married a second time in 1890 to George William Catt, a staunch supporter of woman suffrage. They signed a pre-nuptial agreement granting Carrie two months in the spring and two months in the fall of each year to devote to her suffrage work. He died in 1905, leaving her financially independent and able to work full-time on suffrage.

Louisa Lane Drew

*B*orn for the stage

Louisa's writing is from the book Autobiographical Sketch of Mrs. John Drew, *published in 1899.*

1899

At twelve months old my mother took me on the stage as a crying baby; but cry I would not, but at sight of the audience and the lights gave free vent to my delight and crowed aloud with joy. From that moment to this, the same sight has filled me with the most acute pleasure, and I expect will do so to the last glimpse I get of them, and when no longer to be seen, "Come, Death, and welcome!" I acted (?) all the "children's" parts in the plays then usual—*Damon's* child—and had to be kept quiet with cherries before my last entrance. . . . In Liverpool, I remember playing the brother of "Franken-stein," who is killed by the Monster of Frankenstein's creation, acted by the celebrated T. P. Cooke, and to this hour can remember the horror which possessed me at his look and attitude, my own form dangling lifeless in his arms.

Louisa Lane Drew, actress and theater manager, was born January 10, 1820, in London, England. Her father was an actor and stage manager and her mother was an actress.

Give Her This Day

Louisa made her stage debut at one year of age and remained with the theater all her life.

When she was thirteen, Louisa joined a stock theater company in New York and toured the eastern seaboard, often playing in a different role each night. She married three times, always to Irish actors. She found happiness with her third husband, John Drew, and they had three children.

With Louisa's help, John became America's leading Irish comedian. Although he alternated touring with managing the Arch Street Theater in Philadelphia, Louisa remained in New York playing leading roles. The theater owners eventually offered Louisa the position of theater manager because John was gone so often. In 1863 he died suddenly at the age of 34.

In 1892, after running "Mrs. Drew's Arch Street Theater" for thirty-one years, Louisa moved to New York to live with her son John Jr. She was hailed as the queen mother of the American theater when she died in 1897. She had had a long and glorious career which her descendants continue to this day: two of her children were well-known actors, three of her grandchildren were Ethel, Lionel and John Barrymore, and child star Drew Barrymore of "E.T." fame is her great-great-granddaughter.

Caroline Matilda Kirkland

1845

. . . Few of my fair readers know the real advantages of a thorough acquaintance with the spinning wheel; the expanded chest, the well-developed bust, the firm, springing step which belong to this healthiest and most graceful of all indoor employments.

*P*hysical benefits of spinning

Caroline Kirkland, author, was born January 11, 1801, in New York City. Her widowed Quaker aunt ran a succession of small schools for girls where Caroline was educated.

After her marriage in 1828, Caroline and her husband, William Kirkland, ran a girls' school for several years in Geneva, New York. In 1835 they moved to Michigan, where William was the principal of the Detroit Female Seminary. Caroline taught at her husband's school while raising their family. She had seven children, three of whom died in childhood.

In 1836 William Kirkland bought 1300 marshy acres sixty miles northwest of Detroit and transplanted his family to the village of Pinckney. They lived in a log cabin in a small clear-

Caroline Kirkland's writing is from Western Clearings, *published in 1845.*

ing in the woods for six years. Caroline found the conditions primitive and lonely. To alleviate her sense of intellectual isolation, she began writing long, amusing letters home filled with her observations of the American wilderness. These letters were published in 1839 and 1842.

By 1843 the couple's real estate venture failed and the family moved to New York City. Caroline started a school in their home and continued to write short stories. Three years later her husband drowned, leaving Caroline to support the family.

Caroline became an editor in addition to her writing, and was welcomed in the literary community in New York. Edgar Allan Poe referred to her as "among the literati of New York City."

Mary Phenix

Learning to spin

1897

I learned to spin the Summer after I was twelve. My mother gave me a lesson in spinning and I spun one skein on that day. The next day I spun four skeins and with more ambition than discretion I was quite determined to spin one more skein to make a full day, but my mother said, "No." I had done quite enough for one day. That Summer I spun enough yarn for a large carpet. My cousin, Miriam Boothby (now Mrs. Merrill), lived just opposite and she sometimes brought her wheel to my home and we kept each other company in work, but she could spin faster and easier than I as she was much taller.

Mary Elden Phenix was born January 12, 1827, in Buxton, Maine. Her roots in that town can be traced back to her great-grandfather, one of the first settlers in the mid-1700's. Her parents both came from Buxton and set up a farm together within a mile of their childhood homes, where they remained until their deaths. Mary remained there also until her marriage at age twenty-eight.

Mary wrote her memoirs when she was seventy for her son George. She began with a complete description of her home that included chapters as specific as "beds and bedding" and "chimneys." She detailed the school that she walked to a mile away, even recalling the titles of her textbooks. Other chapters covered clothing, cooking, hairdos and church.

Mary's writing is from a typed copy of her memoirs which is in the Maine Historical Society, Portland, Maine.

Give Her This Day

Ernestine Rose

1851

Not long ago, I saw an account of two offenders brought before a justice in New York; one, for stealing a pair of boots, for which offense he was sentenced to six months' imprisonment; the other, for an assault and battery on his wife, for which offense he was let off with a reprimand from the judge! With my principles I am entirely opposed to punishment. I hold to reforming the erring and removing the causes, as being much more efficient as well as just than punishing; but the judge showed the comparative value he set on these two kinds of property. But you must remember that the boots were taken by a stranger, while the wife was insulted by her legal owner. Yet it will be said that such degrading cases are few. For the sake of humanity, I hope they are; but as long as woman is wronged by unequal laws, so long will she be degraded by man.

Ernestine Rose, women's rights advocate, was born in Poland, January 13, 1810. The only child of a rabbi, she grew up with more liberty and education than was usual for Jewish girls of her time and background. At seventeen she renounced her Jewish faith because it perpetuated the inferiority of women, and left Poland to escape a pre-arranged marriage.

Ernestine lived in Germany, Holland, France and England, working with a group of free thinkers and reformers. In 1835 she co-founded the Association of All Classes and All Nations. The next year she married William Rose, and they moved to New York where she took up the cause of the married women's property bill.

Ernestine was concerned with temperance and anti-slavery movements, as well as the free-thought movement, but her primary cause was women's rights. She became a popular lecturer and was sometimes referred to as the "Queen of the Platform" and spoke at numerous state and national women's rights conventions from 1850 to 1870.

Value of a wife

This excerpt is from a speech Ernestine gave in Boston on October 19, 1851.

Juliet Corson

Good, cheap food

1877

To the Wives of Workingmen:

In planning how to make the wages of the working man provide his family with the necessaries of life, the first point to be considered is the daily supply of food. If this little book shows the laborer's wife how to feed her husband and children upon one half, or one third, or even, in times of great distress, upon the whole of his scanty wages, its objects will be accomplished.

The cheapest kinds of food are sometimes the most wholesome and strengthening; but in order to obtain all their best qualities we must know how to choose them for their freshness, goodness, and suitability to our needs. That done, we must see how to cook them, so as to make savory and nutritious meals instead of tasteless or sodden messes, the eating whereof sends the man to the liquor shop for consolation.

Good food, properly cooked, gives us good blood, sound bones, healthy brains, strong nerves, and firm flesh, to say nothing of good tempers and kind hearts.

Juliet Corson, pioneer in cookery instruction, was born January 14, 1841, in Roxbury, Massachusetts. Her family moved to New York City when she was six, and after her mother's death when she was sixteen, she took her first job.

In 1873 the Women's Education and Industrial Society of New York opened a Free Training School for Women with courses in sewing, shorthand, bookkeeping and proofreading. Juliet added a cooking course the following year, although she had no previous knowledge of cookery. She read many French and German works on the subject, and lectured while a chef prepared the food. The classes were very popular and she was urged to start her own school. In 1876 Juliet opened the New York Cooking School, in her own home, and wrote her first Cooking Manual. She taught the wealthy as well as working girls, and no one was ever turned away because they were unable to pay.

Juliet's writing is an excerpt from the preface of her booklet "Fifteen-Cent Dinners for Families of Six." She paid the expenses herself to print and distribute the first 50,000 copies in 1877 as a consideration to the underprivileged.

Katharine Bement Davis

1913

Many a girl has said to me when arguing the matter of a new relationship and the lack of legal separation from the first, "But, Miss Davis, he did not deserve any consideration!" One girl who has committed bigamy by marrying the second man, gave as her excuse, which I think was perfectly genuine, that she wished to be respectable! In a large proportion of cases of girls sent here for prostitution, one or more men and sometimes as many as six stand ready to marry each as a means of securing her release. These are not always the men with whom the girls have been living nor the men whom they have been supporting. The most extreme case that has come to my attention is that of one of our girls who stopped a man on the street as she was being taken to the train by our officer saying: "She is taking me to prison. Will you marry me to save me?" He said "Yes," and actually wrote me asking to be allowed to do so.

Katharine Bement Davis, social worker and penologist, was born January 15, 1860, in Buffalo, New York.

In 1901 Katharine became the superintendent of the Reformatory for Women in Bedford Hills, New York, and turned the institution into a model penal experiment. She was particularly interested in the rehabilitation of prostitutes, and created the Laboratory of Social Hygiene specifically to study these women.

In 1922 the League of Women Voters named her one of the twelve greatest living Americans of her sex. During her career, Katharine contributed much to prison and social reform. She was creative, straightforward and had a ready wit. The press liked her. They were always supportive of her ideas and brought them before the public in a positive way.

*W*hy prostitutes marry

Katharine's writing is from her article, "A Study of Prostitutes Committed from New York City to the State Reformatory for Women at Bedford Hills." It was included as a supplementary chapter in George J. Kneeland's book, Commercialized Prostitution in New York City *(1913).*

Virginia Clay-Clopton

Husband falsely accused

Virginia's writing is from her book, A Belle of the Fifties: Memoirs of Mrs. Clay, of Alabama, covering Social and Political Life in Washington and the South, 1853-66, *published in 1904. She dedicated the book "To the dear memory of the husband of my youth, Clement Claiborne Clay."*

1904

All day my husband, to whom there had penetrated a rumour of my coming, had been waiting for me, himself tortured by fears for my safety and by the mystery of my delay. The gloomy corridors, in which soldiers patrolled night and day, guarding the two delicate prisoners of State, were already darkening with the early evening shadows when, at last, I saw my husband, martyr to his faith in the honour of the Government, standing within the grating, awaiting me. The sight of his tall, slender form, his pale face and whitened hair, awaiting me behind those dungeon bars, affected me terribly. My pen is too feeble to convey the weakness that overcame me as Lieutenant Stone inserted and turned the key in the massive creaking lock and admitted me. . . .

Virginia Clay-Clopton, Southern socialite and suffragist, was born January 16, 1825, in Nash County, North Carolina. After her mother and sister died when she was three, Virginia was raised by several relatives in Alabama. Her uncle, Secretary of State of Alabama, saw to it that she received a good education and was presented in local society.

When Virginia was eighteen she joined another politically important family through her marriage to Clement Clay, a lawyer and state legislator. The Clays moved to Washington in 1853 when he was elected to the U.S. Senate. Virginia adapted immediately to the Washington social and political scene and flourished in her role as Washington wife until Alabama seceded from the Union in 1861, forcing them to return home.

Mr. Clay was imprisoned in 1865, having been falsely accused of complicity in President Lincoln's assassination. After Clay was released from prison, the couple moved to a small farmhouse on the family plantation, and he retired from political life.

After her husband's death in 1882, Charlotte tried unsuccessfully to run the farm. She returned to Washington in 1886 and one year later married David Clopton, an Alabama Supreme Court justice. After his death, she took the name Clay-Clopton and spent the remainder of her life as an advocate of woman suffrage in Alabama.

Lizzie Scott Neblett

May 27, 1863
Dear Will,

    The mountain of anxiety and dread has been re-moved, the time of exquisite suffering has been passed, and I this morning lie on a bed of ease, a free unshack-led woman once more. Though undeserving I have been dealt with most mercifully and if any poor frail suffering creature ever felt grateful, I do. I thought I should never get through shouting when it was over. Yes, the Dutch gal has come, but she is not Dutch-like in her proportions, a perfect Amazon. . . . She is better developed than any baby I have ever had at any age. Mother just weighed her, nine and three quarters pounds. The fattest thing you ever saw. But, oh, Will I am so sorry, so grieved, that she was not a boy—that was a great damper to my joy after it was over with.

Lizzie Rowan Scott was born January 17, 1833, in Raymond Hinds County, Mississippi. She married William H. Neblett when she was nineteen. They had five children, three girls and two boys. Her husband was fighting in the Civil War at the time she sent him this letter.

Confederate soldier's new baby daughter

Lizzie's letter is in the manuscript collection at the University of Texas at Austin.

Alice Whiting Putnam

1906
I will tell of some playground experiences (in my own yard), where for nearly fifteen years I had the privilege of watching a group of twelve to twenty boys who gathered there almost daily before and after school hours. . . .

    The first really organized play that I recall was a "fire company." Indeed it can hardly be said that there was much engine, and it was the "chief's" wagon, the fire-patrol cart, or the hose cart, as the case might be. Any fellow might be allowed to be chief, and there were often several in one day. . . .

When play is work

Alice's writing is from an article, "The Persistence of Play Activities Throughout School Life; Their Value and Relation to Work," published in the Kindergarten Review, Volume XVI, No. 10, June, 1906.

Then a real engine house was demanded, though hitherto no fault had been found because the carts were kept under the porch, but now that place was no longer satisfactory. The wood of which the house was built was from an old toboggan slide. Limitations were reached here, quite soon, and a 16-year-old boy from Dr. Belfield's Manual Training School was engaged to come to superintend the work, and was at once installed as "the Boss" (and I think he spelled it with a big "B"). These children would never have submitted easily to such domination from teacher or parents as they then endured, and I momentarily expected a "strike," but none came. . . . After the house was finished, it was cleverly fitted up with electrical appliances, bells, gongs, and buttons, and in one corner was a desk with books for records and expenses, etc. Almost every afternoon the boys might be seen astride the ridge pole, or with chairs tilted back, with corncobs in their mouths (I don't think they were smoked, though it might have been so) awaiting an "alarm."

Now, was this play? Yes, surely, and very genuine play in its freedom, spontaneity and delight. Was it work? Yes, creative work, with a definite social idea struggling for realization. . . . Had you seen the responsibility which those children assumed in all of the elaboration of the details which went into the scheme, you could not question the living character of the work.

Alice Putnam, pioneer kindergartner, was born in Chicago January 18, 1841.

Alice married Joseph R. Putnam in 1868. Her interest in kindergarten grew out of a concern for the education of the two eldest of her four children. She went to a training school in Columbus, Ohio and upon graduation opened a kindergarten in her home. Her little school was the foundation of the kindergarten movement in the city of Chicago.

Alice sponsored a training school for kindergartners that she supervised for thirty years. She emphasized freedom, self-expression and social participation, coupled with an open-minded, maternal attitude toward the children.

In 1886 Alice persuaded the Chicago Board of Education to conduct a kindergarten in a public school, and by 1892 there were ten such kindergartens. Her kindergarten concept was accepted and recognized for its early teaching value.

Elizabeth Meriwether

1916

At the time of my marriage I was nearly twenty-six years old, but the man I married was well worth waiting for. Indeed, my dear grandchildren, no woman in all the world ever got a better husband than mine, for no truer, nobler, more unselfish man than Minor Meriwether ever lived. We lived together nearly sixty years and not once in all that time did I ever know him to do a mean thing, not once did we ever have even a little quarrel. In these days of quick and numerous divorces, sixty years of happy companionship with one husband is a record that may merit at least passing mention. Even after more than four score years had whitened my hair and chiseled wrinkles in my once smooth face my dear husband seemed never to see them, seemed to think me as beautiful as in the days of my youth and to love me as much as on the day he asked me to be his bride.

A perfect marriage

Elizabeth Avery Meriwether, writer and woman suffragist, was born January 19, 1824, in Bolivar, Tennessee. Her family moved to Memphis when she was eleven.

In 1850 Elizabeth married Minor Meriwether. She remained in Memphis when her husband enlisted in the Confederate Army at the outbreak of the Civil War. Several unpleasant incidents with Union generals gave her the impetus to move further south to Tuscaloosa, Alabama. There she took up writing and quickly won a $500 newspaper competition.

Elizabeth continued to write all her life, producing many novels, a play and several volumes of popular history. Elizabeth began her work for suffrage in 1876 when she heard that Susan B. Anthony had been jailed in New York for voting. Soon after that incident she rented the Memphis Theater and gave her first lecture. She later recalled: ". . . I remember how my knees shook when I stepped out on the stage of that Memphis Theater to tell the people why I deemed it unwise and unjust to rank women politically with convicts, lunatics and Indians. That was the first time I had ever spoken before a large audience and such was my stage fright, I would have abandoned the attempt then and there had I not felt it was my duty to give my message to the people." She went on to give many speeches to large audiences, and became known for her eloquence.

Elizabeth's writing is from her autobiography, Recollections of Ninety-Two Years, *published prior to her death in 1916.*

Carrie Burnham Kilgore

A freeman, she should vote

1873

Our first inquiry then is whether the word FREEMAN, in *Article III, Section 1, of the Constitution of Pennsylvania, which reads, "In elections by the citizens, every white freeman of the age of twenty-one years . . . shall enjoy the rights of an elector,"* excludes women citizens from the exercise of the right of suffrage?

I claim that this word FREEMAN . . . *includes both sexes and is used only to express condition.*

It is the correlative of the odious, hateful word *slave,* and as the word slave with all its bitterness and degradation is alike applicable to woman as to man, so also is this word *freeman* with all its glory and possibilities.

It is a compound word, composed of two simple words, "FREI," *free* or *true,* and "MANN," a *human being,* and in accordance with the peculiarity of the German compound words, it emphatically expresses the ideas embodied in the two simple words. It does not mean a free man or a free woman, but a free human being. It has no reference to sex in its original, but it does embody the idea that true nobility of character cannot be developed either in man or woman without freedom. This is its precise, and as I shall show Your Honors, its most known significance throughout the ages. . . .

Carrie Kilgore's writing is taken from her book, The Argument of Carrie S. Burnham before Chief Justice Reed and Associate Justices Agnew, Sharswood and Mercur of the Supreme Court of Pennsylvania on the third and fourth of April, 1873, *published by the Citizens Suffrage Association in 1873. Carrie lost this case before the court on the grounds that neither usage nor the state constitution entitled women to vote.*

Carrie Burnham Kilgore, teacher, lawyer and women's rights activist, was born January 20, 1838, in Craftsbury, Vermont. Carrie moved to Wisconsin at age twenty to live with an older sister, where she taught school and worked at getting her own education.

In 1865 Carrie went to Philadelphia, where she renewed her acquaintance with Damon Kilgore, whom she had known in Madison, Wisconsin when he was superintendent of schools. He was now a lawyer and she registered with him as his law student. During this time in Philadelphia, Carrie registered to vote, paid her poll tax but was not permitted to cast her ballot. She argued her own case before the State Supreme Court.

In 1876 Carrie married Kilgore and they had two daughters. For ten years after her marriage she struggled to be allowed to practice law. Finally in 1881 she was admitted to the University of Pennsylvania Law School and became its first woman graduate. After her husband's death in 1888 she took over and managed his law practice.

When Carrie was seventy years old she was the only woman passenger in a hot-air balloon flight over Philadelphia.

Helen Hamilton Gardener

1919

... Having spent my life in using such brain as I possessed in trying to better the condition of women, and having, many years ago, agreed to will my brain to Cornell College (at their request), I hereby confirm that bequest, *provided* a depleting illness or special brain disturbance shall not have produced such brain disintegration as to render it no longer "representative of the brain of women who have used their brain for the public welfare," as was stated in the Cornell request, as their reason for wanting it—to add to the knowledge of the brain quality and characteristics of the "women who think" as against the present statistics based upon the "hospital pick-ups and less fortunate women of the world upon whose brains Science has so far based its conclusions and deductions, which it has tabulated and set over against the results obtained from the examination of the best male brains known to the world."

Her brain to Cornell College

Helen Hamilton Gardener, author and feminist, was born January 21, 1853, in Winchester, Virginia. She was the youngest of six children of the Reverend Alfred G. Chenoweth—her given name was Alice Chenoweth. In 1875 she married Charles Smart, who was eighteen years her senior. They moved to New York City where she took college courses and was exposed to the freethinking and feminist movements.

Her first book was published in 1885 under the name Helen Hamilton Gardener. She used that name from then on both privately and professionally; no one knows why she chose to do so. In 1888 she wrote her most famous piece, "Sex in Brain," to refute a prominent physician who declared that women were inferior to men because their brains were smaller. Helen argued that his findings were invalid because the male brains he had studied were from intelligent, accomplished men, whereas the female brains were from indigents and criminals. She bequeathed her own brain to Cornell University to help provide a suitable specimen for research in the future.

Helen's writing excerpt is from a copy of her will which is among her papers at the Schlesinger Library, Radcliffe College.

Marie Manning

*T*he fourth wife

1944

. . . It is profitable for us all, I think, to remember what a dreary thing it was, only a few generations back, to emerge from childhood and face one's terribly critical twenties. You see, at twenty-five, one was permanently shelved as an old maid. So what did a girl do, who hadn't married early? Well, if she were lucky, she might get a job as an elementary teacher or a governess or domestic, but there weren't enough of such jobs to go around. The usual course was to repair to the home of a married relative and become an unpaid family drudge, supposed to give daily thanks for the "good home" one was imprisoned in.

No wonder that many girls were willing to become second or third wives of unattractive, middle-aged widowers with five or six children, rather than face the ignominy of not having been chosen by any man at all.

Old churchyards, especially in New England, tell the sordid story. We read of the first, second and third wife of Ezekiel, "Gone but not forgotten." Then came Ezekiel. And I've always had a good feminine satisfaction in knowing that his fourth wife was able to bury him.

Marie Manning, journalist and originator of the Beatrice Fairfax column of advice to the lovelorn, was born January 22, 1873, in Washington, D.C.

Marie became a journalist. She was a last-minute replacement for an absent friend at a dinner party, and she found herself seated next to Arthur Brisbane, editor of *New York World*. She told him of her dream of working on a newspaper and he offered her a job.

Marie worked for several years at the *World*. In 1897, Brisbane switched to Hearst's *New York Evening Journal* and many employees, Marie included, followed suit. She and two other woman reporters labored in an obscure corner known as the "Hen Coop" turning out the women's page. One morning Brisbane brought in three letters dealing with intimate personal problems and Marie suggested a separate department to deal with such letters. On July 20, 1898, she debuted as "Beatrice Fairfax"—a name she invented from Dante's Beata

Marie's writing is from her autobiography, Ladies Now and Then, *by Beatrice Fairfax (Marie Manning), published in 1944.*

Give Her This Day

Beatrix and Fairfax County, Virginia, where her family lived.

Beatrice Fairfax's column became an immediate success. At her peak she was receiving 1400 letters a day, mostly from young, unmarried females with romance problems. Marie responded in a forthright, non-emotional manner, her main theme being "dry your eyes, roll up your sleeves, and dig in for a practical solution."

Amanda Berry Smith

1893

An indescribable power

. . . I was in the next room talking with James, my husband. I had gone over to see him. My rent was due, and he had not been over for two weeks, and had not sent me any money. I was not well, and my baby was sick, and I was insisting that James should give me some money, at least the sixty cents that it cost me to come over from New York. But he would not. I was crying and talking, for my heart was almost broken. So, when John Bentley [James' son-in-law] cursed and swore at me, I turned to him quietly, and said: "Why, John Bentley, haven't I a right to come where my own husband is?" But he was fierce. I did not know but he was going to strike me. But I went up to him and looked him in the face, and said to him: "When you have been at my house, haven't I always treated you well? I have never laid a straw in your way in my life; and I don't know why you should speak to me in such a way."

He went on talking and abusing me terribly. There seemed to come an indescribable power over me, and I turned and lifted my hand toward him, and I said to him: "Mind, John Bentley, the God that I serve will make you pay for this before the year is out."

He said: "Well, I don't care if He does. Let Him do it."

He had not more than said the words when he seemed to tremble and stagger. There was a chair behind him, and he dropped down into the chair. I never saw him from that day. This was about two weeks before Christmas, and before the New Year came, John Bentley was dead and buried!

This writing is from Amanda Smith's autobiography, which was written and published in 1893: An Autobiography, The Story of the Lord's Dealing with Mrs. Amanda Smith, the Colored Evangelist, containing an Account of Her Life Work of Faith, and Her Travels in America, England, Ireland, Scotland, India and Africa, as an Independent Missionary.

I always feel sad when I think of it, but I believe that God was displeased with that man for cursing me that day.

Amanda Berry Smith, Protestant evangelist and missionary, was born into slavery on January 23, 1837, in Long Green, Maryland. Although married, her parents were slaves on adjoining plantations until her father was able to buy their freedom. The family moved to Pennsylvania where their house was a stop on the Underground Railroad.

Married in 1854 when she was seventeen, Amanda had two children—one of whom died as a baby, the other in her twenties. In 1856 she became immersed in her religion, which helped her to accept her burdens and tragedies and laid the foundation for her future evangelism. Eight years into their unhappy marriage, her husband left to fight in the Civil War and was killed.

Amanda quickly remarried and had three more children—two of whom died in infancy. Her new husband, Reverend James Smith, soon moved to another part of the state to earn better money, leaving Amanda and her baby in New York City working as a maid and laundress. In 1869, both her husband and remaining child died. It was at this time that she began preaching in the local black churches.

Within a year Amanda had become very popular in both black and white churches. She spent the next twenty years preaching in the U.S., England, India and Africa. In 1892 she returned to a temperance community in Harvey, Illinois, where she devoted the remainder of her life to black orphans.

Kate Waller Barrett

Helping an unwed mother

Kate's writing is from her book, Some Practical Suggestions on the Conduct of a Rescue Home, *published in 1903.*

1903

We must pause here to admit an inmate. A girl mounts the front steps and timidly rings the bell. She feels as if the eyes of every passerby on the street are riveted upon her, and that each one knows her secret. She does not realize that every day a dozen or more ladies and young girls, workers in the Master's vineyard, mount these same steps, and that there is nothing different in her appearance to mark her from them. The door opens and she is greeted by a trim girl whose badge of authority is a neat white apron and muslin cap. She is not stared at as an object of curiosity, as she half feared, but is cordially asked to enter, and is treated as an expected and welcome guest. She is shown into the drawing room, and as she sits down there greets her every evidence of the fact that this is a true home—God's home—and she feels insensibly the safety and the comfort of being cared for, which the very atmosphere of love seems to breathe forth. . . . She is assured that it does not matter what the past has been, the future may be all that she desires to make it. . . .

Katherine Harwood Waller Barrett, leader in the National Florence Crittenton Mission for unwed mothers, was born January 24, 1857, in Falmouth, Virginia.

Kate married Robert S. Barrett, an Episcopal minister, and they had seven children. One night an unwed mother with her baby knocked on the rectory door, seeking help. Kate spoke with her at length and was surprised to discover that she was not dirty or deranged but that they came from similar backgrounds. From this point forward she resolved to help this "outcast class."

Kate assisted her husband in his work with prostitutes, and to learn more about the problem she took the three-year course at Women's Medical College of Georgia. She received an M.D. degree in 1892 and the next year opened her first home for unwed mothers in Atlanta.

Kate wrote to the millionaire evangelist Charles Crittenton asking for building funds. Ten years earlier when his little daughter Florence died he gave up his business career to preach and opened several homes, named for his daughter, to help redeem prostitutes. He immediately sent five thousand dollars, and Kate's home became the fifth in an expanding chain of Florence Crittenton homes.

She visited the homes, held annual conferences, published a magazine and a book, and established a training course for workers in Washington, D.C. Kate believed the mothers should keep their babies instead of placing them for adoption, although she did advise them to move to a new area so as not to disgrace their families.

Clarina Nichols

*K*nitting in the saloon

May, 1869
Wyandotte, Kansas

I read not long since, of a party of ladies, who with their knitting work in hand, took seats in a recently licensed saloon and spent the entire day. Next morning they repaired thither again, and at nightfall were reinforced by more lady knitters, who kept them company through the evening. The saloon keeper packed up next morning and left, declaring that, not a man (he meant customer), had called in the two days. How very much there is to be done, and what a variety of ways and workers is needed to do well and speedily.

Clarina Howard Nichols, newspaper editor and women's rights leader, was born January 25, 1810, in West Townshend, Vermont. She received a good education (for a woman in rural Vermont) and was active in the local Baptist church. At twenty she married Justin Carpenter, a Baptist minister, and moved to New York State. Clarina started a school for girls and had three children of her own. The marriage failed after nine years, and she returned to Vermont, where she obtained a divorce.

She worked as a writer at the *Windham County Democrat* in Brattleboro, Vermont and married the paper's publisher, George W. Nichols. They had one son.

Clarina began her involvement with the women's rights movement in 1847. While concentrating on the legal rights of women to inherit, own and bequeath property, she also worked to obtain the vote for women. She became a very popular speaker. Once when her riverboat ran aground in the Missouri River, she organized a women's rights meeting on board.

Clarina and her husband moved to Kansas in 1854 to be near her children. Mr. Nichols died a year later.

In 1867, she moved to California to live with her son and died there in 1885.

This writing is from a letter Clarina wrote to the editor of the Kansas Daily Commonwealth in 1869.

Julia Dent Grant

1893

It is needless to mention what everyone knows—that Dame Nature was most chary of her gifts to me, no single special talent did she bestow, and of personal charm she was simply miserly. I can only remember my abundance of soft brown hair, a fair complexion, and everyone told me my feet and hands were fairylike. . . .

Julia Dent Grant, wife of President Ulysses S. Grant, was born near St. Louis, Missouri, January 26, 1826. Her education started in a log school near her home. She went to boarding school in St. Louis when she was eleven.

Julia met Ulysses, who had been a classmate of her brother's at West Point, when she was eighteen. The couple fell in love, but her parents disapproved of the young lieutenant. They thought him unimpressive and without prospects. After a long four-year engagement, the couple was allowed to marry. They had four children and a long, happy life together.

Julia was known for her dignity, simplicity and warm hospitality during the eight years she was mistress of the White House. She is buried beside her husband in his great tomb in Riverside Park, New York City.

Thankful for nature's gifts

Julia's writing is from The National Exposition Souvenir: What America Owes to Women, *edited by Lydia Hoyt Farmer, published in 1893.*

Susan Mansfield Huntington

January 5, 1815

How difficult, how hopeless is the task of pleasing everybody! A fortnight since a lady said to me, with a tone and manner which gave peculiar emphasis to the words, "How is it possible you can go out so much, visit your people so frequently, and be engaged in so many charitable societies, without neglecting your family?" This week a different imputation has been attached to my conduct. I am censured for doing so little in a public way, and confining myself so much to my family. I am accused of want of interest in public charities, because I give to them so little of my time and attention. Such different opinions are formed of the same conduct!

Pleasing everyone

Susan Huntington's writing is from a letter to a friend that was included in Memoirs of the Late Mrs. Susan Huntington *by Benjamin B. Wisner, published after her death in 1833.*

But the voice of wisdom bids me, cease from man whose breath is in his nostrils, and study to approve myself to God. As to my conduct, I am very sensible that I do little good in the world, in comparison with what I might do. But whether I could, with propriety, devote more time to the active duties of public charities, I have serious doubt.

Susan Mansfield Huntington was born in Killingworth, Connecticut, on January 27, 1791. Both her father and grandfather were ministers. Joshua Huntington, her husband, was pastor of the Old South Church in Boston. Susan was educated at home by her father and read serious religious books as a very young girl. She wrote poetry, kept a journal and was a prolific letter writer. Her writings are spiritual in content and reveal her compelling desire to lead a God-centered life.

Alice Craven Caborn

*D*akota pioneers

1924

I was certainly a very young and inexperienced woman when I left my home in Iowa the latter part of March in 1883, to come to Dakota Territory. My husband had come ahead with our household goods, the horses, two cows and few other things that he thought might be convenient in a new country.

Aberdeen was our destination, and on the first day of April we started for "our claim" which he had located. By evening we were all settled in our new home, 12 feet square. We had a bed in one corner, a stove in another. Then we had a little cupboard and table. I even put down a carpet, but soon discovered that was a very foolish thing, and it had to come up because it got too dirty. . . .

I remember a bad storm we had that spring. That evening three teams and five men drove up and asked for shelter for themselves and their horses. . . . We had improvised a shelter for our stock by building a frame of lumber and stretching a large tarpaulin over the frame so we told them yes, they could stay. . . .

When the horses were all in, there was not any

Alice's writing is from a series of articles entitled "Edmund's Early History" that she wrote in 1924 for the Ipswich Tribune, *Ipswich, South Dakota.*

Give Her This Day

place for the men, so I moved out the table and trunk and those five men slept with their feet under our bed, and very comfortable, so they said. For three days and three nights that storm lasted, and I cooked for and furnished a place for those men to sleep . . . .

Alice Craven Caborn was born January 28, 1863, in Washington County, Iowa. In 1883 she set off for the Dakota Territory to join her husband who had gone ahead.

Their claim consisted of one hundred acres in Edmunds County. Alice and her husband spent the first two years in a twelve-by-twelve shanty and had to carry water three miles and strain and boil it before use.

Alice wrote a series of articles for the *Ipswich Tribune* in the 1920's portraying the early life of a pioneer. In her concluding article she was fearful that she had given the impression that pioneer life was all hardships, which she felt it was not because "people have a lot to do with our lives, and no finer people ever settled any country than settled Edmunds County."

Hannah Worcester Hicks

September 7, 1862

This is the ninth Sabbath that I have been *a widow*. Two sad, weary months. How many times in past days have I wondered what my future would be—wished that I could have some idea. But oh I did not think it would be as it is. Left a widow, at twenty-eight, with five children growing up around me, and oh, most dreadful of all, my dear husband *murdered*. Oh the bitter, bitter repentance for my unkindness to him. I might have done better, have grieved him less.

. . . This weary, weary time of War. Will the suspense *never* end? I know not what is to become of us. Famine and Pestilence seem to await us. We can only stand and tremble, and dread what next may befall us.

On the night of the 31st of July, rather, the morn of the 1st of August, our house was burnt down. That was the first great trial that my husband was not here to share with me. But truly I hardly felt it a trial, so very little did it seem compared with what I suffered in *losing him* in such a terrible way. Oh for grace to submit in a

*T*rials of war

Hannah's writing is the September 7, 1862, entry in her diary. Hannah's diaries and other valuable Cherokee manuscripts, given by her grandson Homer W. Hicks, are in the Thomas Gilcrease Institute of American History and Art in Tulsa, Oklahoma.

right spirit to *every* trial. I believe my heart is almost dead within me.

Hannah Worcester Hicks was born January 29, 1834 in New Echota, Georgia. Her parents were missionaries to the Cherokee Indians. When the government relocated the Cherokees to Oklahoma via the infamous "Trail of Tears," Hannah's family also moved west to continue their missionary work.

Hannah studied at home and worked at her father's printing office binding books and proofreading. The day after she turned eighteen she married Abijah Hicks, the thirty-three-year-old son of an Eastern Cherokee chief. He had survived the "Trail of Tears" and become a prosperous farmer and merchant.

Hannah and Abijah were married for ten years and had five children. He was murdered in 1862 by Confederate sympathizers.

Catherine Waite

*S*ad consequences of polygamy

1867

THE WIVES OF BRIGHAM YOUNG . . .
Mrs. Mary Ann Angell Young.

This lady is the first living and legal wife of the Prophet. She is a native of New York, and is a fine-looking, intelligent woman. She is large, portly, and dignified. Her hair is well-sprinkled with the frosts of age; her clear, hazel eyes and melancholy countenance indicate a soul where sorrow reigns supreme. She has been very much attached to her husband, and his infidelity has made deep inroads upon her mind. Her deep-seated melancholy often produces flights of insanity, which increase with her declining years.

Mrs. Young seldom receives guests, and her husband himself scarcely ever pays her a visit.

When I looked upon this poor suffering woman, as she sat at church, surrounded by her husband's mistresses, I seemed for the first time fully to realize the true character of that "institution" which has crushed the hearts of many noble women.

Catherine's writing is from her book The Mormon Prophet and His Harem—an Authentic History of Brigham Young, His Numerous Wives and Children, *published in 1867.*

Catherine Van Valkenburg Waite, author, suffragist and lawyer, was born January 30, 1829, in Ontario, Canada. She graduated from Oberlin College in 1853 and married Chicago lawyer Charles B. Waite a year later.

In 1862 President Lincoln appointed Charles to the Utah Territory Supreme Court. They were not warmly received in Utah by the Mormons and returned to Chicago four years later. Catherine was very disturbed by what she saw of the Mormon religion and published *The Mormon Prophet and His Harem* in 1867, condemning their practice of polygamy and its effect on women. She later rewrote the book into a longer form. It contains many grim stories that were told to her by "plural" women who visited with her in secret.

Catherine enrolled in law school in 1885. After passing the bar, she published the *Chicago Law Times* for three years and served as president of the International Woman's Bar Association.

Mary Greenleaf

To Mrs. "JB" of Newburyport
September 24, 1856
We have a good deal to do yet, to prepare for the school. I expect to have the care of thirty-three girls out of school—shall have to cut and fit at least a hundred dresses for them, and teach them to make them properly, besides teaching them cleanliness and almost all domestic duties, and giving them religious and moral instruction. You will ask that I may have grace and strength equal to my day. Hitherto my health has been excellent, and my courage has not failed. I cannot but rejoice I am here, and hope some souls will be savingly benefited by my feeble instrumentality, and if so, how trifling are all the self-denials to be endured!

Chickasaw Indian School

Mary Coombs Greenleaf, missionary, was born January 31, 1800, in Newburyport, Massachusetts. She left school when she was thirteen to care for her ailing mother.

After her mother died (when Mary was fifty-six) she offered her services to the Board of Missions of the Presbyterian Church.

They sent Mary to the Chickasaw Indian School at Wapanucka, Oklahoma. The Chickasaws were a small, scattered tribe of about five thousand. Mary loved caring for the Indian girls in her responsibility. One year after starting her work at the mission, she died of dysentery.

Mary's letter to her friend in Massachusetts was written a few months after her arrival at the mission school. It is contained in the book Life and Letters of Miss Mary C. Greenleaf, Missionary to the Chickasaw Indians, *published by the Massachusetts Sabbath School Society in 1858.*

FEBRUARY

Hattie Wyatt Caraway

January 31, 1939

My dear Mrs. Roosevelt:

I am in receipt of your letter of the twenty-seventh, in which you enclosed an unsigned letter regarding the treatment of negroes in my state by certain minor officials.

I have not had this matter brought to my attention before. The chances are that these statements are exaggerated. However, I will be very glad to take this particular matter up with the Governor and ask that he investigate it and if the statements are true, have him make an attempt to straighten the matter out.

Thanking you for writing me and with kind personal regards, I am

Sincerely yours,

Hattie W. Caraway

Letter to Mrs. Roosevelt

Hattie Caraway was born near Bakerville, Tennessee, February 1, 1876. Her husband, Thaddeus H. Caraway, was a Democratic senator from Arkansas. They had three sons.

Thaddeus died before the expiration of his term in 1931, and the governor of Arkansas appointed Hattie to her husband's seat. She had never worked outside her home.

Hattie was the first woman to be elected to the United States Senate. The voters of her state elected her two times. Hattie was plump and plain, rather motherly-looking, but she won the admiration of her colleagues in the Senate with her intelligence, good common sense, and integrity. She worked hard and had a thorough grasp of the issues that faced her country. When she retired at the last session of the 78th Congress in 1944, the entire Senate rose in a tribute to her, something that is seldom done.

Hattie lost the 1944 campaign to John L. McClellan, whose motto was "Arkansas needs another man in the Senate." She never ran for office again.

This letter from Hattie to Eleanor Roosevelt, written on United States Senate stationery, is in the Franklin D. Roosevelt Library, Hyde Park, New York. It is not clear, from their correspondence, that there was any evidence for Hattie's belief that the complaints of the negroes were exaggerated.

Delia Bacon

Obsession with her work.

Liverpool,
June 1856
Dear Mr. Hawthorne,

. . . Whereas now I am nothing but this work. . . . I would rather be this than anything else. I have lived for three years as much alone with God and the dead as if I had been a departed spirit. And I don't wish to return to the world. I shrink with horror from the thought of it. This is an abnormal state, you see, but I am perfectly harmless, and if you will let me know when you are coming I will put on one of the dresses I used to wear the last time I made my appearance in the world, and try to look as much like a survivor as the circumstances will permit.

Truly yours,
Delia Bacon

Delia Bacon, the originator of the theory that Francis Bacon wrote Shakespeare's plays, was born in Tallmadge, Ohio, February 2, 1811. She started teaching school when she was fifteen and later became a popular lecturer, giving her "Historical Lessons" before large groups of women in New York, Boston and Connecticut.

In 1845-1847 she had an ill-fated romantic relationship with a Yale Divinity School graduate which ended when he refused to marry her. His rejection left her deeply depressed and humiliated. She withdrew from her speaking engagements and became obsessed with her Baconian theory. In England, where she went to research and write a book on her idea, she was befriended by Nathaniel Hawthorne, who was in Liverpool serving as the American consul.

This excerpt of Delia's letter to Nathaniel Hawthorne is from a biographical sketch written by her nephew, Theodore Bacon, in 1888.

Hawthorne was kind to Delia. He read her manuscript and gave her financial help.

Her book was published in 1857. Unfortunately, it received very poor reviews and a good deal of ridicule. Delia was not strong enough to survive this disappointment nor the coming to an end of the effort that had consumed her for so long, and she became insane. She died at the Hartford Retreat for the Insane in 1859. Her Baconian theory is still talked about by students of Shakespeare.

Charlotte Howard Conant

1880

Thursday morning, Miss Howard gave us a lecture in chapel of another kind. Upon our short-comings and long-goings, mostly our long-goings. She mentioned a number of things which we ought not to do. Slamming doors and whistling, *especially* whistling. She said she never knew but one *lady* who whistled and she had taken lessons and practiced until her whistle was the sweetest music, so now the girls all want to know who the lady was. Running through the halls and talking above a whisper after the lights are out are also forbidden. Then idle and flippant words about the faculty are reprehended; neither is it advisable to write frivolous and idle letters to general correspondents on Sunday. This is a *good* place, no doubt of that, and if one obeys all the rules and *regulations*, I should think she was almost perfect.

Charlotte Conant was born in Greenfield, Massachusetts, on February 3, 1862. She graduated from Wellesley College in 1884. Charlotte and her college roommate, Florence Bigelow, started The Walnut Hill School, a preparatory school for girls, in Natick, Massachusetts, in 1893.

*F*reshman writes home

Charlotte's writing excerpt is from a letter she wrote to her family during her freshman year at Wellesley. It is included in A Girl of the Eighties, at College and at Home, *which was compiled by Charlotte's sister Martha Pike Conant after Charlotte's death in 1925. It is a collection of biographical notes, old diaries and letters, and includes several lovely photographs of Charlotte and her family.*

Sarah Norcliffe Cleghorn

1936

I made a great many visits to the jail before I ever knew of what was called the "old part." I assumed, all that time, that I was seeing all the prisoners every week. When somebody happened, one day, to speak about the "old part," I went to see the jailer. "What prisoners are there in the old part? where is the old part? can I go in?"

"Oh, they're misdemeanor prisoners, thirty or forty of 'em—Niggers—in for a short time, a week or two," said he. "No, no, you can't go in—they're a rough lot —wouldn't take a woman in there!"

*V*iolets in a dark prison

"Well, I'm no young girl," I said. "I'm old and tough."

"No telling what they'd say," he replied, shaking his head. "Curse and swear, or worse, probably. If I should let you in, I'd go with you and protect you."

"Well," I said, "I haven't got any pie for them, or any stamps, or magazines. I've only got these violets, about two violets apiece."

They were poor little pale violets, with stems an inch or two long; wild ones, the first of the year.

We went in to the perpetual twilight of the old part, where, in cages much less spacious than those in the "new part," dark forms and faces were glimmering, partly visible. The men seemed sad, gentle and polite; each one accepted his two violets. "Thank you, ma'am."

Sarah Cleghorn, writer and reformer, was born February 4, 1876, in Norfolk, Virginia. Her mother died when she was nine. She and her six-year-old brother were sent to Vermont to be raised by their mother's two unmarried sisters, Aunt Fanny and Aunt Jessie. She had a happy childhood under the loving care of these beloved aunts. She wrote later, "I am a believer in potential motherhood as a quality of the soul rather than of the body. In the case of children coming into the care of aunts or grandparents, there is thrown into this potential motherhood the added force of sisterly or parental tenderness and loyalty."

Sarah graduated from Burr and Burton Seminary in Manchester, Vermont, and attended Radcliffe College and Columbia University. She taught at Manumit School for Workers' Children and Vassar College. Her writing career started when she was thirty-six with pacifist essays and protest poetry. She also wrote several novels.

Sarah organized an unsuccessful effort to abolish capital punishment in Vermont and was very active in prison reform. She never married.

Sarah Cleghorn's account of visiting a prison in Macon, Georgia, is from her autobiography, Threescore, *published in 1936. In his introduction to her book, Robert Frost wrote, "Saint, poet—and reformer. There is more high explosive for righteousness in the least little line of Sarah Cleghorn's poem about the children working in the mill where they could look out the window at their grown-up employers playing golf than in all the prose of our radical-boys pressed together under a weight of several atmospheres of revolution."*

Belle Starr

Mother goes to prison

Feb. —, 1883

My Dear Little One: It is useless to attempt to conceal my trouble from you and though you are nothing but a child I have confidence that my darling will bear with fortitude what I now write.

I shall be away from you a few months baby, and have only this consolation to offer you, that never again will I be placed in such humiliating circumstances and that in the future your little tender heart shall never more ache, or a blush called to your cheek on your mother's account. Sam and I were tried here, John West the main witness against us. We were found guilty and sentenced to nine months at the house of correction, Detroit, Michigan, for which place we start in the morning. Now Pearl there is a vast difference in that place and a penitentiary; you must bear that in mind and not think of mamma being shut up in a gloomy prison. It is said to be one of the finest institutions in the United States, surrounded by beautiful grounds, with fountains and everything nice. There I can have my education renewed, and I stand sadly in need of it. Sam will have to attend school and I think it the best thing ever happened to him, and now you must not be unhappy and brood over our absence. It won't take the time long to glide by and as we come home we will get you and then we will have such a nice time.

Myra Maybelle Shirley ("Belle Starr") was born in Carthage, Missouri, February 5, 1848. She received some elementary-school education in Carthage where her father owned a hotel. During the Civil War the town of Carthage was burned and her family moved to Texas.

Her two brothers were members of roving bands of outlaws. They both were killed in gunfights. She married James C. Reed in 1866. He came from Missouri and had been a confederate guerrilla during the Civil War. Jim Reed raced horses and gambled. Their daughter, Rosie Lee (Pearl), was born in 1868. Belle's husband became an outlaw after killing a man in Arkansas in 1873. The next year he took part in a daring stagecoach robbery and was later murdered by a bounty hunter. Belle went into a common-law marriage with a three-quarter Cherokee renegade named Sam Starr, and lived with him in Cherokee Nation, Oklahoma. Their home became a hiding place for her outlaw friends. Jesse James once hid there for ten days. She charged him room and board. In 1883 Belle and her husband were sentenced to prison for stealing horses.

Her writing here is from a letter she wrote to her fifteen-year-old daughter Pearl before she was taken to the federal penitentiary in Detroit.

Belle loved horses and rode like a cowboy. She was an expert shot and always wore a side arm. She was shot in the back

Belle's letter to Pearl was first published by Samuel W. Harman in Hell On The Border: He Hanged Eighty-eight Men *in 1898.*

A footnote added, "Copied from the original," but there is no reference as to the location of the letter.

and killed by an unknown assailant when she was forty-one.

She was buried in her best riding habit. Her arms were crossed with one of her hands grasping the handle of her six-shooter.

Elizabeth Patterson Bonaparte

Marrying is almost a crime

December 20, 1826
. . . Marrying is almost a crime, in my eyes, because I am persuaded that the highest degree of virtue is to abstain from augmenting the number of unhappy beings. If people reflected, they would never marry, because they entail misery upon themselves when they bring children into the world. I have no desire to see my son married, and I hope he will never have any family.

Elizabeth Patterson Bonaparte was born February 6, 1765, in Baltimore, Maryland. Her family was wealthy, and she was very beautiful. When she was eighteen, Jerome Bonaparte, Napoleon's youngest brother, was presented to her in Baltimore. He was on a return trip to France aboard a French naval ship. Jerome was nineteen. The young couple fell in love, and a few months after they met they were married in a Catholic church in Baltimore.

France never recognized the marriage, and Napoleon would not allow Elizabeth to enter the country. Her son, also named Jerome, was born in England in 1805. Jerome the elder was forced to abandon Elizabeth, and arrangements were made for him to marry Princess Catherine of Wurttemberg, which he did in 1807. Elizabeth obtained a divorce from the Maryland legislature six years later. She spent the remainder of her life making a futile effort to have her son recognized by the Bonaparte family. The obsession with being denied a place for herself and her son consumed her whole life. Elizabeth Bonaparte never remarried and in the end was a lonely, tragic figure. She died in 1879 at the age of ninety-four.

This excerpt of Elizabeth Bonaparte's writing is from a letter to her father written while she was in Italy.

Bethenia Angelina Owens-Adair

North Yakima, Washington
April 14, 1904

Ladies should ride astride

Nothing will preserve woman's grace and her symmetrical form so much as vigorous and systematic exercise, and horseback riding stands at the head of the list, providing she has a foot in each stirrup, instead of having the right limb twisted around a horn, and the left foot in a stirrup twelve or fifteen inches above where it ought to be. If she sits astride her saddle she will relieve herself of those imaginary injurious "jolts" and "jars" received from a rough trotter. This she could not do sitting sidewise. I have been a horseback rider all my life. I was raised on a farm and learned to ride before I can remember. As I grew to womanhood society demanded a side saddle, and I had to adopt it. Some ten years ago, when cross-riding was beginning to be advocated, I adopted the new style. Now, when a pale, delicate, nervous patient is brought to me, especially if from the country, I say: "Now, in addition to your medicine I want you to take a horseback ride every day, but mind you must ride the new style. I forbid the side saddle, and in addition, if you have a flower garden or a vegetable garden, give them special attention, and you will soon be strong and have roses in your cheeks."

Bethenia Owens, physician, was born February 7, 1840, in Van Buren County, Missouri. Her family joined the western migration when she was three and settled on the coast of Oregon.

At fourteen Bethenia married one of her father's hired hands, but it was an unhappy marriage. After four years, she obtained a divorce and the right to take back her maiden name.

Bethenia raised her son alone and supported them by taking in laundry and sewing hats and clothes. At thirty-eight she enrolled in the University of Michigan Medical School and earned her M.D. degree. She was one of the very few women doctors practicing medicine on the Pacific coast during the late 1880's.

Bethenia Owens-Adair's writing is from her book, Dr. Owens-Adair; Some of Her Life Experiences, *published in 1906. It was written in response to a letter in* The Daily Seattle Times *by Dr. M. Tallack, which advocated that the only proper way for women to ride horseback was sidesaddle.*

Clara Crowninshield

Rotterdam
November 4, 1835
Twenty minutes past ten, I must begin my German.
Whereupon I began to draw, for I felt impatient to get
this picture done. Mr. Longfellow came in while I was
at work upon it and criticized my feminine style of
shading. Poor, feeble sex, I wonder we have courage to
undertake anything. I am quite certain that I have not
the slightest talent for drawing, but that is no proof that
no lady may possess the talent.

Clara Crowninshield was born in Salem, Massachusetts, on
February 8, 1811. She was the illegitimate daughter of John
Crowninshield, Jr., a wealthy merchant and yachtsman, and
Elizabeth Howell. She was educated at Miss Cushing's Female
Seminary where she met Mary Potter, who became Henry
Longfellow's first wife. Clara and Mary were good friends,
and she accompanied the Longfellows on a trip to Europe in
1835-1836. Mary Longfellow died while on this trip, and
Clara was in hopes that Longfellow might marry her. Instead,
he married Fanny Appleton [October 6] in Boston in 1843.

*Clara's diary entry comes from
The Diary of Clara
Crowninshield: A European
Tour With Longfellow 1835-
1836.*

Lydia Estes Pinkham

1880
Mrs. Isaac Clark, Sudbury, Mass. Her trouble is in the
ovaries crowding down the organ. Wrote her that her
stomach needs a tonic. Sent her a box of lozenges.
Mrs. F.B. Copeland, Peabody, Mass. Trouble is
with the ligaments and nerves of the womb which causes
a tipping to one side. The compound will strengthen
the nerves and ligaments so that the womb will be held
in its proper place. Sent her pills which with the use of
the Compound will effect a cure. Recommended a
double dose of the Compound.

Lydia Estes Pinkham was born February 9, 1819, in Lynn,
Massachusetts. She grew up in a Quaker family and went to
school at Lynn Academy. She taught school for several years

*The records, through 1925, of
the Lydia E. Pinkham Medicine
Co., and some family papers are
in Schlesinger Library, Radcliffe
College.*

before marrying Isaac Pinkham in 1843. They had five children.

Her family got into serious financial straits in the depression of 1873, and to help out she decided to try selling her homemade vegetable compound. The herbal mixture, made from roots with 18% alcohol added, had an excellent reputation among her family and friends, who used it with good results. It was believed to be especially helpful for "female complaints." She progressed from making small quantities of the compound on her kitchen stove to the development of the Lydia E. Pinkham Medicine Co., which was grossing $300,000 a year at the time of her death in 1883.

Lydia wrote her own advertising and put her picture on the labels of all her products. It has been said that her face may have been the best-known American female face in the nineteenth century. Lydia answered thousands of letters written by women seeking medical advice who were too shy to consult a male doctor. This writing is from her 1880 handwritten record book.

Adelina Patti

1903
It is fortunate that I have natural self-command, for many frightful things have happened in theaters where I have been singing. Once I made a narrow escape in Moscow from burning to death. They wore wide skirts in those days. In turning suddenly, in my dressing room, I overset a spirit lamp, and in an instant my thin draperies were in flames to my neck. I held up my arms as someone threw a blanket around me. It was a marvelous escape, not only for me, but for those about me who were wearing light dresses as well. I sang the performance as usual . . .

. . . In San Francisco it was that I made my narrowest escape, and that was the night a man threw a bomb on the stage.

I had answered two recalls, entering from the center of the scene to make my acknowledgment. When I started to go out a third time, Miss Carolina Bauermeister, who has been with me for years, said, "Don't go from the center this time, go from the wings."

I followed her advice. Had I not, I might have been

The bravery of an opera singer

Adelina Patti's reminiscences are from an interview she gave to William Armstrong. It was included in an article which appeared in the July 11, 1903, issue of the Saturday Evening Post.

---

killed. In the moment that I appeared for that third recall he threw the bomb. Possibly through nervousness, his aim was bad. He had intended to fling it into the box of a banker. Instead it landed in the middle of the stage, just where I would have stood had I entered from the center. The scene that followed was indescribable. "You might have killed Madame Patti," someone shrieked at him.

"I should have been glad if I had," was his answer. "She makes too much money as it is."

Well, when things were quieted the opera went on, and I sang to the end without showing the effects. But then I am not hysterical.

Adelina Patti was born in Madrid, Spain, February 10, 1843. Her Italian mother and father were opera singers on tour in Spain at the time of her birth. When she was still an infant her parents emigrated to New York to pursue their musical careers. Adelina grew up in happy musical surroundings. At the age of four she could sing difficult operatic pieces. When she was eight she performed in public for the first time singing Jenny Lind's "Echo Song" and "Ronda" from *La Sonnambula*. When she was sixteen, she had her operatic debut at the Academy of Music in New York and drew wide acclaim. Her London debut at the Royal Italian Opera in Covent Garden in 1863, when she was eighteen, was a triumph. Charles Dickens wrote on that occasion, ". . . On her first evening's appearance at our Italian Opera—nay, in her first song— [she] possessed herself of her audience with a sudden victory which has scarcely a parallel. . . . This new singer, in her early girlhood, is already a perfect artist—one who will set Europe on fire during the many years to which it may be hoped her career will extend." Verdi called her the greatest singer he had ever heard. Her voice was sweet and had great purity of tone. She remained in London and toured the major cities of Europe for twenty years.

Adelina had three husbands. In 1868 she married a French nobleman whom she divorced seventeen years later. Her second husband, tenor Ernest Nicolini, with whom she had often sung, died after they had been married thirteen years. Her third husband, a Swedish baron, was thirty years younger than she. She had no children. Adelina Patti died in France in 1919 when she was seventy-six, and was buried in Paris.

Lydia Maria Child

A beautiful moment

1845

The other day, as I came down Broome-street, I saw a
street musician, playing near the door of a genteel
dwelling. The organ was uncommonly sweet and mellow in its tones, the tunes were slow and plaintive, and I
fancied that I saw in the woman's Italian face an expression that indicated sufficient refinement to prefer the
tender and the melancholy to the lively 'trainer tunes'
in vogue with the populace. She looked like one who
had suffered much, and the sorrowful music seemed her
own appropriate voice. A little girl clung to her scanty
garments, as if afraid of all things but her mother. As I
looked at them, a young lady of pleasing countenance
opened the window, and began to sing like a bird, in
keeping with the street organ. Two other young girls
came and leaned on her shoulder; and still she sang on.
Blessings on her gentle heart! It was evidently the
spontaneous gush of human love and sympathy. The
beauty of the incident attracted attention. A group of
gentlemen gradually collected round the organist; and
ever as the tune ended, they bowed respectfully toward
the window, waved their hats, and called out, 'More, if
you please!' One, whom I knew well for the kindest and
truest soul, passed round his hat; hearts were kindled,
and the silver fell in freely. In a minute, four or five
dollars were collected for the poor woman. She spoke
no word of gratitude, but she gave *such* a look! 'Will
you go to the next street, and play to a friend of mine?'
said my kind-hearted friend. She answered in tones
expressing the deepest emotion, 'No, sir, God bless you
all—God bless you *all*,' (making a curtsey to the young
lady, who had stepped back, and stood sheltered by the
curtain of the window), 'I will play no more to-day; I
will go *home* now.' The tears trickled down her cheeks,
and, as she walked away, she ever and anon wiped her
eyes with the corner of her shawl. The group of gentlemen lingered a moment to look after her, then turning
toward the now-closed window, they gave three enthusiastic cheers, and departed, better than they came.

*Lydia Child's writing is from
Volume II of* Letters From
New York, *published in 1845.*

*In the years 1843 to 1845
Lydia lived in New York writing
a series of "letters" for the
Boston Courier. The letters
give wonderful descriptions of life
in New York City, from the first
appearance of piped water, to a
grim account of the "dog killers"
roaming the streets clubbing
stray dogs to fight the spread of
rabies. She is thought of as the
first real newspaperwoman.
Mrs. Child published her
newspaper articles in* Letters
From New York (1845). *The
book was so well-received that
eleven editions were printed.*

Lydia Maria Child, abolitionist and author, was born February 11, 1802, in Medford, Massachusetts. She was the foremost woman author of her time. She wrote on a wide variety of subjects. *An Appeal in Favor of That Class of Americans Called Africans*, which she wrote in 1833, is thought of as the first important anti-slavery writing in America. She was the author of the children's song that begins, "Over the river and through the woods to grandmother's house we go." She disliked organizations and lived a quiet life of writing and working for various reforms. She was part of the Underground Railroad, helping slaves to escape. There was a secret tunnel from her house in Wayland, Massachusetts, that led to the nearby Sudbury River. Lydia had no children. Her husband, David, was a dreamer and a poor provider. She loved him dearly and supported them both with the income from her books and articles.

Myra Colby Bradwell

Believing it right to give the ballot to women

Myra Bradwell's writing is from her editorial in the November 7, 1868, issue of Chicago Legal News.

November 7, 1868

We hear a great deal said of late in regard to Woman Suffrage, yet only a few persons are found who have the moral courage and are willing to stand up fairly and squarely and say: "We believe it right to give the ballot to women," about the same number that in our girlhood days were willing to own that a colored man had the God-given right to be free.

But the time *will* come when the opposition to this suffrage movement will melt away before the glorious sunlight of truth and right, as did those old arguments in favor of slavery. Me thinks *human nature* will be about the same then as now—the love of a mother for her darling child will not be lessened—nor the respect and esteem for the noble one who walks by her side, as her protector and guide.

Myra Colby Bradwell, lawyer and crusader for legal reform, was born in Manchester, Vermont, February 12, 1831. Her husband, James Bradwell, was a lawyer. They had three children. James started tutoring Myra in the law early in their marriage and helped her to publish the very successful *Chicago Legal News*, which became an important legal publication.

In 1869 she passed the Illinois bar exam but was denied admission because she was a woman. She took her case to the

Supreme Court and lost there as well. The court stated that it was a matter for states' jurisdiction. When she was fifty-nine, twenty-one years after passing the bar exam, Illinois gave her a license to practice law in her state, and in 1871 she was admitted to practice before the Supreme Court of the United States. She died of cancer when she was sixty-two. At the time of her death, *The American Law Review* wrote that she was "one of the most remarkable women of her generation."

Elizabeth Dwight Cabot

May 20, 1890

My Dear Miss Ellen,

. . . I am doing a little of everything today and wonder whether English women are expected to work in so many different directions at once. First came house-keeping and the sending of letters and parcels, then an hour with my little children who are staying with me. Then an excursion to the greenhouse across the road to see about flowers for my niece Ruth Cabot's wedding. Then to town to see a garden in Hudson Street.

. . . Then a lunch party at Miss Parkman's, Francis Parkman's sister, then to the church for more wedding preparations and then a dear friend to dine and spend the night and I am afraid a sleepy head to entertain her with.

An account of a busy day in Brookline

Elizabeth Dwight Cabot was born in Boston on February 13, 1830. She had a strong civic sense and belonged to many organizations that dealt with social concerns. She had seven sons. Elizabeth worked hard for the Boston Boys' Club, helped manage city-owned tenements for the poor in Boston, and was a member of the Brookline School Committee for many years. In 1888, when she was fifty-eight, she met Ellen Chase, a social worker in England. The two women were alike in their heartfelt concerns for the welfare of the poor and they became good friends, exchanging frequent letters with each other until Elizabeth died in 1901.

Many of Elizabeth Dwight Cabot's letters to Ellen Chase are in the Schlesinger Library, Radcliffe College. All are written on small notepaper and are diary-like in relating the day-to-day events of her life.

Margaret Knight

Famous for her kites

1871

I never cared for the things that girls usually do; dolls never had any charms for me. I couldn't see the sense of coddling bits of porcelain with senseless faces; the only things I wanted were a jackknife, a gimlet and pieces of wood. My friends were horrified. I was called a tomboy, but that made very little impression on me. I sighed sometimes because I was not like other girls, but wisely concluded that I couldn't help it, and sought further consolation from my tools. I was always making things for my brothers. Did they want any-thing in the line of playthings, they always said, "Mattie will make them for us." I was famous for my kites, and my sleds were the envy and admiration of all the boys in town. I'm not surprised at what I've done; I'm only sorry I couldn't have had as good a chance as a boy, and been put to my trade regularly.

Margaret Knight was born in York, Maine, February 14, 1838. From early girlhood she was interested in making things and started inventing when she was twelve years old. She graduated from high school but never went to college. During her lifetime she was awarded twenty-seven patents. Her inventions ranged from an improvement to a paper-feeding machine that would enable it to fold square-bottom bags, to machines for cutting shoes.

She lived in Framingham, Massachusetts, most of her life and worked for several different manufacturing companies there. For a while she had her own shop-workroom in Boston. The inventions didn't bring her financial gain. In her early years she sold them for cash instead of royalties. When she died, her estate was valued at $275.05. At the time of her death, in 1915, the *Framingham News* referred to her as a "woman Edison."

Margaret Knight's writing is an excerpt from a letter she wrote to a friend. It was published in Women in Science, *by H. J. Mozans.*

Julia Archibald Holmes

Pike's Peak,
Aug. 5, 1858

*O*n top of Pike's Peak

Dear Mother,

. . . I have accomplished the task which I marked
out for myself, and now I feel amply repaid for all my
toil and fatigue. Nearly everyone tried to discourage me
from attempting it, but I believed that I should succeed;
and now here I am, and I feel that I would not have
missed this glorious sight for anything at all. In all
probability I am the first woman who has ever stood
upon the summit of this mountain and gazed upon this
wondrous scene, which my eyes now behold. How I
sigh for the poet's power of description, so that I might
give you some faint idea of the grandeur and beauty . . .

Julia Holmes, equal rights advocate, was born in Nova Scotia
on February 15, 1838. Her family first settled in
Massachusetts and later went to Kansas. After her marriage to
James Holmes, the couple traveled from Kansas to Colorado
looking for gold. While on that journey, wearing the reform
bloomer costume, she was the first woman to climb Pike's
Peak. Her writing here is from a letter she wrote her mother
from the top of the mountain.

It is likely Julia's mother sent a
copy of her letter to the
Lawrence *(Kansas)* Republican
so her daughter's story could be
shared. The manuscript copy is
in The Kansas State Historical
Society, Topeka, Kansas.

Leonora O'Reilly

Hull House, Chicago
June 8, 1916

A glorious day for
woman's suffrage

Dear Motherkins,

The big parade is over—it rained in torrents and
the winds blew a gale but on we trudged, colors flying,
slogans held aloft for all to read.

Most wonderful of all, along the line of march
people stood four deep to watch the women go by.

Story has it that just as the antis were saying to the
Republicans, "there is no real demand for the vote"—
we the demanders broke in through every door in the
coliseum dripping wet, with colors flying and spirits

Leonora O'Reilly's many papers
in the Schlesinger Library,
Radcliffe College include this
letter. She and her mother were
very close, and the collection
contains many of the letters they
wrote to each other.

radiant with hope. It was a glorious day for the courage of intelligent womanhood . . .

Leonora O'Reilly, labor leader, women's rights advocate and reformer, was born in New York City, February 16, 1870. She grew up in poverty. Her widowed mother worked long hours in a factory and brought sewing home to do at night. Leonora attended public school for only a few years. At the age of eleven she went to work in a collar factory.

Young Leonora went with her mother to labor and radical meetings. When she was sixteen she joined a neighborhood group of the Knights of Labor and started a club called the Working Women's Society. For several years she was the forewoman in a shirtwaist factory where she worked ten-hour days.

Her friends in the labor movement raised money for Leonora to take time off to go to school. At the Pratt Institute in Brooklyn she took the domestic arts course so that she could become a high-school sewing teacher. She believed that it would be easier for women factory workers to join unions if they had better skills.

Leonora never married. Her adopted daughter died at age five.

This writing is from a letter she wrote to her mother while visiting her friend, Jane Addams, in Chicago.

Sallie Holley

Helping former slaves

Lottsburgh, Virginia
August 3, 1875
There are seven hundred coloured people in this town. Our school keeps from Christmas to Christmas, without vacation, the year round . . . by keeping the doors of our school open, hundreds have learned to read and write. When we first came, they did not know a letter of the alphabet, or the names of the days of the week, could not count on ten fingers or name the state they lived in . . . slaveholders, in shutting out the light of knowledge from the blacks, also shrouded themselves in the gloom of wretched ignorance.

This writing is from A Life For Liberty, Anti-Slavery and Other Letters of Sallie Holley, *published in 1899. It is an excerpt from a printed letter that was probably sent to the North to solicit funds for her school.*

Sallie Holley, abolitionist, was born in Canandaigua, New York, on February 17, 1818. She graduated from Oberlin College in 1851.

After the close of the Civil War, she and her friend Caroline Putnam established a school in Virginia to teach freedmen. The two women taught the former slaves gardening, housekeeping and how to read and write. Sallie never married.

Ida Husted Harper

1883

It's a mistaken idea which girls have that they must be desperately in love with the men they marry. I have seen cases of this kind that exceeded anything ever written in a novel, and I have never yet known of a happy and peaceful marriage to result. It is a short-lived passion, that quickly burns itself out, and lies, a heap of ashes, cold and dead upon the hearth of home. The anticipations which so fervent a love awaken can never be realized, and the keen disappointment causes a reaction that cannot be overcome. *Respect* is the foundation of true love, and we cannot thoroughly respect a man till we have known him long and intimately, have seen him meet with trials and temptations, and overcome them.

Let the man you marry possess your highest esteem, your confidence, your undivided affection; let him find in you corresponding qualities of heart and mind, and you will solemnize the holiest contract on earth—a perfect marriage.

*T*he way to a perfect marriage

Ida Husted Harper, journalist and women's rights advocate, was born February 18, 1851, in Fairfield, Indiana. Ida finished high school when she was seventeen and entered Indiana University as a sophomore. She left after one year to become the principal of a high school in Peru, Indiana.

She married Thomas Winans Harper in 1871 at the age of twenty. He was a lawyer and longtime friend of labor leader Eugene V. Debs, and served as the chief counsel of Debs' union, the Brotherhood of Locomotive Firemen. Soon after her marriage, Ida sent articles to the Terre Haute *Saturday Evening Mail* under a male pseudonym. After doing this secretly for twelve years, she started a weekly column, "A Woman's Opinions," using her own name, and for which she was paid. Ida edited "A Woman's Department" in the

Ida Harper's writing is from her monthly "Woman's Department" section of the April, 1883, Locomotive Firemen's Magazine.

Locomotive Firemen's Magazine for nine years. She divorced her husband in 1890. The couple had one daughter, Winnifred, who also became a writer.

Ida was Susan B. Anthony's official biographer. She spent most of her life working and writing for woman suffrage. She played an important role in the passage of the 19th Amendment on August 26, 1920.

Sara Agnes Pryor

A use for brandy peaches

Charlottesville,
July 1, 1858.
Dear Mrs. Cochran:

May I have your receipt for brandy-peaches? You know Roger is speaking all over the country, trying to win votes for a seat in Congress. I'm not sure he will be elected—but I *am* sure he will like some brandy-peaches! If he is successful, they will enhance the glory of victory—if he is defeated, they will help to console him.

Affectionately,
S. A. Pryor.

Sara Agnes Pryor, author and social leader, was born February 19, 1830, in Halifax County, Virginia. She attended a female seminary in Charlottesville for a brief time but received most of her education from an aunt who tutored her at home. When she was fifteen she had a love story accepted by the *Saturday Evening Post*. Her husband, Roger Atkinson Pryor, was a lawyer and a member of the New York Supreme Court. He won the seat in Congress in 1859 that she makes reference to in her letter. Sara was a founder of the National Society of the Daughters of the American Revolution and a charter member of the Colonial Dames of America. She had seven children. When her husband retired from the court, she began writing books. Her first book was published when she was seventy-three.

Sara Pryor included this letter in her book, My Day, Reminiscences of a Long Life, *published in 1909.*

Elizabeth Carr Miller

1906

I was but nine years old when the Civil War began, but not so young but I vividly recall many things that were said and done. Father was a Republican and of course voted for Lincoln and Hamlin. The Democrat girls called us Lincoln hirelings and black *abolitionists* and many were the quarrels we had at school over the political questions of the day. How our young hearts burned with patriotism when boats laden with blue-coated soldiers passed down the Ohio, and we would wave our sunbonnets and holler "hurrah for Lincoln," or, "hurrah for the Union."

Elizabeth Miller was born February 20, 1852, in a log house on a farm near Rome, Indiana. "Because no boy had come into the family [she was the fourth daughter] my father called me Jim." She received a teaching certificate from the county school. Her first job, when she was eighteen, paid forty dollars a month, and she spent a dollar-and-a-half a week for board and room. Elizabeth married Cortez Miller in 1871, and they had eight children. Her last child was born when she was forty-six. This excerpt of her writing is from a family record she wrote as a Christmas gift to her son in 1910.

Girlhood memories of the Civil War in Indiana

A family record, written by Elizabeth Carr Miller, is in the private papers of Thomas M. Miller, Indianapolis, Indiana.

Alice Freeman Palmer

1897

To a largely increasing number of young girls, college doors are opening every year. Every year adds to the number of men who feel as a friend of mine, a successful lawyer in a great city, felt when talking of the future of his four little children. He said, "For the two boys it is not so serious, but I lie down at night afraid to die and leave my daughters only a bank account." Year by year, too, the experiences of life are teaching mothers that happiness does not necessarily come to their daughters when accounts are large and banks are sound, but that

Why young girls should go to college

Alice Freeman Palmer's writing is taken from "Why Go to College," an article she wrote in 1897. Wellesley College archives contain a collection of her letters and writings.

on the contrary they take grave risks when they trust everything to accumulated wealth and the chance of a happy marriage.

Alice Freeman Palmer was born in Colesville, New York, February 21, 1855. Her graduating class at the University of Michigan in 1876 consisted of sixty-four men and eleven women. She was a dedicated teacher and a champion of college education for women. She went to Wellesley College in 1878 as a professor of history and in 1882 became its second president. Alice resigned five years later, when she was thirty-two, to become the wife of George H. Palmer, a professor at Harvard. The couple had no children.

Isabella Beecher Hooker

Gentlemen who sit in judgment

This excerpt of Isabella's writing is from a speech she gave before the Judiciary Committee of the U.S. Senate. In 1872 it was printed in pamphlet form and included in a memorial tribute to other suffragists.

1872

You sit here, gentlemen, in judgment on my rights as an American citizen, as though they were something different from your own; but they are not . . .

 Our ship of State carries two engines, gentlemen, and was built for them, but heretofore you have used only one, and now you have reached the place where not only two seas meet, but all ocean currents are struggling together for the mastery. The man power alone will not save you, but put on the woman power, and our gallant ship will steady itself for a moment, and then ride the waves triumphantly forevermore.

Isabella Beecher Hooker, suffragist and advocate of women's rights, was born in Litchfield, Connecticut, February 22, 1822. She was a controversial and eccentric figure, often supporting unconventional ideas. The spiritualist cult and belief in séances and mediums were part of her life. At one point she was sure that she would be chosen by spiritual powers to head a matriarchal government of the world. She was an important figure in the National Woman Suffrage Association and was a frequent speaker at Suffrage gatherings.

Emma Hart Willard

Ship Charlemagne,
Oct. 20, 1830
Lat. 49°, Lon. 12R 14'
My Dear Sister:

. . . I have a prospect of realizing the benefit which I expected to my health, from a sea voyage. Yet I have not been seasick, neither have I exercised as much on deck, owing to the roughness of the weather, as I could have wished; but the perpetual motion in which I am kept by the winds and waters; —rocking, and rolling, and tossing; holding with might and main, by some fixed object during the day to keep from being shot across the cabin, and grasping the side of my berth at night for fear of being rolled over the side, all this, though not particularly diverting at the time, is yet very conducive to my health; and seems to put in motion those vital functions, which want of suitable exercise for the body or too much mental exertion had deranged. But not alone to second causes should we attribute the good which we enjoy. . .

Stormy sea voyage

Emma Willard, pioneer of higher education for women, was born February 23, 1787, in Berlin, Connecticut. She was the sixteenth of a family of seventeen children. Emma was encouraged by her father to be intellectual and to set her sights, relative to her sphere in life, higher than most women of her time. When she was thirteen she taught herself geometry and at fifteen enrolled in Berlin Academy. In 1805 she began teaching the younger children at the academy.

Her first husband, Dr. John Willard, was twenty-eight years older than she was. They had one child, John Hart Willard. After Dr. Willard died she married another physician, Christopher Yates. He turned out to be a gambler and fortune hunter, and Emma left him nine months after their wedding. Five years later she obtained a divorce from the state of Connecticut.

In 1819 she moved to Troy, New York, and started the Troy Female Seminary, which later became the Emma Willard School.

Emma lectured and helped organize women's educational societies. She was the foremost reformer of her time in education for women. However, she never became involved in the

Emma's writing here is taken from a letter she wrote to her sister while crossing the Atlantic on a trip to France and England. In 1833 she published her letters and journal written at that time in Journal and Letters from France and Great Britain.

suffrage issue, believing that ". . . even intellectually, the wife may be greater than her husband, and the servant greater than either; but both in the family and in the State, order must prevail; law, human and divine, must have its course; and the good show their goodness by submission. This is one of the trials of this life, by which immortal beings become fitted for a better."

Mary Louisa Hulbert

Life, short and uncertain

April, 1852
Chicago
O my dear husband life is so short and uncertain, it seems very hard that we must be so long separated. Children to bring up and it needs both of us to bring them up as they should be but we must make the best of our lot and try and not sin against God by repining or murmuring. . . . George is so anxious that I shall tell you about our addition to our family that I will just say that the next morning after you left the little cat had seven kittens. I do not know but the birth of them was hastened by the grief of the cat at your departure. She certainly missed you very much.

> Yours in very much love,
> Mary L.

Mary Louisa's letter is at the Chicago Historical Society in the Eri Baker Hulbert and Mary Louisa Walker Hulbert collection, Letters 1836-1852.

Mary Louisa Hulbert was born in Plainsfield, New York, February 24, 1810. She and her husband, Eri Baker Hulbert, had three sons. The family moved from Plainsfield to Chicago to join with Mary Louisa's brother in a business of importing farm implements from the east. They were also the first company to export grain to the east from Chicago.

At the time Mary Louisa was writing this letter in April, 1852, her husband was on his way to California. She never saw him again. Two months later he was killed in an accident.

Give Her This Day

Ida Lewis

May 4, 1889
To Henry King Smith
Dear Sir,

    Yours of April 14 was duly received. Please pardon my long delay in answering. You wish for me to state how many lives I have saved all together since I have had charge of the Light House at Lime Rock Light. I will say in reply 16.

    Respectfully yours,
    Ida Lewis

Lighthouse keeper's note

Ida Lewis was born in Newport, Rhode Island, February 25, 1842. Her father was the keeper of the Lime Rock Lighthouse in Newport Harbor. When she was sixteen, he suffered a paralytic stroke and Ida assumed his duties. Each day she rowed her younger brothers and sister to and from the mainland so that they could attend school. Her good rowing ability enabled her to rescue many people from the sea.

    Ida kept Lime Rock Light for almost twenty years before the federal government in 1879 appointed her the official keeper. She became widely known for her bravery and heroic rescues in the waters of Newport Harbor. When she was in her sixties, Congress and the American Cross of Honor Society awarded her gold medals and the Carnegie Hero Fund gave her a pension.

    When Ida was twenty-eight, she married William H. Wilson, a sailor and fisherman. The marriage was very unhappy and the couple stayed together only a brief time. She believed that divorce was wrong but felt that separation was right if a terrible mistake had been made. She had no children and was never known as "Mrs. Wilson," but was always called "Miss Ida." She died when she was sixty-nine. At the time of her death, she was still in charge of Lime Rock Lighthouse, having been its "keeper" for over fifty years.

Ida's letter to Henry King Smith is in the Gatz collection, at the Historical Society of Pennsylvania, Manuscript Division. There are no collections of Ida's writing in any library or historical society in Rhode Island, or in the National Archives in Washington. This letter may be the only one of hers that was ever saved. She wrote in a beautiful hand.

Katherine ("Sherwood") Bonner

The beginning of an
important relationship

Boston
Dec. 8, 1873
Dear Mr. Longfellow,
I am a Southern girl away from home and friends.
I have come here for mental discipline and study, and to
try to find out the meaning and use of my life. It would
be to me a great happiness and help if I might know
you. May I come and see you please? and if so will you
appoint a day and hour?
With deep respect,
Katherine Bonner
Address
27 Rutland St.

*This letter is in the Henry
Wadsworth Longfellow
collection, Houghton Library,
Harvard University. Katherine
sent it soon after her arrival in
Boston. It was the beginning of
a relationship that lasted until
1883, when she died of cancer at
the age of thirty-four.*

Katherine "Sherwood" Bonner McDowell, author, was born
February 26, 1849, in Holly Springs, Mississippi. She sold her
first story to *The Massachusetts Ploughman* magazine when she
was fifteen. Unhappily married, Katherine left her husband,
Edward McDowell, in 1873 and took her two-year-old
daughter to Boston to pursue a writing career. She wrote
under the *nom de plume* "Sherwood Bonner." Katherine
became Longfellow's assistant and protégé. She dedicated her
novel, *Like Unto Like*, to him.

Laura Elizabeth Richards

How she met her husband

1931
The memory of Class Day, 1869, [at Harvard] is a bright
one. In white and pink, with a pink saucer hat tipped
over my nose, I was proud and happy. The seniors wore
tall hats in '69; they danced around the Tree, they
leaped, pranced, flung themselves about, like young
fauns, if one can imagine a faun in a top hat. They sang
and danced and did many things which I believe were
not done at my grandson's graduation.
One member of the Class of 1869 was not present;
having been born with a dislike of functions, he saw no
reason for enduring one; he took a boat and went down

*This writing is from Laura
Richards' autobiography,
Stepping Westward, written
when she was eighty-one and
published in 1931.*

to the harbor. Fate claims us; there is no escape. The elusive senior and I were to meet, as we had met at dancing school, as we had met again on the stairs at 19 Boylston Place. In the winter of 1869, Henry Richards and I became engaged.

We were young; we had no special prospects, financially speaking; briefly we were to wait two years before thinking of marriage. We waited. . . . Finally we were married on June 17th, 1871, and the Boston bells rang and cannon were fired on Boston Common, and there were fireworks in the evening.

Laura Richards was born February 27, 1850, in Boston, Massachusetts. Her father was Samuel Gridley Howe, the founder of the Perkins Institution for the Blind, and her mother was Julia Ward Howe, the author of "The Battle Hymn of the Republic."

Laura and her husband, Henry Richards, had seven children and enjoyed seventy-one years of married life. They lived in Gardiner, Maine.

Laura started to write when she was ten. She published eighty books in her lifetime. When her seven children were very young, she wrote children's books and poems. As her daughters grew, she wrote novels for young girls, her most famous being *Captain January*. This book sold 3,000,000 copies. Two movies have been made from it, one of which starred Shirley Temple.

Together with her sister Maude, Laura wrote a biography of her mother that received the first Pulitzer Prize for biography.

Laura Richards wrote until the last year of her life. She died when she was ninety-three.

Mary Lyon

Amherst,
April 2, 1835
My Very Dear Mother,
     . . . I think it best to keep myself disengaged from any school, till the new school goes into operation in South Hadley. But the work goes forward very slowly. It will be a great while before I can expect the privilege of laboring there. Will you, my dear mother, pray for this new institution, that God will open the hearts of his

A new college for women

children in its behalf, and that the Spirit of God may rest on its future teachers and pupils, that it may be a spot where souls may be born of God, and saints quickened in their Lord's service? It is my heart's desire that holiness to the Lord may be inscribed upon all connected with it, and that a succession of teachers may be raised up, who shall there continue to labor for Christ long after we are laid in our graves.

Mary Lyon, the founder of Mount Holyoke College, was born in Buckland, Massachusetts, on February 28, 1797. She attended local village schools, and started her own teaching career when she was seventeen in summer schools for little children.

Mary was an energetic, visionary young woman who believed that "there is nothing in the universe I am afraid of but that I shall not know and do all my duty."

She held several good teaching positions before she started on the almost overwhelming task of starting a female seminary for "adult female youth in the common walks of life." Her hopes were to provide women with the same quality of education that was available at the best men's colleges, and that the institution be created on a solid foundation of Christian beliefs. She succeeded, and in 1837, Mount Holyoke Female Seminary opened with its first class of eighty students. Mary thus became the first woman to found a college for women. She was generous and kind, loyal to her friends, and she committed her great energy and intellect to everything she believed in. Mary Lyon died in 1849 and is buried on the Mount Holyoke campus.

Mary Lyon's writing is from a copy of a letter she wrote to her mother, Jemima Shepard Lyon. It is included in The Power of Christian Benevolence, Life and Labors of Mary Lyon *by Edward Hitchcock, president of Amherst College, published in 1851.*

Elizabeth Munson Bayley

Letter to the dead or living

Chehalem Valley, Yamhill County, Oregon
September 20, 1849
Mrs. Lucy P. Griffith, South Charleston, Ohio
My Dear Sister,

It is a long time since I have seen or heard from you, and I don't know whether I am writing to the dead or the living. There is a vast distance between us. The Rocky Mountains separate us. We left Missouri in the year 1845, and started on our pilgrimage to Oregon territory. The fore part of our journey was pleasant.

Give Her This Day

The company we started in consisted of sixty-four wagons. . . . We had no difficulty with the Indians but once. At Fort Hall the Indians came to our camp and said they wanted to trade. They trade horses for wives. Mr. Bayley joked with them, and asked a young Indian how many horses he would give for Caroline [her seventeen-year-old daughter]. The Indian said "three." Mr. Bayley said, "Give me six horses and you can have her," all in a joke. The next day he came after her, and had six horses, and seemed determined to have her. He followed our wagons for several days, and we were glad to get rid of him without any trouble. The Indians never joke, and Mr. Bayley took good care ever after not to joke with them.

Elizabeth Bayley was born in Hartford, Connecticut, on February 29, 1804. She and her husband left Missouri for Oregon with their seven children in 1845. The journey took seven months and twenty-one days over the Oregon Trail. They settled on a donation land claim of one square mile in Chehalem Valley.

The original copy of this letter has never been found. It had been hand-copied and given to the Sabina Ohio News. *I imagine that Elizabeth's sister, Lucy, gave her letter to the newspaper. This was often done so that news from those who had travelled west could be shared. There is a manuscript copy in the Library of the Oregon Historical Society.*

MARCH

Mary Palmer Tyler

1858-1863

I recollect, we children were playing on the floor in the parlor. I was lying down on the carpet when my father rushed into the house, threw open the door of the room saying, "Hurrah, Hurrah!" and, catching me up in his arms, danced a hornpipe round the room singing and whistling in a very extraordinary manner. Mother sat at her work table as usual. She sprang up exclaiming, "Mr. Palmer, what is the matter? What does ail you?" He dropped me instantly, clasped her in his arms, flew around the room kissing her over and over again, and at last exclaimed, "Peace is declared! Hurrah!" and away he flew to spread the joyful news. Mother, as was her wont, expressed her joy by a copious shower of tears. We poor children were too much astonished by the behavior of our revered parents to say anything, but ran out of the house to hear more about the great event.

Mary Palmer Tyler was born on March 1, 1775, in Watertown, Massachusetts. She met her husband-to-be, Royall Tyler, when she was eight years old and he was in his twenties. Mary and Royall were married when she was seventeen. They settled in Brattleboro, Vermont, and had eleven children. Mary survived Royall by forty years. Her "life from the death of her husband was wholly that of a mother, a mother in the widest sense of the word, for she mothered not only her children but the neighbors and the community as well."

Late in her life, Mary's fifth son, William Clark Tyler, gave her a "beautiful book" and "begged her to set down the tales he and his brothers and sisters had loved listening to, that their children and children's children might possess her pictures of the early days of their country."

Peace is declared

Mary's writing, describing the end of the American Revolution, is from her memoirs, written between 1858 and 1863. Her great-grandson submitted the manuscript to G. P. Putnam's Sons, who published Grandmother Tyler's Book—The Recollections of Mary Palmer Tyler *in 1925.*

Sarah Royce

A passage

1849

Our Guide book gave very elaborate directions by
which we might be able to identify the highest point in
our road, where we passed from the Atlantic to the
Pacific Slope. . . . I had looked forward for weeks to the
step that should take me past that point. In the morning
of that day I had taken my last look at the waters that
flowed eastward, to mingle with the streams and wash
the shores where childhood and early youth had been
spent; where all I loved, save O, so small a number,
lived; and now I stood on the almost imperceptible elevation that, when passed, would separate me from all
these, perhaps forever. Through what toils and dangers
we had come to reach that point; and, as I stood looking
my farewell, a strong desire seized me to mark the spot
in some way, and record at least one word of grateful
acknowledgement. Yes, I would make a little heap of
stones.

Nobody would notice or understand it; but my
Heavenly Father would see the little monument in the
mountain wilderness, and accept the humble thanks it
recorded. So I turned to gather stones. But no stone
could I find, not even pebbles enough to make a heap —
and no stick either, not a bush or a shrub or a tree
within reach. So I stood still upon the spot until the
two wagons and the little company had passed out of
hearing; and when I left not a visible sign marked the
place.

Sarah Eleanor Bayliss, was born March 2, 1819, in England.
Her family emigrated to New York when she was an infant.

In 1847 she and her husband Josiah Royce and their
young daughter joined the gold-rush migration to California.
At the beginning of their journey the Royces travelled in a
large wagon train of gold speculators. They soon separated
from the group and continued on alone because the others
would not observe the Sabbath. Sarah kept a "pilgrimage
diary" and wrote a few pencilled lines each day describing their
perilous journey. Once they took a wrong fork and travelled
miles out of their way. Sarah walked to lighten the weak

oxen's load (the Royces were so short of grass they had been taking the straw out of their mattresses to feed the starving oxen).

Along the sides of the trail were piles of belongings that previous pioneers had been forced to abandon to lighten their loads. The Royces eventually had to remove everything but the essentials from their own wagon, since they were running out of time to cross the Sierras before snow fell.

Sarah and Josiah settled in Grass Valley, California, where they reared three daughters and a son under very primitive conditions. She started a school for her children and some of her neighbor's children in her home. After twelve years in Grass Valley the family moved to San Francisco so the children could receive a better education.

Sarah's son, Josiah, became a philosophy professor at Harvard. Thirty years after the gold rush he asked his mother to write an autobiographical account for his book on the history of California. She did this for him, working from her diary and personal recollections. Sarah had a deep faith in God: strong and brave, she was an admirable example of the American pioneer woman.

Sarah Royce's writing recalls crossing the Continental Divide at the South Pass of the Rocky Mountains in southwest Wyoming. It is from her written recollections in A Frontier Lady, Recollections of the Gold Rush and Early California, *published after her death in 1932.*

Anne Gorham Everett

London

December 17, 1841

Papa has been presented to the Queen. She is now at Windsor Castle, and invited Papa there to deliver his credentials and then to dine and pass the night, which he did. The Queen and Prince Albert were very amiable and polite to him, and he had a very pleasant visit. . . . I do not know when Mamma and I are to be presented; perhaps not till after the meeting of parliament. When we have been, then we shall make a business of leaving cards on all the ambassador's and minister's ladies; the cards only are to be left; you do not, at the first visit, go in.

Anne Gorham Everett was born March 3, 1823, in Boston, Massachusetts. She was the oldest daughter of Edward Everett, a prominent Bostonian. Her father was a representative in the U.S. House, governor of Massachusetts, president of Harvard and U.S. minister to Great Britain.

When Mr. Everett was appointed U.S. minister in 1841, the family moved to London. Anne was taught by private

Being presented to the Queen

Anne's letter is to her friend Philippa Call Bush and is included in Memoir of Anne Gorham Everett; with Extracts from her Correspondence and Journal. *The book was privately printed in 1857 for friends and family.*

Anne and her mother were presented to Queen Victoria in April, 1842, just eighteen months before her death.

---

tutors and spoke several languages.

While living abroad Anne became seriously ill. It is surmised she was exposed to malaria from the Pontine Marshes. She died in 1842 when she was twenty years old. Her father wrote: "Young as she was, she had grown up to be my companion and friend, sometimes my adviser, often my exemplar, the object of my tenderest parental love."

Anne's letters and journals reveal her charming, serious personality, her deep faith and love of life.

When Anne died she was temporarily interred in London until her family's return to America in 1845. She was then buried in Mount Auburn Cemetery, Cambridge, Massachusetts, beside her baby sister, Grace.

Myrtilla Miner

*H*er Master's business

Washington
May 17, 1852
My Dear Hannah,

I could not secure a good boarding place near my school, for that is nearly out of town, the people having obliged us to move twice to get out of their way. . . .

Many ladies refused to take me to board because I would teach colored girls, and much else of obloquy and contempt have I endured because I would be about my Master's business. I heed it not, though I am to-night informed that the new mayor will abolish all colored schools. I care not.

October 20, 1852

I love this school of mine profoundly, and have really no idea, when I am with them, that they are not white, recognizing their *spiritual* more than their physical. Some, indeed many, *spirits* with whom I come in contact here seem far darker than they.

Myrtilla Miner was born March 4, 1815, near Brookfield, New York. Her aunt, who operated a private school in her home, inspired her to become a teacher. She picked hops to earn money for her books. Following graduation from the Clover Street Seminary in Rochester, New York, she began her teaching career.

In 1847 Myrtilla spent an unhappy year at a girls' academy in Mississippi. She was appalled by the lack of educational opportunities for slaves, and determined to do

Myrtilla's writing is compiled from letters to her friend Hannah who lived in Pennsylvania. They are included in Myrtilla Miner: A Memoir *by Ellen O'Connor, published in 1885.*

Give Her This Day

something about it. In 1851, with a $100 donation from a Pennsylvania Quaker, she moved to Washington, D.C., and opened the Colored Girls School.

Myrtilla's school soon grew from six to forty pupils. Due to local opposition, she was forced to change locations three times in two years, and occasionally had to brandish a pistol to repel hostile crowds. In 1853, with contributions from Quakers plus $1,000 from Harriet Beecher Stowe's [June 14] royalties from *Uncle Tom's Cabin*, Myrtilla purchased a three-acre lot on the outskirts of town. Her school's one-year program was the only education beyond the elementary level for pre-Civil War blacks.

Myrtilla was forced into early retirement in 1855 due to her fragile health. Nine years later she was thrown from a carriage and died within a few months. Her school continued to operate successfully, and was renamed the Miner Teachers College in 1929. Following the 1954 Supreme Court decision outlawing school segregation, it merged with another institution to form the District of Columbia Teachers College.

Anna Mowatt

Greenfield Hill
July 26, 1846

A close call

I am afraid, my dearest Katie, you will scarcely believe how glad I was to receive your letter unless I answer it without delay. . . . Our last visit to the beach came near favoring a most fatal one to both myself and the children and I cannot help shuddering at the recollection. . . . We had taken the children to bathe and after seeing them enjoy themselves highly in the water my husband told me to drive them home, for he would remain to shoot and return home by another conveyance. For some time we jogged along quite safely, "old Rawbones" proving perfectly obedient to the rein. At last we came to two roads branching different ways and I could not make up my mind which was right, so gave "Rawbones" his own choice, supposing he must guide me toward home. Rawbones was in a brown study, for he took the wrong road, which I presently discovered. At last we found ourselves on the top of a steep hill directly in front of Terry's mill stream. I urged the horse into the water, but before he was half over Rawbones—suddenly

Anna's letter, to her childhood friend Miss Catherine Sargent Huntington, is in the Schlesinger Library, Radcliffe College. The children mentioned are the three Grey children, whom she rescued from the slums and raised as her own.

finding himself immersed up to his breast—quickly lost all respect for his guide. With a very strong effort I frustrated the murderous efforts of the horse and after battling with him a couple of frightful minutes, I turned him towards a narrow little island in the middle of the stream, and persuaded him to lodge the wagon safely upon it. Once on the Island what were we to do? We could neither return nor go on, and there was no assistance within hail. While I was uncertain whether or not to give one of those terrific yells with which Juliet sometimes indulges the startled audience, a gentleman on the road perceived my forlorn-looking self. He drove instantly to the opposite side of the stream and called out, "What has happened? Can I be of any assistance?" I quickly answered, "Show me how to get over there—I can't cross the stream!" "Don't be afraid," he replied very gallantly, "get the children in, and I'll get you safe over here." I obeyed, and in a few minutes was safe on land. Once there I began to tremble violently, and could hardly keep back my tears or help jumping into our delivery wagon and doing something particularly ridiculous in the way of a tragedy queen's heroic tender of thanks. You may well suppose that I was betwixt a smile and a tear all the way home, and the latter almost gained the victory when Captain Nichols coolly informed me that if we had upset in that part of the stream we would have been *drowned "to a certainty."*

Anna Cora Ogden Mowatt, author and actress, was born March 5, 1819, in Bordeaux, France, where her father was working at the time. The family returned to New York City when she was seven, and at fifteen she eloped with James Mowatt, a wealthy lawyer thirteen years her senior.

After Anna developed tuberculosis, the couple left their home on Long Island for Germany's more healthful climate. Her husband also became ill, and they remained abroad for three years.

After returning to the United States, James' health further declined and he lost his fortune through speculation. Anna was forced to assume their support, which she did by writing and giving public poetry readings. In 1845 she wrote a play, "Fashion," a witty satire of New York society life. The play enjoyed enormous success and is still presented today.

Anna became involved with the theater through the success of her play. She debuted as an actress in New York

City and embarked on an eight-year career as one of the foremost actresses on the English-speaking stage. Her husband died in London where Anna was performing. Shortly thereafter her manager committed suicide due to unrequited love for her. She suffered a breakdown and died in 1870.

Lilian Welsh

1925

Always in my lectures in hygiene I was obliged to point out the essential need of the ballot as a tool for securing conditions in the community favorable to health. My opinions on suffrage for women were well-known to the students.

The parade was to take place Monday afternoon. I had two classes meeting from nine to eleven on Monday morning. Very late Sunday night a letter was delivered to me at my home, saying that the sophomore class appreciated the fact that I desired to take part in the suffrage parade in Washington, and they wanted me to be free to do so without feeling that I was neglecting any of my duties. They had, therefore, decided unanimously to "cut" the nine and ten o'clock hygiene classes. As I had no intention of going to Washington until twelve o'clock, I presented myself as usual behind the lecture platform at nine and ten-twenty, but the seats were all empty. The kindness and generosity to me had its reward, in part, as a holiday for them, as the Goucher contingent in the parade was a large one and the students made an entire day of it.

Lilian Welsh, physician and educator, was born March 6, 1858, in Columbia, Pennsylvania.

Lilian received an M.D. degree in 1889 and went on to the University of Zurich for graduate study. After her work in Zurich, she went into private practice in Baltimore with another woman doctor she had met in Zurich, Dr. Mary Sherwood. Because of prejudice against female doctors, they did not have many patients.

In 1894 Lilian decided to leave her practice and teach. She then began her thirty-year affiliation with the recently formed Woman's College of Baltimore (later Goucher College). Lilian wrote about the early years at Goucher: "A

Lilian's writing excerpt here is from her book Reminiscences of Thirty Years in Baltimore, *published in 1925.*

woman who accepted a position in a woman's college in 1890 to develop a department of hygiene entered an unworked field and could practically make of it what she pleased. It seemed to me that the gymnasiums connected with women's colleges should be looked upon as laboratories where one might study the effects of exercise and of mental work upon the health of girls and women."

She was a member of the National American Woman Suffrage Association and marched in numerous street parades. Lilian was also a member of many Baltimore women's organizations as well as a leader in city and state public health work.

Louise Whitfield Carnegie

Leading two lives

Kilgraston,
Sunday, July 1887
Well, Mother darling, as some of the party have gone to church and others are in their rooms I have shut myself in my little sitting room to have a little chat with you. Somehow Sundays I feel more lonely than any other day of the week. I miss the old sweet routine and the great change in my life comes over me more than at any other time. Andrew is sweet and lovely all the time but he is so very different from every other human being. There is not the first particle of pretense about him—he is so thoroughly honest. . . .

I seem to be leading two lives—outwardly I am the mature married woman, while inwardly I am trying to reconcile the old and the new life. I get awfully blue sometimes, but I know it is very wrong to indulge in this feeling and above all to write it to you, but, Mother dear, I feel so much better for it.

Louise Whitfield Carnegie was born March 7, 1857, in New York City. When she was eighteen she met Andrew Carnegie, her future husband, when a friend brought him by the family home. He was twenty-two years older than Louise, the same age as her mother, so at first he paid little attention to her. Over the next few years, however, they discovered they shared many interests and a romance blossomed.

Andrew's mother was possessive and he was overly devoted. Louise broke off their engagement when she realized they could never marry while Mrs. Carnegie was alive. They were finally married in 1887, five months after she died.

Louise's letter, written from Scotland while on her honeymoon, is included in her biography, Louise Whitfield Carnegie—The Life of Mrs. Andrew Carnegie, *by B. Hendrich and D. Henderson, published in 1950.*

Give Her This Day

Suddenly Louise found herself married to one of America's richest men. After years of living in a hotel suite, Andrew was overjoyed to have a home, and Louise became his willing hostess. She aided him in his business and philanthropic interests. Louise spent her life after Andrew's death carrying on his work. She received many honors but, always modest, she accepted them in her husband's memory, saying, "I am the unknown wife of a somewhat well-known businessman."

Emily Elizabeth Parsons

Benton Barracks Hospital
July 8, 1864
My Dear Mother, . . .

*L*ove that heals

One of the boys here is very ill; his father came to see him, and found him asleep. When the boy woke there was his father by his bedside. You may imagine the meeting! The old father sits by the bedside fanning him, and he lies with his hand on his father's knee. . . .

There was another man here very ill, growing worse daily. I wrote to his wife to come to him; and one day when I entered the ward, there she was! I got a warm greeting from her. She brightened him up, nursed him as only a wife can, night and day. I let her stay in the ward, sleeping in the lady nurses' room. He by and by began to mend, and was well enough last week to go home with his wife. If he gets well I do believe it will be due to her; I think she saved his life. Is not that a happy thought for a wife?

Emily Elizabeth Parsons, Civil War nurse, was born March 8, 1824, in Taunton, Massachusetts. Despite being handicapped since childhood by partial blindness, partial deafness and a painful chronic ankle injury, she resolved at the outbreak of the Civil War to become a nurse.

To prepare herself, Emily took 18 months of training at the Massachusetts General Hospital. Her first assignment was a military hospital on Long Island where she was in charge of fifty patients. One year later she was appointed to the Benton Barracks Hospital in St. Louis, the largest military hospital in the west with twenty-five hundred beds. Her appointment was one of the most important given to a woman during the Civil War.

Emily's letter, written to her mother from Benton Barracks Hospital, is included in Memoir of Emily Elizabeth Parsons, *edited by her father and published posthumously in 1880 for the benefit of the Mount Auburn Hospital.*

Although she usually worked sixteen-hour days, Emily loved her work and "her boys." Following the war she started the Cambridge Hospital in her home, caring for destitute families who were unable to pay. The hospital was renamed the Mount Auburn Hospital after her death and is still in operation today.

Emelie Swett Parkhurst

A loved one's absence

1888

The days seemed interminably long—and O so dull! After the tenth day had passed, Emilia walked down every evening to the bluff where she had stood to watch him on the day of his departure—she even called out to him, to make the dead silence of her surroundings less oppressive. Twenty days, and still no signs of the absent one. When three weeks had come and gone, Emilia's anxiety knew no bounds, and towards the evening of the twenty-second day, when her suspense became unendurable, she went to the meadow where the burro was tethered, and throwing her arms about the animal's neck she sobbed, "Good, strong burrito mio, something has happened to your master, and you and I must go and search for him."

Emelie Tracy Swett Parkhurst, poet and author, was born March 9, 1863, in San Francisco, California. Her father, Professor John Swett, was a prominent educator in California and was referred to as "The Father of Pacific Coast Education." He made certain that his own daughter was well-educated.

When she was fourteen, Emelie's first story was printed in the *San Francisco Chronicle*. She continued to write throughout her life, publishing articles, short stores, poetry and biographies. Emelie organized the Pacific Coast Literary Bureau, which later became the Pacific Coast Woman's Press Association.

Emelie's writing is from one of her short stories, "A Legend of Martinez," that was published in the August 1888 issue of Overland Magazine.

Emelie married John Parkhurst, a banker, in 1889. She died three years later when she was twenty-nine.

Hallie Quinn Brown

1939

Our home was a valuable and active station for the Underground Railroad. Many runaway slaves, seeking freedom, found refuge in the garret until they were spirited away to Canada. We children often wondered why our mother baked so many loaves of bread and what was the cause of their speedy disappearance. A family arrived from Texas. They brought with them five children. In complexion, they were white. One saw little suggestion of Negro blood in this family. And yet, officers and masters were pressing hard on their heels. The family was hidden for one week and then, draped in the flag, the stars and stripes, defied the officers who would lay hands on them. Flag-covered, in this manner, they were photographed. For years that picture hung in our home.

Hallie Quinn Brown was born March 10, 1850, in Pittsburgh, Pennsylvania. Her parents were both freed slaves. The family moved to Wilberforce, Ohio in 1870 so she and her younger brother could attend Wilberforce University, a black college. She graduated in a class of six and received a B.S. degree.

Hallie started her teaching career in the South, where she felt most needed during the Reconstruction period. She traveled from Mississippi to South Carolina, Ohio to Alabama, teaching in various public schools and universities. Wherever she settled she always started a night school for black adults who couldn't read.

In the late 1880's Hallie traveled extensively as a lecturer and elocutionist. Her focus was Negro history, temperance and suffrage. As a representative to the International Congress of Women she made two appearances before Queen Victoria.

Hallie's writing is from her unpublished autobiography As the Mantle Falls, *which is in the manuscript collection of the Hallie Quinn Brown Memorial Library, Central State University, Wilberforce, Ohio.*

Eliza Jane Nicholson (Pearl Rivers)

1871

Can a woman travel one hundred miles without taking seven trunks and fourteen bandboxes with her? Grandpa is seventy-five years old and didn't know that such a thing was possible until early last Thursday morning, when cousin Maggie and I came downstairs, dressed for a three day trip to Pascagoula with no other baggage than two small ladies' companions.

The morning was wet and heavy, but two merry girls, and a merrier old gentleman as escort, make a pleasant little traveling party and the fun opened with the carriage door, got out with us at the depot and accompanied us to the end of our jaunt. . . .

The first thing that attracted my attention, after looking around at my fellow passengers, was an old valise that grandpa had shoved under his seat, just behind us; so old and rusty that it looked as if it might have held the extra clothing of Noah when he landed upon Mount Ararat. I declared that it was perfectly outrageous of him to travel with such shabby-looking baggage when escorting young ladies, and proposed to Cousin Maggie that we should pitch it overboard at once; but, remembering that "a bad cloak often covers a good drinker," we concluded to examine the contents and found that among other things the old gentleman had thoughtfully provided himself with a large bundle of lunch and a stout little bottle which he slyly remarked contained toothache medicine.

Eliza Jane Nicholson, poet and journalist, was born March 11, 1849, in Hancock County, Mississippi. After graduating from boarding school she began submitting her poetry to magazines and newspapers under the pen name "Pearl Rivers." At twenty she was included in an anthology of Southern writers.

While visiting her grandfather in 1870 she met Alva Holbrook, owner and editor of the *New Orleans Picayune*. He offered her the job of literary editor, which she accepted despite her family's objections. Eliza and Alva, a man forty-one years her senior, were married two years later. They sold the paper but Alva bought it back after it failed under its new ownership. Unfortunately he died shortly thereafter, leaving his twenty-six-year-old widow with an $80,000 debt. Her family urged her to declare bankruptcy but she was determined to carry on. Her many innovations made the paper suitable for the whole family, and the daily circulation tripled.

Eliza remarried in 1878 and continued to publish poetry and run the *Picayune* until her untimely death at forty-six from influenza.

Eliza's writing is from an article she wrote for the Sunday edition of the New Orleans Picayune *on February 19, 1871.*

Give Her This Day

Jane Arminda Delano

Navy Base Hospital No. 1
Brest, France
Jan. 11, 1919

To give care oneself

The mud was overpowering and only a few boardwalks have been built. In some parts of the camp, it was almost impossible to get through even in the automobile, so one wonders how the nurses have been able to get from ward to ward. . . .

The spirit of the nurses was excellent. In one ward, I met Miss Lord, one of the older Red Cross nurses. She has had a great deal of training school and hospital experience. She told me that never in her life had she found more satisfying work and that she was very happy to have been able to be in charge of a ward and able to take care of the soldiers herself.

Jane Arminda Delano was born March 12, 1862, near Seneca Lake, New York. She was inspired to become a nurse by a friend who had been to India as a missionary nurse.

Jane stood out in her class at nursing school and was rewarded with special duties. Immediately after graduation she was selected to tend the mayor of New York's sciatica. Next she was sent to Florida during a yellow-fever epidemic, followed by Arizona during a typhoid-fever epidemic. She held many administrative positions until 1908, when she began her all-important work of unifying the nursing associations of the Army Nurse Corps and the Red Cross.

During World War I, Jane was able to meet the army's needs, supplying 20,000 professionally trained nurses. She contracted an illness and died in France during a 1919 inspection tour of Red Cross units.

Jane's diary entry, written a few months before her death, is included in The History of American Red Cross Nursing, *published in 1922.*

Christiana Holmes Tillson

1870

A young woman heads west

In 1822 it was still a great event to undertake a journey to Illinois, and many were the direful remarks and conclusions about my going. Your grandmother dreaded my starting without any lady companion, and

was much relieved to find that a Mrs. Cushman, a widow lady, whose husband had been a lawyer in Halifax, and who had but one child—a son, settled near Cincinnati—was waiting an opportunity to go and end her days with her beloved Joshua, and that your father had offered her a seat in our carriage, which offer had been accepted. Your uncle Robert was also to go. The carriage had been built at Bedford, Massachusetts, under your father's directions, expressly for the journey. Your great-grandmother Briggs had seen the carriage pass her house, and in telling how she felt at parting with her eldest granddaughter, and the sadness it had given her to see the carriage that was to take me away, was not aware that she said "hearse" instead of carriage.

How hard it is to shake off the sadness of our young days. Partings, the breaking up of families and home attachments, have always been to me particularly painful, and the sad forebodings I was constantly hearing at that time of the fearful journey, and the dismal backwoods life which awaited me were not calculated to dispel the clouds that would sometimes come over me. I did not know then, as I realize now, that I was more ready to be influenced by fears than by hopes.

Christiana's writing is from her Reminiscences of Early Life in Illinois, *written in 1870 and privately printed at the request of her daughter. She wrote it for her family only, without thought of a large publication. Only five known copies are left of the original book. Her writing excerpt here is copied from the one that belongs to the Historical Society of Quincy and Adams County in Quincy, Illinois.*

Christiana Holmes Tillson was born March 13, 1796, in Kingston, Massachusetts. In October, 1822, she married John Tillson and immediately left for Illinois, where he had been living for three years. Veterans of the War of 1812 had been given 160 acres of Illinois land as a reward; however, many of them did not want to move there and sold to land speculators. Mr. Tillson was such a speculator. He became the first merchant and the first postmaster in Hillsboro, as well as founding Hillsboro Academy and serving as a trustee at Illinois College from its founding until his death. Christiana lived in the first brick house built in the county.

The panic of 1837 ruined the Tillsons financially. They had to leave their beloved Hillsboro for Peoria, where John died unexpectedly in 1853 at the age of 57. Christiana died in New York City, May 29, 1872.

Narcissa Whitman

March 30, 1837

A Cayuse girl

Dear Parents, Brothers and Sisters,

Again I can speak of the goodness and mercy of the Lord to us in an especial manner. On the evening of my birthday, March 14th, we received the gift of a little daughter—a treasure invaluable. During the winter my health was very good, so as to be able to do my work. . . .

The little stranger is visited daily by the chiefs and principal men in camp, and the women throng the house continually, waiting for an opportunity to see her. Her whole appearance is so new to them. Her complexion, her size and dress, etc., all excite a great deal of wonder; for they never raise a child here except they are lashed tight to a board, and the girls' heads undergo the flattening process. . . . Fee-low-ki-ke, a kind, friendly Indian, called to see her the next day after she was born. Said she was a Cayuse te-mi (Cayuse girl), because she was born on Cayuse wai-tis (Cayuse land). He told us her arrival was expected by all the people of the country— the Nez Perces, Cayuses, and Walla Wallapoos Indians, and, now she has arrived, it would soon be heard of by them all, and we must write to our land and tell our parents and friends of it. The whole tribe are highly pleased because we allow her to be called Cayuse girl.

Narcissa Prentiss Whitman, Presbyterian missionary, was born March 14, 1808, in Prattsburg, New York. At sixteen she pledged her life to missionary service but taught school for several years "while awaiting the leading of Providence." In 1834 she responded to a plea for recruits to carry Christianity to the western Indians and was refused as an unmarried woman. Two years later she married Dr. Marcus Whitman, also a Presbyterian missionary, and they set off on the long journey west.

The Whitmans left on the journey west with the Reverend and Eliza Spalding. Years earlier Narcissa had rejected a marriage proposal from Henry Spalding, which added some tension to the difficult trip. They persevered, and Narcissa and Eliza became the first white women to cross the Continental Divide. Marcus and Narcissa established a mission among the Cayuse Indians at Waiilatpu ("the Place of the Rye

Narcissa's letter is from The Coming of the White Women, 1836, as told in the Letters and Journal of Narcissa Prentiss Whitman, *published in 1937 by the Oregon Historical Society.*

Grass") near Fort Walla Walla, Washington. For several years they and their mission prospered.

Narcissa's beloved little daughter, Alice Clarissa, whose birth she wrote about in the above excerpt, drowned in the Walla Walla River when she was two. Narcissa became disheartened after her baby's tragic death and lost interest in her work with the Indians. The Indians became distrustful of the Whitmans, holding them responsible for the large numbers of white immigrants flocking into the region. A measles epidemic, brought by the white settlers, broke out in 1847. Many Indian children died because they had no immunity, while few white children were lost. The Indians believed Dr. Whitman was practicing witchcraft—saving the white children and allowing the Indians to die. This belief resulted in a tragic massacre on November 29, 1847: Narcissa, her husband and twelve others were brutally murdered by Indians from their own mission.

MARCH 15

Alice Cunningham Fletcher

A pathetic parting

Alice's writing is from Volume III of The Morning Star, *a publication of the Indian Industrial School in Carlisle, Pennsylvania.*

1882

The Omaha Indians now face a future wherein their individual powers can find scope for action. . . . Education given to their children means substantial progress. The parents of the children gave up their little ones for five years. . . . The parting was most pathetic. As I looked on the group where the mothers stood with their little ones clinging about their necks, the tears falling plentifully, the fathers nearby, red-eyed but resolute, I wished that all who find it difficult to see a man in an Indian might have been there with me. One old woman who was parting from her elder boy, mingling her grey hair with his glossy black locks as she bent over him, he was her only son save the baby in her arms . . . this woman said to me: "Ah! friend, it is best my boy goes, but my heart cries, and it will cry, but no one shall hear it. . . . I shall think, my boy is learning and will do much in the future when he comes back. . . .

Alice Cunningham Fletcher, ethnologist and Indian reformer, was born on March 15, 1838, in Havana, Cuba. Through a friendship with the director of the Peabody Museum at Harvard she developed an interest in archaeology and ethnology.

At forty-three Alice set off for Nebraska because "after studying ethnology for years in books and museums, she now wished to visit the Indian tribes in their own lodges." She lived with the Omaha tribe and became painfully aware of their poverty, illness, and neglect by the U.S. government, and determined to save their lands. She later said, "I felt that I had found the work which the Creator intended me to do."

In 1886 the Secretary of the Interior sent Alice to Alaska to study the needs of the Indians there. She also worked with the Winnebago tribe of Nebraska for several years and the Nez Perces in Idaho for four years.

Throughout the years Alice had been studying Indian culture, and grateful tribal leaders had given her many artifacts and confided numerous tribal rites. Alice spent her final years writing books on the Plains Indians and transcribing hundreds of their songs to preserve them for the future.

Mary Maverick

A Texas outing

1881

During this summer [1841], the American ladies led a lazy life of ease. We had plenty of books, including novels: we were all young, healthy and happy and were content with each others' society. We fell into the fashion of the climate, dined at twelve, then followed a siesta [nap] until three, when we took a cup of coffee and a bath.

Bathing in the river at our place had become rather public, now that merchants were establishing themselves on Commerce Street, so we ladies got permission of old Madame Tevino, mother of Mrs. Lockmar, to put up a bath house on her premises. . . . Here between two trees in a beautiful shade, we went in a crowd each afternoon at about four o'clock and took the children and nurses and a nice lunch which we enjoyed after the bath. There we had a grand good time, swimming and laughing, and making all the noise we pleased. The children were bathed and after all were dressed, we spread our lunch and enjoyed it immensely. . . . Then we had a grand and glorious gossip, for we were all dear friends and each one told the news from our faraway homes in the "States," nor did we omit to review the happenings in San Anto-

Mary's writing is from her book Memoirs of Mary A. Maverick—San Antonio's First American Woman, *written in 1881 and published in 1921.*

nio. We joked and laughed away the time, for we were free from care and happy.

Mary Adams Maverick was born March 16, 1818, in Tuscaloosa, Alabama. She married Samuel A. Maverick when she was eighteen. After their marriage the couple traveled to San Antonio, Texas, where they were among its earliest settlers. She wrote about leaving home:

"December 7, 1837, we set off for Texas. With heavy hearts we said goodbye to Mother, and my brothers and sisters. Mother ran after us for one more embrace. She held me in her arms and wept aloud and said: 'Oh, Mary, I will never see you again on Earth.' I felt heartbroken and often recalled that thrilling cry; and I have never beheld my dear Mother again." At sixty-three Mary wrote her memoirs of the early years in Texas at the urging of her children. She devoted three chapters to the Indians, claiming there were "one thousand and one incidents" with the Comanches, who from 1838 to 1842 "made life very unsafe on the frontier and were always within dangerous proximity to us."

She died when she was eighty. All but four of her thirty-four grandchildren were present at her funeral.

Sarah Edgarton Mayo

The powers of the moon

Sarah's letter to her friend Luella Case is in the Hooker Collection at Schlesinger Library, Radcliffe College.

October 21, 1841
Shirley Village, Massachusetts
. . . Do you see how brightly the moon is shining tonight—and do you think of me, poor moonstruck thing that I am? I do not know what association there exists between the moon and absent friends, but certain am I that I never look on the one, without thinking most tenderly of the other. There is not, I think, an object in nature that has such strange, half melancholy and half blissful influence upon me as the clear bright moon. I can never write about it—it is too spiritual and glorious for words—am I not *lunatic?*

Sarah Edgarton Mayo, author and poet, was born March 17, 1819, in Shirley, Massachusetts. She was the tenth of fifteen children and grew up in a large mansion amid a cheerful and loving family.

Sarah spent her first twenty-seven years in her parents' home in Shirley, living the life of a scholar and writer. The beautiful natural scenery of the surrounding countryside influenced her writings. She contributed many pieces to the *Universalist and Ladies' Repository*, a Boston publication, where she served as assistant editor from 1839 to 1842. From 1840 to 1848 she edited the *Rose of Sharon*, a Universalist gift annual.

Sarah married Amory D. Mayo in 1846. He was often sickly and decided to renounce his strenuous teaching career and devote his life to the Gospel ministry. In 1846 he became pastor of the Independent Christian Society in Gloucester, Massachusetts.

Although it was her husband who was in fragile health, it was Sarah who met an untimely death at twenty-nine. In his memoirs of his wife Mr. Mayo does not define her fatal illness other than to state she felt slightly indisposed on Monday and Tuesday evenings, and by Sunday sunset she was dead. She was buried in the cemetery of her beloved village of Shirley.

Rose Coghlan

1919

Every one else had remarked how beautiful I looked. I certainly was a strapping girl for 14.

However, I said my speeches well. The next day I was handed the part of the Widow Melnotte, the mother of Claude, which was played by Barry Sullivan, the great Irish actor. . . as Claude Melnotte he was not ideal. He was then over 50. Perhaps his mother looked younger than her son in this case.

But nothing mattered to me then. I had made good, and the great man took my hand after the play, speaking these words: "Young lady, you have a career before you if you study seriously and earnestly. Your faults are those of youth. Those you will outgrow. Your wonderful voice you will retain, I feel assured." I flushed, thanked him, and made a vow to myself that I, too, would become a star.

The flush of youth

Rose Coghlan was born March 18, 1852, in Peterborough, England. She idealized her older brother Charles; after he became an actor, she followed suit.

Rose made her debut in Scotland when she was thirteen and went on to star on the London stage. In 1872 she arrived in America and became a leading actress in Wallack's Theatre in New York City. Rose was famous for her voice, described by one theatre critic as "rich, mellow, utterly

Rose's writing is from an article in the September 21, 1919, Boston Sunday Herald entitled "Rose Coghlan, Famous Actress, Tells Her Life Story—First of Four Installments of Autobiography of a Star Who Knew Everybody and Saw Everything."

individual and capable of every gamut of emotion from mirth to scorn or plea for mercy or tragic intensity."

She was married and divorced twice and never had children. In later years her career faltered as the tastes of the times changed and her dramatic style of overacting became passé. She had to declare bankruptcy three times and spent her last four-and-a-half years at St. Vincent's Retreat for Nervous and Mental Diseases, Harrison, New York.

Maria Patton Chamberlain

Letter from Hawaii

Maria's writing is from a letter to her sister, written when Maria was seventy years old. It is contained in Volume II of Missionary Letters—1816-1900 at the Knight Library, Hawaiian Mission Children's Society, Honolulu.

Honolulu
July 29, 1873.
My dear Sister Ann

Your very acceptable letter dated March 19th 1873 was safely received and ought to have been answered before now.

I wonder if it occurred to you while writing the date that it was my birthday. Yes I am now in my seventieth year and cannot expect my pilgrimage to be lengthened out much beyond my three score years & ten. Yet God has been very gracious to me, and continued my health and strength and vigor, beyond many who commenced life about the time I did.

. . . I must now tell you of one of the saddest things which has ever happened to me, in all my life. I have lost my parental patrimony, and I have almost lost my confidence in man. I went to Boston in 1860 and handed it over myself, to Mr. Henry Hill, whom in integrity and uprightness I regarded but little lower than the angels, and he passed it over to his son, without legal security & he has failed, & involved all his father's funds and all mine. I do not think that Mr. H. Hill meant to defraud me, but he had too much admiration for, & too much confidence in his son. He has written me he hopes to get into business (*he is eighty years old*), and transmit funds, to me again.

I had been quite economical of my funds, and had in his hands when he ceased paying me interest (two years ago) five thousand dollars.

I do not think I shall suffer, tho' I may not be able to keep as much help as I should be glad to, in my declining years. The Board allowed me three hundred and fifty per year, and I have a furnished house and lot secured to me.

I am very much attached to this climate and I want, unless some very unpropitious event occurs, to live & die in the house where my husband & I lived and labored together, 21 years, and I have lived a widow 23 years.

Maria Patton Chamberlain, Hawaiian missionary, was born on March 19, 1803, in Salisbury Township, Pennsylvania. She became a teacher and decided early on that she wanted to do missionary work. Although unmarried, she set off for Hawaii on the ship *Parthian* in 1827.

Five months after her arrival in Hawaii, Maria married Levi Chamberlain, an accountant and superintendent of secular affairs for the Mission.

Maria and Levi had seven children. In addition to raising her own large family, she nursed many young mothers and took care of many babies that were not her own. She referred to herself as a "keeper at home."

Mary McLeod Maybee

1915

*T*he old well

When I was between forty-five and fifty years old I visited my birthplace in Canada. The loved ones were all gone and I walked down the smooth beaten pathway to the old well and looked in, and caught the reflection of my face and I said, "Why does age come on us unaware and flush the blossoms from our cheeks and luster from our eyes and sprinkle our hair with frost?" and the answer seemed to come: "Calm content and the pleasures of the imagination, and a firm faith in the power of the all Wise are a rich compensation for thy loss. Go thy way and never again question the wisdom of the Almighty, for it is His plan that we shall grow old."

Mary McLeod Maybee was born March 20, 1855, in Zephyr, Canada. She married William Maybee from Richmond, Virginia, and they had three children.

Mary and William were Methodist Missionaries in India and China for many years. Upon their return they established

Mary's writing is from the private collection of Verna Payer who lives in Old Mystic Connecticut. Mary was Verna's great aunt.

the Methodist Orphanage in Richmond. Mary was a poet and artist. She led a long, productive life and died in Daytona Beach, Florida, when she was ninety-three.

Arozina Perkins

A romantic view

Fort Des Moines, Iowa
January 2, 1850
My dear Brother,
     . . . I am boarding in a family from Missouri. There is the man, woman, and two children, which latter I have as scholars. There are three rooms, one of which, the parlor, I occupy. Shall I describe it to you? Well, in one corner stands a bed, in another a table covered with books, a clock and my accordion, between the two windows, under the looking glass is a stand—no—I happen to have it pulled out by the stove just now, to write on. Behind me is a sofa, and beneath a carpet. My two trunks are part of the furniture, and my rough box which I obtained so quickly in my hurry at Hartford is under the bed, with my go-to-meeting bonnets in it. . . .

     This is a very fine pious family, and I enjoy myself very much. Mr. E. spends most of his time reading and Mrs. E. just minds her own business, as every woman ought to. The diet too just suits me, for we have plenty of cornbread, mush, and milk.

Arozina Perkins, teacher, was born March 21, 1826, in Johnson, Vermont.

     Arozina was deeply religious and spent a good deal of time thinking about her reason to be on earth. She came to believe that God had planned a special mission for her in the west and she applied for a teaching position through the National Popular Education Board.

     After a six-week journey Arozina arrived in Fort Des Moines, Iowa. She kept a detailed diary of her pioneering experience. Her romantic, idealized vision of the west turned to disillusionment which caused her to doubt her self-worth. She never got over her feelings of loneliness and her heart was broken when the minister she had hoped to marry ended the relationship.

     Arozina returned east and died at age twenty-eight of a "disease of the respiratory organs."

Arozina's letter to her brother Barnabas is in the Connecticut Historical Society, New Haven, Connecticut.

Laura Jean Libbey

April 16th 1887.
472 Putnam Ave., Brooklyn.
Mr. Bonner:

Respected sir: I have your letter of recent date—kindly pardon me for the delay in replying.

I have closed the story with the thirteenth installment. I never make them longer unless requested to lengthen them.

I am awfully sorry so much repetition occurred. I shall try to avoid it in future. You need not be afraid that I will fall into any of the habits of your workers—I promise you I will not. I will write *young love stories*—pure, bright—with a vein of deep romance and pathos running through them—a story for the masses.

And about the new story—I shall have to ask—as before—a little time to get it up.

The conversation we had the second time I saw you, made a deep impression upon me—I mean about the train stopping in front of that farmhouse and your thoughts which you jotted down in a notebook.

You pictured that scene so vividly—so much so—that I have not forgotten it, and the thought occurred to me of opening my new story with a cheerful farm scene.

A cheery old farmer with two pretty young daughters—the youngest his idol—etc., etc.

Something of that kind perhaps. I think you would be highly pleased with it. Trusting you have not been delayed in any way by my not replying sooner, I remain

Yours with much respect
Laura J. Libbey

Laura Jean Libbey, author, was born March 22, 1862, in Brooklyn, New York. Her first writing was published in the *New York Ledger* while she was still in her teens. For the next decade she contributed many serials and articles to popular weekly magazines.

Laura produced over sixty romantic novels during the 1880's and 1890's which were printed in cheap paper volumes that sold for between fifteen and twenty-five cents. Although the critics described her work as melodramatic and repetitious,

Birth of a novel

Laura Jean Libbey's letter to Robert Bonner, editor of the New York Ledger, *is in the Rare Books and Manuscripts Division of the New York Public Library. Several years after this letter was written, she broke off her association with the* Ledger *because Bonner continued to complain about the similarity of her plots.*

she had a faithful following, primarily among young working girls who loved her stories and bought millions of copies of her books.

Fannie Merritt Farmer

A cookbook is more than recipes

Fannie's writing is from the preface of The Boston Cooking School Cook Book, *published in 1896.*

1896

With the progress of knowledge the needs of the human body have not been forgotten. During the last decade much time has been given by scientists to the study of foods and their dietetic value, and it is a subject which rightfully should demand much consideration from all. I certainly feel that the time is not far distant when a knowledge of the principles of diet will be an essential part of one's education. Then mankind will eat to live, will be able to do better mental and physical work, and disease will be less frequent.

Fannie Merritt Farmer, cooking teacher, dietician and author, was born March 23, 1857, in Boston, Massachusetts. At sixteen she was struck with paralysis in her left leg which left her with a permanent limp.

Fannie worked for a while as a mother's helper, and she became an excellent cook. She then enrolled in the two-year course at the Boston Cooking School. After graduation she remained as the assistant principal, and in 1894 became head of the school.

In 1896 Fannie published *The Boston Cooking School Cook Book*. The publisher thought her book a risk and required her to pay for the publication costs. It has been revised and re-printed eleven times, and has been translated into French, Spanish and Japanese.

As Fannie became increasingly concerned with proper diet for the sick, she trained nurses and hospital dieticians and lectured at Harvard Medical School. She considered her *Care and Cookery for the Sick and Convalescent*, published in 1904, her most important work.

Frances Jane Crosby

1903

On entering the Institution for the Blind I knew many
poems by heart and had already cultivated a strong love
for the poetic art. My teachers did not encourage me to
write poetry; often they would take from me my poetic
works. This grieved my heart. One day Dr. Combe of
Boston came to examine our craniums. As he touched
my head and looked into my face he remarked, "And
here is a poetess; give her every possible encouragement. Read the best books to her, and teach her to
appreciate the finest there is in poetry. You will hear
from this young lady some day."

   This was as music to my soul. I had waited long for
someone to encourage me to adhere to what I already
felt was to be my lifework, hymn-writing.

A poet is discovered

Frances Jane (Fanny) Crosby, poet and hymn writer, was born
March 24, 1820, in Putnam County, New York. She became
permanently blind when she was six weeks old.

   Fanny enrolled in the New York Institution for the Blind
in New York City when she was fifteen. She had written
poetry since childhood, which went largely unnoticed until the
visit of Dr. Combe mentioned here in her writing. Thereafter
her teachers taught her poetry and encouraged her to write.
She became somewhat of a celebrity at the school and was frequently called upon to recite her poetry for visiting dignitaries.

   After Fanny completed her education she remained at the
school as a teacher until 1858. That year she married Alexander Van Alstyne, another blind former pupil and teacher.
They moved to Brooklyn, had one child who died in infancy,
and stayed together until his death in 1902.

   While she was at the Institution for the Blind, Fanny
started to publish her poetry. She also collaborated with a
music instructor on approximately sixty songs—some of which
became popular favorites. That was the beginning of her
hymn-writing. It has been estimated that Fanny wrote
between 5500 and 9000 hymns. She used many different
pseudonyms, so it is difficult to know the exact number. The
very popular "Safe in the Arms of Jesus" was her favorite.
Although her hymns were nondenominational, they found
special favor with the Methodists, who, for a time, annually
observed a Fanny Crosby Day.

*Fanny's writing describing her
meeting with the well-known
phrenologist Doctor George
Combe is from her autobiography*
Fanny Crosby's Own Life
Story, *published in 1903.*

Matilda Joslyn Gage

*W*rongly taught

1881

Mary Somerville, the most eminent English mathematician of this century, was publicly denounced in church by Dean Cockburn of York; and when George Eliot died a few weeks since, her lifeless remains were refused interment in Westminster Abbey, where so many inferior authors of the privileged sex lie buried.

Contempt for women, the result of clerical teaching, is shown in myriad forms. Wife-beating is still so common, even in America, that a number of states have of late introduced bills especially directed to the punishment of the wife-beater. Great surprise is frequently shown by these men when arrested. "Is she not my wife?" is cried in tones proving the brutal husband has been trained to consider this relationship a sufficient justification for any abuse.

Matilda Joslyn Gage, women's rights activist, was born March 25, 1826, in Cicero, New York.

In 1845 Matilda married Henry Gage, a merchant, and they had four children. She made her first appearance on the lecture stage at the National Woman's Rights Convention in 1852.

In 1875 Matilda became the head of both the National and the New York State suffrage associations. She became discouraged with the slow pace of woman suffrage and blamed the churches which educated men to a "belief in woman's inferiority." She eventually resigned from all organizations to form her own radical one, the Woman's National Liberal Union.

Matilda supported woman suffrage until her death at seventy-one, even writing a speech from her deathbed to commemorate the fiftieth anniversary of the first women's rights convention. Her lifelong motto, "There is a word sweeter than Mother, Home, or Heaven; that word is liberty" is carved on her gravestone.

Matilda's writing is from the chapter "Woman, Church and State" in Volume I of the History of Woman Suffrage, *edited by Elizabeth Cady Stanton, Susan B. Anthony and Matilda Joslyn Gage, published in 1881.*

Margaret Miller Davidson

Saratoga,
June 1, 1838.

June is at last with us, my dear cousin, and the blue-eyed goddess could not have looked upon the green bosom of her mother earth attired in a lovelier or more enchanting robe. I am seated by an open window, and the breeze, laden with the perfumes of the blossoms and opening leaves, just lifts the edge of my sheet, and steals with the gentlest footsteps imaginable to fan my cheek and forehead. The grass, tinged with the deepest and freshest green, is waving beneath its influence; the birds are singing their sweetest songs; and as I look into the depths of the clear blue sky the rich tints appear to flit higher and higher as I gaze, till my eye seems searching into immeasurable distance. Oh! such a day as this, it is a luxury to breathe. I feel as if I could frisk and gambol like my kitten from the mere consciousness of life.

A day in June

Margaret Miller Davidson, poet, was born March 26, 1823, in Plattsburgh, New York. The Davidson family was a sickly one and seven of the nine children preceded their parents to the grave. Although the father was a doctor, he was unable to help medically or financially. The mother, despite being chronically ill herself, managed the finances and raised and educated the children.

Margaret's older sister, Lucretia, was a poet of some renown. She died of tuberculosis just shy of her seventeenth birthday, when Margaret was only two and a half. Lucretia adored her baby sister and often predicted, "She must, she will be a poet!" Mrs. Davidson took this as a prophetic statement and undertook her daughter's education in English, religion and the classics, and encouraged her to write poetry.

Margaret also developed tuberculosis, and although the family took many vacations and moved frequently in search of a healthful climate, nothing could prevent the advancement of the disease. Washington Irving met Margaret when she was twelve and he remarked: "The soul was wearing out the body. I felt convinced that she was not long for the world; in truth, she already appeared more spiritual than mortal."

Margaret and her sister Lucretia were both beautiful, bright, delicate children. Edgar Allen Poe described Margaret as a "fairy child" and the whole country became enthralled with the romantic concept of the sisters' lives, deaths and

Margaret's letter, written to her cousin a few months before her death, is contained in Biography and Poetical Remains of the Late Margaret Miller Davidson, *by Washington Irving, published in 1841.*

---

poetic works. Their poetry was similar; flowery verses concerning nature, love, sickness and death. Margaret's poems are longer than her sister's and have a stronger religious theme. After her death when she was fifteen, sixty of Margaret's poems were published with her biography by Washington Irving. She is buried in the village graveyard at Saratoga, New York.

Florence Finch Kelly

*T*he urge to be different

1939

Why should a raw, green girl of the Kansas prairies, away back in the very Victorian early 1880's, have broken away so determinedly from all that she had known, and gone off alone without money, friends or influence, to earn her living and make her life in distant cities about which she knew little, in a profession of which she knew even less? That sort of thing was "not done" in those days. A girl stayed at home quietly and helped with the housework until she married and had a home of her own to take care of, or, if she shunned matrimony, she lived with her father and mother until they died and then room was made for her in the home of a married brother or sister or some other relative.

. . . My own conviction as to the propulsive force that sent me eastward from a Kansas farm is that it was an inner something as inborn and compelling as the urge that sets a-wing the migrating bird, yearning for distant climes, and that it would have caused the same action no matter what my environment had been.

Florence Finch Kelly, journalist, was born March 27, 1858, in Girard, Illinois. When she was eleven her family moved to Kansas.

Florence always wanted to be an author. Her father objected to her desire to attend college so she taught for two years to earn the tuition herself and enrolled in the University of Kansas. Her father eventually relented and paid for her final three years. She graduated in 1881 and moved to Boston, where she started her writing career at the *Globe*.

She left the paper after three years to help another *Globe* employee, Allen P. Kelly, start a newspaper in Lowell, Massachusetts.

Their paper, the *Lowell Bell*, failed, but Florence and Allen Kelly were married in December, 1884. They had two sons.

Florence's writing is from her autobiography, Flowing Stream—The Story of Fifty-six Years in American Newspaper Life, *published in 1939.*

94

Give Her This Day

The couple moved from place to place for many years working on newspapers in San Francisco, New Mexico, Los Angeles and Philadelphia.

In 1906 Florence began working at the *New York Times Book Review*, where she remained a mainstay for the next three decades.

Florence's childhood dream of being a novelist persisted throughout her life, and she did write five novels and a book of Western stories. Her books were well-received, but it was as a journalist that she was both known and respected.

Alice Higgins Lothrop

1916

Drawing the line

I was much impressed recently when a quiet, middle-aged, kind-hearted relative of mine was explaining to me the utterly shocking conduct of her young maid, after it had been explained to her by the modern social point of view. "You see," said she, "they say it is a weakness she has." It is all true, our recognition of "wellness," our understanding and sympathy with mental and moral irresponsibility, and I wouldn't lose a bit of our insistence on our collective responsibility for all the sins of the universe; but nevertheless, unless someone begins soon, and pretty soon, to preach the doctrine of individual responsibility for sin, we shall be helping to create a mean-spirited race.

Alice Higgins Lothrop was born March 28, 1870, in Boston, Massachusetts. When she was twenty-eight she entered the Associated Charities of Boston as an agent-in-training. Within five years, she became general secretary.

Alice was successful due to her good organizational skills. She had many innovative ideas, made quick decisions and chose able assistants. She was especially adept at organizing emergency relief after the San Francisco fire in 1906, two local Massachusetts fires in 1908 and 1914, and the Halifax explosion in 1917.

Although Alice resigned from her executive position at the Associated Charities following her marriage to William Lothrop in 1913, she remained an active social worker in the field until her death in 1920.

Alice's writing is from a speech she gave in May, 1916, before the National Conference of Charities and Correction in Indianapolis.

Amelia Huddleston Barr

*The joy of love

Amelia's writing is from the last book she wrote, All the Days of My Life: An Autobiography—The Red Leaves of a Human Heart, *published in 1913.*

1913

I had told Robert that the first thing was to get my father's and my mother's consent to our marriage, and he went to Kendal the following day for this purpose, arriving there about four in the afternoon. . . . Mother was making some school pinafores for Alethia, and Robert's knock did not interest her at all. . . . But when the girl opened the parlor door and Robert entered she was astonished. However, my name and the letter he brought from me put him at once in Mother's favor, and in a few minutes he was telling her how dear I was to him, and that I had promised to be his wife in July, if my father and mother approved it. He stayed to tea with my parents, and had a long conversation with them, and they were thoroughly satisfied that I had chosen well and wisely. As if I had had any choice in the matter! The event had been destined, even when I was born, and Robert Barr only a lad of seven years old.

    . . . I returned home, and the days went by in a dream of happiness. Robert came home every Friday or Saturday to Kendal, and we rode over to Windermere, if it was fine weather, and strolled about its laurel woods, whispering to each other those words which lovers have always said, and always will say, even till time shall be no more—unless, the march of what is called "progress and efficiency" puts love out of the question altogether. It was a wooing that fitted wonderfully into my happy girlhood, blending itself with my childhood memories, with the wind and the sun, and the mountains and lakes I loved. And I took with a grateful heart the joy sent me—a joy glorified by all the enchanting glamours and extravagant hopes of youth and love.

Amelia Edith Huddleston Barr, novelist, was born March 29, 1831, in Ulverston, Lancashire, England. Her father was a Methodist minister.

    Amelia began teaching at sixteen until her marriage to Robert Barr, a Scotsman, in 1850. One year later they emigrated to the United States and settled in Chicago. In Chicago Robert became an accountant and Amelia opened a school in their home. Robert was very outspoken, so much so that he made an enemy of a very powerful Chicago politician. After a threat on his life, he had to leave the city.

The Barrs relocated in Austin, Texas, and prospered there for nine years. In 1866, after moving to Galveston, the whole family contracted yellow fever. Robert and the three boys died, and as soon as Amelia was strong enough she left for New York with her three remaining daughters.

During the next decade she supported her family by writing over one thousand articles and poems for religious magazines and newspapers. Her first novel appeared in 1875. Thereafter, she wrote at least two novels a year until her death. All of her eighty-one books contained simple, folksy characters with cheerful sentimental plots and strong religious overtones.

Jessie Donaldson Hodder

October 26, 1913

Darling, you'll never have a stepfather, don't worry—I promised both you and Olive that long ago and I never have broken a promise made to either you or her. Furthermore, your Daddy was my only love and no one has ever wanted to take his place nor have I ever seen anyone I would put in his place. God bless you, dear, and keep you pure and true to all your ideals. . . .

Jessie Donaldson Hodder, prison reformer, was born March 30, 1867, in Cincinnati, Ohio.

She entered into a common-law marriage with Alfred LeRoy Hodder in 1890 and had a son and a daughter. In 1897 Hodder began teaching at Bryn Mawr College and he sent his little family to Switzerland, promising to join them soon. He never left America but renounced their marriage and married another woman in 1904. Shortly thereafter Jessie's daughter died and Jessie contemplated suicide.

In 1906 Jessie returned to the United States and found work as a housemother at an industrial school for girls. She specialized in counseling unwed mothers. In 1910 she was appointed superintendent of the Massachusetts Reformatory for Women in Framingham.

Jessie transformed the Framingham reformatory into a model institution. Many European penologists visited the prison, and it served as an example for the women's prison in Belgium. In 1925 she was the only female delegate to the International Prison Congress in London.

*S*he won't remarry

Jessie's writing selection is from a letter written to her son J. Alan when he was sixteen. Her letters are in the Schlesinger Library at Radcliffe College.

Harriet Talcott Buckingham

Life on the trail

May 4, 1851

Mr. & Mrs. Smith have had the carriage so arranged that a bed can be made of the seats, and when the curtains are all buttoned down there is a comfortable sleeping apartment. The little girl and I sleep in one of the big covered ox wagons in which is a nice bed—really makes a cosy little low roofed room, it has a double cover—Mr. Smith has a coop fastened on behind the carriage which contains some fine white chickens—three hens and a rooster. We let them out every time we camp, and already they seem to know when preparations are made for moving and will fly up to their place in the coop. . . .

August 18, 1851

The crickets are large, often an inch and a half or two inches in length—black & shiny, the Indians make soup of them—they catch them by driving them into pits dug for this purpose—they are dried for winter use. It's laughable to see our white chickens try to swallow them. It often takes two or three efforts to get one disposed of, they are so numerous that one cannot avoid stepping on them.

Harriet Talcott Buckingham was born March 31, 1832, in Norwalk, Ohio. She left for Oregon in a wagon train when she was nineteen with her aunt and uncle and younger brother.

Harriet kept a detailed journal of her trip west beginning May 4, 1851.

Shortly after her arrival in Oregon, Harriet met and married Samuel A. Clarke, a Portland businessman. They had four children. After Harriet's death in 1890, her husband wrote a two-volume history of Oregon which he lovingly dedicated "as a remembrance of the lovely character and beautiful soul of the woman whose life was blended with mine, and was a blessing to all who knew her."

Harriet's writing is from her diary, which was donated to the Oregon Historical Society by her daughter Sarah.

APRIL

Agnes Repplier

1886

Nowadays anxious parents and guardians seem to labor under an ill-founded apprehension that their children are going to hurt themselves by over-application to their books, and we hear a great deal about the expedience of restraining this inordinate zeal. But a few generations back such comfortable theories had yet to be evolved, and the plain duty of a teacher was to goad the student on to every effort in his power.

Agnes Repplier was born April 1, 1855, in Philadelphia. Her formal schooling was short-lived, as she was expelled from two boarding schools for failing to obey the rules.

    Agnes began writing short stories for local periodicals to augment the family's income after her father lost most of his money in 1871. In 1884 Father Hecker, founder of *Catholic World*, commissioned her to write an essay. Thereafter she abandoned fiction in favor of essays, publishing eighteen volumes during her lifetime.

    Agnes received an honorary degree from the University of Pennsylvania in 1902, followed by degrees from Temple, Yale, Columbia, Marquette and Princeton. She published her last essay in *The Atlantic Monthly* when she was eighty-four.

*F*ashion in education

Agnes' writing is from her article, "Children Past and Present," which appeared in the April, 1886, issue of The Atlantic Monthly.

Laura Fish Judd

1860

An idea prevailed in the earlier years of the mission that the children could not be trained here, but must be sent to the fatherland. I shall never forget some of those heart-rending parting scenes. Little children, aged only six or seven years, were torn away from their parents, and sent the long voyage around Cape Horn, to seek homes among strangers. They have sometimes fared hard during those long voyages, without a mother's care, with no one but the rough sons of Ocean to nurse and watch them. They have sometimes fallen into the hands of selfish, exacting guardians, and been unkindly

*C*hildren of missionaries

Laura's writing is an excerpt from her book, Honolulu Sketches of Life Social, Political and Religious, in the Hawaiian Islands from 1828-1861, *published posthumously in 1880. It was reprinted in 1928 and has been called one of the landmarks of Hawaiian literature.*

dealt with or sadly neglected. Their pillows have been wet with childhood's tears, as they thought of their far-off homes, and felt the need of parental sympathy and tenderness.

Laura Fish Judd, Hawaiian missionary, was born April 2, 1804, in Plainfield, New York. She experienced a religious conversion when she was seventeen which marked the beginning of her interest in missionary work.

Dr..G. P. Judd had been accepted for mission work in the Sandwich Islands provided he found a wife to accompany him. He decided to ask Laura Fish, practically a stranger, to marry him, and asked his uncle to propose for him. Laura accepted immediately and they were married in September, 1827. Six weeks later they began the five-month voyage to Hawaii.

Dr. and Mrs. Judd were dedicated, hard-working missionaries from 1828 to 1842. They were buried side by side in the Nuuanu Cemetery under the headstone: "They were lovely and pleasant in their lives, and in their death they were not divided."

Harriet Prescott Spofford

*N*ot so gentle

1895
One might suppose that Priscilla, gentle as tradition represents her, would have been attracted by the fire and spirit of the brave Captain. But perhaps she was not so very gentle. Was there a spice of feminine coquetry in her famous speech to John Alden, for all her sweet Puritanism? Or was it that she understood, and was the first in this new land to take her stand upon it?

Harriet Elizabeth Prescott Spofford was born April 3, 1835, in Calais, Maine. When she was fourteen, her father abandoned the family to seek his fortune in Oregon. Mrs. Prescott and the five children settled in Newburyport, Massachusetts, Harriet's home until her death.

In 1851, Harriet won a contest with an essay analyzing Hamlet's insanity. She began writing stories for weekly magazines to support the family. Soon she was publishing novels, short stories, poetry, children's books and travel books, producing an enormous volume of work during her sixty-year career. By the late 1800's, she was one of the most popular female writers in America.

Harriet's writing about Priscilla Alden is from Three Heroines of New England Romance, *published in 1895.*

Give Her This Day

Dorothea Dix

June 29, 1883

Dear Sir and friend,

. . . How well I remember with comfort and cheer your calls when I was at Danville. You did not suspect the good you were doing me. Your presence bringing to recollection so much you had written, inciting to a deeper hope and trust, in a Divine Providence.

I do not think, Mr. Whittier, you have ever realized the wide-reaching blessing, and good, of your published works.

My opportunity for knowing very much of this has been large, by personal expression, and more through letters.

In saying this to you I am both honest and earnest.

But, dear sir, we must all know, in a degree at least, the influence of our lives. . . .

The influence of our lives

Dorothea Lynde Dix was born April 4, 1802, in Hampden, Maine. Her father was frequently absent, and her mother was a semi-invalid, forcing Dorothea to assume the care of her two younger brothers. Occasional visits to her grandparents in Boston opened her eyes to the educational opportunities outside of her Maine village. When she was twelve, Dorothea moved in with her grandmother. Two years later, she opened her first school for young children.

When Dorothea was thirty-nine, she began teaching a Sunday school class at a Cambridge jail; this was to change her life. She was horrified to discover many of the female inmates were not criminals but merely insane, and their cells were filthy and unheated. She began a study of every Massachusetts prison and her findings were grim. She described prisoners who were "confined in cages, closets, cellars, stalls, pens! Chained, naked, beaten with rods, and lashed into obedience." She spoke before the legislature in 1843 and eventually persuaded them to allocate funds to expand and improve the mental hospital at Worcester, Massachusetts.

Dorothea carried her work into the states of Rhode Island and New York. In 1845, she prodded New Jersey into building its first mental hospital at Trenton. She travelled thirty-thousand miles during the next three years, presenting her pleas against neglect and cruelty to the mentally ill before ten state legislatures.

Dorothea was appointed superintendent of army nurses

Dorothea's letter to John Greenleaf Whittier, written when she was eighty-one, is in the Houghton Library Manuscript Collection, Harvard University.

during the Civil War. Following the war, she resumed her
work with prisons and mental institutions until her death
in 1887.

Mary Jane Holmes

A woman in love

1855
And Jenny was very happy. Blithe as a bee she flitted
about the house and garden, and if in the morning a tear
glistened in her laughing eyes as William bade her
adieu, it was quickly dried, and all day long she busied
herself in her household matters, studying some agreeable surprise for her husband, and trying for his sake to
be very neat and orderly. Then when the clock pointed
the hour for his return, she would station herself at the
gate, and William, as he kissed the moisture from her
rosy cheek, thought her a perfect enigma, to weep when
he went away, and weep when he came home!

Mary Jane Hawes Holmes was born April 5, 1825, in Brookfield, Massachusetts. She began school when she was three
and showed an interest in writing when she was six.
      Mary Jane met Daniel Holmes, her future husband, while
she was teaching. They lived in Kentucky for three years after
their marriage before moving to New York, where they lived
the rest of their lives. She began writing shortly after settling
in New York, often using her experiences in Kentucky as the
basis for her novels. After Mary Jane's first book was
published in 1854 she published one a year for over forty years.
Her novels were all similar; she wrote "a good, pure, natural
story, such as mothers are willing their daughters should read,
such as will do good instead of harm." Her sales totaled more
than forty million and often libraries stocked twenty to thirty
copies of each title.

*Mary Jane's writing is from her
novel,* The English Orphans
or Home in the New World,
published in 1855.

Eliza Gurney

August 18, 1863

Esteemed Friend, Abraham Lincoln—

Many times since I was privileged to have an interview with thee, nearly a year ago, my mind has turned toward thee with feelings of sincere and Christian interest; and as our kind friend, Isaac Newton, offers to be the bearer of a paper messenger, I feel inclined to give thee the assurance of my continued hearty sympathy in all thy heavy burdens and responsibilities, and to express not only my own earnest prayer, but, I believe, the prayer of many thousands whose hearts thou hast gladdened by thy praiseworthy and successful efforts "to burst the bands of wickedness and let the oppressed go free."

A message of support

Eliza Paul Kirkbride Gurney was born April 6, 1801, in Philadelphia. After her mother died, she was sent to boarding school, but had to return home after three years to nurse her ailing father. After his death she became engaged to John Howell. However, he too died within the year.

Eliza then devoted herself to her Quaker religion. From 1832-1835 she travelled with Hannah Backhouse, a well-known English Quaker minister. They visited seventeen states and Canada. In 1836, she accompanied Hannah on a journey of ministry throughout Scotland and England.

In 1841, Eliza was recorded as a minister of the gospel by the Quaker Monthly Meeting in Darlington, England, Hannah's hometown. Three months later she married Joseph Gurney, a banker, Biblical scholar, and Friends minister. Eliza and her husband spent the next six years, until his death, on a travelling ministry in France and Switzerland.

Following the deaths of her husband and her close friend Hannah Backhouse, Eliza relocated to New Jersey where she continued to labor as a travelling minister. In 1862 she visited President Lincoln to give him her support for his efforts to end slavery. They spent forty-five minutes in conference, ending with them kneeling together in prayer.

Eliza's letter to President Lincoln, in answer to his specific request to hear from her, is included in Memoirs and Correspondence of Eliza P. Gurney, *edited by Richard Mott, published in 1884.*

Anna Thomas Jeanes

Words from the store

1870
My idea has been to extend a knowledge of simple
words to those Indians, too old for school. . . . The
store goods with the words applicable to buying and
selling I imagine may prove desirable to the older
Indians. Would it not be worthwhile to allow the more
intelligent children, as they become familiar with the
words, to take home the baskets of store goods, and
other objects (for a limited time) and each, in turn, teach
their friends? . . .

Anna Thomas Jeanes was born April 7, 1822, in Philadelphia,
the youngest of ten children in a devout Quaker family. Anna
never married and led a quiet life, studying painting and the
different religions of the world. She took a particular interest
in Buddhism.

The last of Anna's siblings died in 1894, leaving all the
accumulated Jeanes' wealth to her. She spent the remaining
twelve years of her life dispensing her inheritance of over two
million dollars.

Anna gave most of her money to the Pennsylvania Yearly
Meeting of Friends and to various black charities. Her main
concern was "the poor little Negro cabin one-teacher rural
schools." She donated more than one million dollars to the
Negro Rural School Fund to improve education in elementary
schools. "Jeanes teachers" were sent from school to school to
assist and advise the local teachers.

*Anna's letter to her friends Tom
and Mary Lightfoot is in the
Anna Jeanes Collection at the
Friends Historical Library,
Swarthmore, Pennsylvania.*

Albion Fellows Bacon

An angry voice

1914
Before I started off on a tour, I went again to the homes
of the poor, to burn within my mind a more vivid image
of their wretchedness, to get the figures of their
enormous rentals, and to rouse afresh the anger that
blazed within me, that I might kindle it in others. . . .

I envied the lecturers who could talk all the time
about pretty things, and hated the reek and ruin of the
slums, more than ever. But the truth had to be told.

And here was such an opportunity. I might never see this audience again. They *must* know and care.

If only one could have a cast-iron body and a vulcanised larynx! I heard with amazement the feats of endurance of my club sisters, who toured our state and other states with vigour unabated. I had come to the place where the range of five or six cities laid me low, at the seventh I was asleep on my feet, and at the eighth I was speechless from exhaustion.

Albion Fellows Bacon, housing reformer, was born April 8, 1865, in Evansville, Indiana. Her childhood was spent in the tiny country town of McCutchanville. She married Hilary E. Bacon, an Evansville banker, in 1888. They had four children. Albion became interested in housing reform after she volunteered for the sanitation committee of Evansville's Civic Improvement Society and saw the local slums for the first time.

Albion believed that the slums bred vice and disease and that filthy, unsanitary housing was the major cause of the misery she perceived. She developed the idea of including tenement regulation in the state building code.

She wrote hundreds of letters, pamphleted the legislature, and traveled the state speaking for her cause. In 1913 she triumphed when the legislature passed a law regulating all residences, other than single-family dwellings, in all Indiana cities.

Albion's writing is from her autobiography, Beauty for Ashes, *published in 1914.*

Mary Elizabeth Lightner

June 7, 1863

A gathering of saints

Monday we landed at Omaha in a heavy rainstorm; rode to Florence, six miles, without a cover from the rain, and stopped at a cabin, laid down in damp bedclothes; next night had the cholera and was sick three or four days, and my babe had bowel complaint very bad. Thursday some immigrants arrived with the smallpox. Two are dead and ten more sick. One of the number spent the evening with us; we shook hands with them; they said nothing about the disease; the next day they were sent to the hills, where tents were provided for them. On Saturday seven hundred persons from England arrived here en route for Salt Lake. This is the gathering place for those who intend crossing the plains. Today, saints

Mary's writing from her journal was published in the Utah Genealogical and Historical Magazine, Volume XVII, 1926.

---

from Africa and Denmark arrived here. Their tents were scattered over the hills, and when the campfires were lit up at night the scene was beautiful to behold. It makes me think how the children of Israel must have looked in the days of Moses, when journeying in the wilderness.

Mary Elizabeth Rollins Lightner was born April 9, 1818, in Lima, New York. She married Adam Lightner when she was twenty and they had ten children.

Adam was a carpenter so the family moved frequently, following the construction booms. They lived in Illinois, Missouri, Wisconsin, Minnesota and Nebraska until they finally settled in Utah.

Mary was an active member of the Mormon Church, having been baptized into the faith when she was twelve. Her husband never became a Mormon.

Louise Chandler Moulton

An unfair contest

Madrid,
1897
This brilliant creature made hot work for the banderill-eros, and held even the matador for a long time at bay; but at last he gamely died, and the black mules dragged him away, as they had done his brothers before him.

By this time I thought I knew enough about bull-fights, and I left. . . .

My sympathies were all with the bulls. . . . They alone were doomed with absolute certainty from the start. Even the horses might escape; and at worst their torture was but for a moment. The men were only in just enough danger to make the thing exciting, and there were ninety-nine chances out of a hundred that they would come off scatheless; but the bull, let him bear himself ever so bravely, was to be made an end of.

Louise Chandler Moulton was born April 10, 1835, in Pomfret, Connecticut. She published her first poem when she was fifteen.

In 1855 Louise married William U. Moulton, an older man who published a Boston literary weekly that carried her work. She quickly established their elegant Boston home as a

Louise's writing is from her book of travel sketches, Lazy Tours in Spain and Elsewhere, *published in 1897.*

Give Her This Day

gathering place for local and visiting literary society. Although she continued to write, she was most successful at recognizing and promoting new talent.

In 1876 the Moultons bought a home in London and for the next thirty years Louise presided over a weekly salon there for six months of the year, plus her Friday salon in Boston the other half of the year.

When she died she bequeathed over nine hundred books, mostly first editions and presentation copies, to the Boston Public Library.

Mary Richardson Walker

Friday, July 26, 1839.
To Rev. E. Walker,

My Dear Husband I find it in vain to expect my journal will escape your eyes & indeed why should I wish to have it [so]? Certainly my mind knows no sweeter solace than the privilege of unbosoming itself to you. It frequently happens that when I think of much I wish to say to you, you are either so much fatigued, so drowsy or so busy that I find no convenient opportunity till what I would have said is forgotten. I have therefore determined to address my journal to you. I shall at all times address you with the unrestrained freedom of a fond & confiding wife. When therefore you have leisure & inclination to know my heart, you may here find it ready for converse.

*I*ntimate messages

Mary Richardson Walker, missionary and diarist, was born April 11, 1811, in West Baldwin, Maine. She started a diary when she was twenty-two which she kept for fifty-seven years.

Mary wrote to the American Board of Commissioners for Foreign Missions in hopes of receiving a mission, but was refused because she was single. A friend introduced her to Elkanah Walker, knowing both of them wished to be missionaries. They become engaged a few days after they met and were married in March, 1838, with Mary wearing a black wedding gown to symbolize her grief at parting from her family.

After a difficult journey across the country, Elkanah and Mary started their missionary life near Spokane. Elkanah wrote two primers in the Flathead Indian language, and Mary started a school to teach the children.

The American Board ceased its operations in Oregon in

Mary's writing is an 1839 entry from her diary, which is located at the Huntington Library, San Marino, California.

1847, and Mary and her husband and eight children moved to Forest Grove, Oregon. When her husband died in 1877, Mary revealed in her journal how sad and lonely she was without him. She wrote, "I think of so many things I want to tell Mr. Walker. I realize more and more how much I loved him more than anyone else."

Mollie Moore Davis

A bold story

1897

I have endeavored to sketch, in rather bold outlines, the story of Texas. It is a story of knightly romance which calls the poet even as, in earlier days, the Land of Texas called across its borders the dreamers of dreams.

But the history of Texas is far more than a romantic legend. It is a record of bold conceptions and bolder deeds; the story of the discoverer penetrating unknown wildernesses; of the pioneer matching his strength against his savage; of the colonist struggling for his freedom and his rights. . . .

Mollie Evelyn Moore Davis was born April 12, 1844, in Benton County, Alabama. When she was eleven the family moved to Texas to try farming. In 1860 she had her first poem printed in the *Tyler Reporter*, and was listed in the government census as "poetess."

Mollie published numerous poems and stories over the next two years. Her work caught the eye of Edward Cushing, the editor and publisher of the *Houston Telegraph*. He invited her to move into his home, to broaden her education through study in his library and by associating with cultivated people. She remained there five years.

Mollie was married in 1874 to Major Thomas Davis, a Galveston tobacco merchant. She continued writing, turning away from poetry to prose. Her novels, set in Texas, presented a humorous yet accurate picture of Texas life.

Mollie's writing is from The Story of Texas Under Six Flags, *published in 1897.*

Helen Maria Winslow

1900

My cruel parents established a decree, that we must never have more than one cat at a time. After a succession of feline dynasties, I remember fastening my affections securely upon one kitten who grew up to be the ugliest, gauntest, and dingiest specimen I ever have seen. In the days of his kittenhood I christened him "Tassie" after his mother; but as time sped on, and the name hardly comported with masculine dignity, this was changed to Tacitus, as more befitting his sex. He had a habit of dodging in and out of the front door, which was heavy, and which sometimes swung together before he was well out of it. As a consequence, a caudal appendage with two broken joints was one of his distinguishing features. Besides a broken tail, he had ears which bore the marks of many a hard-fought battle. But I loved him, and judging from the disconsolate and long-continued wailing with which he filled the house whenever I was away, my affection was not unrequited.

Helen Maria Winslow was born April 13, 1851, in Westfield, Vermont. Her father was a composer and opera singer and her mother was a poet and a linguist.

Following her mother's death and her father's remarriage, Helen settled in Boston with her three sisters. She began writing stories and poetry which were published in local magazines. Journalism, however, was her forte. She joined the staff of the *Boston Transcript* and later the *Boston Advertiser* and *Saturday Evening Gazette.*

Helen was one of six co-founders of the New England Woman's Press Association. She served as treasurer of that organization as well as vice-president of the Press League.

Just one cat

Helen's writing is from Concerning Cats—My Own and Some Others, *published in 1900.*

Harriet Livermore

A parting

1845

In May, 1824, that month of opening flowers, I left the mansion of my earthly parents again, and roved abroad. . . . My parents did not oppose it at all. I believe they long since determined to suffer me to take my own way. My mother reminded me of my feeble health, and said she thought home the best place for me. I took leave of my parents, and brothers, and sisters, with an aching heart, not knowing but our next meeting might be at the bar of a Holy God; and as soon as the carriage turned from the door, gave vent to my grief. The tears did not drop, they flowed in torrents from my eyes that had just looked upon my earthly father, perhaps for the last time.

Harriet Livermore was born April 14, 1788, in Concord, New Hampshire. When she was twenty, she accompanied her father to Washington while he served Congress. She became engaged in 1811 to Moses Elliott, but his parents forced him to terminate the relationship. Harriet felt this was divine punishment for her "wild and irregular" personality, so she turned fervently to religion.

Harriet spent the next two years reading the Bible in search of a religious credo. She left the Episcopal faith of her birth and tried the Congregational, Quaker and Baptist churches until she had a nervous breakdown in 1824. After that she proclaimed herself a "solitary eclectic" and a "Pilgrim stranger."

Harriet published her first book, based on scripture readings, and used the proceeds to finance her evangelical work. She travelled throughout New England, sometimes on foot, preaching to all who would listen.

Harriet's interpretation of the Bible convinced her in 1832 that the millennium was approaching. She decided to await the Lord's arrival in Jerusalem. Between 1837 and 1862 she made ten Atlantic crossings for this purpose. She died in poverty in 1868 at the Blockley Almshouse in Philadelphia.

Harriet's writing is from Harriet Livermore, the Pilgrim Stranger, *published by a distant relative, Reverend Samuel Livermore, in 1884.*

Give Her This Day

Elizabeth Boynton Harbert

1871

Calico days

Well, one morning I was washing the dishes, and everything went wrong. I put the biscuits in the closet, and set my pan of dishwater in the oven, and then hunted for it, (and oh! you know what funny things I can do); and then I commenced talking to myself, and I said it's just another "every day;" I don't have any more best days at all. They are all real calico days, and faded calico at that; and so I leaned on the old table and looked out the window, and just wished and wished that I was a boy, so that I could earn money, and go to college, and be somebody.

Elizabeth Boynton Harbert was born April 15, 1843, in Crawfordsville, Indiana. Five years after graduating from the Terre Haute Female College with honors, she published her first book.

In 1870, Elizabeth married Captain W.S. Harbert, a lawyer, and continued her writing career. She was editor of the women's department of Chicago's *Inter-Ocean*, which made her a familiar household name throughout the West.

In addition to her career, Elizabeth found time to participate in many charitable activities and frequent lecturing for womans suffrage.

Elizabeth's writing is from her second book, Out of Her Sphere, *published in 1871.*

Grace Livingston Hill

1929

An aunt's insight

I recall a Christmas long ago when I was just beginning to write scraps of stories myself, with no thought of ever amounting to anything as a writer. [My aunt's] gift to me that year was a thousand sheets of typewriter paper; and in a sweet little note that accompanied it she wished me success and bade me turn those thousand sheets of paper into as many dollars.

It was my first real encouragement. The first hint that anybody thought I ever could write, and I laughed aloud at the utter impossibility of its ever coming true.

Grace's remembrance of her Aunt Isabella Alden [November 3] is from the preface she wrote for Alden's last novel, An Interrupted Night, *published in 1929.*

But I feel that my first inspiration for storytelling came from her, and from reading her books in which as a child I fairly steeped myself.

Grace Livingston Hill, novelist, was born April 16, 1865, in Wellsville, New York. She was encouraged to write at an early age by her mother and her aunt, both of whom had written children's books. Grace borrowed her aunt's typewriter and wrote her first book at ten, and published her first book at twenty-two.

After Grace married Reverend Thomas Hill in 1892, she stopped writing to devote herself to home and church duties. However, her husband died suddenly in 1899, and she resumed writing to support herself and her two young daughters.

In 1908 Grace had her first popular success with a historical romance. Thereafter, she wrote two or more novels a year until her death at eighty-one, totalling seventy-nine books with sales of over three million. Although the time and locale varied, her plots always involved a sweet young woman who found true love and strong religious faith after a series of misadventures.

Susan Fenimore Cooper

Return of the robins

Wednesday, 22d.—1850

... This morning, to the joy of the whole community, the arrival of the robins is proclaimed. It is one of the great events of the year, for us, the return of the robins; we have been on the watch for them these ten days, as they generally come between the fifteenth and twenty-first of the month, and now most persons you meet, old and young, great and small, have something to say about them. No sooner is one of these first-comers seen by some member of a family, than the fact is proclaimed through the house; children run in to tell their parents, "The robins have come!" Grandfathers and grandmothers put on their spectacles and step to the windows to look at the robins; and you hear neighbors gravely inquiring of each other: "Have you seen the robins?" ... It was last night, just as the shutters were closed, that they were heard about the doors, and we ran out to listen to their first greeting, but it was too dark to see them. This morning, however, they were found in their

Susan's writing is from the 1887 new and revised edition of Rural Hours.

native apple trees, and a hearty welcome we gave the honest creatures.

Susan Fenimore Cooper, author, was born April 17, 1813, in Scarsdale, New York. She spent most of her life in the small village of Cooperstown, which had been founded by her grandfather. Susan's father was the well-known author James Fenimore Cooper. She was his copyist and in 1876 wrote a series of prefaces to a new edition of his works.

In addition to working with her father, Susan's literary career included novels, biographical sketches and magazine articles. Her best work, *Rural Hours*, was centered around life in Cooperstown. It was first published in 1850 and reprinted many times in America as well as London. Susan represented the third generation of her family to write about Cooperstown.

Mary Baptist Russell

December 14, 1893

Sharing a perspective

I trust, dear Gussie, you are a little easier, a little improved; still, whatever God allows is for your good, so continue to say often, "God's holy will be done." One such act of conformity in time of trial is, according to St. Augustine, more meritorious than thousands of acts of love when all goes smoothly.

I hope your dear mamma is well. Give her my love and best wishes, and your papa, too, the same. Ask them to pray for me sometimes.

Mother Mary Baptist Russell was born April 18, 1829, in Newry, County Down, Ireland. As a child she watched her mother administer to the needy during the Great Famine, and when she was nineteen she entered the Kinsale Convent of the Sisters of Mercy. Upon receiving her habit she took the name Sister Mary Baptist.

In 1854, the first archbishop of the recently established San Francisco diocese sent a plea to Ireland for assistance. Sister Mary Baptist left Kinsale for California with eight nuns and novices. They were needed immediately to help care for the victims of an Asiatic cholera epidemic which lasted six months. Shortly thereafter, as Mother Mary Baptist, she founded St. Mary's Hospital, the first Catholic hospital on the west coast.

Nursing was the primary activity of Mother Baptist and her Sisters of Mercy. However, they also became involved in

Mother Baptist's letter to a young girl confined to bed with a spinal disease is included in The Life of Mother Mary Baptist Russell, Sister of Mercy, *written by her brother Matthew Russell and published in 1901.*

all aspects of the community. They started an adult night school, a shelter for homeless women and prostitutes, several Catholic high schools and a home for the aged and infirm. The Sisters regularly visited local prisons, offering religious instruction and comfort to inmates on death row. After Mother Baptist's death at sixty-nine, the *San Francisco Bulletin* described her as the "best-known charitable worker on the Pacific Coast."

Lucretia Garfield

Center of attention

Lucretia's writing is from her diary which is in the Manuscript Division, Library of Congress.

March 12th, 1881
Held our first morning Reception for all the great roaring world. For two hours we took the hands of the passing crowd without a moment's intermission. Before the first hour was over I was aching in every joint, and thought how can I ever last through the next long sixty minutes. But the crowd soon made me forget myself, and though nearly paralyzed, the last hour passed more quickly than the first.

Lucretia Rudolph Garfield was born April 19, 1832, in Garretsville, Ohio. In 1850, she enrolled in the Western Reserve Eclectic Institute, which had been recently founded by her father and other members of the Disciples of Christ.

While attending the Eclectic Institute, Lucretia befriended James Garfield, a poor farm boy. They married in 1858, and he was elected to the Ohio Senate the following year. They bought a farm in Mentor, Ohio, known as "Lawnfield," and had seven children.

Following James' election to the United States presidency, Lucretia assumed her duties as First Lady in March, 1881. However, she contracted malaria within two months and was sent to Elberon, New Jersey, to convalesce. While she was there, President Garfield was shot at a Washington railroad station. He lingered for eighty days until he finally succumbed. Lucretia outlived her husband by thirty-six years, supported by a fund of $360,000 that was raised by public subscription and a Congressional grant.

Adelia Smith Johnson

1911

Love is rather a silly thing to have three meals a day
of . . . I used to tell the girls when I hired them, I'd
rather have a case of measles in the house than a girl
in love.

I'm getting rather dissipated lately and go to see the
pictures every Saturday night, and sometimes in the
middle of the week. How is that for an old lady? One
can get quite a lot of amusement for ten cents! . . .

Well we are never young but once, and then not
very long.

Adelia Maria Smith Johnson was born April 20, 1846, in
Richford, Vermont. In 1865 she married William Prescott
Johnson, also of Richford, and they had three sons.

She and her husband moved to Wells River, Vermont, in
1873 where he was deputy sheriff. They bought the Wells
River Boarding House and Livery Stable, which Adelia ran
until her husband's death in 1906. In the years following the
closing of the boarding house she did practical nursing.

A Vermonter's perspective

*Adelia's writing is from a letter
she wrote to her granddaughter
in 1911 and was included in her
great-granddaughter Eunice K.
Halfmann's* Clothespins and
Calendars, Recollections of
the Past, *published in 1985.*

Belle Case LaFollette

1911

"What do Washington women talk about?" I am asked.
Altogether too much about the weather. Women in official life come from all parts of the country, have widely
varied experience as well as much in common. They are
intelligent, and have insight. They might discuss current
events, politics, religion, education, philosophy.

But there is nothing of the French salon or English
drawing room in the social life of Washington. I often
wonder why. Women appear fearful their opinions will
be interpreted as an echo of their husband's. You often
hear them say, even in trivial matters, where it could
really make no difference, "I speak for myself," or "this
is my own, not my husband's view."

*W*ashington gossip

*Belle's writing is taken from her
syndicated column "Thought for
Today" that she wrote for the
North American Press
Syndicate, Series XVI,
November 11, 1911.*

Belle Case LaFollette was born April 21, 1859, in a log cabin in Summit, Wisconsin. After graduating from the University of Wisconsin, she taught for two years until her marriage to a former college classmate, Robert LaFollette.

In 1883 Belle entered the University of Wisconsin Law School, becoming the first woman to receive a law degree from that university. Although she was admitted to the bar, she never actually practiced, but her legal training was a great help to her husband's career. She was an active participant during Robert's three terms in Congress, serving as his secretary and administrative assistant.

In 1906 Robert was elected to the U.S. Senate. Three years later, he and Belle created *LaFollette's Magazine*. She edited the "Women and Education Department," writing articles on health, child care, political news and Washington social life. In 1913 Belle spoke in favor of woman suffrage before her husband's colleagues, the Senate Committee on Suffrage.

At the time of her death in 1931, the *New York Times* editorialized that she was possibly "the most influential of all American women who had to do with public affairs in this country."

APRIL 22

Olive Logan

Life on the stage

Olive's writing is from her book, Women and Theatres, *published in 1869.*

1869

I referred the other night to decent young women who are not celebrities,—merely honest, modest girls, whose parents have left them the not very desirable heritage of the stage, and who find it difficult to obtain any other employment, being uneducated for any other. When these girls go into a theatre to apply for a situation now, they find that the requirements of managers are expressed in the following questions,—

"1. Is your hair dyed yellow?

"2. Are your legs, arms, and bosom symmetrically formed, and are you willing to expose them?

"3. Can you sing brassy songs, and dance the can-can, and wink at men, and give utterance to disgusting half-words, which mean whole actions?

"4. Are you acquainted with any rich men who will throw you flowers, and send you presents, and keep afloat dubious rumors concerning your chastity?

"5. Are you willing to appear to-night, and every

night, amid the glare of gas lights, and before the gaze of thousands of men, in this pair of satin breeches, ten inches long, without a vestige of drapery upon your person?

"If you can answer these questions affirmatively, we will give you a situation; if not, there's the door."

Olive Logan, actress, lecturer and author, was born April 22, 1839, in Elmira, New York. Her father, Cornelius Ambrosius Logan, was an early well-known American actor.

Olive was carried on stage for her first role as a child. At fifteen she made her formal debut on the Philadelphia stage and was highly successful until she retired at twenty-nine to join the lecture circuit. Theater historian George Odell claimed, "She was too homely to act" but was "a clever speaker."

Olive married William Sikes in 1871 and moved to Cardiff, Wales where her husband was the American consul. She lectured and wrote plays until his death in 1883 plunged her into poverty. Olive lost her mind in 1909 and was placed in an asylum where she died a few months later. She was buried in a pauper's grave.

Penina Moïse

1841
> Hope, Laughter and Sleep accidentally met
> One day in the valley of tears
> There they strove by their spells to make mortals
>   forget
> The briars Life's tree ever bears.

Hope, Laughter and Sleep

Penina Moïse, poet and writer of Jewish hymns, was born April 23, 1797, in Charleston, South Carolina. After her father died when she was twelve she helped support her family by making lace and doing embroidery work.

Penina studied and wrote poetry at night, often by moonlight. Her verse was published in many east coast newspapers and ladies' magazines. She was devoutly religious, remaining single rather than marry out of her faith. In 1841 she began composing hymns for her congregation, Temple Beth Elohim. Many of these hymns are still sung today in American Reform Jewish congregations.

Penina's writing is the first verse of her thirteen-verse poem "Hope, Laughter and Sleep," which is included in the book Secular and Religious Works of Penina Moïse, *published posthumously in 1911 by the Charleston section of the Council of Jewish Women.*

Susan Dimock

The joy of achievement

50 Mothingen, Zürich
Oct. 25, 1868
Dr. Cabot,
Dear Sir,

You were so kind as to be interested in my search for a good medical college, and to say that you would like to hear from me, and I have great pleasure in being able to tell you of my success. Altogether I am entirely content and very happy.

I have eight hours daily in the University, five or six for lectures and two or three for discussions, which last—I enjoy extremely. Three times a week I give an English lesson, and Saturday aft. and Sunday I have free to spend as I please, generally in the mountains.

I hope to get my degree here in three and a half years, and then to spend a year in Paris, pass my examinations there also, and get that degree too to take home to the Mass. Med. Society.

I am very truly yours,
Susan Dimock

Susan Dimock was born April 24, 1847, in Washington, D.C. As an only child, she received an excellent education at home until she was sent to boarding school at age thirteen. While there, her studies in Latin sparked her interest in medicine.

Susan's father died during the Civil War and her family lost most of its property. Susan and her mother resettled with relatives in Massachusetts. In 1866 she began studying at the New England Hospital for Women and Children. Her application to Harvard Medical School was declined due to her sex, and Massachusetts General Hospital would only allow her to study under certain restrictions. Determined, she applied to the University of Zürich, where she was accepted and graduated in three years with high honors.

Upon her return to Boston, Susan was appointed to a three-year residency at New England Hospital. Her administrative and surgical skills so impressed the hospital's board that they renewed her term for three more years. She asked to take five months' leave of absence between terms and set sail for Europe with two women friends. Ten days into the voyage the

Susan's letter is in the Sophia Smith Collection, Smith College, Northampton, Massachusetts.

steamer ran aground on an island off the coast of England, killing almost everyone on board. Susan's body was recovered and returned to Boston for burial.

Constance Cary Harrison

Paris
Sunday 20 Jan. 1867

Went today, by way of variety, to the American Chapel, and prayed faithfully for "the President of the United States and all in authority." The Congress, however, I consider past praying for, and so discreetly withheld my Amen. . . .

   · Mr. St. Martin came to dinner, and held us to our engagement to walk in the Bois. The great ponds were covered with skaters this evening. . . .

   I will admit that it was a very gay scene. Oh! These astonishing French people! They sit on snow-covered benches under leafless trees for friendly chats, and their hapless infants are trotted back and forth through freezing winds and the thermometer 14 degrees below zero!

*P*arisian impressions

Constance Cary Harrison, author, was born April 25, 1843, in Lexington, Kentucky. During the Civil War she lived with an aunt and uncle in Richmond, Virginia. Constance and her three cousins were popular society belles in the Confederate Capital and it was during this time she met her future husband, Burton Harrison, President Davis' private secretary.

   While living in Richmond, Constance published her first book, *Blockade Correspondence*. After her marriage to Mr. Harrison in 1867, the couple settled in New York, where he practiced law. Over the next twenty years, Constance produced numerous novels, magazine articles, short stories and historical sketches, plus an etiquette book and her own memoirs.

Constance's diary is part of the Papers of Burton Harrison and Family collection, Carton #9, Manuscript Division, Library of Congress.

Martha Farnsworth

A dubious beginning

Tuesday
September 3, 1889
. . . My last day of *"Single Blessedness"* so must make the most of it: it all seems so strange, yet I'm happy as can be.
Wed. 4

My Wedding Day, and I pray God to bless it . . . I have felt *so sad* all day and it has been hard to keep back the tears: my eyes have been full most all day but not one dropped. I'm determined not to cry on my wedding day. I love Johnny and I know he does me, yet it seems tho' he has thought more of how things shall look, at the wedding, than of me; he has hurried me all day and not given me one little pleasant word concerning what is to be. My heart feels hungry and not satisfied.

Martha Farnsworth was born April 26, 1867, in Mt. Pleasant, Iowa. Her family moved to Kansas when she was five.

Martha began a diary when she was fourteen and kept it for the next forty years until there were sixteen volumes totaling more than four thousand pages. Her writings revealed her strong determination as she coped with her marriage to Johnny Shaw, a drunkard who was unable to hold a job. She worked as a waitress to support them until his death from consumption after four years of marriage.

Martha later married Fred Farnsworth, a postman. She had taken up the cause of temperance because of her experiences with her first husband, and she threatened her second husband that if she ever saw him take one drink she would leave him. Apparently he refrained from alcohol, as they spent twenty-nine happy years together.

Martha learned to roller skate when she was thirty-eight and at forty-two she became the first woman in Topeka to swim across a local lake.

Martha's writing is from her journal, which is in the manuscript department of the Kansas Historical Society, Topeka, Kansas.

Alice Morse Earle

1893

Ice water and brown bread

I often fancy I should have enjoyed living in the good old times, but I am glad I never was a child in colonial New England—to have been baptized in ice water, fed on brown bread and warm beer, to have had to learn the Assembly's Catechism . . . to have been constantly threatened with fear of death and terror of God, to have been forced to commit Wigglesworth's "Day of Doom" to memory, and after all, to have been whipped with a tattling stick.

Alice Morse Earle was born April 27, 1851, in Worcester, Massachusetts. Her parents were avid antique collectors, and their house was described as "a veritable museum." Through them, she acquired an appreciation and understanding of fine antiquities and colonial America.

In 1874, Alice married Henry Earle and moved to his Brooklyn Heights home, where she lived for the rest of her life.

In 1891, Alice had her first article published in *The Atlantic Monthly* as well as her first novel; both concerned America's colonial past. She produced seventeen books and more than thirty articles on the subject in the next twelve years. She did extensive research in various historical societies and libraries and became well-known in her field.

Alice's writing is from Customs and Fashions in Old New England, *published in 1893.*

Frances Smith Griswold

1871

God's design

The young mother knelt in the darkness, beside her sleeping child. It was her first bitter grief. The little innocent had blessed her life for one short year. . . .

If mothers could but put aside their anguish, and see only the joy of the ransomed! Yet this is not God's design for us. He wills that we shall feel the tearing away of the heart-tendrils as they cling too closely to the objects of our love. He knows that by the very strength

Frances' writing is from Asleep, *published in 1871.*

of our affection, and the deep yearning grief, we shall be drawn after our beloved ones, until we reach them in the golden City.

Frances Irene Burge Griswold was born April 28, 1826, in Wickford, Rhode Island. Her father, rector of St. Paul's Narragansett Church for twenty years, played a large part in influencing her spiritual and educational life.

Frances wrote her first book when she was twenty-seven and published thirty-two more, as well as countless newspaper articles, during her lifetime. Her *Bishop and Nanette* series were widely used in Episcopal Sunday school classes, and *Asleep,* her most popular, best-selling book, was a comfort to many people during periods of grief after the death of loved ones.

Following the death of her first husband, Frances married Judge Elias Griswold, a distant relative, and settled in Brooklyn, New York.

APRIL 29

Lucia Loraine Williams

Serenade in the wilds

July 1, 1851

Camped on the Platte. Last night we were awakened by serenaders. Five horsemen circled around the carriage, singing "Araby's Daughter." It was a beautiful night. We were surrounded by bluffs in a little valley and on being awakened by their song, seeing the panting steeds and looking around upon the wild country it seemed as though we were transplanted into Arabia. They were beautiful singers from Oregon. Said they were exiles from home. Mr. Williams arose. They sang "Sweet Home" and several others. Invited us to stay and celebrate the 4th. Said they would make us a barbecue, but we were anxious to get on and the affliction that we had just suffered unfitted us for such a scene.

Lucia Loraine Bigelow Williams was born April 29, 1816, in Vermont. She married Elijah Williams, a widower with two sons, and they had a son and a daughter of their own.

In 1851 the entire family set off on the long overland journey west. Their ten-year-old son was killed in an unusual accident when he fell from the wagon and the wheels ran over his head.

They settled in Salem, Oregon, in a house across the

Lucia's diary belongs to her great granddaughter Helen Stratton Felker of Tacoma, Washington. She presented it to Kenneth L. Holmes for inclusion in his Covered Wagon Women *(published in 1984).*

street from the State Capitol. Elijah practiced law and Lucia was one of the founders of the First Congregational Church. There is a stained-glass window at the church commemorating her activities that can still be seen today.

Mary Dimmick Harrison

1889
Executive Mansion, Washington.
My Dear Mrs. McCulloch,

*A*n invitation

　　Mrs. Harrison receives her friends informally Friday afternoons between three and four o'clock, and will be very glad to see yourself and friends at one of these afternoons. She also holds her first public reception next Saturday afternoon from three to five.

　　Owing to the crowd at the evening receptions, it has become necessary to issue cards for the few who are admitted through the South Entrance and Mrs. Harrison takes pleasure in sending one to you for the next reception. I am very truly yours,

　　Mary Scott-Dimmick
　　January twentieth

Mary Dimmick Harrison was born April 30, 1858, in Honesdale, Pennsylvania. She married Walter Dimmick, a lawyer from her hometown in 1881. He died of typhoid fever three months later.

　　Mary's mother's sister, her beloved Aunt Carrie, was married to Benjamin Harrison, twenty-third president of the United States. After Mary was widowed, her aunt invited her to move into the White House. She lived there for two years, helping her aunt and uncle with their duties.

　　Mary's aunt passed away just as President Harrison lost his bid for reelection. Three and a half years later Mary, age thirty-seven, and Benjamin, age sixty-two, were wed. His two children were opposed to the marriage and never accepted their stepmother.

　　Mary and Benjamin settled in Indianapolis and enjoyed all the honors bestowed upon an ex-president. They had a daughter in 1897. Benjamin Harrison died four years later. Mary relocated to New York and always retained her interest in politics, attending her last Republican convention at the age of eighty-two.

Mary's letter, written on behalf of the first Mrs. Harrison, is in the Manuscripts Division, Lilly Library, Indiana University, Bloomington, Indiana.

M A Y

Mary Harris Jones (Mother Jones)

1925

An army of women

The fight went on. In Coaldale, in the Hazelton district, the miners were not permitted to assemble in any hall. It was necessary to win the strike in that district that the Coaldale miners be organized.

I went to a nearby mining town that was thoroughly organized and asked the women if they would help me get the Coaldale men out. This was in McAdoo. I told them to leave their men at home to take care of the family. I asked them to put on their kitchen clothes and bring mops and brooms with them and a couple of tin pans. We marched over the mountains fifteen miles, beating on the tin pans as if they were cymbals. At three o'clock in the morning we met the Crack Thirteen of the militia, patrolling the roads to Coaldale. The colonel of the regiment said, "Halt! Move back!"

I said, "Colonel, the working men of America will not halt nor will they ever go back. The working man is going forward!"

"I'll charge bayonets," said he.

"On whom?"

"On your people."

"We are not enemies," said I. "We are just a band of working women whose brothers and husbands are in a battle for bread. We want our brothers in Coaldale to join us in our fight. We are here on the mountain road for our children's sake, for the nation's sake. We are not going to hurt anyone and surely you would not hurt us."

They kept us there till daybreak and when they saw the army of women in kitchen aprons, with dishpans and mops, they laughed and let us pass. An army of strong mining women makes a wonderfully spectacular picture.

Well, when the miners in the Coaldale camp started to go to work they were met by the McAdoo women who were beating on their pans and shouting, "Join the union! Join the union!"

They joined, every last man of them, and we got so enthusiastic that we organized the streetcar men who promised to haul no scabs for the coal companies. As

Mother Jones' writing is from the chapter, "How The Women Mopped Up Coaldale," in her autobiography, published in 1925.

there were no other groups to organize we marched over the mountains home, beating on our pans and singing patriotic songs.

Mary Harris Jones, labor agitator, known as "Mother" Jones, was born May 1, 1830, in Cork, Ireland. Her father came to America when she was five and as soon as he became a U.S. citizen he sent for his wife and family.

Mary worked for a while in Chicago as a teacher and then a dressmaker before moving to Memphis, Tennessee. In 1861 she married Mr. Jones, a staunch member of the Iron Molders' Union. In 1867 a yellow-fever epidemic swept through Memphis killing mostly the poor, as the well-to-do fled the city. "One by one, my four little children sickened and died. My husband caught the fever and died. I sat alone through nights of grief. No one came to me. No one could. Other homes were as stricken as mine. All day long, all night long, I heard the grating of the wheels of the death cart." She served as a volunteer nurse until the plague ended, after which she returned to Chicago and resumed dressmaking.

Mary lost everything she had in the Great Chicago Fire of 1871 and had to take shelter at St. Mary's Church. During that time she spent many evenings attending meetings of the Knights of Labor in a building next door to the church. She became acquainted with the labor movement through the Knights of Labor, who had organized after the Civil War to fight industrial slavery. She regarded those early labor leaders as "saints and martyrs," and "decided to take an active part in the efforts of the working people to better the conditions under which they worked and lived."

From the 1880's on Mary Jones became "Mother" Jones, a leader in the working-class fight against low wages, long hours and terrible working conditions. She had no permanent home, but found lodging wherever she went, always traveling from one industrial area to another.

Mother Jones celebrated her hundredth birthday with a large party, and telegrams poured in from across the country. She died seven months later. Buses brought miners from all over the state to her funeral, which was broadcast through loudspeakers to a crowd of between ten and fifteen thousand people. She was buried beside her "boys" in the Union Miners' Cemetery in Mount Olive, Illinois.

Mary MacLane

1902

I write every day. Writing is a necessity—like eating. I do a little housework, and on the whole I am rather fond of it—some parts of it. I dislike dusting chairs, but I have no aversion to scrubbing floors. Indeed, I have gained much of my strength and gracefulness of body from scrubbing the kitchen floor—to say nothing of some fine points of philosophy. It brings a certain energy to one's body and to one's brain.

But mostly I take walks far away in the open country. Butte and its immediate vicinity present as ugly an outlook as one could wish to see. It is so ugly indeed that it is near the perfection of ugliness. And anything perfect, or nearly so, is not to be despised. I have reached some astonishing subtleties of conception as I have walked for miles over the sand and barrenness among the little hills and gulches.

My subtle thoughts

Mary MacLane was born May 2, 1881, in Winnipeg, Manitoba. Her father died when she was eight and the family relocated in Butte, Montana. At nineteen she kept a diary for three months which she sent off to a Chicago publisher, who published it within the week. *The Story of Mary MacLane by Herself* became an instant best seller and the talk of the nation. Her provocative thoughts, shocking sexual revelations, and unorthodox behavior propelled Mary into the spotlight, as everyone wanted to learn more about this strange girl who prowled the cemetery at night.

Mary's book was banned from the local library because of its unflattering portrait of Butte and its townspeople. However, offers came in for her to lend her name to a cigar and a drink, and the term "MacLaneism" was coined to describe previously conventional young ladies whose behavior changed radically after reading the book. In the first month alone eighty thousand copies were sold, earning $17,000 in royalties.

Most importantly to Mary, her earnings enabled her to leave her detested Butte. For the next eight years she traveled up and down the east coast, acting outlandishly and making avant-garde statements. One of her first acts upon returning home in 1910 was to referee a prizefight.

In 1917 Mary again left Butte for Chicago, where she wrote and starred in the movie "Men Who Have Made Love

Mary's writing is from her first book, The Story of Mary MacLane by Herself, *published in 1902.*

To Me," a film that generated as much controversy through its sensationalism as her book had twenty years previously.

Following the movie, Mary's life began a downward plunge. Her three books were no longer selling, and her passion for gambling and the high life had reduced her to poverty. She died when she was forty-eight, alone in a shabby hotel room in Chicago.

Caroline White Willard

A cruel custom

Chilcat Mission
Haines, Alaska
1882

Old superstitions make the people very cruel and heartless. Of all the customs, there is not one, I think, which gives me so much trouble as that of marrying their children and selling them. In spite of us, so far, there are in our village several child-wives from nine or ten to thirteen years of age. One dear girl was given by her parents to her father's brother, a great brutal fellow, who already had a wife, almost blind, with several feeble, idiotic children. This little one was a gentle, delicate and beautiful girl of about nine or ten years. When I see her now, I almost want to run away; for I feel tempted to do something desperate. Her little face is bruised and swollen; her eyes are bloodshot, and their expression would bring tears to your eyes. She sits in that dark, cold hut with only those most repulsive beings about her, sewing away for them like a little old woman, all child-life forever gone.

Caroline McCoy White Willard was born May 3, 1853, in New Castle, Pennsylvania. As a child she already showed an interest in missionary work, reading stories of missionaries and organizing her young friends into a missionary society.

When Caroline was eleven, she contracted a serious illness from which she was not expected to recover. She lay in her bed, near death, accepting the inevitable. One day, without any reason, she revived and rapidly recovered. She and her parents concluded that God must have work on earth for her to accomplish. As soon as she was strong enough she was carried into her church, where she made a public declaration of her faith in Jesus.

Caroline's writing is from Life in Alaska, *edited by her sister, published in 1884. Happily, a few months after writing this discouraging letter she was able to rescue the little girl and place her in her boarding school for girls.*

In 1879, Caroline married Eugene Willard. A few months later they departed for Alaska, where they had accepted teaching positions under the Board of Home Missions of the Presbyterian Church. They established boarding schools for boys and girls at their Chilcat Mission.

Priscilla Merriman Evans

1885

We landed in Boston on May 23rd [1856], then travelled in cattle cars three hundred miles to Iowa City. We remained in Iowa City three weeks, waiting for our carts to be made.

. . . When the carts were ready we started on a three-hundred-mile walk to Winterquarters on the Missouri River. There were a great many who made fun of us as we walked, pulling our carts, but the weather was fine and the roads were excellent and although I was sick [from pregnancy] and we were tired out at night, we still thought, "This is a glorious way to come to Zion."

We began our journey of one thousand miles on foot with a handcart for each family, some families consisting of man and wife, and some had quite large families.

. . . My husband, in walking from twenty to twenty-five miles per day [had pain] where the knee rested on the pad [as a young boy he had lost his left leg at the knee in an accident]. The friction caused it to gather and break and was most painful. But he had to endure it, or remain behind, as he was never asked to ride in a wagon. . . .

. . . We reached Salt Lake City on October 2, 1856, tired, weary, with bleeding feet, our clothing worn out and so weak we were nearly starved, but thankful to our Heavenly Father for bringing us to Zion. William R. Jones met us on the Public Square in Salt Lake City and brought us to his home in Spanish Fork. I think we were over three days coming from Salt Lake City to Spanish Fork by ox team, but what a change to ride in a wagon after walking 1330 miles from Iowa City to Salt Lake City!

Priscilla's writing excerpt is from a short autobiography she wrote in 1885. She condensed and copied it from her journal written years before. It was reprinted in Volume IX of Heart Throbs of the West, published in 1948 by the Daughters of the Utah Pioneers in Salt Lake City.

Priscilla Merriman Evans was born May 4, 1835, in Pembroke-shire, Wales. She was baptized into the Church of Latter-day Saints when she was seventeen despite her father's strong objections.

Shortly after she and Mormon Elder, Thomas Evans, were married in 1856, they came to the United States. Upon arrival they joined Captain Bunker's Third Handcart Party, becoming a part of an extraordinary migration of three thousand Mormon immigrants who walked from Iowa City, Iowa, to Salt Lake City, Utah. No one was allowed to ride in a wagon. They all walked, pulling their hickory carts behind them.

Thomas farmed for several years after settling in Utah and was not successful at it. He sold his farm and started a store. He was soon called away to England on a mission. Priscilla was left to raise their children and run the business. In 1877, when she was forty-two, her twelfth child was born. Thomas' health was not good after his return from overseas, so they sold their home and store on Main Street and built a small house outside of town where they lived out their days. Priscilla concluded her writing with her life motto: "Not to look back—but forward" and said that she had always "thanked the Lord for a contented mind, a home and something to eat."

Lucy Larcom

Childhood

Lucy's writing is from her autobiographical book, A New England Girlhood, *published in 1889.*

1889

It is one of the most beautiful facts in this human existence of ours, that we remember the earliest and freshest part of it most vividly. Doubtless it was meant that our childhood should live on in us forever. My childhood was by no means a cloudless one. It had its light and shade, each contributing a charm which makes it wholly delightful in the retrospect.

Lucy Larcom, poet, was born May 5, 1824, in Beverly, Massachusetts. Her father died when she was a young child, forcing her mother to move the family of ten children to Lowell, where she worked in the textile mills. Lucy's education soon ended as she joined her older sisters in the factory.

Lucy worked in the mills for ten years. To relieve the tedium she wrote poetry, taking her topics from nature, local people and folklore. She had an intense Christian faith and always thought of her poetry as an extension of that faith, a way to achieve good.

Mary Clemmer Ames

1873

Then it is heavenly to "loaf;" but it is not much to tell about. If it is loafing to bask on a bank, in the full blaze of the sun, through an entire August afternoon, making intimate acquaintance with bugs and "things"—the cunning workers of the ground and the murmuring nations of the air—then I am a born loafer. Let the sun burn and tan me; I "loaf" on in imperturbability of soul. Pretty field-bugs, that live in the grass, are such delightful society, compared with tedious people. If you have never found this out, do try. My closest companions during the last month have been grasshoppers. They will not leave or forsake me. There is one actually hopping on my paper at this moment. The amount of time I spend in mending their legs and helping them out of tight places should insure me their gratitude as the benefactor of their race.

Mary Clemmer Ames, journalist and author, was born May 6, 1831, in Utica, New York. Her family was large and of limited means. As a result she obtained little formal education, and she rushed into an early marriage with Daniel Ames, a Methodist minister, in 1851. It was an unhappy marriage. She permanently separated from her husband in 1865, and received a divorce in 1874.

Mary moved to Washington, D.C., resumed her maiden name, and took up writing to support herself. She became very successful. For ten years she wrote a column entitled "Woman's Letter from Washington" for the New York religious weekly *The Independent*. Her letters commented on the political issues of the day, and to gather information she spent many hours in the ladies' gallery of the House and Senate. Mary was so adept at writing that she received five thousand dollars' salary during her last year at the paper—reputedly the largest amount ever paid to an American newspaperwoman up to that time.

In addition to her newspaper work she published three novels, two volumes of political articles and a book of poetry.

Mary believed "the best thing that can happen to any woman is to be satisfactorily loved, to be taken care of, to be made much of, and to make much of the life and the love utterly her own in her own home." At long last she found

A born loafer

Mary's writing is from the chapter "Northern Vermont in August" in her book, Outlines of Men, Women and Things, *a collection of her newspaper articles, published in 1873.*

happiness when she married Edmund Hudson, a Washington journalist, in 1883. They honeymooned in Europe, but she was stricken with paralysis soon after their return and died of a cerebral hemorrhage eight months later.

Varina Howell Davis

Candidate's wife

Washington
June 6th 1846
My dear Mother, my best dearest friend,

To-day I am so miserable I feel as if I could lay down my life to be near you and Father. It has been some time a struggle between Jeff and me, which should overcome the other in the matter of his volunteering....

I found out last night accidentally that he had committed himself about going. I have cried until I am stupid.... Jeff thinks there is *something* the matter with me, but I *know* there is not.... If Jeff was a cross, bad husband, old, ugly, or stupid, I could better bear for him to go on a year's campaign, but he is so tender and good that I feel like he ought never to leave me—I won't weigh you down with my troubles....

Varina Howell Davis was born May 7, 1826, on her parents' plantation, "Marengo," in Louisiana. She first met Jefferson Davis when she was seventeen and they were married two years later in 1845.

The Davises went to Washington in 1847 after he had been elected to the Senate. Later he was appointed Secretary of War. Varina was well suited to her role as social hostess, a role that was augmented in importance because the First Lady, Jane Pierce, disliked all public appearances.

After Mississippi seceded in 1861, Jefferson Davis was selected president of the Confederacy, and they took up residence at the executive mansion in Richmond. When the capital fell in 1865 they were forced to flee, but Jefferson was seized and imprisoned. Varina spent two years trying to secure his freedom, then joined him at Fortress Monroe.

Davis was finally released in 1867 and became an insurance salesman. Varina had difficulty coping with their diminished existence and suffered from depression and hypochondria. She had a nervous breakdown in 1876. With the passage of time post-war anger subsided, and Jefferson Davis became a Southern hero. Life for Varina became meaningful again.

Varina's letter to her mother is included in Jefferson Davis— Private Letters, 1823-1889, *edited by Hudson Strode, published in 1966.*

Augusta Evans Wilson

1859

Reader, marriage is not the end of life; it is but the beginning of a new course of duties; but I cannot now follow Beulah. Henceforth, her history is bound up with another's. To save her husband from his unbelief, is the labor of future years. She had learned to suffer, and to bear patiently; and though her paths look sunny, and her heart throbs with happy hopes, this one shadow lurks over her home and dims her joys. Weeks and months glided swiftly on. Dr. Hartwell's face lost its stern rigidity, and his smile became constantly genial. His wife was his idol; day by day, his love for her seemed more completely to revolutionize his nature. His cynicism melted insensibly away; his lips forgot their iron compression; now and then, his long-forgotten laugh rang through the house. Beulah was conscious of the power she wielded, and trembled lest she failed to employ it properly.

Augusta Evans Wilson, novelist, was born May 8, 1835, near Columbus, Georgia. At seventeen she published her first book anonymously, and at twenty-three she published the novel *Beulah* under her own name. A contemporary writer, Mary Virginia Terhune, called it "the best work of fiction ever published by a Southern writer." The tremendous sales of the book brought the Evans family from abject poverty to a comfortable financial state.

During the Civil War Augusta was so pro-South that she broke off her engagement to a man who supported Lincoln. She wrote anonymous propaganda articles for an Alabama paper, and her third novel, *Macaria*, was forbidden reading to Union troops.

At thirty-three, Augusta married a wealthy neighbor twenty-seven years her senior, Colonel Lorenzo Wilson. She produced a total of nine romance novels which brought her royalties averaging $10,000 per year for thirty years.

Augusta's writing is from her novel Beulah, *published in 1859.*

Belle Boyd

*B*lood was boiling in her veins

Belle's writing is from her book, Belle Boyd in Camp and Prison, *published in 1866.*

1866

A party of soldiers, conspicuous, even on that day, for violence, broke into our house and commenced their depredations. . . .

They had brought with them a large Federal flag, which they were now preparing to hoist over our roof in token of our submission to their authority; but to this my mother would not consent. Stepping forward with a firm step, she said, very quietly, but resolutely, "Men, every member of my household will die before that flag shall be raised over us."

Upon this, one of the soldiers, thrusting himself forward, addressed my mother and myself in language as offensive as it is possible to conceive. I could stand it no longer; my indignation was roused beyond control; my blood was literally boiling in my veins; I drew out my pistol and shot him. He was carried away mortally wounded, and soon after expired.

Belle Boyd, Confederate spy, actress and lecturer, was born May 9, 1844, in Martinsburg, Virginia.

Belle was passionately devoted to the South, and in 1861, when she was seventeen, commenced her espionage work. At first she obtained information from admiring Union officers and passed it on to Confederate officers via messenger. Belle graduated to courier and fared well due to her excellent riding skills and knowledge of the area. By 1862 she had become famous in the North and the South. Secretary of War Edwin Stanton had her imprisoned twice, after which she was banished to the South for the duration of the war.

Just shy of her twentieth birthday Belle set sail for England carrying Confederate dispatches, but her ship was seized by a Union vessel, and she was sent to Canada under penalty of death if recaptured. Five months later she married the Union naval officer who had captured the ship, thus ending her service to the Confederates.

Belle returned to the United States from England after the death of her husband and acted in stock companies for a few years. She married again, had four children, and divorced to marry an actor seventeen years her junior. From 1886 until her death in 1900 Belle toured the country giving dramatic recitals of her war escapades. She stressed the union of North and South and her lectures were very popular nationwide. She died of a heart attack at a speaking engagement in Wisconsin.

Persis Sibley Black

May 9, 1841
Our little circle of young ladies is lessening. Miss Louisa Tripp and Miss Lucinda Williams are both published. I think them both good matches, but I don't envy them—I had rather go to my school, much as I dread it, but it isn't leaving home for life.

May 13, 1841
. . . We all avoid the expression which so naturally occurs, "while you are gone," as much as we can, for it is painful to all. The time seems long, for notwithstanding my philosophy teaches me that I shall live but one day at a time, I look at the whole. The engagement is greater than any I have ever perform'd, and it started me to think I could hardly get away from it even should my parents or brother be ever so sick. I dread it, and yet I am not sorry to go.

May 14, 1841
This is National Fast Day in consequence of the death of President Harrison.

I left home at 7 o'clock this morning for Belfast. My heart has not been so heavy for years. I could not give the parting words, for tears.

Leaving home

Persis Sibley Andrews Black was born May 10, 1813, in Paris, Maine. She was a schoolteacher until she married Charles Andrews in 1842. He was a member of Congress when he died suddenly after ten years of marriage.

Persis remarried Alvah Black, also of Paris, and they had one son. She kept a diary for over twenty years that revealed what type of person she was: introspective, pious, and dedicated to her family. She also had a sense of humor: one entry described an evil man who had abandoned his wife and had many mistresses, "a man openly bad—but he can sing, and therefore was tolerated in the choir."

Persis' diary is in the Maine Historical Society, Portland, Maine. These May entries relate to her taking a teaching position in Belfast, Maine.

Phoebe Stanton

Letter from the trail

May the 9th 1847
Dear Brothers and Sisters,
. . . We are now one hundred and ten miles from St. Joseph. It will be four weeks tomorrow since we left home. . . .

There is a great deal of wild fruit in this country. The people look coarse and plain here but appear to be clever. . . . I have to close my letter before we start with the cattle coming now my opportunity for writing is poor as I have to write on a small box in the wagon with every kind of noise around me. Forgive me scribbling for I have written the most of it with the oxen hitched to the wagon. . . . I hope you will get ready by next spring and come. Farewell, remember I am your affectionate Sister,

Phoebe Stanton

Phoebe Fail Stanton was born May 11, 1815, in Virginia. A few months shy of her sixteenth birthday she married Alfred Stanton, a twenty-three-year-old farmer. They lived in Indiana for sixteen years and had five children. In 1847 the family went west on the Oregon Trail.

The Stantons settled in Salem, Oregon. They filed a claim on six hundred and forty acres under the law which granted three hundred and twenty acres to each spouse. Many local farmers had decided to raise fruit, and Alfred followed their example. They soon had a thriving nursery with over three thousand trees.

Phoebe participated annually in the Marion County Agricultural Society and the Oregon State Fair, entering fruit from their orchards. She was a consistent winner with her dried apples and plums, preserved pears and peaches, crab-apple jelly and currant wine.

Phoebe's letter to her brothers and sisters is from Covered Wagon Women—Volume I, *edited and compiled by Kenneth Holmes, published in 1983.*

Fanny Butterfield Newell

Cabot, Vermont
December, 1811
On the evening of the fourth of December, 1811, my firstborn was introduced into the world, to the joy of all present. I said in my heart, he shall be called Ebenezer; for hitherto the Lord has helped me. Three days after, by means of neglect, I took a violent cold, and a fever followed. O what a wonder that I am alive on the shores of time.

. . . For several days I had little knowledge of what passed around me. The terror of death was upon me, and I expected soon to pass its dismal vale.

Then an awful, glorious, interesting scene was open to my view; and whether I was in the body or out of the body, I cannot tell; God knoweth. This one thing I know, that I had no knowledge of anything that transpired below the sun on this earth. Neither did I see anything with my natural eyes; for they were covered with several thicknesses of cloth, to protect them from the light, which gave me pain. In the first of my vision I thought that I had taken leave of all earthly friends, and was taken up a little from the earth; from thence looking down I saw my body, from which my spirit had so lately taken her flight. I saw also my companion and friends weeping around the poor, lifeless clay, and thought God had taken all natural affection from me, for I felt no degree of sorrow.

Fanny Butterfield Newell was born May 12, 1793, in Sidney, Maine. She married Reverend Ebenezer Newell, a traveling Methodist minister, when she was seventeen.

The life of an itinerant minister was difficult. They were continually travelling, crisscrossing Maine, New Hampshire, and Vermont in their covered wagon. At night they slept in the wagon or prevailed upon the kindness of strangers.

Fanny died of consumption one month shy of her thirty-first birthday and was buried in Sidney, Maine.

At heaven's gate

Fanny's writing is an entry in her diary from December, 1811. It is contained in Memoirs of Fanny Newell: Written by Herself and Published by the Desire and Request of Numerous Friends, *published in 1833.*

Linda Gilbert

*B*ooks in jail

Linda's writing is from a letter soliciting funds from Reverend George H. Hepworth, written in April, 1875. It is included in her book, Sketch of the Life and Work of Linda Gilbert, *published in 1876.*

1876

I am anxious to furnish every jail and house of detention, where men and women who are more or less criminal are confined, with a library. Prisoners have nothing to look at but the blank walls of their cells, and nothing to think of except their sins, and though this latter may be a very fruitful theme, it is not always a profitable one. They would gladly read good works, and the value of such an influence cannot be overestimated. You must not forget that a man who would care nothing for a book when he is with his boon companions, is oftentimes very grateful for it when he is alone. I have known cases again and again, where men have not only been brought to repentance for the past, but to a radical reformation, by means of the few books and pictures to which they have had access.

Linda Gilbert, prison welfare worker, was born May 13, 1847, in Rochester, New York. Her daily walk to school each day took her past the Cook County Jail, and she grew to pity the inmates. One day a prisoner asked to see her textbooks, and she returned several times to see him with books from her father's library. She decided that when she grew up she would establish a library at that prison.

At seventeen Linda made good her promise and set up a library with an inheritance she had received. This encouraged her to do more, and she resolved to put a library in every prison in the state.

Linda formed the Gilbert Library and Prisoner's Aid Fund in 1873. She visited prisoners, bringing them gifts and writing letters for them. After a prisoner's release she often would provide him with clothing, shelter, train tickets or a job.

Linda Gilbert, as the *New York Tribune* once commented, was a "powerful dreamer," and she accomplished a great deal of prison reform.

Anna Laurens Dawes

1885

The readers of *Good Housekeeping* have already been told
that the happiness of married life depends upon a knowledge of bread making, and that the real cause of the
prevalence of divorce is too little education in beefsteak.
The world is deluged with essays upon "How to make
home happy," and disputes on the perennial topic of the
extent to which children should be disciplined; but we
have heard little or nothing of the uses and abuses of
chairs.

A serious problem

Anna Laurens Dawes was born May 14, 1851, in North Adams,
Massachusetts. Her father was a United States senator.
    Anna began her writing career when she was twenty,
publishing newspaper and magazine articles, book reviews and
short stories. One of her articles on American prisons was read
twice before Congress and published in the Congressional
Record.
    Anna was a trustee of Smith College as well as a member
of numerous charitable, missionary and literary societies.

*Anna's writing is from her
article, "The Science of Chairs,"
from the September 5, 1885,
issue of* Good Housekeeping
magazine.

Annie Fellows Johnston

1929

Along this street one summer morning, nearly thirty
years ago, came stepping an old Confederate Colonel.
Everyone greeted him deferentially. He was always
pointed out to newcomers. Some people called attention to him because he had given his right arm to the
lost cause. . . .
    This morning a child of delicate flower-like beauty
walked beside him. She was pushing a doll buggy in
which rode a parrot that had lost some of its tail feathers, and at her heels trailed a Scotch-and-Skye terrier.
    "She's her grandfather all over again," remarked a
lady. "I call her 'The Little Colonel.' There's a good
title for you, Cousin Anne. Put her in a book."

*I*dea for a book

*Annie's writing is from her
book,* The Land of the Little
Colonel: Reminiscence and
Autobiography, *published in
1929.*

It was out of that remark that the first volume of the series grew.

Annie Fellows Johnston was born May 15, 1863, in Evansville, Indiana. Annie read avidly as a child and published her first poem when she was sixteen.

Following an extensive European tour, Annie and her sister Albion [April 8] were married in a double ceremony in 1888. Annie married her cousin William Johnston, a widower with three children.

After William's death in 1892, Annie was forced to turn to her writing as a means of support. She published her first book two years later, and in 1896 produced her most popular book, *The Little Colonel*. She wrote while standing at a high desk, and by the time of her death at sixty-eight, she had written fifty children's books with sales of over one million copies.

Elizabeth Palmer Peabody

*N*ot the person

June 30, 1886
It is because I believe marriage is a sacrament, and nothing less, that I am dying as an old maid. I have had too much respect for marriage to make a conventional one in my own case. I am free to say that had Hawthorne wanted to marry me he would probably not have found much difficulty in getting my consent; but it is very clear to me now, that I was not the person to make him happy or to be made happy by him, and Sophia [September 21] was. If there was ever a "match made in Heaven" it was that, as I think you will agree. . . .

Elizabeth Palmer Peabody was born May 16, 1804, in Billerica, Massachusetts. She received an unusual education for a woman of her time: she spoke ten languages and avidly pursued studies in philosophy, theology, history and literature. Elizabeth began teaching in her teens, and through her work associated with leading New England intellectuals such as Bronson Alcott, Horace Mann, Emerson and Hawthorne.

In 1840 Elizabeth moved to Boston and opened a bookstore in her front parlor. She specialized in books on radicalism, and her shop quickly became the headquarters of the Transcendentalists. She also began publishing books, thus becoming the first female publisher in Boston.

Elizabeth's writing, concerning her sister Sophia's marriage to Nathaniel Hawthorne, is from Letters of Elizabeth Palmer Peabody, American Renaissance Woman, *edited by Bruce Ronda, published in 1984.*

From 1850 to 1884 Elizabeth wrote ten books, fifty articles, and gave hundreds of lectures on Christian-Transcendental education for children. In 1860 she opened the first kindergarten in the United States, modeled after the German kindergarten movement of Friedrich Froebel.

Elizabeth was active and influential until her death when she was ninety. It has been suggested that Henry James' character Miss Birdseye in *The Bostonians* was inspired by Elizabeth's life.

Mary Edwards Bryan

Thomasville,
January 28th [1860]
My Dear Mr. Mann:

I thank you very much, for the letter, for the friendly suggestions it contained and for the praise you have given me in the kindness of your heart and which will stimulate me to try and deserve it. I am glad that I have at last found what I have wanted and needed so long—one who will criticise me and point out faults which I can remedy. We young writers wither up at public criticism, but it does us good to have a friend show how we may improve.

Mary Edwards Bryan was born May 17, 1838, near Tallahassee, Florida. Her mother educated her at home on their isolated plantation.

Mary eloped with Iredell Bryan and moved to his home in Louisiana when she was sixteen. Her father found her and took her back to Georgia, where she had her first child. She wrote for, and became the editor of, the *Georgia Literary and Temperance Crusader*.

In 1860 Mary rejoined her husband in Louisiana and continued her writing career. She wrote novels and many articles for the major Southern magazines. In 1885 she moved to New York, where she edited the *Fireside Companion* and *Fashion Bazaar*. Mary returned to the South where she lived the last years of her life.

*W*elcome criticism

Mary's writing is from a letter she wrote to her editor, William Mann. It was included in the article "A Georgia Authoress Writes to Her Editor: Mrs. Mary E. Bryan to W.W. Mann," Georgia Historical Quarterly, December 1957, Volume XLI, Number 4.

Harriet Low Hillard

Sunday, May 24, 1829

Embarked on board the *Sumatra*, bound to Manila, and thence to Macao, where I shall probably take up my residence for the next four years; and for you, my dear sister, shall this journal be kept. I left home at five o'clock (in the morning) with feelings not to be described nor imagined but by those who have been placed in a similar situation. We were escorted out as far as Baker's Island by a few friends from Salem, which made it rather pleasanter for me, though I cannot say that I enjoyed anything that took place that day. The morning was as delightful as it could be, with a fresh breeze that soon wafted us beyond the sight of our native land. About nine our party left us. However, I behaved like the heroine I had resolved to be! At ten I began to be seasick; and, though I suffered nothing in comparison to some people, it was enough to make me feel a state of utter *hopelessness*, and prostration of *strength* and *spirits* such as I never before knew nor desire to feel again.

May 29

Every day I take a lesson in the rigging of the ship. I now know the head from the stern, and likewise that it is a difficult matter for a ship to cut the water with her taffrail, which is more than I once knew. That is not the extent of my knowledge, but I shall keep the rest to myself. I think I am rather an apt scholar!

Harriet Low Hillard was born May 18, 1809, in Salem, Massachusetts. She was the second oldest of twelve children of Seth Low, a prosperous New England merchant-shipmaster. The Low family ran a large shipping business through the ports of Salem, New York, London and Canton, China. In 1829 Harriet's aunt and uncle were departing to work abroad for five years. He was to head the shipping business in Canton while his wife resided in Macao, where he would spend summers and holidays. Mrs. Low was not in the best of health and her husband wanted her to have a pleasant companion, so it was arranged that Harriet would accompany them.

Harriet spent five years in China. She became secretly engaged to a Mr. Wood while she was in Macao, but when she informed her uncle, he disapproved of her choice and forced

Harriet's letters, written in journal form to her sister, Mary Ann Low, are in the Low-Mill family papers in the Manuscript Division of the Library of Congress.

her to break off the engagement. Harriet was brokenhearted and despondent for months until she came to realize that her uncle had been correct. Two years after her return home, Harriet married John Hillard and moved to London, where he was a partner in a large bank.

In 1848 John's bank failed. The family, which now included five daughters, was forced to return to the United States, where they moved in with Harriet's father in Brooklyn, New York.

Fidelia Bridges

December 3, 1906

Dear Annie,

I smile at your suggestion of a "boarder" for me. The need of companionship could never be so dire, as to tempt me to that. . . . I need no protection—my house is in no way isolated—a row of neighbors are opposite. Kindly disposed people. . . .

My trustworthy servant, who has been with me for 12 years—will leave me in the spring to make a home of her own, and I shall find it hard to fill her place—And the man who has been my treasure for garden and furnace, for three years, has done the same thing—so I seem to be outliving the props of my old age. But I will be inspired by your fine courage.

Most affectionately,

Fidelia

Fidelia Bridges was born May 19, 1834, in Salem, Massachusetts. Her parents both died when she was fifteen, leaving an older sister to provide for the family. She relocated them to Brooklyn, New York, where she opened a school, but Fidelia did not enjoy teaching and soon quit to concentrate on her drawing lessons.

In 1860, Fidelia began studying in Philadelphia with William T. Richards, a leading disciple of the English Pre-Raphaelite school. Two years later, she had her own studio but remained close to Richards. He helped her exhibit at the Pennsylvania Academy of Fine Arts and also found patrons to buy her work.

Fidelia's early works were done in oil, but by 1871 she had switched to watercolor. Her subjects were always those of

A long life

Fidelia's letter to her sculptor friend Anne Whitney, written at age seventy-two, is included in the Anne Whitney Papers, Wellesley College Archives, Wellesley, Massachusetts.

birds, wildflowers, pastoral scenes. From 1875 on, she only painted birds, illustrating several books in addition to a line of greeting cards.

Dorothea Payne Madison

Perilous moments

August 23, 1814
Dear Sister,

Will you believe it, my sister? We have had a battle or skirmish near Bladensburg and here I am still, within sound of the cannon! Mr. Madison comes not. May God protect us! . . . Mr. Carroll has come to hasten my departure and is in a very bad humor with me, because I insist on waiting until the large picture of General Washington is secured, and it requires to be unscrewed from the wall. This process was found too tedious for these perilous moments. I have ordered the frame to be broken and the canvas taken out. It is done! and the precious portrait placed in the hands of two gentlemen of New York for safekeeping. And now, dear sister, I must leave this house or the retreating army will make me a prisoner in it by filling up the road I am directed to take. When I shall again write to you, or where I may be tomorrow, I cannot tell!

Dorothea Payne ("Dolly") Madison, wife of the fourth president of the United States, was born May 20, 1768, in Guilford County, North Carolina. Her first husband, John Todd, Jr., and infant son died during a yellow-fever epidemic. Dolly and her surviving son stayed on in Philadelphia, where she met Virginia Congressman James Madison and married him.

Although James was seventeen years older than Dolly, their temperaments complemented each other, and they had a happy life together. While he was introspective and uncomfortable with guests, Dolly excelled at making light conversation and putting people at ease.

In 1801 President Jefferson appointed Madison Secretary of state, and they moved to Washington. Since both Jefferson and his vice-president were widowers, Dolly filled the role of hostess at presidential functions. Their home was always open to diplomats, politicians and foreign travellers.

As First Lady, Dolly continued her role as social hostess, and her immense popularity helped to increase her

Dolly's letter to her sister, describing the British invasion of Washington, is included in The National Exposition Souvenir: What America Owes to Women, *published in 1893.*

husband's popularity. She secured her place in history in 1814 when the British captured and burned Washington. As the White House was burning, Dolly managed to salvage many important items before she fled, including the Declaration of Independence and the famous portrait of George Washington by Gilbert Stuart.

Anna Brackett

1894

Southern courtesy

For a Northern woman it was sometimes difficult to be calm; when we could neither listen to the prayers offered from the pulpits nor read the newspapers; when threatening anonymous letters came to our hand, and we grew tired with the constant strain and uncertainty— even then, and perhaps even more than before, to cross the threshold into an atmosphere of peace and unfailing courtesy. Those girls came from homes that were full of bitter feeling and opposition to the North, but there was never an ungentle look or word from them to their Northern teachers. The schoolroom was an asylum, a safe and sure place for us; and what this meant of good breeding and loyalty is comprehensible perhaps only to those who have spent their lives in contact with young and warm-hearted girls.

Anna Callender Brackett, educator, was born May 21, 1836, in Boston, Massachusetts. She was educated in private and public schools in Boston.

After teaching in Massachusetts for several years, Anna took a job as vice-principal of a girls' school in Charleston, South Carolina, but the firing on Fort Sumter and subsequent blockading of Southern ports forced her to flee North. She spent the next eleven years teaching in Massachusetts and Missouri until she opened a private girls' school in New York City, which she ran for the next twenty-three years.

Anna's methods were very advanced for her time: she gave no written exams or grades, and felt that teachers were responsible for instilling their pupils with morals as well as information. Following her death in 1910, her students started an endowment fund in her honor which became a graduate fellowship of the American Association of University Women.

Anna's writing, describing her Civil War experiences in South Carolina, is from an article in the May, 1894, issue of Harper's New Monthly Magazine.

Mary Cassatt

December 28, 1922

Dear Mr. St. Gaudens,

. . . It may interest you to know what Degas said when he saw the picture you have just bought for your Museum. It was painted in 1891 in the summer, and Degas came to see me after he had seen it at Durand-Ruels. He was chary of praises but he spoke of the drawing of the woman's arm picking the fruit and made a familiar gesture indicating the line and said no woman has a right to draw like that. . . . If it has stood the test of time and is well-drawn, its place in a museum might show the present generation that we worked and learnt our profession, which isn't a bad thing. My best wishes to you and Mrs. St. Gaudens for the coming year. May it bring you all this troubled world can give of good.

Sincerely yours,

Mary Cassatt

Mary Cassatt was born May 22, 1844, in Allegheny City, Pennsylvania. Her father never had a serious career, so in 1851 he decided to take the family on a long tour of Europe. They spent the next four years in France and Germany. The art Mary saw throughout the European museums inspired her to become a painter.

In 1861 Mary entered the Pennsylvania Academy of Fine Arts, but she found the academy's teaching methods uninspiring and determined that she should study abroad. Her first piece was accepted by the Paris Salon in 1872. Degas admired one of her paintings at the Salon and invited her to join his new group of independent artists, the "impressionists." She and Degas became good friends, and she participated in four of the eight impressionist exhibits.

Mary brought her work to the United States in the late 1870's, introducing impressionism to America. She also encouraged her brother and other wealthy American art patrons to invest in the new movement.

Mary began experiencing eye trouble in 1910 and, within two years, had cataracts on both eyes. She continued to paint but her work was coarse and unappealing. By 1920 she was completely blind.

Mary's letter to Homer Saint-Gaudens, the Director of Fine Arts at the Carnegie Institute, Pittsburgh, Pennsylvania, is included in Cassatt and Her Circle—Selected Letters, *edited by Nancy Mowll Mathews, published by Abbeville Press Publishers in 1984.*

Margaret Fuller

April 12, 1840

My dear friend,

    Yesterday was the first day of spring we have had since February. I went into the woods and read a little book called *Nature* through for the first time. It's strange that it should be the first, but you read it to me initially, and so since whenever I have opened it, I missed the voice and laid it aside. I was pleased to feel how much more truly I understood it now than at first. Then I caught the melody, now I recognize the harmony! The years do not pass in vain.

Margaret Fuller was born May 23, 1810, in Cambridgeport, Massachusetts, the first of nine children. Her father was disappointed that she was not a boy, so he educated her as one. She studied English, Latin, history and literature so constantly that she later recalled she had "no natural childhood."

    In her twenties, Margaret began teaching. She became acquainted with all the New England intellectuals, forming an especially close friendship with Ralph Waldo Emerson. The New England Transcendentalist movement was well under way, and Margaret became a leader. For five years she presided over the Conversations, gatherings of Boston's intelligentsia to discuss topics such as ethics, mythology, art and religion. In 1840 she joined Emerson and others to found *The Dial*, a quarterly journal of Transcendentalist sentiments.

    In 1844, Margaret moved to Horace Greeley's home in New York City and began writing for his *New York Tribune*. Two years later she was sent abroad as a foreign correspondent. In 1849, she married the Marchese d'Ossoli, a Roman nobleman ten years her junior.

    Margaret began writing the history of the Roman revolution, which she believed was her most important work. Their house was under police surveillance, and she found it impossible to get her book published in Italy, so she unwillingly resigned herself to return to America. Only a few hours out of New York Harbor, their ship hit a sandbar and broke up. Margaret, her husband and their young children drowned.

Better later

Margaret's letter to Ralph Waldo Emerson is in the Houghton Library Manuscripts Collection, Harvard University.

Ynez Mexia

The roar of the Pongo

1933

I established camp a few miles above the Pongo, at the mouth of the Rio Santiago, which heads in the Ecuadorean Andes. José joined me in a few days, the canoes and paddlers were sent down the river, and, as if awaiting that, the rainy season began with unprecedented violence and the rivers rose and rose until the roar of the Pongo could be heard for miles.

For three months I camped there, collecting botanical specimens and making short excursions. . . .

Ynez Mexia was born May 24, 1870, in Georgetown, D.C., while her father was there representing the Mexican government.

Ynez was married and widowed twice by 1908. Following the death of her second husband she moved to San Francisco, where she did social work. She began taking courses at the University of California and in 1925, at age fifty-five, she took a botany course on flowering plants that would change her life. That summer she took her first field trip to Mexico and gathered five-hundred species of plants.

Ynez's article, "Three Thousand Miles Up the Amazon," appeared in the February, 1933, Sierra Club Bulletin, Volume 18, Number 1.

Ynez had the personality of an explorer and was happiest when alone and isolated from civilization. She made several expeditions to Mexico, as well as to Alaska, Brazil, Peru, Ecuador, Argentina, Bolivia and Chile. She was extremely professional, prepared her specimens well, and kept copious notes. She died of lung cancer when she was sixty-eight.

Leta Stetter Hollingworth

Wicked new ideas

1927

It is of record that the perambulator was deplored as wicked and dangerous when it was first invented. The true mother, it was said, carried her child "as God intended." The physician who first used anesthetics to lighten the pains of childbirth was set upon for a scoundrel. At present birth control is condemned in religion and in law. . . .

Leta's writing is from the "The New Woman in the Making," an article in the October, 1927, issue of Current History, Volume 27, Number 1.

Each woman, even now, who sets out upon a way of

life different from that of the dependent housewife, is still an explorer.

Leta Anna Stetter Hollingworth was born May 25, 1886, near Chadron, Nebraska.

She graduated from the University of Nebraska in 1906. Two years later she married Harry L. Hollingworth. They moved to New York City where Harry became a professor of psychology at Columbia. Leta resumed her studies and obtained a Master's degree from Columbia in education and sociology, plus a teaching certificate in educational psychology.

In 1914 she was appointed to New York City's first civil service position for a psychologist. She became interested in the new field of clinical psychology and completed her Ph.D. degree. Her research revolved around the psychology of women and her theory that any limitations attributed to women were due to society, and not to biological differences.

Mary Andrews Denison

1854

Is it not a beautiful sight to meet, amidst the throng of fashionable women, a pretty rosebud of a young girl, with the dawn of womanhood stealing over her fair, open brow, modestly moving along the pavement? Her dress is simple, unassuming; rich, perhaps, but unmarred by folds, ruffles or buttons. No jewelry offends the sight, in the glare of day. Her eye, now drooping, now glancing timidly, but innocently, upon the passersby, seems the reflected beam of a pure and happy heart. Her demeanour is ladylike, her movements are full of grace, because so natural and unstudied. . . . Every gentleman of refinement cannot but pay the passing tribute of an admiring glance upon one so fitly representing what all women should be, on a public street—unassuming, modest, and elegantly but neatly attired.

A woman properly dressed

Mary Ann Andrews Denison, writer, was born May 26, 1826, in Cambridge, Massachusetts. At twenty she married Reverend Charles Denison, a man seventeen years her senior. He was the assistant editor of the *Boston Olive Branch*, an anti-

Mary's writing is from her book, What Not, published in 1854.

slavery paper. Encouraged by her husband's literary interests, Mary began submitting articles to the *Olive Branch* and other magazines.

Mary's first book was published in 1847 and launched a long career that eventually included more than eighty novels with total sales of over one million. Her standard formula combined romance and adventure with religious overtones of virtue always conquering evil.

The Denisons travelled frequently to England and British Guiana as well as throughout the United States. In addition to her fiction, Mary wrote hundreds of articles describing their travels for American and British newspapers and magazines. She continued to write until she was over eighty years old.

Amelia Bloomer

Childhood recollections

1889

My earliest recollections are of a pleasant home in Homer, Cortland County, New York. Here was I born, and here the first six years of my life were passed. But little of these early days can now be recalled after sixty years have been added to them, yet there are a few incidents that are so deeply impressed upon memory, that they seem but the occurrence of a week ago. . . . A scene comes before the mind's eye of my brother and myself looking from an upper window, and seeing some Indians knocking at the door of a small untenanted house opposite to us. My brother, who was a few years older than myself, called out, "Come in." The Indians opened the door and stepped in, then out, and looked up and around sorely puzzled at hearing a voice, but seeing no one, while my brother and I laughed and danced behind the blind at the trick which we had played upon them.

Several children were on their way to school. One little girl jumped upon the wheel of a wagon which stood in front of a house, intending to get in and ride to school. The horse became frightened while she stood on the wheel, and ran away, throwing her violently to the ground and injuring her severely. The mirth of childhood was turned to sadness, and we trudged on to

Amelia's writing is from Life and Writings of Amelia Bloomer, *edited by her husband and published in 1895.*

school, after seeing her unconscious form carried into the house. I could not have been over four or five years old when these things happened, but they are deeply engraved on memory's tablet.

Amelia Jenks Bloomer, reformer, was born May 27, 1818, in Homer, New York. When she was seventeen, she started teaching school in a nearby village. There she met and became engaged to Dexter C. Bloomer, a young law student. The young couple were married in 1840, with the word "obey" omitted from her vows.

In 1849 she started a temperance paper, the *Lily*. It became the forum for women reformers. Dress reform became a major issue in the early 1850's, when Elizabeth Cady Stanton's cousin, Lizzie Miller [September 20], appeared in full Turkish pantaloons and a short skirt. Women's outfits until that time had consisted of long, cumbersome skirts, at least six full petticoats, and tightly laced whalebone corsets, all of which weighed twelve to fifteen pounds. Mrs. Stanton and Amelia adopted the new pantaloon style and Amelia defended it in the *Lily*. National newspapers picked up the story, subscriptions to the *Lily* doubled, and Amelia was swamped with requests for patterns and information on this new outfit that had become known as the "Bloomer Costume." She wore nothing else for about six years until she came to feel that the controversial attire drew away from her more important reform causes and she stopped wearing it.

In 1855 the Bloomers moved from New York State to Council Bluffs, Iowa, where they remained for the rest of their lives.

Annie Maria Barnes

1890

Manners

The breakfast consists of rhinoceros meat, which the industrious hunters of the day before have provided, a porridge of Indian meal into which the gravy has been mixed, and potatoes roasted in the ashes. But in whatever manner each little black child awaits his breakfast, they are all careful to receive it in identically the same fashion; that is, with but one hand outstretched. To receive the bowl with two would be altogether the very worst evidence of bad manners and not at all in keeping with the strict forms laid down in the Lepelole code of

Annie's writing is from Children of the Kalahari: A Story of Africa, *published in 1890.*

juvenile training. That they may eat it afterward either with one hand or two plunged into the gravy-stirred porridge, and serving as the mode of conveyance to the mouth, matters not, so that only one hand is out-stretched in receiving.

Annie Maria Barnes was born May 28, 1857, in Columbia, South Carolina. She had an article published in the *Atlantic Constitution* when she was eleven. Her work was noticed by the editor, and she became a regular correspondent at fifteen.

Like many Southerners, the end of the Civil War left the Barnes family in financial ruin. Annie turned to her writing, producing mainly children's stories. In 1887 she started *The Acanthus*, a paper for juveniles. The literary content was excellent and it enjoyed some popularity, but she was unable to make it a financial success.

Annie published the first of many novels in 1885. Her most popular work was *The Children of the Kalahari*, a child's tale of Africa, which had enormous sales in America and England.

MAY 29

Elizabeth Allston Pringle

A diary begins

November 7, 1875
I have determined to write down from day to day what happens to me for my own future satisfaction. I often wish I had done so during the past ten or twelve years, when so many important changes have taken place in my life that it seemed to me there is nothing left to happen. We are settled married people without chil-dren—five years of married life have passed so rapidly that I feel but little older than the day I took those cares upon me.

Elizabeth Allston Pringle was born May 29, 1845, at Canaan Seashore, the family's summer home, near Pawley's Island, South Carolina.

The Civil War was disastrous to the Allston family: Mr. Allston died during the war and the family lost all but one of their seven plantations, "Chicora Wood." Elizabeth was residing at home when she met and married John Pringle of the "White House," a plantation eight miles down river.

Elizabeth had a happy marriage, cut short after only six years by John's sudden death. She was able to purchase the

Elizabeth's diary is in the Allston-Pringle-Hill Collection, South Carolina Historical Library, Charleston, South Carolina.

Give Her This Day

"White House" from her husband's family and, against all advice, decided to manage it herself. Following her mother's death, Elizabeth assumed control of "Chicora Wood" as well, raising livestock and poultry in addition to rice. She successfully ran both plantations, turning a profit until the early 1900's, when a combination of violent weather and newly invented mechanized rice cultivators drove most of the Carolina plantations out of business.

During all her years managing rice plantations, Elizabeth found time to write, mostly stories and plays. She received many rejection slips until her first piece was finally accepted by the *New York Sun* when she was fifty-eight. She published two notable works: *A Woman Rice Planter* and *Chronicles of Chicora Wood*, before her death in 1921.

Josephine Preston Peabody

London,
24 May, 1907
Dearest Mother:

Consideration for honeymooners

I must quench your suspense and tell you how perfectly lovely all my new family has been to me.

They all behaved alike in their affection and consideration. By consideration I mean that we never *once* had to hear a *single* foolish, jocular, or sentimental personality about honeymoons or young married people or anything of the kind;—of the cheapening and odious kind that relations and old friends think they can permit themselves. And that seems to me the topmost reach of good taste and pleasantness. I really cannot thank them too much. Among so *many* relations it simply wasn't to be thought of that nobody should do or say anything silly and jarring. But nobody did. . . .

Josephine Preston Peabody, poet and dramatist, was born May 30, 1874, in Brooklyn, New York. After her father died in 1886 she was sent to Dorchester, Massachusetts, to live with her grandmother.

When she was thirteen Josephine started mailing poems to various magazines and a few were published. At nineteen she began a correspondence with the editor of *The Atlantic Monthly*. He printed one of her poems and arranged for her to attend Radcliffe College on a two-year scholarship.

Josephine's letter, describing her first meeting with her husband's family while on honeymoon in England, is included in Diary and Letters of Josephine Preston Peabody, *published in 1925.*

Josephine married Lionel Marks, a Harvard professor and native of England, in 1906. While in Europe on her honeymoon she wrote the first copy of "The Piper," a verse drama based on the legend of the Pied Piper of Hamlin. It was published in 1909 and she entered it in the Stratford Prize Competition, which she won out of a field of 315 entries. It was performed in London and New York and brought her literary recognition on two continents.

Jessie Benton Frémont

A passage

1887

Among my earliest memories of the White House is the impression that I was to keep still and not fidget, or show pain, even if General Jackson twisted his fingers a little too tightly in my curls; he liked my father to bring me when they had their talks, and would keep me by him, his hand on my head—forgetting me of course in the interest of discussion—so that sometimes, his long, bony fingers took an unconscious grip that would make me look at my father, but give no other sign.

Jessie Ann Benton Frémont was born May 31, 1824, near Lexington, Virginia. Her father was the well-known senator from Missouri, Thomas Hart Benton, and their house was a gathering place for politicians, military men, clergy, pioneers and trappers. Jessie's mother was a semi-invalid, so Jessie was called upon at an early age to act as hostess.

When Jessie was sixteen she met and married Lieutenant John Frémont of the Army's Topographical Corps. They had five children.

During the 1840's Frémont led four government expeditions to the west. Each time he returned Jessie wrote his reports, which were meant to encourage migration by mapping out the easiest routes and most appealing locations for settling. His report of 1845-6, written by Jessie and published both as a Senate document and as a book, is believed to have had greater influence upon people going west to settle than any other writing at that time.

Jessie's writing is from her autobiography, Souvenirs of My Time, *published in 1887.*

JUNE

Caroline Lee Hentz

May 30, 1836

School again. Alternate coaxing and scolding, counsel and reproof, frowns and smiles—Oh! what a life it is. Oh woe's me—this weary world, I am oft tempted to say. Yet Man is doomed to earn his subsistence by the sweat of the brow & the fire of his brain & why not woman also? . . .

*W*eary work

Caroline Lee Whiting Hentz was born June 1, 1800, in Lancaster, Massachusetts. When she was twenty-four, she married Nicholas Hentz, a moody Frenchman prone to fits of jealous rage.

During their first ten years together, they moved from Massachusetts to North Carolina, Kentucky, Ohio and Alabama in search of suitable work. They were forced to flee Ohio after Nicholas overreacted from jealousy due to his wife's friendship with another man. They relocated in Alabama where they ran a succession of boarding schools. Caroline had begun writing as a child and had several pieces published during her early marriage. Her first novel, which appeared in 1846, was very well-received. However, her chores maintaining the school with approximately twenty boarding pupils left little time for creativity. Due to Mr. Hentz's jealousy, Caroline retired more and more from society, preferring to share his unusual hobbies of raising silkworms and collecting insects.

In 1849, with her children grown and her husband a "miserable hypochondriac—unfit to work," Caroline turned to her writing. In six years, she published eight novels and seven collections of short stories, earning a reasonable income. Her novels presented a romantic idea of Southern plantation life and were extremely popular for more than thirty years.

Caroline's diary is in the Southern Historical Collection, University of North Carolina Library, Chapel Hill.

Helen Herron Taft

1914

Since the ex-President was not going to ride back to the White House with his successor, I decided that I would. No president's wife had ever done it before. . . .

Of course, there was objection. Some of the

*B*reaking tradition

Inaugural Committee expressed their disapproval, but I had my way and in spite of protests took my place at my husband's side. . . .

We entered the official coach at four and were slowly driven down through the Capitol grounds to Pennsylvania Avenue, and thence to the White House.

. . . The expected and expectant crowds were thronging the sidewalks and filling the stands, and our greeting from them was all that my fancy had pictured it.

For me that drive was the proudest and happiest event of Inauguration Day. Perhaps I had a little secret elation in thinking that I was doing something which no woman had ever done before. . . .

My responsibilities had not yet begun to worry me, and I was able to enjoy, almost to the full, the realisation that my husband was actually president of the United States and that it was this fact which the cheering crowds were acclaiming.

Helen Herron Taft, wife of the twenty-seventh president of the United States, was born June 2, 1861, in Cincinnati, Ohio. At twenty-two, "weary of frivolities," she organized a salon for intellectual discussion. One of the members was a young lawyer, William Taft, whom she married after a three-year courtship.

Helen played a central role in shaping her husband's career. She became his close confidante and advisor.

Following Taft's election, Helen assumed her duties as First Lady enthusiastically. However, within the first year she suffered a nervous collapse which left her stamina and speech impaired, so that she was unable to participate in official functions. Following his presidency, William taught law at Yale, and Helen recovered in the quieter Connecticut lifestyle.

The Tafts returned to Washington in 1921 when he was appointed chief justice of the Supreme Court.

Helen died in 1942 and is buried beside her husband in Arlington National Cemetery.

Helen Taft's writing is from her autobiography, Recollections of Full Years, *published in 1914.*

Eliza Merrill

July 13, 1836

For eight months past he [her year-old son Samuel] has been afflicted with diarrhea which was brought on by drinking the water . . . this spring he had three fits which called forth all my feeling. He has one tooth which came through last night. Can creep and walk by a bench, is very active. At about seven months ago we began to correct him and he now sits still in my lap during prayers. This has been a great trial. I plainly see the need of foresight to keep him from forming bad habits. . . .

The Otoes are very fond of him and he of them. Oh that his heart may early be given to the Saviour and to his work of mercy upon the earth.

A mother's hopes

Eliza Wilcox Merrill, missionary to the Otoe Indians, was born June 3, 1800, in Charleston, New York.

In May of 1830 Eliza married Reverend Moses Merrill. They moved to Michigan where he preached and she taught school for two years until the Baptist Missionary Union appointed them as missionaries. They travelled to Bellevue, Indiana Territory (now Nebraska), two hundred miles from any white settlement. There they established a mission for the Otoe Indians. They built a school, preached through an interpreter, and offered spiritual and medical counseling. Eliza and her husband learned the Otoe language and translated and printed a spelling book, two reading books and a hymn book, *Wdtwhtl Wdwdklha Eva Wdhonetl*, so the Indians could sing hymns in church.

Reverend Merrill died of consumption in 1840. Eliza found the lawlessness, sickness and drunkenness to be too much for her to manage alone and she returned east the following year.

Eliza's writing is from her journal which is in the Moses Merrill Collection at the Nebraska Historical Society, Manuscript Division, Lincoln, Nebraska.

Mary Hanchett Hunt

Drinkers beware

1884

You have learned enough about your body by this time, to understand that when people are sick, it is generally their own fault; either they have not been taught how to care for their bodies, or they are heedless in spite of their knowledge.

But sometimes one is sick or suffers very much, because of wrong things that his parents or grandparents did. Does this seem strange? Someone has told you, perhaps, that you have your father's hair and eyes, but that your mouth and chin are like your mother's.

You have heard of children who were quick-tempered, or generous like their parents. Not only property, but faces and character are inherited. Our lives are very closely linked with those of our "blood-relations," and evil tendencies, as well as good impulses, descend from them to us.

Over in the poorhouse is a man who does not know so much as most children four years old. He cannot learn to read or write; he is an idiot. And this is because he is the child of drinking parents whose poisoned lifeblood tainted his own.

Many men and women are insane because they inherit disordered bodies and minds, caused by the drinking habits of their parents; and the descendants of "moderate drinkers" suffer in this way, as well as those of the drunkard.

Mary Hannah Hanchett Hunt was born June 4, 1830, in South Canaan, Connecticut. She graduated from the Patapsco Female Institute and stayed on to co-author science textbooks with the principal, Almira Phelps [July 15]. In 1852 she married Leander Hunt, a salesman, and moved to Massachusetts.

Mary's writing is from her textbook, A Temperance Physiology for Intermediate Classes and Common Schools, *published in 1884.*

Mary believed that temperance should be taught in the schools, based on scientific principles which proved the evils of alcohol. In one year alone, Mary spoke before 182 meetings in ten states.

She launched a campaign in Vermont to pass a state law requiring temperance to be taught in public schools. In 1882

Vermont was the first state to pass the law, after which she travelled to many states to lead the fight. By 1901 every state had legislated her plan, and over twenty-two million children were receiving "scientific temperance instruction."

Miriam Folline Leslie

1884

While I was paying $80,000 of my husband's debts, I spent but $30 for myself, except for my board. I lived in a little attic room, without a carpet, and the window was so high that I could not get a glimpse of the sky unless I stood on a chair and looked out. When I had paid the debts and raised a monument to my husband, then I said to myself, "Now for a great big pair of diamond earrings," and away I went to Europe, and here are the diamonds. The diamonds are perfect matches, twenty-seven carats in weight, and are nearly as large as nickels.

Miriam Folline Leslie was born June 5, 1836, in New Orleans. In 1857 she married Ephraim Squier, an amateur archaeologist. His articles describing his Central American explorations earned him the job of editor of Frank Leslie's *Illustrated Newspaper.*

Through her husband's work Miriam came in contact with Frank Leslie, the flamboyant Englishman who had built a major publishing empire in the United States. She began contributing articles and soon became editor of his *Lady's Magazine* and *Lady's Journal.*

In 1867 the Squiers traveled abroad with Mr. Leslie. He secretly reported Mr. Squier's arrival to his British creditors, so that he was detained for several weeks while Miriam and Frank traveled on together. Seven years later they were married after obtaining divorces from their respective spouses.

After Miriam married Frank Leslie, she continued to work two days per week and spent the remaining time entertaining at their mansion in Saratoga. Frank's publishing business had been overextended for some time, so that he left Miriam a bankrupt company when he passed away in 1880. She legally changed her name to "Frank Leslie" and took over active management of his holdings. She cut the number of magazines from twelve to six and quickly brought them back into the black. She became known as "the Empress of Journalism."

Indulging herself

Miriam's writing is from a speech she gave at the annual New York State Suffrage Society Meeting in 1884. It is included in Volume 3 of History of Woman Suffrage, *edited by Elizabeth C. Stanton, Susan B. Anthony and Matilda J. Gage, published in 1886.*

Miriam died in 1914, leaving half of her $2,000,000 estate to Mrs. Carrie Chapman Catt for "the furtherance of the cause of Woman's Suffrage."

J U N E 6

Annie Fields

Old, poor and forgotten

1883
It is a cause for wonder to see how many aged and in-firm persons are left to pine away in the attics of cities, forgotten by their own people, and receiving fifty cents a week to pay their rent from some relief society. . . .

I found two sisters living in a scant, squalid fashion. They were Scotch by birth, and had been dressmakers, but had outlived their custom and their usefulness. They were getting small doles which they chiefly spent in drink "to keep up their spirits." They would not tolerate the idea of being sent away. . . .

Annie Adams Fields, author, literary hostess and social welfare worker, was born June 6, 1834, in Boston, Massachusetts. She married James T. Fields, a partner in the famous Boston pub-lishing firm of Ticknor and Fields. Although he was seventeen years her senior, they enjoyed a long, happy life together.

Her marriage thrust Annie into the center of the New England literary scene. She made their beautiful Beacon Hill home a haven for well-known writers, including Longfellow, Whittier, Hawthorne, Lowell and Emerson. Annie had a keen critical eye, and her husband relied on her judgment to assist him in appraising the merits of proposed manuscripts.

Annie's writing is from her book, How to Help the Poor, *published in 1883, a handbook for charity workers which sold 22,000 copies in two years.*

After James' death in 1881, Annie published three volumes of poetry and many reminiscences of their well-known friends. She also became interested in social welfare work and founded the Associated Charities of Boston.

J U N E 7

Susan Elizabeth Blow

How taste is weakened

1899
The taste of little girls is often corrupted by expression-less dolls, badly painted and badly dressed. The musical taste of boys is coarsened by tin trumpets and poor

drums. Many children are allowed to bang on the piano. Many are injured by all kinds of ugly and tawdry playthings, and by badly drawn and crudely colored pictures . . . we forget that all true beauty implies strength and simplicity, and we warp the taste of children by the excessive luxury of our homes.

Susan Elizabeth Blow, kindergarten educator, was born June 7, 1843, near St. Louis, Missouri. While on a trip to Germany in her late twenties she became acquainted with the kindergarten work of Friedrich Froebel and studied his teaching techniques.

After her return to the United States, Susan asked the school board of St. Louis to provide one classroom and one salaried teacher, and in return, she would supervise without pay. They accepted her offer, and in September, 1873, the first kindergarten in St. Louis opened.

By 1880 kindergartens had been accepted throughout the St. Louis public school system and served as a model for the movement as it spread around the country. Susan started a school to train teachers and spent her entire life in the advocacy of kindergartens. A full-length portrait of Miss Blow hangs in the Missouri State Capitol.

Susan's writing is from her article, "Letters to a Mother on the Philosophy of Froebel," in Volume XLV of the International Education Series, published in 1900.

Mary Lucinda Bonney

1893

Seeing from newspapers that Senator Vest, of Missouri, had been pressing Congress for thirteen years to open the Oklahoma lands to settlement by whites amazed me. A senator, I said, urging that injustice! A moral wrong upon our government! It took hold of me. I talked about it to one and another. One day my friend, Mrs. A. S. Quinton, visited me in my room. I told her the story and of my deep feeling. Her heart and conscience were stirred. We talked and wondered at the enormity of the wrong proposed by Senator Vest, and that Congress had listened. Then and there we pledged ourselves to do what we could to awaken the conscience of Congress and of the people. I was to secure the money, and Mrs. Quinton was to plan and to work.

Mary Lucinda Bonney was born June 8, 1816, in Hamilton, New York. She taught in a succession of schools along the

Moral outrage

Mary's writing, protesting the invasion of the Indian Territory, is from A Woman of the Century, edited by Frances E. Willard and Mary A. Livermore, published in 1893.

east coast for fifteen years. In 1850, in order to give her mother a home, she co-founded the Chestnut Street Female Seminary in Philadelphia, later renamed the Ogontz School for Young Ladies. Mary served as principal for thirty-eight years.

Mary became interested in the plight of the Indians through a woman's home missionary circle she started at her church. In 1879 she circulated a petition endorsing the honoring of treaties to end the white development of the Indian Territory. She obtained thirteen thousand signatures and delivered them in a three-hundred-foot roll to President Rutherford B. Hayes. The following year she drafted another petition with fifty thousand signatures. Her third petition, calling for the end of Indian reservations, was signed by 100,000 people.

When Mary was seventy-two, she travelled to London to attend the Centenary Conference on the Protestant Missions of the World. While there, she met and married Thomas Rambaut, a Baptist minister. They shared two happy years together until his death.

Mary E. Barnes

Boarding-school lament

May 11, 1846

Dear Father,

It is little more than four weeks since I left Old Woolwich to be shut up in prison among old maids that are cross enough to bite a board nail in three pieces. . . . Take the teachers and scholars together and they are the most unsocial set I ever came across in my life. They are so haughty and independent that they would not speak to anyone in the shape of a new scholar even if they met them, as the saying is, in their porridge dish....

I have been so homesick since I came here that I have hardly known whether I was in the land of the living or not. I have cried half of the time, and been as ugly as sin could make me the other half.

Mary's letter, written while she was a student at the Charlestown Female Seminary, is in the Maine Maritime Museum Manuscript Collection, Bath, Maine.

Mary E. Barnes was born June 9, 1827, in Old Woolwich, Maine. Her father was a prosperous master mariner, so he was away from home frequently. As the eldest daughter in a family of nine children, Mary was called upon to run the household for her sickly mother.

When Mary was eighteen, she was sent to the Charlestown Female Seminary, a Catholic school run by nuns.

She was miserable there but remained through graduation, after which she returned to the family home in Maine. She died suddenly when she was twenty-four.

Rebecca Latimer Felton

1919

A writer and her readers

My attachment to the readers of the Georgia newspapers is something like the affection that an aged grandmother feels towards her great-grandchildren. We understand each other, and generally we think alike. Numbers of these readers (in their loving confidence) have named children for me. I prize their affection. I wish for them Heaven's richest blessings when their faithful old friend can write no more!

Rebecca Ann Latimer Felton was born June 10, 1835, near Decatur, Georgia. She graduated in 1854 from Madison Female College, at the head of her class. She married Dr. William Felton the same year.

The Feltons strongly supported the Confederate cause during the Civil War. They were forced to flee their home when Sherman marched through Georgia. Upon their return, they found the fields overgrown and the house destroyed. They spent the next several years rebuilding. Dr. Felton ran for Congress in 1874 as an Independent. Rebecca became his press secretary and campaign manager.

Rebecca assisted her husband in his political career for the next twenty years. She wrote for the newspapers and lectured on women's rights, temperance and prison reform. She was instrumental in creating the Georgia Training School for Girls in 1915.

Rebecca's writing is from Country Life in Georgia in the Days of My Youth, *published in 1919 when she was eighty-two years old.*

Addie Hunton

1920

*N*o turning back

And now there was no turning back. Months ago the war zone was just six hundred miles from the coast of France—but now the United States was at war, and as we stepped on the gangplank, war-zone passes were surrendered. We were crusaders on a quest for Democracy! How and where would that precious thing be found?

Addie D. Waites Hunton was born June 11, 1875, in Norfolk, Virginia. She married William Hunton, the descendant of a freed slave who had come to Norfolk to establish a Young Men's Christian Association for Negroes in 1893.

From the beginning of their marriage Addie helped her husband with his Y.M.C.A. work. In 1907 the National Board of the Young Women's Christian Association appointed her secretary for projects among Negro students.

At the outbreak of World War I, Addie had been recently widowed and her children were grown, so she threw herself into Y.M.C.A. efforts. Upon her arrival in France in 1918, she was one of three black women allowed to work with the 200,000 segregated black troops. She augmented the usual canteen services to include a literacy course, Sunday discussion groups, and other educational, religious, athletic and cultural activities for the Negro soldiers who came for rest and relaxation.

Addie was proud that the Negroes' model behavior won the respect of the French, but resentful that her own country practiced discrimination. She devoted the rest of her life to working for the betterment of her race.

Addie's writing is from her book, Two Colored Women with the American Expeditionary Forces, *co-authored with Kathryn Johnson, published in 1920.*

Grace Mouat Jeffris

Keeping fit

Grace's letter is in the private papers of her great-great-granddaughter Ann Jeffris Miller of Evergreen, Colorado.

February 8, 1878
Willie, you must take a great deal of outdoor exercise or else you will be sick and Pa will certainly make you come home. You know, Johnny Orcket, what a strong healthy boy he was. He has been confined in a store very close for two or three years and now they have had to take him to the insane asylum. His mother is nearly frantic over him. Will, you must walk out every day, a good long walk, as that is all the exercise you can have that is good for anything. If you lose your health you are good for nothing, mentally or physically. Take warning before it is too late.

Grace Mouat Jeffris was born June 12, 1831, in the Shetland Islands off the north coast of Scotland. At fourteen her family

Give Her This Day

emigrated to Janesville, Wisconsin, where she remained her entire life.

Grace married a carpenter and they had several children. Grace wrote frequently to her son Will while he was attending Beloit College in Beloit, Wisconsin. The letters often admonished him to be careful of his health. She offered many creative suggestions such as "you might get 5¢ worth of rhubarb root and eat a piece as large as two peas when you go to bed that is very good to act on the liver and it will not hurt you."

Hannah Chandler Ropes

July 6, 1862

Smiling their thanks

We are expecting a hundred more today. All we now have were in Porter's division and are from Michigan and Pennsylvania. When one of the Michigan boys with a *dreadful* arm was led in to give his name, I lifted the canteen from his neck and he said, "Oh, lady! there are three other boys from the same place with me, *do* let them lie down close by me." And he was not willing to move any till they came, so I went along them all and asked for the "boys who came from Michigan" and all the four had broken arms! I took hold of their sleeveless coats and led them all up together. Every time I go by them they smile upon me their thanks, for their cots are side by side.

Hannah Ropes was born June 13, 1809, in New Gloucester, Maine. She married William Ropes in 1834, settled in Massachusetts, and had four children. Five years after their marriage Hannah converted to the Swedenborgian religion, and gradually she and her husband grew apart. He eventually left the family, moved to Florida, and never returned.

Hannah's nephew gave her a copy of Florence Nightingale's book, *Notes on Nursing*, which inspired her to become a nurse. In June, 1862, she arrived in Washington to offer her services to the Union and was assigned as matron in the Union Hotel Hospital.

Hannah was shocked by the hospital conditions and angered at the administration. After failing to obtain satisfaction from the head surgeon and the surgeon general, she bypassed regular military procedure and went directly to Secretary of War Edwin Stanton. Her actions resulted in a complete inspection of the hospital, followed by a change of

Hannah's letter to her daughter, written soon after her arrival at Union Hospital, is among a collection of her letters in the Skinner Ropes Manuscript Collection, Special Collections Division, General Library, University of California, Riverside.

administration after the head surgeon and the steward were arrested. It was an astounding achievement for a woman nurse single-handedly to challenge the establishment and win.

Hannah's career as an army nurse was cut short after seven months when she died of typhoid fever.

Harriet Beecher Stowe

Kind concern

1873

How much dogs suffer mentally is a thing they have no words to say; but there is no sorrow deeper than that in the eyes of a homeless, friendless, masterless dog. We rejoice, therefore, to learn that one portion of the twenty thousand dollars which the ladies of Boston have raised for "Our Dumb Animals" is about to be used in keeping a *home* for stray dogs.

Let no one sneer at this. If, among the "five sparrows sold for two farthings," not one is forgotten by our Father, certainly it becomes us not to forget the poor dumb companions of our moral journey, capable, with us, of love and its sorrows, of faithfulness and devotion.

Harriet Beecher Stowe was born June 14, 1811, in Litchfield, Connecticut. After her mother's death when she was four, she and her eight siblings were raised by their father, a Congregational minister. He instilled in all his children the need to achieve personal fulfillment through public service.

When Harriet was twenty-four, she married a widower, Calvin Stowe. They had five children. She turned to writing to increase the family's meager income as well as to alleviate her feelings of being "a mere drudge with few ideas beyond babies and housekeeping." Her first collection of stories was published in 1843, after which her literary talent supported the family.

Harriet felt driven to change humanity through her work and, remembering her father's prayers for "poor, bleeding Africa," decided to write the story of slavery. She looked upon this task as a mission; she could turn a whole nation away from the injustice of slavery.

The result of her labors was *Uncle Tom's Cabin*, initially published in 1851 in serial form in the anti-slavery newspaper, *National Era*, and in book form the following year. It was an instant success, selling over 300,000 copies in one year. Its influence was to be far-reaching.

Harriet's writing is from Palmetto Leaves, *published in 1873.*

Adah Isaacs Menken

1868

I am as wild and as earnest in my dressing room, and woe to the unlucky creature who displeases me, or opposes me in look or deed! I always get a clear stage. Everybody strives to please me as slaves do a master. They think I am crazy at night. My attention cannot be turned to any subject but the stage as long as the piece lasts. I see and hear nothing else. I feel nothing but the character I represent. To be so intense requires a soul. Can this be the same soul that breathes in my poems the very air of Heaven? I have written these wild soul-poems in the stillness of midnight, and when waking to the world next day, they were to me the deepest mystery.

Adah Isaacs Menken was born June 15, 1835 near New Orleans. In her attempt to fabricate a romantic background, she managed to hide most details of her past. She was born Adah Bertha, although at various times she used the names of Delores and Adle, and a poetry book she said she wrote under the pen name "Indigena" was never written.

It is known that Adah was married and divorced four times. Her first marriage occurred in 1856, and she turned to the theater as a means of support when her husband lost all his money in the panic of 1857. She enjoyed instant success, performing in the Midwest and New York City.

In 1859 Adah married a prizefighter, believing her first husband had divorced her. He announced to the press that he hadn't, causing a scandal, and her second husband abandoned her. Deciding to make use of this notoriety, Adah began acting the role of "Mazeppa," which climaxed in a scene of her nude, lashed to a galloping horse. She wasn't actually nude, wearing flesh-colored tights and a loincloth, but the audience loved it, she became a star, and the press called her "the most perfectly developed woman in the world."

Adah played Mazeppa to enthusiastic crowds in America and Europe until she collapsed in Paris in 1868 and died within the month.

Her powerful soul

Adah's writing is from her article, "Notes on My Life," in the September 6, 1868, New York Sunday Times.

Luella Dowd Smith

*E*mpty heart

1887
My heart is as my house—alone;
    Its mirth and hope have fled.
It hears no answer from its own;
Its singing-birds of youth have flown;
    Its loves are with the dead.

The welcome waits—the love-feast spread,
    Poor foolish heart—in vain!
In vain your tears of grief are shed.
There is no waking for your dead.
    The soul of love is slain.

Luella's writing is from her poem "Your House is Left Unto You Desolate," which is included in her book of poetry, Wind Flowers, *published in 1887.*

Luella Dowd Smith was born June 16, 1847, in Sheffield, Massachusetts. Her parents were both teachers, so she was educated by them at home, or in schools they operated. She taught school and Sunday school herself until her marriage in 1875 to Dr. Henry Smith.

Luella and Henry resided in Sheffield for nine years, after which they took an extended trip abroad and returned to settle permanently in Hudson, New York. Luella had begun writing as a child, and she continued writing all through her married life. She wrote both poetry and prose, publishing her first book, *Wayside Leaves*, in 1879. Her strong religious beliefs and upright moral fiber were reflected in her work. Luella's interest in the temperance cause led her to write a series of temperance stories for children.

Susan La Flesche Picotte

A job application

June 13, 1889
To the Honorable Commissioner of Indian Affairs:
Dear Sir:

I hereby make application for the position of Gov't physician to the Omaha Agency Indian School.

I am an Indian girl and a member of the Omaha tribe. . . . I entered the Woman's Medical College of

Philadelphia in the Fall of 1886, graduating last March and receiving my degree as Doctor of Medicine.

Receiving an appointment to serve as one of the six interns of the Woman's Hospital of this city, I entered the hospital May 1st as one of the six physicians appointed.

I have a good opportunity to see many patients every day, see many operations and gain all the experience I can before returning to my people.

I feel that I have an advantage in knowing the language and customs of my people, and as a physician can do a great deal to help them.

Very respectfully,
Susan La Flesche, M.D.

Susan La Flesche Picotte was born June 17, 1865, on the Omaha reservation in northeastern Nebraska. Her father, Chief Joseph (Iron Eye), was a strong leader, concerned with the alcoholism that plagued his people. Susan graduated in 1886 from the Hampton Institute in Elizabeth, New Jersey, receiving a gold medal for her high academic achievements.

The Woman's National Indian Association, co-founded by Mary Lucinda Bonney [June 8], had recently begun a scholarship program. Susan accepted their aid to finance her studies at the Woman's Medical College of Pennsylvania. She finished the three-year course in two years, graduating at the top of her class of thirty-six. Following a year's internship at the Philadelphia Woman's Hospital, she returned to her tribe to practice medicine.

In 1894 Susan married Henry Picotte, who was half-Sioux, half-French. After his death in 1905, she and her two sons moved to the newly formed town of Walthill on the Omaha reservation. Following her father's ideals, she led a delegation to Washington to demand that liquor not be sold on the Omaha and Winnebago reservations. As one of the first town residents, she became a guiding spirit in the community.

Susan's letter of application for a job that she did indeed get is from the Record of the Indian Bureau, Item #15736, National Archives, Washington, D.C.

Jane Lampton Clemens

The bright side

June 18, 1855
Dear Children,

Sometimes I forget everything. I said Mollie I am very sorry I did not speak to Judge Moore last night here. Mollie said I had a long talk with Judge Moore. I then asked why she and Orion did not ask Dr. Bancroff, and Mollie said they were both here. I have no recollection of seeing them or Judge Moore that evening. . . . I forget everything but I don't find my mind is all wrong. . . . I have a new set of teeth made in a new way. I think I shall like them. Livy I am afraid you and Sam will think they will not do. But I am delighted with them. . . .

Jane Lampton Clemens was born June 18, 1803, in Adair County in southern Kentucky. Jane and her sister were raised by their widowed father, who had a talent for failure in every business enterprise he tried. As a result they existed at the poverty level. Lack of funds did not stop Jane from becoming a flirtatious Southern belle besieged with suitors.

Jane married John M. Clemens, a pioneer lawyer. Despite constant traveling and very little money, Jane maintained her optimism, sense of humor and interest in all things new and different. She imbued these qualities in her four children, the youngest being Samuel, whom the world came to know as "Mark Twain."

Jane's letter to her son, Samuel, and his wife was written on the eve of her eighty-second birthday. It is included in Jane Clemens, The Story of Mark Twain's Mother *by Rachel M. Varble, published in 1964.*

Elizabeth Marbury

Better single

1923
Many of my friends expected me to marry young and well; and when I never married at all, great was their astonishment. I will now tell the truth as to why I never married and then the subject can be dismissed.

I can honestly say that I never had a really good offer. The best was but anemic. I attracted all the lame ducks that were limping about, I was the lodestar of the weaklings; the youths who trailed me were poor affairs

Elizabeth's writing is from her autobiography, My Crystal Ball, *published in 1923.*

---

as a rule, and to prove that my estimate of them was correct, not one in after life ever demonstrated any real value and never achieved any conspicuous accomplishment.

Elizabeth Marbury was born June 19, 1856 in New York City. She received a well-rounded education, studying Latin before she was seven and attending a play every Friday night. At twenty-nine she raised five thousand dollars for a charity benefit which brought her to the attention of a successful theatrical producer. He suggested that she seek a career in the business side of the theater.

Three years later Elizabeth co-produced "Little Lord Fauntleroy" on the stage and launched her new career. She became the American and English representative of the Socit de Gens de Lettres, the French writers' organization. For fifteen years she protected their works through copyrights, collected royalties, and ensured proper translations. Her business grew rapidly, and she opened offices in Paris, London, Berlin and Madrid.

Elizabeth weighed over two hundred pounds and smoked four to five packs of cigarettes daily. Despite her weight, she had tremendous energy and required little sleep. She read up to five plays a day, selecting the new hits for the coming theater season.

Beginning in 1914 Elizabeth devoted herself to the French war effort, for which she was awarded medals from both the French and Belgian governments. At the end of the war she represented the Knights of Columbus, spending many months talking to the troops waiting to go home. She later wrote that this was the most enjoyable experience of her life.

Elizabeth died in New York City when she was seventy-seven. Her elaborate funeral at St. Patrick's Cathedral was attended by the mayor and the governor.

Mary Smith Garrett

1893

*W*ell-taught

In past ages the deaf were the victims of deliberate as well as ignorant cruelty. In the present age they are no longer deliberately drowned, as in ancient Rome, nor exposed to die, as under the laws of Lycurgus, but they are still largely sufferers from a modified form of the ignorance which formerly ranked them with imbeciles. . . .

Mary's writing is from a speech she gave before the Congress of Women at the 1893 World's Columbian Exposition, Chicago.

I know of three mothers who were fortunate enough to realize what they could accomplish for their deaf infants, and who have taught them to read the lips so well, and also to talk, that now that these children are grown up, no one would take them to be stone deaf. They are all women; two of them have married hearing men, and the third is a bright, happy girl of twenty-one, who is studying art in Chicago, on exactly the same footing with the hearing. . . .

Mary Smith Garrett was born June 20, 1839, in Philadelphia. She and her sister Emma became interested in the education of the deaf. After teaching at the Pennsylvania Institute for the Deaf and Dumb, Mary opened her own school in 1885 in Philadelphia.

Mary was a firm believer in teaching the deaf to speak and read lips, rather than use sign language. She felt that vocal training of deaf children should start at a very young age so as to free them from "the needless loneliness of the Ghetto of Silence."

In 1891 Mary and her sister started the Pennsylvania Home for the Training in Speech of Deaf Children Before They Are of School Age. Emma was the principal for two years, until she committed suicide. Mary then assumed the position until her own death thirty years later. There was, at the time, a controversy over the benefits of speech training versus sign language. Mary was instrumental in obtaining passage in 1899 and 1901 of two Pennsylvania laws requiring all state deaf institutions to offer training exclusively by the oral method.

Theodosia Burr

A daughter's letter

Theodosia's letter to her father while he was in exile in England is included in Correspondence of Aaron Burr and His Daughter Theodosia, *edited by Mark Van Doren, published in 1929.*

August 1, 1809
Indeed, I witness your extraordinary fortitude with new wonder at every new misfortune. Often, after reflecting on this subject, you appear to me so superior, so elevated above all other men; I contemplate you with such a strange mixture of humility, admiration, reverence, love and pride, that very little superstition would be necessary to make me worship you as a superior being; such enthusiasm does your character excite in me.

When I afterward revert to myself, how insignificant do my best qualities appear. My vanity would be greater if I had not been placed so near you; and yet my pride is our relationship. I had rather not live than not be the daughter of such a man.

Theodosia Burr was born June 21, 1783, in Albany, New York. Her father, Aaron Burr, doted on his only child, supervising her education and giving her lessons in skating, dancing and music. Following her mother's death when she was eleven, Theodosia and her father became even closer. They began their frequent correspondence, which ultimately totaled thousands of letters. As she grew older, she assumed the role of hostess on their estate overlooking the Hudson.

When Theodosia was seventeen, the same year her father became vice-president of the United States, she was married to Joseph Alston of South Carolina. Her father's career began a downward spiral following his duel with Alexander Hamilton in 1804. When he was arrested and imprisoned for treason in 1807, Theodosia moved to Richmond to be near him. The following year she went to New York under an assumed name to say good-bye to him before he left for England. Theodosia felt the repercussions of her father's actions and told him "the world begins to cool terribly around me."

Aaron Burr returned to New York in 1812. Theodosia set sail from South Carolina on the pilot ship *Patriot*, joyfully looking forward to her long-awaited reunion with her father. However, the ship disappeared at sea with no trace of survivors.

Caroline Healey Dall

1874

An unrecognized burden

If boys are preparing for college, they do not have to take care of the baby, make the beds, or help to serve the meals. A great many girls at the high schools do all this. Then, if a man who is a student marries, he is carefully protected from all annoyance. His study is sacred, his wife does the marketing. If his baby cries, he sleeps in the spare room.

So far, women have written in the nursery or the dining room, often with one foot on the cradle. They must provide for their households, and nurse their sick, before they can follow any artistic or intellectual bent.

Caroline's writing is from a collection of essays by several women, Sex and Education, A Reply to Dr. E.H. Clarke's "Sex in Education," *published in 1874.*

Caroline Wells Healey Dall was born June 22, 1822, in Boston, Massachusetts. She received an excellent private-school education, and her father hoped she would have a literary career. However, she was more interested in religion and working with the underprivileged. At fifteen she started one of the first nursery schools for working mothers in Boston.

In 1844 Caroline married Charles Dall, a Unitarian minister. They had two children, but the union was not a happy one. After eleven years together he went to India as a missionary, where he remained, except for occasional brief visits home, until his death thirty-one years later. Left alone at home to raise her family, Caroline committed herself to the cause of women's rights.

She wrote, taught, and periodically preached in Unitarian churches until her death in 1912.

JUNE 23

Anne Elizabeth McDowell

Initial success

1856

Contrary to the predictions and most earnest hopes of the opponents of woman's rights to live by her own industry, we have reached the last number of the first volume of the *Advocate*. It has been a year of trial and struggle; but we have, thanks to the kind friends who have practised rather than preached, been able to place our paper on a footing which ensures it another year's existence, and, we trust, a long and useful life.

Anne Elizabeth McDowell was born June 23, 1826, in Smyrna, Delaware. Little is known of her childhood. When she was twenty-nine, she started a weekly newspaper, the *Woman's Advocate*.

Anne's idea for her paper was to devote it "to the elevation of the female industrial class." She did this by employing only female typesetters and printers, who received the same wages as men.

After financial losses forced her to close her paper, Anne worked as editor of the Philadelphia *Sunday Dispatch* and later the *Sunday Republic*. She established a library for female employees of Wannamaker's Department Store, known as the McDowell Free Library. Her activities were greatly diminished in later years by an illness that left her paralyzed in one leg and dependent on braces to walk.

Anne's writing is from her editorial "The End of the Volume" in the January 5, 1856, edition of the Woman's Advocate.

Esther Belle Hanna

May 11, 1852

Started this morning before 6 o'clock. Got along comfortably last night—heard wolves howling very near us, the first I ever heard, they make a singular mournful noise. We have a bad time today crossing the sloughs, they are so deep, and very hard on our cattle. Our mules get along well; our carriage is very comfortable and we have a real nice little bedroom of it at night, shut it all up close, let down the backs of the seats, spread our mattress, hung up our clothes on the hooks which are put in all around. I have my looking glass, towel etc., hung up and everything in order. Got some beautiful wildflowers today, they grow in profusion on the prairie. We passed two newly made graves yesterday and one today, just by the roadside. O how hard to think of being left alone by the wayside!

Esther Belle McMillan Hanna, pioneer, was born June 24, 1824, in Canonsburg, Pennsylvania. She married Reverend Joseph A. Hanna, a Presbyterian minister, in 1852. One month later they set off on their long and perilous journey west to the Oregon country.

Esther kept a detailed journal of their trip from May 4, 1852, when the wagon train departed St. Joseph, Missouri, until October 28, 1852, when they arrived in Oregon City. They began with eighty people and twenty wagons but due to sickness, wagon disasters, and disagreements over whether or not to travel on the Sabbath, their numbers decreased to eighteen people and five wagons. Esther and Joseph walked the last seventy miles of their two thousand mile journey. All their oxen but one had died and the mules were too weak to carry a rider.

The Hannas established the second Presbyterian Church to be founded in Oregon at Corvallis. The church was first organized in their home with only four members. Esther had four children and lived in Corvallis the rest of her life.

Heading for Oregon

Esther's writing is from her travel diary that she kept on the six-month trek to Oregon. Six weeks after she wrote with such delight about their cozy wagon they were forced to cut it in two, make a small cart of it to lighten the oxen's load, and burn the remainder. A copy of Esther's diary is located at Pacific University, Forest Grove, Oregon.

Olive Thorne Miller

*T*he happy minstrel

1881

Hearing the sweet song of a cat-bird, I seized an opera glass, and looked over the neighboring yards till I found him perched on the roof of a pigeon-house, singing with great energy. Several pigeons were also on the roof, and seemed interested in the stranger entertaining them. Suddenly, in the middle of a burst of song, the minstrel darted like a flash among them, evidently for pure fun, for he did not touch one of them, and returned instantly to his song. Wild panic, however, seized the pigeons, and although he was a mere atom among them, they flew every way, and would have shrieked with terror had they been able.

Olive Thorne Miller was born June 25, 1831, in Auburn, New York. Her father believed that success was always just around the corner, so, as a result, her childhood was spent moving and living in new places, from New York to Missouri, with stops in Ohio, Wisconsin and Illinois. Shy and bookish, Olive began writing stories as a child.

Olive moved to Chicago when she married Watts Miller in 1854. Her husband's family thought "the dish cloth was mightier than the pen" so she temporarily put her writing aside to devote herself to her home and four children. In 1870 her first story was published. It was followed by hundreds more, all stories and nature sketches for children.

In 1880 Olive became interested in the study of birds. This new focus led her to write on the subject, producing her finest works. She became one of the most popular writers on birds in her time, respected by lay people and professionals alike.

Olive's writing is from her article, "The Tricks and Manners of a Cat-Bird," Harper's New Monthly Magazine, *Volume 70, June 1881.*

Give Her This Day

Sarah Pierce

Litchfield.
Jan. 13, 1842.
My Dear Emma

    You must not expect that your old aunt will be able to write to you very often, as her bodily weakness is great, and her eyes very poor. I was glad to see your last letter written so handsomely and without any mistakes in the spelling. I hope you will be careful to acquire a good style, and a handsome mode of writing letters and notes, as they show a woman's education on more occasions than almost anything else she is called to perform. . . .

*S*how your education

Sarah Pierce was born June 26, 1767, in Litchfield, Connecticut. Her father died when she was fourteen and her brother, the paymaster general of the Continental Army, assumed responsibility for his six siblings. He sent Sarah and her older sister to school in New York to become teachers.

    In 1792, Sarah returned to Litchfield and opened a school. At first she taught in her dining room and had only two or three pupils. The school's reputation grew until local citizens provided a building. It was enlarged in 1827 and incorporated as the Litchfield Female Academy. Sarah taught the usual academic subjects plus needlework, painting, dance and physical education. The enrollment was as high as 130 during her forty-year tenure.

    Sarah participated in Litchfield's centennial celebration in 1851, during which the keynote speaker praised her for giving "a new tone to female education" in the United States. She died the following year when she was eighty-five.

Sarah's letter to her niece is included in Chronicles of a Pioneer School from 1792 to 1833, *which was compiled by Emily N. Vanderpoel and published in 1903.*

Ednah Dow Cheney

1902
My great-grandmother was named Ednah Hardy, and the name Ednah, then unusual, has been kept in the family for four generations, and always spelled with the "h." I have always fought for the "h," and with good

*H*idden blessing in a name

reason; for my Hebrew friends tell me the "h" is a sacred letter, and means "the favor of God."

Ednah Dow Littlehale Cheney was born June 27, 1824, on Boston's Beacon Hill. She received an excellent education in local private schools and became acquainted with intellectuals such as Emerson and Bronson Alcott. She attended Margaret Fuller's [May 23] "Conversations" which awakened her philosophical and literary interests. She admired Miss Fuller so profoundly that she later wrote, "I absorbed her life and thoughts, and to this day I am astonished to find how large a part of 'what I am when I am most myself' I have derived from her."

Ednah married Seth Cheney from a prominent Connecticut silk manufacturing family in 1853. He died within three years, leaving her with a young daughter. Ednah became interested in medical education for women and was secretary, later president, of the newly formed New England Hospital for Women and Children. During and after the Civil War, she helped relocate freed slaves, and organized Boston teachers to travel to the South to work.

Ednah's writing is from Reminiscences of Ednah Dow Cheney, *published in 1902.*

Anne Wilson Goldthwaite

*R*emembering Mammy

1935

The early years of my life were the golden age. They were filled with love and warmth and ease and approbation. I remember only happy things. . . .

My Mammy was of tremendous importance to me and I to her. She was inordinately proud of my good looks and my bad temper, especially the latter. In a group of nurses with their charges, I have heard her boast of my misdeeds.

Years later, on my eighth birthday, Mammy gave me a golden ring, like a wedding ring, and a filigree breastpin to remember her by when I was grown. She lies buried in a Negro graveyard in Texas, and there is a stone at her head with her name carved deep so that we children might always find her. We are now far from her grave. I have lost all of her presents, and I am conscious of guilt; but if I can write her name—Nancy Sykes—into this book I shall have atoned.

Anne's writing is from her twenty-eight-page "Reminiscence" in the Archives of American Art, Smithsonian Institute, Washington, D.C.

Give Her This Day

Anne Wilson Goldthwaite was born June 28, 1869, in Montgomery, Alabama. As a child she loved sketching and painting. After her boyfriend was killed in a duel when she was twenty-one, her uncle encouraged her to move to New York City to study art.

Anne settled in New York and never again resided in the South, although she never lost her affection for the region and used it as the subject of much of her artwork.

In 1906 Anne went to Paris to study. She met many of Europe's leading artists and was among the founders of the Académie Moderne. Anne always painted familiar, homey scenes of life, such as a hen house or a Negro and his mule working a field.

Anne returned to New York just prior to World War I. She taught at the Art Students League and produced a prolific amount of work until her death in 1943. Her paintings hang in many of America's museums, including the Metropolitan Museum of Art, the Art Institute of Chicago and the Library of Congress.

Celia Thaxter

1873

A child's excitement

In the long, covered walk that bridged the gorge between the lighthouse and the house we played in stormy days, and every evening it was a fresh excitement to watch the lighting of the lamps, and think how far the lighthouse sent its rays, and how many hearts it gladdened with assurance of safety. As I grew older I was allowed to kindle the lamps sometimes myself. That was indeed a pleasure. So little a creature as I might do that much for the great world!

Celia Laighton Thaxter was born June 29, 1835, in Portsmouth, New Hampshire. In 1839, her father took the job of lighthouse keeper on White Island, nine miles off the coast of Portsmouth, the smallest of the Isles of Shoals. Celia and her two brothers were educated by their father on this tiny island of less than three acres. Her childhood memories formed the basis for all her future writings.

Mr. Laighton moved the family to Appledore, the largest island of the group, when Celia was twelve. He went into partnership with Levi Thaxter, opening the summer hotel "Appledore House." The inn became a popular gathering

Celia's writing is from her article "Child-Life at the Isles of Shoals" in the May, 1876, issue of The Atlantic Monthly.

place for New England artists and writers.

When Celia was sixteen, she married Levi Thaxter, fifteen years her senior. She had rarely left the islands and found it difficult adjusting to life on mainland Massachusetts. She began writing poetry as an outlet for her homesickness. Her first poem was published in 1861 in *The Atlantic Monthly*.

Celia socialized with most of Boston's well-known literary figures. Her close friend, the poet John Greenleaf Whittier, convinced her it was "destiny to produce poetry." She published six volumes of poems during her lifetime and was one of the best-known American female poets. She never wrote about people, but always about the ocean, the rocks, and the plant and animal life of her beloved Isles of Shoals.

Mabel Cratty

Life is good

1925

I may be a strange person, but I do find life good. Perhaps I am not so sensitive to the tiny filaments of pain, but in spite of what my life has brought and still presents—the suffering of those I love—of those from whom I am responsible, who depend on me, the needs and woes of many, many friends—I am still so *sure* that life is good, and has more to be rejoiced over than to mourn. If we have work, useful work to do, we can't be completely unhappy. We can be measurably content.

Mabel Cratty was born June 30, 1868, in Bellaire, Ohio. As a child she idolized her aunt, a Methodist missionary in India. Following graduation from Ohio Wesleyan University in 1890, Mabel hoped to join her aunt in India, but family responsibilities prevented her from doing this.

Mabel taught school at various institutions until 1900 when she was made principal of the Delaware, Ohio, high school. Friends initially involved her in the Young Women's Christian Association, which she joined in 1902. Within two years she had resigned her high-school position to move to Chicago and become the associate general secretary of the American Committee of the Y.W.C.A. Two years later she resettled in New York City to become the general secretary, the post she held until her death.

Mabel's letter is included in Mabel Cratty—Leader in the Art of Leadership, *by Margaret E. Burton, published in 1929.*

JULY

Florence Nicholson Coates

1916

A gifted reader can bring tears to the eyes of almost any one by repeating certain poetry. And the tears will be brought by the beauty of the things repeated. People are not really moved by what is ugly. Ugliness in poetry they may find clever and interesting. But it is only beauty that "snatches the breath and fills the eyes with tears."

Florence Nicholson Coates was born July 1, 1850, in Philadelphia. She was well-educated at private schools in America, a convent in Paris and a music academy in Brussels.

Florence married William Nicholson when she was twenty-two and had one son before her husband passed away. Two years later, she married Edward Coates, a member of a prominent Philadelphia family. They had one daughter who died in infancy.

Between 1900 and 1914, Florence published over fifty poems and enjoyed popular success. She often gave dramatic recitations of her works, accompanied by her piano playing. Her "Ode on the Coronation of King George V" was publicly read in Great Britain and presented to the King.

The Federation of Women's Clubs unanimously elected Florence Poet Laureate of Pennsylvania. She passed away a few years later when she was seventy-six.

Florence's writing is from her article, "Godlessness Mars Most Contemporary Poetry," in the December 10, 1916, New York Times *magazine section.*

Grace Raymond Hebard

1907

The most hazardous and the most significant journey ever made on the Western Continent—a journey that rivals in daring and exceeds in importance the expeditions of Stanley and Livingstone in the wilds of Africa—a journey that resulted in the greatest real estate transaction ever recorded in history and gave to the world riches beyond comprehension—was piloted by a woman. . . .

In honor of this Indian girl, Sacajawea, the only

Grace's writing is from her article, "Pilot of First White Men to Cross the American Continent," in the 1907 Journal of American History.

woman who accompanied the Lewis and Clark expedition into the northwest, memorials are being erected.

Grace Raymond Hebard was born July 2, 1861, in Clinton, Iowa. Her father died soon after her birth, leaving her mother to raise four young children alone. Grace was a sickly child, unable to attend school, so she was educated at home by her mother. She must have been an excellent teacher, as Grace was able to enter the University of Iowa and graduate with a degree in engineering.

The Hebards moved to Wyoming soon after Grace's graduation. She took a drafting job in the United States Surveyor General's office where she was the only woman among forty men. She soon became interested in the fledgling University of Wyoming and was named to its board of directors in 1891.

Grace received her Ph.D. from Ohio Wesleyan and was admitted to the Wyoming Bar in 1898. Sixteen years later she was admitted to practice before the Supreme Court of Wyoming. She was also a professor of economics at the university as well as its first librarian. Somehow, with all these activities, she still found time for sports, becoming state champion in both golf and tennis.

Grace retired from teaching in 1931 to devote herself to writing books and articles about Wyoming's history, its Indians and their reservations. All the local Indians loved and trusted Grace; the Shoshonis adopted her into their tribe and called her "the good woman, the woman with one tongue."

Charlotte Perkins Gilman

The first kiss

1935

One year there was a handsome Harvard boy in the party, who invited me out to sit on the rocks in the moonlight. Thus romantically placed, he confided to me that he had kissed more than one girl for what he was sure was the first time. Replying, I soberly inquired if he did not expect to marry some day, which he admitted. "When you first kiss the girl you mean to marry, don't you wish that to be her 'first time'?" Yes, he did. "Then don't you see that every time you kiss these other girls first you are robbing some other man of that dear pleasure?" He saw. Our conversation continued

Charlotte's writing is from her autobiography, The Living of Charlotte Perkins Gilman, *published in 1935.*

on a most friendly and confidential basis, but I noticed that next night he took one of the pretty waitresses out on the rocks—they were nice neighborhood girls.

Charlotte Anna Perkins Stetson Gilman, author and lecturer, was born July 3, 1860, in Hartford, Connecticut. In 1884 she married an artist, Charles Stetson, and they had one child.

Within a year of her marriage Charlotte became extremely depressed, often spending whole days in her bed sobbing. After a trip to California without her husband she noticed her condition had improved dramatically and concluded that she had to leave her husband to preserve her mental health. She suffered aftereffects from her breakdown, however, for the rest of her life, which she referred to as living in "dreary twilight."

Charlotte moved to Pasadena, California, and supported herself, her daughter and her mother by writing short stories and poetry and giving lectures. She travelled the country, speaking on a variety of topics pertaining to women and socialism. In 1898 she published her most important book, *Women and Economics*, which still commands a place in American feminist literature. She encouraged women to develop their own earning power so as not to be dependent on men. She proposed "common nurseries" where mothers could leave their children.

Charlotte married George Gilman, her first cousin and seven years her junior, in 1900. She still could not enjoy the role of housewife and continued writing and lecturing. In 1932 she was told she had breast cancer and, always the realist, she quickly bought and hid enough chloroform so that she could end her life before her suffering was too great. She killed herself in 1935.

Mary Florence Denton

Kyoto, Japan
July 21, 1890
Pardon me for speaking so plainly but I do think that you at home who are sending money here to bring girls to America and are taking care of them while they are there, are doing a very foolish thing. . . . I have yet to meet a Japanese whom I think improved by America. When they come home disliking their own people and unable to live as Japanese live, not able to eat Japanese

Not improved

Mary's writing, from a letter to the American Board of Commissioners for Foreign Missions, is included in Mary Frances Denton and the Doshisha *by Frances Clapp, published in 1955.*

food and altogether out of sympathy with everything Japanese, then I think America has been a positive evil.

Mary Florence Denton was born July 4, 1857, in a mining camp in Nevada County, California. While teaching in Pasadena, she met the Reverend and Mrs. Gordon, missionaries on furlough from Japan. They acquainted her with the Doshisha Schools in Kyoto.

Defying her parents' wishes, Mary volunteered for missionary service. In October, 1888, she arrived in Japan and began her association with the Doshisha that would last her entire life. The Doshisha consisted of a boys' and girls' high school, a nursing school and a theological seminary. A women's junior college was added in 1912. Mary rotated between schools as needed, but primarily taught English, the Bible and Western-style cooking. Her marble cake was so popular that she was asked to bake it when the Empress of Japan visited the campus in 1924.

When Mary reached retirement age, she refused to return to America. She remained in Japan during World War II and died there in 1947.

Hannah Johnston Bailey

Freedom flawed

1896

When travelling in Turkish dominions last spring I slept with the flag of my country over my bed and felt more secure on account of it. That flag, our own "Old Glory," is respected by all nations. I was told by Turkish officials that my passport would not be honored in some parts of their domain unless supplemented by one signed by their own officers, and I obtained such a one at great price; but they did not refuse to let me keep my flag, or tell me I must carry their Turkish ensign in order to pass through their territory unmolested. I loved to exhibit our beautiful stars and stripes and tell what they meant and tell of the free institutions and of the greatly advanced privileges of women which this flag protected, but I could not say what I desired most of all to say, that all the women of America would have a voice in their own Government.

Hannah's writing is from her annual President's Address before the Maine Woman's Suffrage Association in 1896.

Hannah Clark Johnston Bailey was born July 5, 1839, in Cornwall-on-the-Hudson, New York. Her father was a Quaker minister, and through him she became committed to the cause of pacifism.

Hannah taught school for ten years until her marriage to Moses Bailey, a Quaker widower, in 1868. He died after fourteen years, leaving Hannah with enough income to pursue her reform interests.

Hannah was very active as a Sunday-school teacher and as a board member of Quaker schools. She also worked for the Temperance and woman's suffrage movements. She was most concerned with ending all forms of violence, opposing lynching, capital punishment, prizefighting and, most importantly, war.

Hannah distributed pacifist literature and lectured all over the United States. She believed the best place to begin was with the country's youth. To this end she encouraged mothers to forbid playing with army toys and opposed military drills in schools and the draft system.

The outbreak of World War I dashed Hannah's dreams of peace. After suffering a mental and physical collapse, she died in 1923.

Ellen Martin Henrotin

The present hysteria on the subject of Prostitution and teaching of Sex Hygiene does not make for a wise action and will not materially assist in solving the problems. It goes far deeper than homes for women, reformatories and refuges. The whole concept of life must be changed, enlarged and purified. . . .

We hear much of a new morality, but we never see its formulated codes. After all is said and done, virtue in a man or woman must be spontaneous and it is the duty of this awakened generation to formulate the principle of "duty towards the race."

Ellen Martin Henrotin was born July 6, 1847, in Portland, Maine. She spent much of her childhood abroad, attending schools in London, Paris and Dresden. Soon after returning to America and settling in Chicago, Ellen met and married Charles Henrotin. They had three sons.

In 1893 Ellen was appointed vice-president of the Board of Lady Managers of the World's Columbian Exposition and

Awakening a generation

Ellen's writing is from her undated paper, "Psychology of Prostitution," which is included in the Henrotin Collection at Schlesinger Library, Radcliffe College.

was reponsible for its strong feminist emphasis. Her administrative abilities were noticed and led to her election as president of the General Federation of Women's Clubs. During her period of leadership, the number of American women's clubs doubled. She was particularly interested in improving the conditions of the working woman and in ending prostitution. She prepared reports, lectured tirelessly and organized her club members to this end.

Mary Atkins

*T*houghts at sea

December 31, 1863
Lon. 148° 38' E.: La. 27x 06'
The wind is W.N.W. which drives us a little to the eastward off our course. The sea breaks over the bow every few minutes and seems as if it would sweep everything before it. Today I have seen enough of a sea voyage and think hereafter I shall prefer traveling by land, or, what is better, not at all. The ship rolls so fearfully one can scarcely sit or stand. The only comfort is bed.

One year ago today was spent at Col. Narasythy's with Mary Loughlin. Little thought I then I should be nearly across the Pacific today. Mary in Virginia City and I here. How strange is life! What will close of another year bring? This, so far as I know, finds all of my sisters and brother still alive.

Mary Atkins was born July 7, 1819, in Jefferson, Ohio. She began teaching in rural schools when she was sixteen. While still teaching she attended Oberlin College, graduating with honors in 1845.

Mary grew restless teaching in eastern schools and contemplated missionary work in Siam. She went instead to California, where women comprised less than ten percent of the population. She took over as principal of the three-year-old Young Ladies' Seminary at Benicia, near San Francisco. Under her leadership the school turned a profit and gained a wide reputation.

Mary's writing, describing her voyage to the Far East, is from The Diary of Mary Atkins: A Sabbatical in the Eighteen Sixties, *published by Mills College in 1937.*

In 1863 Mary took a sabbatical to the Far East, stopping en route to visit the Oahu College, which was run by a missionary couple, Cyrus and Susan Mills. A year later she sold the Benicia Seminary to the Millses. They incorporated it into the Mills Seminary, which later became Mills College.

Give Her This Day

Maria White Lowell

Rome
January 6, 1852
Dearest Lois,

I was exceedingly glad to get your nice long letter this morning, and pulled it out of James's hand who always likes to look a long time at all our letters before he opens them, speculating upon the outside, upon post marks, or upon anything which will allow him to linger over the unbroken seal. But I who think the cream of the letter is to be found within, do not enjoy this kind of grace before the meal, but prefer to taste at once. It is delightful to think that you have a little baby named Clara. I had it always upon my list of names. It has such a pretty meaning too and yet is simple and uncommon. Clara Howe sounds very sweet.

Maria White Lowell has born July 8, 1821, in Watertown, Massachusetts. She and her sisters were educated by a governess at home, after which they attended the Ursuline Convent School, the fashionable place at the time for daughters of wealthy Bostonians. A Know Nothing mob burned the convent down when she was thirteen, ending her formal education. She then joined the group of young women at Margaret Fuller's [May 23] "Conversations." She was hoping to discover "What were we born to do? and how shall we do it?"

In 1840 Maria became engaged to James R. Lowell, a twenty-one-year-old law student. He found law boring but was unsure if he could make a living with his poetry. Maria encouraged him to become a poet as a means of bringing an uplifting message to man. They were married four years later when he felt his literary work was producing enough income to support a family. Maria also wrote poetry, which he helped her to publish in magazines and anthologies.

Maria had four children in five years, two of whom died as infants. So many pregnancies and so much tragedy took a toll on her health. The family left for Italy in 1851 to try to revive her spirit. However, her only son died in Rome the following year. Maria said she was "tired of broken promises" and dared not plan a future for her one remaining child. She died soon after at the age of thirty-two.

To a friend

*Maria's letter to her friend Lois
(Mrs. Estes Howe) is included in*
The Poems of Maria White
Lowell with Unpublished
Letters and Biography, *edited
by Hope Vernon, published in
1936.*

Sara Parton

A mother's pleasure

1857

Of course you know that "Napkin" is Louis Napoleon's little baby; perhaps you don't know that his mamma does not nurse him herself. I wonder does she know how much pleasure she loses by not doing it? I wonder does she know how sweet it is to wake in the night, and find a baby's soft little hand on her neck, and his dear little head lying upon her arm? I wonder does she know how beautiful a baby is when it first wakes in the morning, raising its little head from the pillow, and gazing at you with its lustrous eyes and rosy cheeks, so like a fresh-blown dewy flower? I wonder does she know how delicious it is to give the little hungry rogue his breakfast? No, no; poor Eugenia! poor empress! She knows nothing of all this. She has had all a mother's pain, and none of a mother's pleasure. She hires a woman to nurse and sleep with little "Napkin."

Sara Payson Willis Parton, author and newspaper columnist, was born July 9, 1811, in Portland, Maine. Her family moved to Boston when she was one year old. At twenty-six she married Charles Eldredge and had three children.

After the death of Charles and a brief unhappy second marriage which ended in divorce, Sara unsuccessfully tried to support herself by sewing and teaching. She decided to try writing and launched her career under the name "Fanny Fern." Soon magazines and newspapers were printing her amusing articles.

Her first book, published in 1853, became an instant best-seller both in America and England. The following year she published two more successful books, earning her more than ten thousand dollars in royalties in two years. The owner of the *New York Ledger* hired her at one hundred dollars per week, thus making her one of the first women columnists in the United States.

Sara's writing is from The Play-Day Book: New Stories for Little Folks, *published in 1857.*

Sara remained with the *Ledger* for the rest of her life. In 1856 she married James Parton, a biographer eleven years her junior. Her daughter Ellen lived with them, and after Sara died her daughter became Parton's second wife.

Cordelia Lewis Scales

October 29, 1862

My dear darling Loulie:

   . . . I was taken very sick very sudden one morning.

   . . . I felt perfectly well when I got up, & was walking across the floor, when I was taken with congestion of the lungs & I fell before Pa, who was close by, could catch me. . . .

   For one week Dr. Gray did not leave me; he stayed with me night and day. I never was so completely humbled in my life as I was by this spell. And Lou what do you think, they shingled my hair & it was so long & even I had learned to braid & tuck it up like a grown lady. You do not know how becoming it was. I have enough to make me a beautiful braid. Dr. Gray was afraid I would have congestion or inflammation of the brain was the reason he cut it off, for he kept ice to my head all the time after the hair was cut. I wish you could see me now with my hair parted on the side with my black velvet zouave on & pistol by my side and riding my fine colt, Beula. I know you would take me for a Guerilla. I never ride now or walk without my pistol. Quite warlike, you see. We have had the house full of our soldiers every since the Yankees left.

Cordelia Lewis Scales was born July 10, 1843, at the family mansion, "Oakland," near Holly Springs, Mississippi. During the Civil War Northern troops occupied "Oakland" at least six different times, and during the peaceful intervals her family aided the Confederate soldiers from nearby camps.

   Cordelia carried on a frequent correspondence with her school friend, Lou, who lived thirty miles away, filling her in on the constantly changing events at her home. In one letter she described how one thousand black Republicans (the 26th Illinois Regiment) camped on her property for two weeks. Next came the 90th Illinois Irish Legion, whom she felt treated her family better because "the Irish were all Democrats."

   Cordelia was very brave and never refrained from voicing her pro-South opinions. When one Northern major was departing he warned her that he would reduce the South to starvation, and she replied, "I had rather starve to death in the South than be a beggar in the North."

A young Confederate

Cordelia's letter to her friend, Lou Irby, is in The Mississippi Historical Society, Jackson, Mississippi.

Susan Bogert Warner

A mighty power

1851

When Ellen was able to begin her letter the reading of it served to throw her back into fresh fits of tears. Many a word of Mrs. Montgomery's went so to her little daughter's heart that its very inmost cords of love and tenderness were wrung. It is true the letter was short and very simple; but it came from her mother's heart; it was written by her mother's hand; and the very old re-membered handwriting had mighty power to move her.

Susan Bogert Warner was born July 11, 1819, in New York City. When she was seventeen, her father purchased Constitu-tion Island, a wooded retreat in the Hudson River near West Point. Susan and her younger sister Anna learned to cook, gar-den, cut firewood and row to the mainland for supplies. Following the panic of 1837, they lost most of their money and possessions, driving both sisters to careers in writing.

Susan published her first book in 1851 under the pseu-donym "Elizabeth Wetherell." Public tastes at the time favored romantic, moralistic tales exactly like Susan's, so she enjoyed instant success. Her debut novel was the first by an American to reach sales of one million. Susan dropped her pen name and continued to publish at least one, sometimes two or three, books per year for the next thirty years. One novel sold ten thousand copies the day it appeared in the stores.

Both Susan and her sister regularly taught Bible classes to the West Point cadets. Susan died at sixty-five and Anna sur-vived her by thirty years. They were buried side by side at West Point, on a grassy knoll overlooking their Constitution Island home.

Susan's writing is from her first book, Wide, Wide World, *written under the pseudonym "Elizabeth Wetherell" and published in 1851.*

Eliza Rotch Farrar

*T*ravelling

Eliza's writing is from her autobiography, Recollections of Seventy Years, *published in 1866.*

1866

Travelling is one of the few pleasures of this world that does not perish in the using. Southey said, "It is more delightful to have travelled than to travel," and I think he is right. The most prosperous journeys have their anxieties and disappointments, and sight-seeing is so fatiguing as sometimes to destroy all enjoyment; but in retrospect, all that was unpleasant is forgotten, and we only live over the most delightful part of our experiences.

Eliza Rotch Farrar was born July 12, 1791, in Dunkirk, France, to American parents. Her father, a Quaker whaling merchant, had gone to Europe to try to establish a tax-free whaling port. Forced to leave France during the Reign of Terror, he moved his whaling industry to a small Welsh town. Eliza and her seven siblings were raised by governesses at their elegant Welsh estate, "Castle Hall."

When Eliza was twenty-eight her father lost his fortune speculating in the price of whale oil, and she was forced to live with her grandparents in New Bedford, Massachusetts. Nine years later she married John Farrar, a mathematics professor at Harvard.

Eliza wrote numerous books for children although she never had children of her own. She published her most important book, *The Young Lady's Friend*, in 1836. It was among the first American etiquette books and became popular on both continents.

Madeleine Vinton Dahlgren   J U L Y   1 3

1884   *I*nto Hades

One debilitating April morning, after a sleepless night, he sat at the breakfast-table in his dressing-gown, and ordered the morning's paper. In it he read the announcement of the marriage of Mme. De Beaulieu. Five minutes later a groan, followed by the thud of a heavy fall, was heard by the faithful Pat Maloney, who ran quickly and found the Senator foaming at the mouth and breathing stertorously.

The sixteen doctors sent for pronounced it apoplexy, just as his soul, in charge of its attendant demons, fell into Hades.

Madeleine Vinton Dahlgren was born July 13, 1825, in Gallipolis, Ohio. She was educated at Monsieur Picot's Boarding School in Philadelphia and in the Convent of the Visitation in Georgetown, D.C. Her mother and brother died when she was a child, so she had to learn quickly to assume the

Madeleine's writing is from her romantic novel, A Washington Winter, published in 1884.

role of companion and hostess to her father, a congressman.

At the age of thirty, Madeleine married Daniel Goddard, Assistant Secretary of the Interior Department. She was widowed after five years and returned to her father's Washington home with her two children. She began writing, publishing her first collection, *Idealities*, in 1859 under the pen name Corinne. She supported her family through her writing, and by translating religious and political essays from the French, Spanish and Italian.

Madeleine married John Dahlgren in 1865, and they had three children. Once again she was widowed after five years, and once again she returned to her father's house and resumed her writing. In the 1880's she switched from nonfiction to fiction, producing romantic, highly dramatic novels that were frequently serialized in popular magazines.

Amanda Douglas

A beauty's decline

1868

Martha was a beauty and a belle. She flirted away her halcyon days, was vain, imperious, selfish, and faded into a fretful "old maid." As years passed she became an invalid, and aggravated trifling disorders by lack of regular living and exercise, and passionate indulgence in temper. She had turned the point of half a century now, was wrinkled, thin and sallow, but persisted in keeping up those youthful habits least becoming to age.

Amanda Minnie Douglas was born July 14, 1838 in New York City. She was a sickly child, prone to reading and storytelling. As an adult she turned her talent for weaving tales into a career as an author.

Amanda published her first book, which was immediately successful, when she was twenty-eight. She had sold the copyright, however, and received little recompense. She held onto the copyrights of her subsequent books; approximately twenty-five were published in the next twenty years.

Amanda's writing is from her novel, Claudia, *which was published in 1868.*

As a hobby, Amanda enjoyed inventing things. One of her inventions, which she had patented, was a folding frame for a mosquito net.

Almira Lincoln Phelps

1836

Exhortations to duty from female pens, though the sentence be not constructed with the strength of Johnson, or the periods rounded with Addisonian elegance, may affect the hearts of other females. The lot of women is in many respects the same for all: we are mothers, wives, daughters, and in the performance of our duties appertaining to our various relations, need assistance from the experience of others. We can render mutual benefits by the suggestions of individual experiences, and as it is often that the most humble and unpretending are the most exemplary, such should be encouraged to write for the ladies' periodicals; because everything dictated by nature and good sense is valuable and interesting.

Almira Hart Lincoln Phelps was born July 15, 1793, in Berlin, Connecticut, the youngest of seventeen children. She received her first formal schooling from her sister Emma Willard, later the founder of the Troy Female Seminary.

After a series of teaching jobs, Almira married Simeon Lincoln in 1817. Their first child died in infancy and Simeon passed away three years later, leaving Almira a widow with two toddlers. Financial need forced her to move to Troy, New York, to teach at her sister's school.

In 1829 Almira published her first textbook, *Familiar Lectures on Botany*, followed by books on chemistry, geology and natural philosophy. Her imaginative texts helped to bring the sciences into the standard curriculum.

Almira married John Phelps, the widowed father of one of her students, in 1831. After a few unsuccessful attempts at opening a school, they took over the Patapsco Female Institute in Maryland, Almira serving as principal and John as business manager. Almira turned the school into a respectable Southern copy of the Troy Female Seminary with the purpose of taking "away from females their helplessness."

*M*utual benefits

Almira's writing is from an article she submitted to American Ladies Magazine, *Vol. IX, 1836.*

Marietta Holley

A state of mind

1883

Tom compared in his mind her fresh wild-rose loveliness with the professor's bony daughters—the only females he had been accustomed to seeing—and his heart beat more rapidly beneath his shining vest; she being a few years older than himself only added to her charms. For Tom's mind at this time was in the state usual to nineteen years.

Between the careless flowery path of boyhood and the calm region of manhood, there is an intermediate realm, paved thoroughly with self-conceit, a realm of hair oil, and gushing, though fickle, admiration for the opposite sex; but above all, and beneath all, matchless assurance and wisdom beyond all wisdom of later years. Tom Maynard was journeying through this realm.

Marietta Holley was born July 16, 1836, on the family farm in Jefferson County, New York. She began writing poetry as a young child, for which she was teased by her brothers. Her formal education ended at fourteen when financial difficulties forced her to give piano lessons to help support the family. She persisted with her writing, however, and her poems and stories were printed in several popular magazines.

In 1871 Marietta wrote the first comic narrative of the series that was to make her wealthy and famous. She created the characters Samantha Allen, the proper wife of Josiah Allen, and Betsy Bobbet, the eccentric old maid. She wrote twenty volumes about these characters, the last being published in 1914. Her books were enormously popular, with huge sales that enabled Marietta to command a $14,000 advance fee.

Marietta's writing is from her short story, "Katy Avenal," in Miss Richards' Boy, and Other Stories, *published in 1883.*

Although Marietta was asked to join the W.C.T.U. and the National Woman Suffrage Association, she preferred not to be affiliated with any groups. However, she worked her reform ideas into her books, covering women's rights, temperance, poor labor conditions and racial problems.

Mary Fenn Davis

1875

While the world is marching onward with such majestic strides in the paths of Science, Art and Literature— while printing presses, and steam presses, and railroad cars, and telegraph wires, and ocean steamers, and labor-saving machines are multiplying among us, can it be that the Soul stands still? Can it be that the light which two thousand years ago irradiated for a brief period a small portion of the moral horizon, is all that will ever be demanded by the race? Are the wings of the Spirit to be forever fettered, while mentality is seeking deeper depths and soaring to loftier heights?

Mary Fenn Davis was born July 17, 1824, on her father's farm in Clarendon, New York. Her parents were devout Baptists, and her father was an early crusader against alcohol.

Mary graduated with honors from Ingham University in 1846, then married Samuel Love, a teacher from Buffalo. On a visit to Boston they met Andrew Davis, the "Poughkeepsie Seer and Clairvoyant." After hearing his talk on "Spiritualism, Harmonial Philosophy, and Marriage and Divorce," Mary became a convert. She travelled to Indiana soon after to obtain a divorce, leaving her two children to be raised by their father.

Mary and Andrew Davis were married in 1855. Using his powers as a clairvoyant, he pronounced their marriage "a spiritually perfect union." She edited the *Herald of Progress*, a Spiritualist newspaper, and lectured frequently on woman's suffrage, temperance and the Harmonial Philosophy.

After thirty years together, Andrew announced that he had been misinformed by the spirits and their union did not, in fact, have the proper harmony. He had their marriage annulled and quickly remarried a young student. Mary was so shocked that her health became weakened, and she died a year and a half later.

Let loose the Spirit

Mary's writing is from Danger Signals: An Address on the Uses and Abuses of Spiritualism, *published in 1875.*

Helen Mar Gougar

For the vote

Helen's writing is from a speech she gave before the Senate Committee on Woman Suffrage, March 7, 1884. It is included in Volume IV of History of Woman Suffrage, *edited by Susan B. Anthony and Ida Husted Harper, published in 1902.*

1884

The older empires of the earth are sending to the United States a population drawn very largely from the asylums, penitentiaries, jails and poorhouses. They are emptying those men upon our shores, and within a few months they are intrusted with the ballot, the law-making power in this republic. . . . I, as an American-born woman, enter my protest at being compelled to live under laws made by this class of men while I am denied the protection that can only come from the ballot. While I would not have you take this right from those men whom we invite to our shores, I do ask you, in the face of this immense foreign immigration, to enfranchise the tax-paying, intelligent, moral, native-born women of America.

Helen Mar Jackson Gougar was born July 18, 1843, in Litchfield, Michigan. She was educated at home and at local Hillsdale College until financial necessity forced her to accept a teaching job when she was fifteen. She married John Gougar four years later.

In the late 1870's, Helen became involved with the woman suffrage and temperance movements. She discovered she had excellent skills as a speaker and went on the lecture circuit throughout the state of Indiana. She was so effective as a campaigner for the Republican Party that the Democrats tried to defame her character. She sued for slander and won a $5,000 settlement. However, the stress of the experience turned her hair permanently white.

Helen became disillusioned with the Republican Party because of their vacillation on temperance and woman suffrage issues and joined the National Prohibition Party.

Alice Dunbar-Nelson

Sunday, December 4, 1921
Century Club to hear Madame Inouye, the little Japanese woman, teacher of Domestic Science in the University of Tokyo, who is here interesting the American
women in disarmament. . . .

She wanted to have the women ask her questions. I
was much amused. The American public does not want
to be uplifted, ennobled—it wants to be amused. The
women wanted to know of her school life! It made me
think of myself, and some of the burning messages I
bring to audiences, and then they want me to recite a
dialect poem! She told about the school, but I sympa-
thized with her.

Alice Dunbar-Nelson was born July 19, 1875, to a middle-class
black family in New Orleans. She graduated in 1892 from the
two-year teachers' program at Straight College. Three years
later she published her first book, *Violets and Other Tales*, which
contained twelve poems and seventeen short stories.

The young black poet Paul Laurence Dunbar saw her
picture and read one of her poems in the Boston paper. Tremendously impressed, he began a two-year correspondence
with her. They finally met at a reception in his honor in New
York City on the eve of his departure for a lecture tour in
England. They became engaged that night.

Alice and Paul were married in 1898. Soon after, she
published her second book of "local-color" tales of French and
Creole characters set in New Orleans. They separated after
only four years of marriage, and Alice returned to teaching.
For the next eighteen years, she was the head of the English
department at a Delaware high school.

In 1920 Alice became the first black woman to serve on
Delaware's Republican State Committee. Defying a threat of
dismissal from her teaching job, she attended a conference at
the Ohio home of presidential candidate Warren G. Harding
to decide the party's position on racial problems. After losing
her teaching post, as threatened, she became associate editor of
the *Wilmington Advocate*, a weekly paper dedicated to the fight
for equal rights for black citizens.

Missing the message

Alice's writing is from Give
Us Each Day—The Diary
of Alice Dunbar-Nelson,
*edited by Gloria Hull,
published in 1984.*

Francesca Janauschek

A studious actress

1877

If people who go on the stage were more serious and better students, they would not have half the temptation and trouble they have now. At any rate, they would have something to talk about besides their dresses and their neighbors' doings. I hate gossip and I like study. If there was nothing left for me to study, I should have to invent something.

Francesca Roman Magdalena Janauschek, known as "Fanny," was born July 20, 1829, in Prague, Bohemia. She took ballet lessons as a child, but her real talent was in acting. By sixteen, she was playing major roles in Prague, and left soon after to conquer the German stage. For the next twenty years she was a major European star, touring throughout Germany, Austria and Russia.

In 1867 Fanny brought her own troupe of actors for a lengthy American tour, always performing in German as she spoke not a word of English. The well-known theatrical producer Augustin Daly promised her that if she could speak English she would be a great success, so she spent the next year studying. She later recalled, "I went into the country, took four professors, one for reading, one for grammar, one for pronunciation and the other to go over my roles with me. I studied twelve and fifteen hours a day. . . ."

Fanny's writing is an excerpt from an unknown article. It is included in her file in the Harvard Theatre Collection, Cambridge, Massachusetts.

Mr. Daly presented Fanny to New York theatergoers in numerous English-speaking roles such as Lady Macbeth and Elizabeth of England. In the late 1860's, she was one of the most popular women in her profession, praised by critics for her "imperious carriage, fiery declamation and noble gesture."

Sarah Maria Mousley

A wild prairie scene

Sarah's diary was typed from the original by a descendant, Mrs. Robert Snow, and donated to the Utah State Historical Society, Salt Lake City.

July 27, 1857

In the afternoon of this day I was called to witness the most terrific of all scenes, a stampede on the plain. The cattle started almost all together and Oh my father my heart sickens as I recall the scene and my soul is grieved in memory of the painful occurrence. I beheld men thrown, women leaping from their wagons, children screaming as team after team ran on in wild confusion dashing headlong on the wild prairie without power to impede their progress in the wild scene of apparent death. God gave me presence of mind sufficient to remain in my wagon which I did and alone except the unseen guardian who in God's wisdom did not leave me alone but shielded me from the shafts of the destroyer. I set or remained unhurt and beheld the cattle stopped and their affright calmed in answer to my fervent prayer.

Sarah Maria Mousley was born July 21, 1828, in Centreville, Delaware. When she was twenty-nine her family decided to move to Utah because of the anti-Mormon sentiment in the east. They took a train to Iowa City and went the remaining way by wagon train.

Shortly after their arrival in Salt Lake City, Sarah, age thirty, and her youngest sister Amanda, age twenty-one, were both wed to Angus M. Cannon, a leader of the Mormon Church. He originally only wanted to marry Amanda, but Brigham Young would not perform the ceremony unless he took the older sister as his first wife. Sarah had six children and Amanda had ten. Two more wives were brought into the family and Angus fathered a total of twenty-seven children.

Emma Lazarus

34 East 57th St.
Monday
December 1880
My Dear Mr. Stedman,

I return with many thanks Mrs. Fields' [June 6] poems. They seem to me very sweet, graceful and delicate, but what you say about their resemblance to my own work, confirms me more than ever in the opinion I have long held of my verses—that they are not of the slightest value or importance to the world. Here is a woman who takes the same interest that I take in purely poetic and classical thoughts, and evidently has the same desire to refine her thought and to rid her mind of everything prosaic and trivial and what does she accom-

She wished to stir, to awaken

Emma's letter to the critic and anthologist E.C. Stedman was found inside his copy of her first book of poetry. It is included here from an article published in the January, 1958, issue of Boston Public Library Quarterly.

plish. Nothing to stir, to awaken, to teach or to suggest, nothing that the world could not equally well do without! . . .

Emma Lazarus, poet and author, was born July 22, 1849, in New York City. She grew up in a wealthy, cultured environment with private education.

Emma published her first volume of verse when she was seventeen. Soon after that she met Ralph Waldo Emerson at a social gathering and began a long correspondence with her "mentor." She published her second volume of poetry four years later which was well received in both England and the United States.

Emma's family belonged to the oldest Jewish congregation in New York City, but she stopped attending services at an early age and showed little interest in Jewish history. She experienced an abrupt change in 1881-2 when the assassination of Czar Alexander II of Russia set off an outburst of Jewish persecution and a mass exodus of Jews to America. Emma anticipated the Zionist movement by ten years, advocating a national Jewish homeland in Palestine. She helped to establish the Hebrew Technical Institute in New York City to offer vocational training to displaced Russian Jews.

Emma is remembered by generations for the lines of her sonnet, "The New Colossus," inscribed on the pedestal of the Statue of Liberty:

Give me your tired, your poor,
Your huddled masses yearning to breathe free,
The wretched refuse of your teeming shore.
Send these, the homeless, tempest-tost to me,
I lift my lamp beside the golden door!

JULY 23

Charlotte Cushman

In mid-career

Charlotte's letter to her mother is from the book Charlotte Cushman: Her Letters and Memories of Her Life, *published in 1878.*

London
May 1, 1845
To Mother

I have just returned from the theatre, after acting the new play for the second time ["Infatuation" by James Kenny]. It has not succeeded; but my word was pledged to do it, and I have kept my word. It may, perhaps, do me some little injury, but I can afford a trifle, and my next play will bring me up. I am tired; I have acted four times this week, and I act to-morrow night again. Everything goes on finely; I am doing well, and I hope my star may continue in the ascendant. I have given myself *five years more*, and I think at the end of that time I will have $50,000 to retire upon; that will, if well invested, give us a comfortable home for the rest of our lives, and a quiet corner in some respectable graveyard.

Charlotte Saunders Cushman, actress, was born July 23, 1816, in Boston, Massachusetts. At thirteen she left school to work as a domestic but continued taking singing lessons. In 1835 her voice teacher arranged for her theatre debut. She was an instant success and audiences loved her.

After her first appearances on the London stage, the *London Sun* wrote: "Since the memorable first appearance of Edmund Kean in 1814, never has there been such a debut on the boards of the English theatre." She gave a performance for Queen Victoria in 1848 followed by two triumphant return tours of the United States.

Charlotte saved her money and invested it wisely, so that by the age of thirty-six she announced her retirement from the theatre. Thereafter she travelled between homes in London, Rome, Boston and Newport, entertaining her artistic group of friends.

Jean Webster

1912

Dear Kind-Trustee-Who-Sends-Orphans-to-College, . . .

I must say, however, that when I think about you, my imagination has very little to work upon. There are just three things that I know: You are tall. You are rich. You hate girls.

I suppose I might call you Dear Mr. Girl-Hater. Only that's sort of insulting to me. Or Dear Mr. Rich-Man, but that's insulting to you, as though money were the only important thing about you.

Maybe you won't stay rich all your life; lots of very clever men get smashed up in Wall Street. But at least you will stay tall all your life! So I've decided to call you Dear Daddy-Long-Legs. I hope you won't mind.

Daddy-Long-Legs

Jean's writing is from her most popular children's book, Daddy-Long-Legs, *published in 1912.*

Jean Webster was born July 24, 1876, in Fredonia, New York. Christened Alice Jane, she chose the name "Jean" in boarding school. While attending Vassar College, she wrote a weekly column in the *Poughkeepsie Sunday Courier* to earn extra money. She also began writing the popular Patty Stories, which were collected and published in 1903 with the title *When Patty Went to College*.

Jean made several trips abroad following graduation and turned her experiences into books. Her own personal favorite was *The Wheat Princess*, written during the winter she spent in a convent in Italy's Sabine Mountains.

Upon her return to America, Jean settled in Greenwich Village. She did philanthropic work in orphanages, which led to her best-selling book, *Daddy-Long-Legs*, about a miserable orphan who was finally set free at seventeen when an anonymous man sent her to college. In 1914 Jean adapted it for the theater, and in 1919 it was made into a movie with Mary Pickford.

In 1915, Jean married Glenn McKinney, a New York lawyer. She died the following year giving birth to her daughter, Jean Webster McKinney, who survived.

Anna Symmes Harrison

Coping with loss

Anna's writing is from "Short Family Papers; Anna Harrison to John Cleves Short," in the Manuscript Division of the Library of Congress.

Northbend August 29, 1854
My dear Nephew,

I feel very sincerely for you and my dear Mary in the loss of your dear babe. I well remember my feelings at the death of my dear Infant, I thought it was like tearing my heart asunder. To mourn we must, but we must try to keep from mourning, very dark are the ways of Providence to us, shortsighted Mortals—but we cannot often feel it so to be.

Anna Symmes Harrison, wife of the ninth president of the United States, was born July 25, 1775, in Flatbrook, New Jersey. After her mother died she was raised by her grandparents for fourteen years until her father remarried and sent for her to join him in Ohio. She stopped en route in Kentucky to visit her sister, where she met William Henry Harrison, a young army officer. Against her father's objections Anna and William were married in 1795. Despite Harrison's success, her father never liked him, and it was fifteen years before he treated him civilly.

As William forged a political career steering him towards

the presidency, Anna assisted him as a charming hostess. She also provided him with a pleasant home life as she raised their nine children. Unfortunately, she wasn't able to serve as First Lady, as illness forced her to miss the inauguration, and one month later, as she was packing for Washington, her husband died suddenly of pneumonia.

Elizabeth Wormeley Latimer

1892

Christmas Day of that sad year [1871] arrived at last, and New Year's Day, the great and joyful fête-day in all French families. A few confectioners kept their stores open, and a few boxes of bonbons were sold; but presents of potatoes, or small packages of coffee, were by this time more acceptable gifts. Nothing was plenty in Paris but champagne and Colman's mustard. The rows upon rows of the last-named article in the otherwise empty windows of the grocers reminded Englishmen and Americans of Grumio's cruel offer to poor Katherine of the mustard without the beef, since she could not have the beef with the mustard.

Here is the bill-of-fare of a dinner given at a French restaurant upon that Christmas Day:

Soup from horse meat.

Mince of cat.

Shoulder of dog with tomato sauce.

Jugged cat with mushrooms.

Roast donkey and potatoes.

Rat, peas, and celery.

Mice on toast.

Plum pudding.

One remarkable feature of the siege was that everybody's appetite increased enormously. Thinking about food stimulated the craving for it, and by New Year's Day there were serious apprehensions of famine.

Elizabeth Wormeley Latimer was born July 26, 1822, in London. She travelled extensively throughout Europe and Africa in her youth and resided in London and Paris. In her twenties after the family returned to the United States, she published several novels.

Champagne and mustard

Elizabeth's description of Paris during the Franco-Prussian War in 1871 is from her book, France in the Nineteenth Century, 1830-1890, *published in 1892.*

Elizabeth married Randolph Latimer in 1856 and they settled in Maryland. She did not write for twenty years while she raised her family. However, during the last thirty years of her life she produced a tremendous amount of work: novels, magazine articles, histories and translations from the French and Italian. Elizabeth loved history and the exploits of royalty, military men and explorers. Her best works were about such historical figures.

Linda Richards

A happy home

Linda's writing is from Reminiscences of Linda Richards—America's First Trained Nurse, *published in 1911.*

1911

We had in our grandfather's house a very comfortable and happy home. He was my most intimate friend. I would sit upon his knees brushing his snow-white hair, and would confide to him all my school joys and sorrows. I received much valuable advice from him during these talks. My grandfather was a very religious man, and we always attended church and Sunday school. On Sunday afternoons grandfather always went for a walk. He was thin and over six feet in height, and I was small and stout, and had to trot to keep up with him. He seldom talked to me on these long walks, but I could not have been hired to remain at home. There was nothing hard in my young life; hardships began with hospital life, where the first years were indeed very hard.

Linda Richards was born July 27, 1841, near Potsdam, New York. At thirteen she joined the Free Will Baptist Church during a religious revival. She showed an early interest in nursing, administering to sick neighbors in her village, and became determined to study medicine. She held onto her dream through seven years of factory work, finally training at Boston City Hospital in 1870 as an assistant nurse. She transferred to the newly formed school at the New England Hospital for Women and Children and received their first diploma in 1873.

Linda travelled to England in 1877 to fulfill her "long-cherished plan" of studying under Florence Nightingale. Upon her return to Boston, she helped establish a nursing school at Boston City Hospital based on the Nightingale system.

In 1886 Linda moved to Japan to open the first nursing school at the Doshisha Hospital in Kyoto. She did evangelical work in addition to her teaching, and considered the five years she spent in Japan to be the happiest of her life.

Ill health forced Linda to return to America, where she continued working to improve nursing education until her retirement when she was seventy.

Frances Campbell Sparhawk

1925

One day in the garden room Whittier spoke laughingly of some early stories of his that he had recently found when rummaging in the garret. He assured his listener—the writer—that they were not so bad! No persuasion, however, could induce him to show them, or even tell her more about them. But not a few of his poems have a dramatic touch which suggests that had he not been reformer and poet, he would have been famous in romance.

*H*idden talent

Frances Campbell Sparhawk was born July 28, 1847, in Amesbury, Massachusetts. She was a sickly child, unable to attend school. She accompanied her father, a physician, on his rounds and benefited greatly from his wisdom. Another influence upon her youth was the poet John Greenleaf Whittier, a neighbor with whom she formed a close friendship.

In her twenties, Frances wrote stories for papers and magazines, and published her first book in 1881. A concern for the American Indian led her to visit numerous reservations and Indian Schools. She spent some time at the Carlisle Indian School where she edited the school paper, *Red Man*. She turned these experiences into two popular books published in 1890 and 1892.

Frances' writing, referring to herself in the third person, is from Whittier at Close Range, *published in 1925.*

Isabella Marshall Graham

1811

. . . One year and three months will complete my three score and ten. I do not know one individual alive, whom I knew in my school days; it has been the case for many years . . . my children under God, care for me. I

*T*hree score and ten

have my dear little room, my bible and books founded on it. I have a dear Pastor, and Christian friends . . . my cup runs over with blessings.

Isabella Marshall Graham was born July 29, 1742, in Lanarkshire, Scotland. She married Dr. John Graham, a local widower, in 1765. They moved to Canada, where he was physician to a British Army Regiment.

Eight years later they were transferred to Antigua, but John passed away shortly after their arrival. Isabella was left penniless, pregnant with her fifth child. She returned to Scotland to live with her father.

Isabella opened a small school in her home which expanded into a girls' boarding school in Edinburgh. In 1789 she returned to America and opened a new school in New York City. Within a few years her daughters all married well-to-do New York merchants, and Isabella was free to devote herself to her philanthropic interests.

Isabella's writing is from a letter she wrote to a friend and is included in The Power of Faith Exemplified in the Life and Writings of the Late Mrs. Isabella Graham, *published in 1816.*

She co-founded the Society for the Relief of Widows and Children, one of the first charities in the United States. She gave religious instruction to orphans and children in the public almshouse, and visited prisoners and inmates of the lunatic asylum. Shortly before her death at seventy-one, she established a weekend school for young people who worked in factories, to further their education.

JULY 30

Susan Shelby Magoffin

*E*xperiencing mysteries

1846
Thursday July 30
Well this is my nineteenth birthday! And what? . . . . I am sick! Strange sensations in my head, my back, and hips, I am obliged to lie down most of the time. . . .
August 1846, Thursday 6
The mysteries of a new world have been shown to me since last Thursday! In a few short months I should have been a happy mother . . . Friday morning 31st of July my pains commenced . . . after midnight all was over. I have been in my bed till yesterday [a week]. An Indian woman in the room below me . . . gave birth to a fine healthy baby and in half an hour after she went to the River and bathed herself and it. Never could I have believed such a thing, if I had not been here. . . .

Susan's writing is from Down the Santa Fe Trail and Into Mexico: The Diary of Susan Shelby Magoffin, 1846-1847, *edited by Stella Drumm, published in 1926.*

Susan Shelby Magoffin was born July 30, 1827, in Arcadia, Kentucky. Her grandfather was the first governor of the state. In 1845 she married Samuel Magoffin, a neighbor twenty-six years her senior.

Samuel and his brother James had been taking yearly caravans of goods from Independence, Missouri, to Mexico and back. Six months after their marriage, Samuel left for his annual journey. Although raised on a plantation in luxurious style, Susan chose to accompany her husband west, thus becoming the first white woman to travel the Santa Fe Trail.

Susan kept a diary of their trip from June 11, 1846, to September 8, 1847. She was pregnant during the journey, caught yellow fever in Matamoras, and gave birth to a stillborn son. They later settled in Barrett's Station, Missouri, and had two daughters. Susan died suddenly when she was twenty-eight.

Sarah Alden Ripley

1845

Transition

Who can call life tame when it is so full of wonder and sorrow and love? . . . I once thought a solitary life the true one, and, contrary to my theory, was moved to give up the independence of an attic covered with books for the responsibilities and perplexities of a parish and a family. Yet I have never regretted the change. Though I have suffered much, yet I have enjoyed much and learned more. The affections as they multiply, spread out in rays to the circumference, but the soul returns, not driven back by desertion, but willingly, to its true centre, the God within.

Sarah Alden Ripley was born July 31, 1793, in Boston, Massachusetts. She married the Reverend Samuel Ripley and they had nine children.

The Ripleys opened a boarding school for boys in their home to accommodate fourteen pupils. Sarah taught Greek and Latin. She was known to be one of the foremost Greek scholars in the country.

Sarah was an avid reader and a popular figure in the intellectual circles of her time. Following her death, her close friend Ralph Waldo Emerson wrote, "her delight in books was not tainted by any wish to shine, or any appetite for praise or influence."

Sarah's letter to her friend and future son-in-law, George Simmons, is included in Worthy Women of Our First Century, *by O.J. Wister and Agnes Irwin, published in 1877.*

AUGUST

Maria Mitchell

1878

An astronomer's journey

I had a friend who lived in Denver, and she was visiting me. I sought her at once, and with fear and trembling asked, "Have you a bit of land behind your house in Denver where I could put up a small telescope?" "Six hundred miles," was the laconic reply!

I felt that the hospitality of the Rocky Mountains was at my feet. Space and time are so unconnected! For an observation which would last two minutes forty seconds, I was offered six hundred miles, after a journey of thousands.

A journey from Boston to Denver makes one hopeful for the future of our country. We had hour after hour and day after day of railroad travel, over level, unbroken land on which cattle fed unprotected, summer and winter, and which seemed to implore the traveler to stay and to accept its richness. It must be centuries before the now-unpeopled land of western Kansas and Colorado can be crowded.

Maria Mitchell was born August 1, 1818, on Nantucket Island, off the Massachusetts coast, when Nantucket was the greatest whaling port in the world. One of her father's jobs was to rate the whaling fleets' chronometers by checking them through stellar observations. As a child, Maria began assisting him out on the widow's walk of their house. She witnessed her first solar eclipse at the age of twelve. When asked in later years how she became an astronomer, she replied, "In Nantucket people quite generally are in the habit of observing the heavens, and a sextant will be found in almost every house."

Maria became the librarian of the Nantucket Athenaeum when she was eighteen, holding the position for the next twenty years. The library was only open afternoons, so Maria was free to roam the stacks during the mornings, studying whatever pleased her. After dinner, she joined her father in the observatory he had built on the roof of the Pacific Bank. His lookout became a station of the United States Coast Survey, and they made thousands of observations to determine time, latitude and longitude.

On October 1, 1847, using her two-inch Dollong telescope, Maria discovered a new comet. After it was proven that she was indeed the first person to see the comet, it was named

Maria's journal entry, describing her trip to Denver to observe a solar eclipse, is included in Maria Mitchell, Life, Letters and Journals, *compiled by Phebe Mitchell Kendall, published in 1894.*

for her. She became famous worldwide and was awarded a gold medal by the king of Denmark.

In the early 1860's, Matthew Vassar was preparing to open his female college. He wanted to add someone of Maria's reputation to his first faculty, so he offered to build her an observatory with a twelve-inch telescope (the third largest in the country at that time). Maria hesitated, doubting her own teaching credentials since she had never attended college herself. She decided to try, and was one of Vassar's greatest teachers for the next twenty-three years.

Eliza Orne White

*T*he invalid

1898

Elsie was ill again. Poor Elsie had had so many little illnesses of late, and demanded so much sympathy, that her friends were beginning to tire of her pretty invalid ways. First there was the cold she took by going out in her slippers on Christmas Eve, which was very careless of her, as her husband did not fail to point out; and then there was the attack of grippe she had, after her cousin Helen's wedding, when she would insist upon wearing a low-necked gown, contrary to Dr. Reycroft's orders; and now that the east winds of May had arrived, her neuralgia returned.

Eliza Orne White was born August 2, 1856, in Keene, New Hampshire. An early childhood influence was her mother's closest friend, Lucretia Hale [September 2], author of the children's book *The Peterkin Papers*. Eliza later wrote, "Aunt Lucretia was the most perfect companion for any child. She never made you feel you were an inferior."

Eliza followed in the footsteps of her Aunt Lucretia, publishing her first children's story at the age of eighteen. She went on to write forty books. Some were for adults, but the majority were humorous children's books set in New England, detailing the perils of growing up.

Eliza eventually went deaf and spent the last thirty years of her life totally blind. Nonetheless, she retained her vivid imagination and continued to write prolifically, publishing her last book, *When Esther was a Little Girl*, seventy-five years after the appearance of her first collection of short stories.

Eliza's writing is from A Lover of Truth, *published in 1898.*

Give Her This Day

Ada Matilda Bittenbender

1891

Woman's influence in the court room as counsel is pro-
motive of good in more than one respect. Invectives
against opposing counsel, so freely made use of in some
courts, are seldom indulged in when woman stands as
the opponent. And in social impurity cases, language, in
her presence, becomes more chaste, and the moral tone
thereby elevated perceptibly. But there should be one
more innovation brought into general vogue, that of the
mixed jury system. When we shall have women both as
lawyers and jurors to assist in the trial of cases, then, and
not until then, will woman's influence for good in the
administration of justice be truly felt.

Ada Matilda Cole Bittenbender was born August 3, 1848, in
Macedonia, Pennsylvania. She married Henry Bittenbender, a
lawyer, in 1878, and they moved to Osceola, Nebraska.
      Ada taught school in Nebraska and edited the *Osceola
Record*, a Republican newspaper. She gradually became an
active feminist, helping to organize the Nebraska Woman
Suffrage Association. In 1882 she served as president of that
organization. Meanwhile, she had been studying law with her
husband's guidance. She became Nebraska's first female
attorney and joined her husband's practice as his partner, frequently trying cases in state and federal courts.
      From 1883 to 1889 Ada was superintendent of temper-
ance legislation on the Nebraska W.C.T.U., and in 1887 she
took on the same role for the National W.C.T.U. She also
served as their lawyer, spending a great deal of time in Washington, D.C. She gave up both positions in the early 1890's to
return to Nebraska and her lucrative private practice.

*Ada's writing is from her
chapter "Women in Law" in
*Woman's Work in America,
edited by Annie Meyer,
published in 1891.*

Esther Hill Hawks

*Hopkinton
Aug. 21st, 1856*

Bless you my darling husband for that precious letter! It
was just what my soul craved. I wanted some loving
words from you and I have got them. I was beginning

*Esther's letter is in the Hawks
Papers, Manuscript Division,
Library of Congress.*

to feel that you were angry at me for staying away so long. So I had pictured over and over again our meeting. I should come into the store and you would just *nod* a little, perhaps touch the ends of my fingers, looking *tremendously* sober all the time, I should stand round trying to look very indifferent, for a few minutes then go into the little room and have a real hard cry. Then there would be bitter words on both sides and "after the storm cometh the sunshine"—but now I *know* we shall meet without the clouds for I am coming home on Saturday if it is possible.

Esther Jane Hill Hawks was born August 4, 1833, in Hookset, New Hampshire. When she was seventeen, she accompanied her friend, Helen, to Manchester to visit Helen's brother, Dr. John Milton Hawks. Esther was smitten instantly, but he continued to play the field for several years, visiting churches and sewing circles to look over women.

Esther and Milton were married at last in 1854 and settled in Florida. While there she taught at a private school in a Methodist church and risked imprisonment for violating the law by running a school for Negro children.

Upon their return to New Hampshire, Esther began an informal yet intense study of medicine. She became determined to be a doctor and enrolled at the New England Female Medical College. She graduated two years later with six other women.

At the outbreak of the Civil War, Esther went to Washington to volunteer her services as a doctor, or at least as a nurse. However, the federal government was not hiring female doctors, and Dorothea Dix, Superintendent of Army Nurses, would only hire middle-aged, plain women. Esther, a known beauty, five feet seven inches tall with long curly hair, did not qualify. She returned to Manchester, and Milton went South instead to do war work.

After the war the Hawks resettled in Florida, but Esther felt isolated and unfulfilled. In 1870 she returned alone to Lynn, Massachusetts, where she opened a medical practice with a friend and classmate from medical school. Her practice flourished, primarily treating women with gynecological problems. Upon her death the minister eulogized, "She has been doing God's work in the world."

Clara Bewick Colby

1900

The way up the heights of woman's advancement has been long and steep, but it has not been dreary. The greatest men of the century have walked with us; poets have sung for us; prophets have inspired us with visions of success; statesmen have made courts and forums ring with eloquence in our behalf; stones have blossomed into roses; scorn has become applause; timidity, opposition and indifference have changed into a grand chorus of appeal for women's equality before the law. Let us then close the nineteenth century with a convention which shall be a jubilee for our successes and the preparation for the twentieth century, which is to be not man's nor woman's but humanity's.

A glorious century

Clara Dorothy Bewick Colby was born August 5, 1846, in Gloucester, England. Her father moved the family to a farm near Windsor, Wisconsin, when she was three. Clara attended the University of Wisconsin, taking the regular men's curriculum rather than that of the University's "Female College." The president threatened to withhold her degree, but relented, and she was named valedictorian and Phi Beta Kappa.

Clara pursued graduate studies in French, Greek and chemistry while earning a living teaching Latin and history. In 1871 she married Leonard Colby, and they moved to Beatrice, Nebraska, where he set up a law practice. They adopted two children: a three-year-old orphan from the streets of New York who died as a young man, and a Sioux Indian baby whom Leonard found in her dead mother's arms after the Battle of Wounded Knee. As an adult, she performed in Wild West shows and early Western movies.

Clara established a free library in Beatrice in 1873 and initiated a series of lectures through which she met many leading suffragists of the day. She became a convert, and helped organize the Nebraska Woman Suffrage Association, of which she was president for thirteen years. From 1883 to 1909, she published and edited the weekly *Woman's Tribune*, one of the major voices of the women's movement.

Clara's writing is from a speech she gave before the thirty-second annual convention of the National Woman Suffrage Association in 1900. It is included in Democratic Ideals—A Memorial Sketch of Clara B. Colby, *edited by Olympia Brown, published in 1917.*

Susie King Taylor

Black woman travels
south

1902

On February 3, 1898, I was called to Shreveport, La., to
the bedside of my son, who was very ill. He had been
traveling on business when he fell ill, and had been sick
two weeks when they sent to me. I tried to have him
brought home to Boston, but they could not send him,
as he was not able to sit and ride this long distance; so
on the sixth of February I left Boston to go to him. I
reached Cincinnati on the eighth, where I took a train
for the south. I asked a white man standing near—before I got my train what car I should take.

"Take that one," he said, pointing to one.

"But that is a smoking car!"

"Well," he replied, "that is the car for colored
people." I went to this car, and on entering it all my
courage failed me. I have ridden in many coaches, but I
was never in such as these. I wanted to return home
again, but when I thought of my sick boy I said, "Well,
others ride in these cars and I must do likewise," and
tried to be resigned, for I wanted to reach my boy, as I
did not know whether I should find him alive. . . .

I got to Marion, Miss., at two o'clock in the morning, arrived at Vicksburg at noon, and at Shreveport
about eight o'clock in the evening, and found my son
just recovering from a severe hemorrhage. He was very
anxious to come home, and I tried to secure a berth for
him on a sleeper, but they would not sell me one, and he
was not strong enough to travel otherwise. If I could
only have gotten him to Cincinnati, I might have
brought him home, but as I could not I was forced to let
him remain where he was. It seemed very hard, when his
father fought to protect the Union and our flag, yet his
boy was denied, under this same flag, a berth to carry
him home to die, because he was a Negro.

Susie's writing is from her book,
Reminiscences of My Life in
Camp, *published in 1902.*

Susie King Taylor was born a slave August 6, 1848, on one of
the Sea Islands off the coast of Savannah, Georgia. Her
mother married at thirteen and had nine children, of whom
Susie was the eldest. At seven she went to Savannah to live

with her grandmother, where she learned to read and write illegally. She was taught by a free woman in her home and she "went every day about nine o'clock, with her books wrapped in paper to prevent the police or white persons from seeing them."

In 1862, when the Union soldiers began firing on Fort Pulaski, Susie and many others fled to St. Simon's Island under the protection of the Union fleet.

About six hundred men, women and children were on St. Simon's during the War. Susie took charge of a school and had forty pupils. Later they were transferred to a camp in Beaufort, South Carolina, where Susie worked as a laundress and continued to teach and nurse the sick. She married Edward King, a liberated slave who served in the first Negro regiment of the Grand Army of the Republic. The first black troops did not receive any pay for eighteen months, and Susie didn't receive any money for her services for four years and three months, but she "was glad, however, to be allowed to go with the regiment, to care for the sick and afflicted comrades."

In 1866 the regiment was mustered out, and Susie and her husband returned to Savannah. She opened a school in her home as there were no public schools for Negro children. "I had twenty children at my school, and received $1.00 a month for each pupil. I also had a few older ones who came at night."

Sergeant King died in 1866 while Susie was expecting their first child. She had to give up teaching, place the baby with her mother, and take up domestic work. She worked in the South until 1873 when she moved to Boston. There she worked as a maid for four years until her marriage to Russell Taylor. "All this time my interest in the boys in blue had not abated. I was still loyal and true, whether they were black or white. My hands never left undone anything they could do towards their aid and comfort in the twilight of their lives." In 1886 she organized the Boston branch of the Women's Relief Corps and became its president in 1893.

Alice James

February 2nd 1892

This long slow dying is no doubt instructive, but it is disappointingly free from excitements: "naturalness" being carried to its supreme expression. One sloughs off the activities one by one, and never knows that they're gone, until one suddenly finds that the months

The narrowing circle

Alice's writing is from Alice James: Her Brother—Her Journal, *published in 1934.*

have slipped away and the sofa will never more be laid upon, the morning paper read, or the loss of the new book regretted; one revolves with equal content within the narrowing circle until the vanishing point is reached, I suppose.

Alice James was born August 7, 1848, in New York City. She was the youngest of five, and the only daughter in a family of dynamic achievers; one brother was the psychologist William James, and another was the novelist Henry James. Alice had to develop quickly a strong intellect and bold manner just to be able to participate in dinner-table conversations.

Mr. James uprooted his family frequently, travelling through Switzerland, France and England for extended periods. Alice and her brothers felt like "hotel children." Upon settling in Cambridge, Massachusetts, when she was sixteen, she had her first nervous breakdown, after which she had recurring bouts of illness.

At the age of thirty, Alice went into a severe depression from which she never totally recovered. Her parents' deaths four years later left her financially comfortable. She departed for England to visit her brother Henry, but became ill en route and rarely left her bed thereafter. She began a journal, recording her innermost thoughts and fears as her illness progressed. She died of cancer in Kensington, England, at the age of forty-three.

AUGUST 8   *Alice Gordon Gulick*

Correcting a child

Santandei, Spain
February 23, 1877
Dear ones at home:

The last number of Henry Ward Beecher's paper, *The Christian Union*, contained some very lengthy advice to parents on the training of their children. Among other things the writer remarked that they should never say "you shall" or "you must not" but rather "I prefer that you should or should not do so and so." Jamie was in mischief this morning. That is, he had taken a towel and dipped it in water, and was slapping it on the floor in imitation of the Spanish washer-women, and it became necessary to correct him. So I said gently, "Jamie I prefer you should not do so." He did not even

Alice's letter is in the Gulick Collection, Houghton Library, Harvard University.

Give Her This Day

look up. Then William rose to his feet and said, "Jamie, we jointly prefer you should cease that "ar mork!" He slapped all the more vigorously—and by actual experiment we found that the old fashioned "thou shall not" had more power.

Alice Winfield Gordon Gulick was born August 8, 1847, in Boston. After graduating from Mount Holyoke Seminary, she stayed on as a teacher. On October 3, 1870, she married Alvah Kittredge, a tutor at nearby Amherst College, but he was very ill and died the next day.

Alice remarried the following year to Reverend William Gulick. He had been raised in Hawaii by missionary parents and planned to continue in their footsteps. Within a week of their wedding, William and Alice, plus his brother and his wife, sailed for Spain.

Alice came to feel her best efforts were through education, so in 1877 she opened a boarding school with five girls. The school, known as the Colegio Norte Americano, grew in size and reputation as teachers from America came to assist. In 1892 she undertook the establishment of a school for higher learning, patterned after United States women's colleges such as Mount Holyoke and Wellesley.

Alice made five speaking tours of the United States to raise funds for her International Institution for Girls in Spain. The long years of labor and travel took their toll, and she contracted tuberculosis in 1903 and died within the year.

Elizabeth Schuyler Hamilton

Albany, New York
August 11, 1804
To William S. Smith
President of the Society of Cincinnati
Sir,

Consolation

To the distress of a heart so deeply afflicted as mine from the irreparable loss of a most amiable and affectionate husband. I trust the respectable society in which you preside will impute the delay of the Acknowledgment for their consolatory letter . . . the wounded heart derives a degree of consolation from the tenderness with which its loss is bewailed by the virtuous, the wise and humane, and also from that high honor and respect with

Elizabeth's writing is included in the Hamilton Papers, Manuscript Division, Library of Congress.

which the memory of the dear deceased has been commemorated. . . .

> I am Sir with great respect your Obedient Servant
> E. Hamilton

Elizabeth Schuyler Hamilton was born August 9, 1757, in Albany, New York. She married Alexander Hamilton in 1780; the couple had eight children. In 1789 Hamilton was appointed as the first secretary of the treasury in the newly formed United States government, and Elizabeth became a prominent member of political society.

In 1804, three years after Elizabeth's oldest son had been killed in a duel, Alexander was killed in his well-publicized duel with Aaron Burr. Elizabeth spent the last fifty years of her life preserving and enhancing her husband's reputation.

Elizabeth gathered every word Alexander wrote for publication, and was especially intent on proving that he had penned most of Washington's Farewell Address. She was assisted by her son John who shared her belief in his father's outstanding abilities.

Eliza Frances Andrews

*I*ndignant

May 14, 1865

On my way to church I had a striking illustration of the difference between our old friends and our new masters. The streets were thronged with rebel soldiers, and in one part of my walk, I had to pass where a large number of them were gathered on the pavement, some sitting, some standing, some lying down, but as soon as I appeared, the way was instantly cleared for me, the men standing like a wall, on either side, with hats off, until I had passed. A little farther on I came to a group of Yankees and negroes that filled up the sidewalk, but not one of them budged, and I had to flank them by going out into the dusty road. It is the first time in my life that I have ever had to give up the sidewalk to a man, much less to negroes! I was so indignant that I did not carry a devotional spirit to church.

Eliza's writing is from The War-Time Journal of a Georgia Girl, *published in 1908.*

Eliza Frances Andrews was born August 10, 1840, at Haywood, her parents' plantation near Washington, Georgia. Her father was a lawyer, and he encouraged all his eight children to study and read. Eliza, called "Fanny," received an A.B. degree in the first graduating class from La Grange Female College.

The Civil War divided the Andrews family. Although he owned two hundred slaves, Mr. Andrews was a Unionist opposed to secession, while all his children were avid Confederates. Late in 1864, after Sherman's March to the Sea, Fanny and her younger sister were forced to leave their plantation. It was during this period that she decided to become a writer, and upon returning to Haywood she declared she would never marry, in order to pursue her career.

Fanny published several magazine articles, but her father's death in 1873 forced her to teach out of financial necessity. She taught French, literature and botany at various institutions through 1903, but continued writing in her spare time. Her first novel was published in 1876 and enjoyed some success. She produced other novels, but her most important work was her Civil War diary, which she published forty years after writing it.

Octavia Walton Le Vert

Paris
1857
The ladies' dresses were very brilliant, and precious jewels sparkled on their bosoms. But to the vast circumference of the *petticoats* our eyes have not yet become accustomed. They resemble half-inflated balloons, just rising from the ground, and the wearers appear compelled to push the skirts along as they walk. The *courtesy*, or *curtsy* now in vogue, is most extraordinary. The ladies can no longer move back a step or two, and incline forward (as was their custom formerly), without knocking over some small man by the weight of their petticoats; therefore, instead of bending forward, they give a sudden "duck down." . . .

Octavia Celeste Walton Le Vert was born August 11, 1811, at Bellevue, her grandfather's home near Augusta, Georgia. She was privately tutored and specialized in languages.

In 1835, the Walton family moved to Mobile, Alabama. The following year, Octavia was married to Dr. Henry Le Vert. They had five children.

Octavia published her first book in 1857, a two-volume work describing her European journeys. Her writing,

The latest fashion

Octavia's writing is from her Souvenirs of Travel, *published in 1857.*

recounting tales of society life abroad, catered to the mid-nineteenth century romantic imagination.

Dr. Le Vert died during the Civil War, and the family fortune was lost. Octavia was shunned by local residents for having opposed secession and for entertaining Union officers, so she resettled in New York City. She was a co-founder of Sorosis, one of the first women's clubs.

A U G U S T   1 2

Katharine Lee Bates

A vision of America

1930

America the Beautiful was written in its original form, more literary and ornate than the present version, in the summer of 1893. I was making my first trip west. After visiting at Chicago the World's Fair, where I was naturally impressed by the symbolic beauty of the White City, I went on to Colorado Springs. Here I spent three weeks or so under the purple range of the Rockies, which looked down with surprise on a summer school. This had called to its facility several instructors from the east. . . . My own subject, which seemed incongruous enough under that new and glowing sky, was English Religious Drama.

We strangers celebrated the close of the session by a merry expedition to the top of Pike's Peak, making the ascent by the only method then available for people not vigorous enough to achieve the climb on foot nor adventurous enough for burro-riding. Prairie wagons, their tail-boards emblazoned with the traditional slogan, "Pike's Peak or Bust," were pulled by horses up to the halfway house, where the horses were relieved by mules. We were hoping for half an hour on the summit, but two of our party became so faint in the rarified air that we were bundled into the wagons again and started on our downward plunge so speedily that our sojourn on the peak remains in memory hardly more than one ecstatic gaze. It was then and there, as I was looking out over the sea-like expanse of fertile country spreading away so far under those ample skies, that the opening lines of the hymn floated into my mind. That the hymn has gained, in these twenty-odd years, such a hold as it

Katharine's writing is from An Autobiography in Brief of Katharine Lee Bates, *privately printed in 1930.*

has upon our people, is clearly due to the fact that Americans are at heart idealists, with a fundamental faith in human brotherhood.

Katharine Lee Bates, poet, English professor and author of "America the Beautiful," was born on August 12, 1859, in Falmouth, Massachusetts. Her father died when she was an infant, leaving his widow with four children and very little money.

Katharine was able to go to Wellesley College with the generous help of her brother and graduated in 1880. She taught for several years at Dana Hall, a girls' preparatory school. She loved the school and it was difficult for her to leave it when she was offered a professorship at Wellesley in 1886. She eventually became the head of the English literature department and was a major force in policy formation at the young college.

Katharine had been interested in writing since childhood. Once, while quarantined in a Boston attic for twenty-eight days after being exposed to smallpox, she passed her time writing a children's story for a prize contest. She won $700 and used the money for her first trip to Europe. She traveled frequently to Europe and wrote prolifically to supplement her salary: travel books, children's books, textbooks. Poetry, however, was her first love. Six volumes of her verse appeared in her lifetime and two were published posthumously.

Katharine is best known for her poem, "America the Beautiful," inspired by her first trip west. The only payment she ever received for writing America's unofficial second national anthem was a small check from the weekly journal, *The Congregationalist*, where it was first published on July 4, 1895.

Lucy Stone

1855

The last speaker alluded to this movement as being that of a few disappointed women. From the first years to which my memory stretches, I have been a disappointed woman. When, with my brothers, I reached forth after the sources of knowledge, I was reproved with "It isn't fit for you; it doesn't belong to women." Then there was but one college in the world where women were admitted, and that was in Brazil. I would have found my way there, but by the time I was prepared to go, one was

A determined woman

Lucy's writing is from a speech given before the National Convention in Ohio in 1855. It is included in Volume I of History of Woman Suffrage, *edited by Elizabeth Cady Stanton, Susan B. Anthony and Matilda Joslyn Gage, and published in 1881.*

opened in the young State of Ohio—the first in the United States where women and negroes could enjoy opportunities with white men. . . .

In education, in marriage, in religion, in everything, disappointment is the lot of woman. It shall be the business of my life to deepen this disappointment in every woman's heart until she bows down to it no longer.

Lucy Stone was born August 13, 1818, near West Brookfield, Massachusetts. As a child, she was already aware of the inferior role women played to men; her mother believed that a husband ruled his family by divine right. After reading in the Bible that men should rule women, Lucy felt the translation must have been incorrect. She decided to attend college, study Greek and Hebrew, and rectify the situation.

In 1843, supporting herself through teaching and house-work, Lucy entered Oberlin College. She learned in her Greek and Hebrew courses that certain Bible passages regarding women's roles had indeed been misconstrued, and she used this in later years as part of her forceful argument for women's rights.

Lucy had always said she would never marry so that she would "call no man master." However, a persistent Henry Blackwell courted her for two years, reassuring her that she could continue her women's rights work with his assistance. They were married in 1855, but Lucy retained her last name. The phrase "Lucy Stoner" came into vernacular to signify a married woman who kept her maiden name.

Lucy worked tirelessly for her cause, writing and lectur-ing, until a few months before her death at age seventy-five. Always testing new boundaries, Lucy requested her body be cremated, thus becoming the first person cremated in New England.

Charlotte Fowler Wells

Conversing with spirits

Charlotte's writing is from a report on spiritualist meetings in New York City. It is included among the Charlotte Fowler Wells papers in the Department of Manuscripts at Cornell University Library.

1850

When being asked if they the spirits had any directions to give for our guidance during the evening, they asked for the alphabet and spelled, "shut out the light," which being put in the hall they expressed satisfaction, and we seated ourselves around the table and joined hands, keeping perfectly quiet, when, to our surprise, in the

---

course of a few minutes Almira was much affected mag-
netically and Edward passed to the superior condition
for the first time. . . . After a few minutes, he said, "the
past is an *atom* to what is before us. God is everything.
The Earth is a part of God. What do we mean by Eter-
nity and the Universe? Imagination is far below its conception." . . .

After conversing with the spirits of some of his old
friends, and receiving directions for the next Wed. evening, he joined hands with us, and after apparently watching the departure of spirits as they soared aloft, he awoke
and knew nothing of what happened until we told him.

Charlotte Fowler Wells was born August 14, 1814, in Cohoc-
ton, New York. She was educated at local schools, supple-
menting her knowledge by self-instruction at home. She
began her teaching career when she was nineteen.

In the early 1830's Charlotte became enthralled with
phrenology through the influence of her brothers Orson and
Lorenzo, the earliest and most fervent devotees of the new
American fad. Phrenology was the Austrian science which
taught that there were physiological and cranial determinates
of character. The Americans took it one step further: once
character was determined by cranial examination, it could be
altered.

Orson and Lorenzo established a phrenological center in
New York City in 1835 which included a museum, lecture-
booking office and publishing house. They asked Charlotte   to
join them, and for the next sixty years she handled all the
practical aspects of phrenology: teaching, giving character
readings, writing, editing and proofreading.

Charlotte married Samuel Wells when she was thirty.
He had planned to become a doctor, but abandoned the idea
after hearing her brother's lecture. He joined them as an
assistant and, following the wedding, became a partner in the
family business. The Fowler and Wells Company was the
mainstay of phrenology in the United States. When she was
eighty, Charlotte still contributed articles to the *Phrenological
Journal.*

Mary S. Logan

A long partnership

1913

To tell my own story is to tell that of my famous husband, General John A. Logan. Our marriage was a real partnership for thirty-one happy years. I shared his thoughts and plans no less when he was a senator than when he was a prosecuting attorney in southern Illinois. We were working in the harmony of a common purpose, whether I was in the kitchen improvising a meal for his friends when he was running for the legislature, or entertaining in Washington after his fame was secure and his influence nationwide. With him I witnessed the stirring events in which he was a leader on the borderland of the Confederacy, where he raised his Union regiment. We were together whenever possible during the war. I travelled with him on his political campaigns after the war. Thus I came to know not only the eminent soldiers and public men of his time, but the men in the ranks who believed in him and followed him, whether to Vicksburg and Atlanta or in his political battles.

Mary Logan, political wife, writer and magazine editor, was born August 15, 1838, in Petersburgh, Missouri.

At the age of seventeen Mary married John Alexander Logan. They moved to Illinois where he practiced law and launched a political career. Mary accompanied him on all his campaigns and her cheery personality and good political sense helped elect him to the United States Congress.

During the Civil War John left Washington to lead a volunteer regiment and was quickly promoted to general. Mary placed their two children with relatives in Illinois and joined him, following him from battlefield to battlefield to aid in whatever way she could. After the war she suggested that a spring day be set aside to decorate the graves of the war dead. John, taking her advice, sponsored the legislation declaring May 30th a national holiday to be known as Memorial Day.

General Logan died in 1886 and Mary began writing to augment her income. She published two books of memoirs: *Thirty Years in Washington* and *Reminiscences of a Soldier's Wife*. She edited *Home Magazine* for seven years, wrote a manual on health and manners, and co-wrote *The Part Taken by Women in American History* with her daughter.

Mary's writing is from her autobiography, Reminiscences of a Soldier's Wife, *published in 1913.*

Helen Mary Knowlton

1899

A true artist

True artist that he was, he was sympathetic in a high degree, needing the sympathy of other artists, but rarely receiving it. A few friends he had—some of them artists, but quite as many who were not—to whom he could speak freely of his work, his doubts and fears, as well as his hopes and successes. He regarded the art-sentiment as all-essential; and would say, sometimes, with intense seriousness: "Painting, only, is worth the while."

Helen Mary Knowlton was born August 16, 1832, in Littleton, Massachusetts, the second of nine children. In the early 1860's she moved to Boston to study painting, opening her own studio in 1867.

In 1868, Helen and a few other women asked the well-known artist William Morris Hunt to teach a class. He agreed, and taught for three years until he decided he wanted more time for his own artwork. Hunt asked Helen to assume the class. She taught for four years, until she too decided she needed more time for painting and to write a book on Hunt's teaching techniques.

Helen gradually turned away from landscape painting to portraiture, her first work being a huge likeness of Hunt. She continued to paint as well as write art criticism for two Boston newspapers until well into her seventies.

Helen's writing is from Art-Life of William Morris Hunt, *published in 1899.*

Charlotte Forten Grimké

1864

*R*estless spirits

Little colored children of every hue were playing about the streets, looking as merry and happy as children ought to look, now that the evil shadow of Slavery no longer hangs over them.

The first day at school was rather trying. Most of my children were very small, and consequently restless. Some were too young to learn the alphabet. These little ones were brought to school because the older children—in whose care their parents leave them while at

Charlotte's writing is from her article, "Life on the Sea Islands," which appeared in Volume XIII of The Atlantic Monthly, *May, 1864 .*

work—could not come without them. We were therefore willing to have them come, although they seemed
to have discovered the secret of perpetual motion, and
tried one's patience sadly. But after some days of positive, though not severe treatment, order was brought
out of chaos, and I found but little difficulty in managing and quieting the tiniest and most restless spirits!

Charlotte Forten Grimké, black teacher and author, was born
August 17, 1837, in Philadelphia. Her father tutored her at
home rather than send her to Philadelphia's segregated
schools. In 1856 she began teaching at a grammar school in
Salem, Massachusetts, the first black teacher to instruct white
children in that area.

 The Union forces during the Civil War occupied a group
of islands off South Carolina where abandoned plantations
harbored a great number of uneducated slaves. The Union
organized programs of educational, medical and financial aid
for this newly freed population, and Charlotte volunteered to
go there in 1862 as a teacher.

Phoebe Yates Pember

*B*eyond modesty

1879

. . . The circumstances which surround a wounded man,
far from friends and home, suffering in a holy cause and
dependent upon a woman for help, care and sympathy,
hallow and clear the atmosphere in which she labors. In
the midst of suffering and death, hoping with those
almost beyond hope in this world; praying by the bedside of the lonely and heart-stricken; closing the eyes of
boys hardly old enough to realize man's sorrows, much
less suffer by man's fierce hate, a woman *must* soar
beyond the conventional modesty considered correct
under different circumstances.

Phoebe Yates Levy Pember was born August 18, 1823, in
Charleston, South Carolina. Just prior to the outbreak of the
Civil War, she married Thomas Pember, but he died of tuberculosis in 1861. Phoebe then joined her family at the home of
relatives in Marietta, Georgia.

 Phoebe was tense and unhappy in the small house at
Marietta. When she was offered the post of matron at

Phoebe's writing is from A
Southern Woman's Story,
published in 1879.

Chimborazo, a large army hospital near Richmond, she accepted immediately. She was in charge of housekeeping and diet for thirty-one wards; during the course of the war, she and her assistants tended to more than fifteen thousand soldiers.

Phoebe's salary of forty dollars per month was so inadequate that she wrote magazine articles at night for extra money. Supplies and help were constantly short at the hospital. In one letter home in 1863 she wrote, "I have not been able to cook, and everything for seven hundred sick men has to be cooked under my eyes by two black imps of fourteen."

Phoebe stayed at Chimborazo through its occupation by Union forces in April, 1865. In 1879 she published her wartime reminiscences as *A Southern Woman's Story.*

Florine Stettheimer

1929
New York

    At last grown young
    With noise
    And colour
    And light
    And jazz
    Dance marathons and poultry shows
    Soul-savings and rodeos
    Gabfests and beauty contests
    Skytowers and bridal showers
    Speak-easy bars and motor cars
    Columnists and movie stars.

Young New York

Florine Stettheimer was born August 19, 1871, in Rochester, New Hampshire. She began painting lessons in New York in her early twenties. When the family moved abroad, she continued her studies in Munich, Stuttgart and Berlin.

The Stettheimers returned to America at the outbreak of World War I. Florine and her two sisters opened an art salon in New York City that became legendary. The three women entertained well-known artists, authors and art critics of the day.

Florine had her first one-woman show in 1916, but she attracted little attention and had no sales. Thereafter, she refused to exhibit her work and would not sell any of her paintings, smiling and saying she liked them too much herself and preferred to keep them.

Florine's poem is included in Florine Stettheimer, *by Henry McBride, published in 1946 by the Museum of Modern Art, New York City.*

In 1934 Florine designed the costumes and sets for the opera "Four Saints in Three Acts," the first time a renowned American artist worked in the theater. She then began her series of four large masterpieces, the "Cathedrals."

Florine refused to sell her work right up to her death at seventy-three. Fortunately, she had abandoned her idea of having her paintings buried with her in a mausoleum, so her sister Ettie inherited over one hundred pieces. In 1946 the Museum of Modern Art gave her an impressive memorial show, and in 1966 Columbia University established the Florine Stettheimer Room in its Art Center.

Maria Louise Pool

*A*n old dog

1898

A rough brown dog sat at the very edge of the tumble-down breakwater. He was looking steadily seaward. He was evidently old, and he was scarred by many fights; but his sunken mouth, from which he had lost many teeth, showed that he would not fight again victoriously.

He was gaunt from a lifetime of insufficient food, but yet he had the air of a dog who is loved.

Sometimes he turned from his gaze at the sea and glanced behind him at the child who was sitting in a wheelbarrow a few feet away. Every time he glanced thus he slightly wagged his stump of a tail, and the child smiled or she said in a soft voice:

"Good Boss!"

And then Boss wagged harder; but he could not give much attention to his companion, for his whole heart was with that bent old woman who was up to her waist in the water by the outermost ledge. It was there that the Irish moss grew, and at low tide the woman could gather it.

Maria Louise Pool was born August 20, 1841, in East Abington, Massachusetts. She attended local public schools where her talent for writing was soon discovered. As a teenager she began contributing to the *Galaxy* and other popular magazines.

In 1870 Maria moved to New York City and commenced her career as a journalist. She wrote humorous, yet touching, essays on New England country life which earned her a wide readership in the *New York Tribune* and the *Evening Post*.

Maria's writing is from her collection of short stories, Boss and Other Dogs, *published in 1898.*

Give Her This Day

Maria published her first novel in 1887. She continued to produce one or two books a year until her premature death at fifty-seven at her home in Massachusetts.

Mary Lovell Carpenter

July 10, 1873

Dear Aunt Martha, . . .

A difficult start

We arrived here a week ago last Monday after a journey of two weeks. . . . George did not ride ten miles of the whole distance, two hundred miles. The older children took turns riding and driving. We camped in our wagon and I cooked our meals by campfire. . . . Our circumstances now are very discouraging. George is haggard and worn, for his mind is ill at ease and he works very hard. There is no chance to earn anything in this region. . . the grasshoppers have destroyed the gardens here, so all we have is a few potatoes growing. Our appetites are good, which seems rather unfortunate. Our house is but a leaky ten-foot shanty. . . . It makes it worse, I expect a confinement in October. I try to trust God's promises, but we can't expect him to work mir- acles now a days. . . . Even if we do freeze or starve in the way of duty, it will not be a dishonorable death. I laid awake almost all night one night worrying about it but that didn't do any good. "Sufficient to the day is the evil thereof."

Mary Lovell Carpenter was born August 21, 1840, in Rochester, Minnesota. Following high school, she married George Carpenter, a local farmer.

At the age of thirty-three, Mary and George and their children resettled in Marshall, Minnesota, near the South Dakota border, in hopes of finding "better circumstances." After a difficult start, they prospered in the newly settled region. Mary remained in Marshall until her death at the age of eighty-five.

Mary's letter, describing her family's move to southern Minnesota, is from the Mary E. Lovell Carpenter and Family Papers, in the Minnesota Historical Society collection.

Emily Chubbuck Judson

A happy place

1846

It is a happy place, that district school; overflowing with the genuine cream of fun; gay, busy, mischief-hatching, and gloriously mischief-executing . . . I cannot imagine what creates the undefinable longing for the "last day" . . . the "last day" is carefully watched for; and, despite the old adage, it comes at last; while, with smooth aprons and cleaned faces, and all bedecked in holy day finery, the future statesmen and (provided success attend some of the reformers of the present day) stateswomen, sally forth to the place of action.

Emily Chubbuck Judson was born August 27, 1817, in Eaton, New York. Her father's failed attempts at farming plunged the family into poverty; Emily was required to work in a woolen mill at the age of ten.

Emily studied on her own while she labored at the mill, so that she was able to leave it for a teaching job when she was fifteen. She taught for eight years, while contributing anonymous stories and poems to the local papers. The Sheldon sisters, headmistresses of the Utica Female Seminary, were so impressed by Emily's perseverance that they awarded her a year's scholarship. She stayed on as a teacher of English composition.

Emily wrote a popular series of children's books which earned her enough to purchase a home for her destitute parents. She also contributed numerous magazine articles under the pen name "Fanny Forester." At twenty-eight, she was introduced to the Reverend Adoniram Judson, the fifty-seven-year-old founder of the American Baptist Mission in Burma. He wished to hire her to write a memoir of his second wife who had recently died. He proposed marriage soon after their first encounter.

Emily and Adoniram were married in 1846 and set sail for Burma immediately. She had two children, one of whom died as an infant, plus five children from Judson's previous marriages. Following his death in 1850, she returned to America with her brood, exhausted and sickly. She died of tuberculosis a few years later at the age of thirty-six.

Emily's writing is from Alderbrook—A Collection of Fanny Forester's Village Sketches, *published in 1864.*

Amélie Louise Rives

1923

Curtain

She makes a sudden spring to the door, opens it, and is
without before any can stop her. They hear her voice
dying away, calling: "Take courage, poor soul! Courage! Courage! I am coming! I am coming to you!"
As the door is closing on her, Donal rushes towards it,
though the others try to keep him back. He tears it
open in the wind and struggles out. No sooner has he
done so, than he is flung violently back into the room,
half-stunned. As the door slams to and fro in the wind,
before anyone has thought to fasten it, a sudden gust
blows out all the lights and wild, little trilling laughter is
heard outside, rising and falling. "Ah, ha-ha-ha! Ah,
ha-ha-ha!"

Amélie Rives was born August 23, 1863, in Richmond,
Virginia. She spent her childhood in Mobile, Alabama, and on
the family's country estate, "Castle Hill," in Virginia. She
began writing when she was nine. Her family rarely read and
never criticized her work, so she was free to develop her forceful, unique style.

In 1886, Amélie published a story anonymously in *The
Atlantic Monthly*. Her tale of the sixteenth century became
popular in America and England, and she was soon revealed as
the author.

Amélie married John Chandler, grandson of John Jacob
Astor, in 1888. The union was not a happy one. Following
their divorce, she married Prince Pierre Troubetzkoy, a Russian artist, and continued her literary career until well into her
seventies.

*Amélie's writing is from the end
of the first act of her three-act
play, "November Eve,"
published in 1923.*

Kate Claxton

1894

A career in the theater

I know of no other vocation except literature in which a
woman stands on a footing of absolute equality with a
man. If an actress is capable of doing as good work as
an actor, she receives the same remuneration that he

does. As for the temptations that are supposed to surround a young girl who goes on the stage, they don't exist to any greater extent than the evil influences that are brought to bear on a girl in any other calling that takes her out of her home and family surroundings.

Kate Claxton was born August 24, 1848, in Somerville, New Jersey. Following a quick marriage and divorce in 1865, she decided on a career in the theater. Although her father had written several plays and acted in amateur theater, he was strongly opposed to Kate's career choice. She persevered and made her stage debut in Chicago in 1869.

Kate moved to New York and acted regularly at the Fifth Avenue Theater and the Union Square Theater. In 1874 she first played Louise, the blind girl, in *The Two Orphans*, the role which made her famous. Although she took other parts over the years, it was Louise who brought her the most success.

During one performance of *The Two Orphans* in 1876, the Brooklyn Theater caught on fire and burned to the ground, killing more than two hundred. This catastrophe became a part of Kate's public image, and some considered her an omen of disaster. The following year she narrowly escaped another fire at the Southern Hotel in St. Louis. She was married and divorced two more times, five of her six children died in infancy, and the sixth committed suicide the same year that Kate retired from the theater.

Kate's writing is from an interview in the December 8, 1894 issue of the New York Dramatic Mirror.

Ann Bryant Smith

Domestic happiness

August 16, 1802
My good man and I left our bed a little after five. I milked the cow, he made the fire, I prepared our breakfast, he ground the coffee and drove the cow to pasture. After a delightful repast he went to his store, I to washing our dishes, making our bed, taking care of the milk and sweeping the rooms. Oh ye voluptuous and idle, dissipated people. I pity you because ye know not the pleasure of domestic happiness. My God, I thank thee that thou hast given me a mind capable of enjoying this kind of bliss.

October 11, 1802
I have passed twenty happy years with my good husband.

Ann's writings are from her journals, which are in the Maine Historical Society, Portland, Maine.

August 26, 1806

My husband and his wife rode fourteen miles this morn and returned at 6 o'clock, took our breakfast, passed the day together in the store. We are now snug in our chamber, *he* counting his money, *I* writing.

August 28, 1806

My good man and I have had a most delightful ride this morn, we set out a short time after sunrise and returned after eight. Rode about eighteen miles, part of the way through a charming country, on our route we had one of the finest views I ever saw. The prospect was so fine that I regretted my not being a landscape painter. I am not capable of describing its beauties so shall not attempt it. Helped my husband in the store and altered a gown.

August 30, 1806

My good husband and his wife rode this fine morn with the sun and had another charming ride. No two persons I believe ever enjoyed each other's company better or ever desired less to be apart.

March 30, 1807

It is the opinion of the writer of this Diary that more persons decay of REST, than WORK. It is her intention not to fall by the former.

April 13, 1807

I am employed this day in washing, ironing, mending, doing house work, reading, writing and knitting. Variety enough for the most whimsical woman.

Ann Bryant Smith was born August 25, 1763, in Newmarket, New Hampshire. She married Eliphalet Smith, also of Newmarket, when she was nineteen. They had one son who died when he was six years old.

Ann kept a journal from 1800 to 1830. She and her family lived in Portland, Maine. She led a simple life as a homemaker and helpmate to her husband, whom she adored. He suffered from rheumatism and she suffered from migraines, toothaches and earaches. Despite this they were both cheerful and willing to do what needed to be done.

Ann often helped her husband in his dry goods store. They made the journey to Boston together several times a year to purchase merchandise for the store. In October, 1803, she wrote: "We have bought more than we shall sell this season I fear." During the same trip she attended her first play with a friend but enjoyed her walk to the theater over Beacon Hill more. She said: "It is the last as well as the first play I ever intend to see acted." On a buying trip in 1806 they went to a cotton factory in Pawtucket, Rhode Island, where she was startled to see "there were one hundred persons employed, 7/8ths of them are children."

With humor Ann summarized her life and journal: "Mrs. Smith was a truthful, conscientious, generous and amiable woman. Her family were always attended by her in terms of most affectionate regard. If this journal should ever come into the possession of any who should make an unworthy use of any part of her writings or any animadversion upon her work, it would be better that her friends should have destroyed her manuscripts."

Annie Wittenmyer

*D*runken women

1873

There are thousands of women to-day among the higher classes, who are more or less under the influence of liquor every afternoon, or who occasionally take a spree.

I have seen women elegantly dressed, living in palatial residences, who were so drunk that they could not get out of their carriage without the aid of a footman.

. . . Much of the increase of drunkenness among women, I believe, may be traced to the free use of Patent Medicines.

Most of these compounds are liquors, variously drugged.

Taken month after month, an appetite for stimulants is created, and something stronger is required.

From what I have been able to gather, I am persuaded that more persons are made drunkards by their use than are cured of disease.

Annie Turner Wittenmyer was born August 26, 1827, in Sandy Springs, Ohio. In 1847 she married William Wittenmyer, a local merchant. They had five children, but only one survived infancy.

During the Civil War, Annie was elected by the legislature as the first sanitary agent for the state of Iowa. She received a pass from Secretary of War Stanton, approved by

Annie's writing is from Women's Work for Jesus, *published in 1873.*

Give Her This Day

President Lincoln, which enabled her to enter onto the bat-
tlefields where she ministered to the wounded. She came
under fire many times, but when warned of danger she answered, "I am safe: He covers me with His feathers and hides
me under His wings."

In 1863, Annie created the Soldier's Orphans' Home in
Iowa and became the first president of the Woman's Christian
Temperance Union, serving her first five years without salary.
She started her own magazine, *Christian Woman*, which she
edited for eleven years. Her efforts were responsible for establishing the Kentucky Soldier's Home and for the passage of a
law by the Fifty-second Congress to pension army nurses.

Julia Marlowe

1928

The night came at last. The audience was small. "The
beautiful young actress" was entirely unknown, and the
trumpets of our advance man lured few people to the
play. But that did not affect me at all. I was launched
on my adventure and I was trying my wings. Many
another night I was to face just such a scanty gathering,
but always I was learning—learning—trying out on the
stage what I had concluded to do in my own room, stor-
ing up in my eager mind experience for the victory of
which I felt assured. I really felt like Longfellow's
young man who bore the banner with the strange
device, "Excelsior." I must not fail.

Julia Marlowe, christened Sarah Frances Frost, was born
August 27, 1866, in Upton Caldbeck, England. Her father
fled to America in 1870, believing he had put out a neighbor's
eye with his whip during a race. He settled in Ohio, changed
his name to Brough, and sent for his family. As a child Fanny
was drawn to the theater and bought her first Shakespeare
book from a travelling salesman, paying on the installment
plan with her twenty-five-cents-a-week allowance.

When she was twelve she answered a newspaper ad and
joined the chorus of a juvenile opera company. The manager's
sister-in-law, Ada Dow, saw Fanny's talent and took her under
her wing. "Aunt Ada" rented a small apartment in New York
City, where they studied and rehearsed for three years. At the
end of that time, Fanny chose the stage name "Julia Marlowe,"
and began her acting career.

Sure of success

Julia's writing is from Julia
Marlowe's Story, *edited by her
husband, E. H. Sothern. It was
in manuscript form at the time
of his death in 1933 and was
published in 1954 according to a
provision in Julia's will.*

Julia was insistent on playing only Shakespearean roles and on directing her own productions. As a result, she refused offers from many well-known managers, until financial necessity forced her to desert Shakespeare. In 1904, however, she teamed with Edward H. Sothern, and they became the foremost exponents of Shakespeare in the American theater at that time. They were married in 1911 and continued touring intermittently until their final retirement in 1924.

Julia outlived her husband by seventeen years. She lived at New York's Plaza Hotel, doing church work and reading to the blind.

Lucy Webb Hayes

Starting a campaign

Fremont,
Oct 25th 1875
My dear old Darling—

I am as happy as any young girl over your letter, indeed we are a joyous family every day we think of the happiness in store for us—Soon to have you home— then all things look bright. Pleasant congratulatory letters from friends still coming and every once and a while a sweet morsel for the old wife comes too. I had a delightful time at Cleveland—and then in addition Scott was so good and lovely—I am really proud of him—I am so glad you went to Philadelphia and glad to have you remain this long—not that the old wife is at all bitten by the Mania—but it does her heart good to have you know—and I am so glad so happy so *proud* to be your wife. . . .

Lucy Ware Webb Hayes, wife of the nineteenth president of the United States, was born August 28, 1831, in Chillicothe, Ohio. She was the first female student to enroll at Ohio Wesleyan University. When her family relocated to Cincinnati, she graduated from Wesleyan Female College in that city, giving one of the commencement orations.

Lucy had already met Rutherford B. Hayes, a lawyer, when she was sixteen, and they renewed their friendship in Cincinnati. They were married in 1852.

During the Civil War, Rutherford was an officer in the Union Army and Lucy accompanied him, positioning herself at his headquarters where she nursed the injured and wrote letters home for the soldiers. Her "boys" adored her, calling

Lucy's letter to her husband at the beginning of his bid for the presidency is in the Rutherford B. Hayes Papers, Rutherford B. Hayes Presidential Center, Spiegel Grove, Fremont, Ohio.

her "Mother Lucy." Following the war, she founded the Ohio Soldiers' and Sailors' Orphans' Home while her husband began his political climb in Congress and as governor.

Following Rutherford's election as president, Lucy played a more active role as First Lady than had many of her predecessors. She was a gracious hostess, and together they presented a pious, wholesome, family image. Lucy, called "Lemonade Lucy" by her opponents, is best remembered for her total ban on liquor in the White House at all times. She felt temperance was best achieved through education and example. In gratitude, the W.C.T.U. presented a portrait of Mrs. Hayes to the White House.

Henrietta Woodford

Nov. 9, 1858
My Very Dear Parents,

I believe I have not told you what a feat the mice accomplished while I was up to Mr. H's. They are great to monopolize. They took every yeast cake that I had. I did not think they would touch them. Well, I suppose you wonder what we have done all this time; but we have had bread and good bread without yeast, though perhaps not quite as good as with yeast. It is the Kansas way of making bread. I find almost every one uses what is called *salt rising*. It is nothing but flour and a little salt, which by standing in a warm place about six hours will be light as yeast. I don't know but you, Ma, have known of it before, but I never heard of such a thing. It certainly is very little trouble.

*K*ansas bread

Henrietta Woodford was born August 29, 1840, in West Avon, Connecticut. She attended Mount Holyoke Seminary for one year until family responsibilities forced her to leave.

Henrietta's brother, the Reverend Oswald Woodford, was a missionary Congregational minister who had gone west to establish his church in Kansas. His wife Pauline died giving birth to a daughter and he brought the child home to Connecticut for his family to raise. It was decided that Henrietta should return to Kansas with him to help ease the pain of his bereavement and take charge of his domestic affairs.

Henrietta remained in Kansas from 1858 to 1859. Although it was desolate frontier, unlike anything she had been

Henrietta's letter home from Grasshopper Falls, Kansas, is included in Establishing a Church on the Kansas Frontier: The Letters of the Reverend O. L. Woodford and His Sister Henrietta, 1857–1859, *edited by Virginia McLoughlin, which appeared in the* Kansas Historical Quarterly, *Volume XXXVII, 1971.*

accustomed to in New England, she grew to like it. She wrote her parents: "I am feeling now very much at home. Sometimes I think for a minute that it is almost strange that I am so contented." She worked hard to please her brother and make him comfortable, spending much time reading to him, as he had eye trouble.

Mary Austin Holley

Lady patriots

1836
The ladies of Texas during the passing struggle—more patriots even than the men—have displayed much of the Roman virtue, encouraging the citizens, and keeping up the chivalry of the volunteers by expressions of enthusiasm and by fêtes as well as by a careful attention to their wants. They have not yet been called upon to shoulder the rifle and mount the war-steed, but with the occasion will come the spirit to do so.

Mary Phelps Austin Holley was born August 30, 1784, in New Haven, Connecticut. She was raised by an uncle following her father's death when she was ten.

In 1805, Mary married Horace Holley, a Congregational minister. They settled in Lexington, Kentucky, when he was offered the presidency of the newly formed Transylvania College. Mary complained bitterly about the lack of culture on the frontier, but she endured for nine years. They returned to New England by ship in 1827, but they both caught yellow fever during the voyage, and Horace died.

Mary became a governess to support herself and her young son, but she longed for the comfort of family ties. In 1831 she departed for Texas where her brother lived, as well as her cousin Stephen Austin, one of the founders of Texas. She published a book of "historical, geographical and descriptive observations" of Texas which was instrumental in promoting emigration and annexation. Mary died of yellow fever in 1846.

Mary's writing is from Texas, *published in 1836.*

Louise Khiele Scovel

1897

Boston discovers Chicago

This afternoon I went out to the conference and heard Jane Addams of the Hull House. She is quite charming and her personality is certainly very interesting. She is a bright, ready speaker, really very witty. Her paper was upon the condition of affairs in their ward—(the 19th I think) and the methods of the aldermen. She spoke particularly of Powers. After she finished, questions were in order, among others, Mr. Maloy (who is an old man, very delightful, student of Emerson and Browning) asked with a rather "Bostonian air," whether she thought it would do any good to go out there and start a Browning Club. I can hardly explain or analyze the manner this was asked in—it was a trifle cynical, and taking it for granted they had never *heard* of such a thing in Chicago.

Miss Addams replied that they *had* already several Browning Clubs at Hull House, and some from the Browning Clubs were among those who voted for Powers! It takes Boston people some time to see a joke, especially if it is at their expense, but finally they began to feel the force of this and from a gentle murmur at the first, they gradually broke into applause, after which Mr. Maloy remarked in a rather subdued manner that if Browning did not help them he didn't know what *would*.

Louise Gilman Khiele Scovel was born August 31, 1868, in Preston, Minnesota, where her father was minister of the Presbyterian church. Louise attended local schools until 1897 when she went to Boston to study at Dr. & Mrs. Curry's school of public expression. In 1900 she married Carl W. Scovel, a Presbyterian minister. They had one son, born in 1902.

In 1904 the couple settled in New York State and remained there until 1932. Louise helped her husband in his ministry—teaching Sunday school, cooking at church suppers, entertaining at home.

Carl died of a heart attack in 1932. Louise went to China the next year to be with her son, who was a medical missionary. She lived in a small gray brick house with an amah and a servant. Her grandson, Carl Scovel, remembers having tea

Louise's letter was written three years before her marriage, while she was attending school in Boston. It is part of a private collection of her grandson, Carl Scovel, minister of King's Chapel, Boston, Massachusetts.

and cookies at his grandmother's: "She often wore a shawl and insisted on good behavior, was formal but also very kindly. She was the true picture of a Victorian Lady."

Louise stayed in China nine years participating in the social life of the mission. She taught English to the Chinese, and tried to learn Chinese herself, but found it difficult. On one New Year's Day she thought she was saying, "Congratulations! Have a happy New Year!," but she was actually saying, "A rooster! Put on the vegetables!"

In 1941 Louise returned to America after being warned by the American Consul that hostilities might break out between the United States and China. In 1946 she returned to China, although she was not well. She had Parkinson's disease and spent the last two years of her life in bed. She died in Canton in 1948 and was buried there. In 1980 her grandson tried to locate her grave, but the cemetery was in poor condition and he could find no trace of it. There is a stone to her memory in Clinton, New York, near her husband's grave.

SEPTEMBER

Phebe Noyes Brett

Farmington, Maine
April 19, 1854
Dear Fred,

Will not you my dear Fred be one of the happy group who are now seeking an interest in the blessed redeemer? I know full well that you will never repent that you give your heart this early to God and thereby secure an interest in that haven of rest which is prepared by our Father in heaven for all those who love him and serve him while here in this lower world. Be assured you can never more easily make a full consecration of yourself to God than at the present time. Disease may seize you and thus suddenly you may be ushered into the presence of the most high God and happy, thrice happy will it be for you if you are found ready—"for in such an hour as ye think not, the son of man cometh." . . .

Phebe Noyes Brett was born September 1, 1805, in Minot, Maine. She was able to trace her ancestry back to James Noyes, a knight who fought with William the Conqueror at the Battle of Hastings.

At the age of twenty-five, Phebe married Rufus Brett, a blacksmith from Minot. They settled in Farmington, Maine, where he was a town assessor for many years. Phebe had nine children, delivering her last daughter when she was forty-six years old.

Phebe was a devout Christian and a diligent mother who was dearly loved. A few weeks after her death, her daughter Emma wrote to her brother Theodore, "I cannot dispel the illusion that she is here still. Her presence is felt constantly and throughout the house but more especially in the sitting room, where the last of her precious life was spent and where the light from those dear loving eyes faded out forever."

A mother's wish

Phebe's letter to her eighteen-year-old son, who had gone to Boston as a mercantile apprentice, is among the personal papers of her great-great-grandson William S. Edgerly, of Cambridge, Massachusetts.

Lucretia Peabody Hale

A desert tableau

1886

. . . Mrs. Peterkin sat alone in front of the Sphinx, alone, as far as her own family and friends were concerned, and yet not alone indeed. A large crowd of guides sat around this strange lady who proposed to spend the day in front of the Sphinx. Clad in long white robes, with white turbans crowning their dark faces, they gazed into her eyes with something of the questioning expression with which she herself was looking into the eyes of the Sphinx.

Lucretia Peabody Hale was born September 2, 1820, in Boston. She came from a prominent family, descendants of the famous patriot Nathan Hale. Lucretia and her sister Susan [December 5] never married. As adults they shared a home, and financial necessity forced Lucretia to turn to writing. In 1858 she published the first of many stories in *The Atlantic Monthly*, followed shortly by her first novel.

In 1868, Lucretia created her well-loved family, the Peterkins, for a story in the children's magazine *Our Young Folks*. Many stories followed and were collected in *The Peterkin Papers* and *The Last of the Peterkins*, two books that continue to be cherished by children today.

Lucretia's writing is from The Last of the Peterkins, *published in 1886.*

Sarah Orne Jewett

*T*he happiness in books

148 Charles Street, Boston
January 23, 1899
My dear friend:

I thank you sincerely for your most kind letter, and I wish to tell you how much pleasure it gives me to know that you like my stories.

I am sure that you must like a great many other books since you like these stories of mine. And I am so glad, because you will always have the happiness of finding friendships in books, and it grows pleasanter and pleasanter as one grows older. And then people in books are apt to make us understand 'real' people better,

Sarah's letter to young Mary Mulholland is in Special Collections, Colby College, Waterville, Maine.

and to know why they do things, and so we learn sympathy and patience and enthusiasm for those we live with. . . . It is just the same way that a beautiful picture makes us quicker to see the same things in a landscape. . . .

Good-bye, dear Mary, I send you many thanks for your letter and my kindest wishes. I hope that you will be as busy and as happy as can be and never be without plenty of friends—in books and out of them.

Yours affectionately,
Sarah O. Jewett

Sarah Orne Jewett was born September 3, 1849, in South Berwick, Maine.

She moved to Boston in 1878 and at that time became close friends with Annie Adams Fields [June 6], wife of publisher James Fields. After his death the two women lived together.

Through her association with the Fieldses and the encouragement she received at their literary salon, Sarah began writing. In 1877 she published her first book, going back to her Maine roots for location and characters. Thereafter all her books were of the "local color" school, revealing the "hidden fire of enthusiasm" in the New England spirit.

Sarah's writing career came to an end on her fifty-third birthday when she was thrown from her carriage and suffered injuries from which she never recovered.

Sarah Childress Polk

March 27, 1843

Dear Husband, . . .

A shared burden

I must confess that I feel sad and melancholy at the prospect before me, or I should say before you, the fatigue, exposure and absence for four months cannot present to me a bright prospect. I have not the assurance that the body and constitution can keep up under such labours as you have to go through, and it is only the hope that you can live through it that gives me a prospect of enjoyment. But we beg and pray that you will take care of yourself and do not become too much excited. . . .

Your affectionate Wife Sarah Polk

Sarah's letter to her husband is in the Manuscript Division of the Library of Congress.

Sarah Childress Polk, wife of the eleventh president of the United States, was born September 4, 1803, in Rutherford County, Tennessee. She first met her future husband, James Polk, when he was a classmate of her brother's at nearby Murfreesboro Academy. They became reacquainted a few years later when he began coming regularly to Murfreesboro as clerk of the State Senate.

Sarah took a strong interest in her husband's career, which led from the legislature to fourteen years in Congress. He was elected to the presidency in 1844. She was indispensable to him as secretary, political advisor, nurse and emotional confidante. Her experience with official gatherings and her ability to make light, pleasant conversation compensated for her introverted husband.

Sarah was devoutly religious and saw to it that the Sabbath was strictly observed in the White House. She also banned dancing at all functions. James Polk died three months after leaving office, when he was fifty-four.

Sarah lived for the next forty-two years at Polk Place, the Nashville estate James had provided for their retirement. She rarely left the house except for Sunday church services. She was revered as a national treasure: the Tennessee legislature called on her during each session, and every prominent person or group that came to Nashville did the same.

SEPTEMBER 5 ## *Amy Cheney Beach*

*V*oyage to Europe

1912
You see I am a staunch believer in the possibilities offered for a musical education in our own country, for I have studied only in America; indeed, since I am a very bad sailor, I have never quite summoned the requisite courage until this year to attempt a voyage across the ocean. Indeed I had almost concluded that until the journey could be made by some other way—perhaps by a flying machine—I should have to forego the pleasure of travel in Europe.

Amy's writing is from "A Conversation on Musical Conditions in America," which was recorded by Arthur Wilson, and published in the January, 1912, issue of The Musician, *Volume XVII, Number 1.*

Amy Marcy Cheney Beach was born September 5, 1867, in Henniker, New Hampshire. Her mother was a pianist and singer, and became Amy's first music teacher. She began singing, with perfect pitch, at the age of one, and began composing simple waltzes by four. At six, she demanded piano lessons, so her mother allowed her three per week.

Amy made her debut as a pianist in 1883. Two years

---

later, she performed with the Boston Symphony Orchestra; her performance was described in the *Boston Evening Transcript* as "thoroughly artistic, beautiful and brilliant."

Amy's concert appearances became infrequent following her marriage to Doctor Henry Beach, a surgeon twenty-four years her senior. She became interested in composing instead. Her husband encouraged her in this endeavor and recommended she study by herself instead of with a teacher, believing that formal study might rob her work of some of its originality. She began her Mass in E-flat major in 1886, an elaborate piece for vocal quartet, chorus, orchestra and organ, which took three years to complete. It was first performed on February 7, 1892, by the Handel and Haydn Society of the Boston Symphony Orchestra, the first work by a woman ever performed by them. She received a standing ovation.

During her lifetime, Amy composed one hundred and fifty classical works in addition to church music, choral works and popular songs, firmly establishing herself as one of America's foremost female composers.

Catharine Esther Beecher

1835

One thing is certain, if religious influences are banished from our national system of education, every denomination will be injured in its most vital interests. For one who would be proselyted by a sectarian teacher, ten would be ruined by vice and irreligion consequent on the neglect of moral and religious influences.

Religion in school

Catharine Esther Beecher was born September 6, 1800, in East Hampton, Long Island. Her father was Lyman Beecher, the famous Presbyterian minister.

Catharine became a schoolteacher in Connecticut at the age of twenty-one and soon became engaged to Alexander Fisher, a mathematics professor at Yale. However, he died at sea four months after their engagement, which Catharine saw as a divine judgment. Her father's interpretation was that God had chosen her for a vocation beyond ordinary women.

In 1823 Catharine and her sister Mary opened the Hartford Female Seminary. She resigned in 1831 because she was suffering from mental confusion that made her feel she was "approaching insanity." She accompanied her father to Cincinnati where he took over the presidency of Lane Theological Seminary.

Catharine's writing is from her "Essay on the Education of Female Teachers for the United States," written at the request of the American Lyceum, and delivered at their annual meeting on May 8, 1835.

Catharine's experiences in the west convinced her that America was "courting bloodshed and anarchy" by not educating its children properly; there were two million children growing up beyond the reach of schools. Through her efforts, the Mt. Vernon Church in Boston created a society for "sending pious female teachers to the west." Catharine assisted a similar organization in Cleveland, and between the two groups over five hundred teachers went west.

Alice Chipman Dewey

Teaching a child

1903

. . . Children have their own method, their own mental ways at four years of age. It is the business of the teacher to find out these ways, and through them to lead the child to other ways. It may be possible to wrong a child by trying to give him by means of a gift, a knowledge of the three dimensions of space of which he gained complete control at the age of nine or twelve months by going up and down stairs, or by climbing in and out of a high chair.

Alice Chipman Dewey was born September 7, 1858, in Fenton, Michigan. Her parents died when she was a child, so she and her younger sister were raised by their maternal grandparents.

Alice enrolled at the University of Michigan and graduated in 1886. As a junior she had met John Dewey, a philosophy professor, and they were married soon after her graduation.

John and Alice moved to Chicago where he had been asked to head the philosophy department of the newly established University of Chicago. Through the auspices of his department, Alice helped him start an elementary school, known as the Laboratory School, where his ideas could be translated into practice. The school tested his philosophical and psychological concepts, and the principles which evolved set the course for educational reform for the next fifty years. In 1904 both Deweys resigned from the university in a dispute with the administration over Alice's role as principal of the Laboratory School.

Alice's writing is from her article, "The Place of the Kindergarten," in The Elementary Schoolteacher, Volume III, Number 5, January, 1903.

The Deweys and their five children then travelled extensively in Europe. One of her sons died of typhoid in Ireland and, although they adopted an Italian boy of the same age, Alice never fully recovered her former stamina, and her health declined.

Phoebe Wilson Couzins

Women bear the torch

1884

At the gateway of this nation, the harbor of New York, there soon shall stand a statue of the Goddess of Liberty, presented by the republic of France—a magnificent figure of a woman, typifying all that is grand and glorious and free in self-government. She will hold aloft an electric torch of great power which is to beam an effulgent light far out to sea, that ships sailing towards this goodly land may ride safely into harbor. So should you thus uplift the women of this nation, and teach these men, at the very threshold, when first their feet shall touch the shore of this republic, that here woman is exalted, ennobled and honored; that here she bears aloft the torch of intelligence and purity which guides our Ship of State into the safe harbor of wise laws, pure morals and secure institutions.

Phoebe Wilson Couzins was born September 8, 1839, in St. Louis, Missouri. During the Civil War she assisted her mother, a nurse for the Western Sanitary Commission, and developed her position on women's rights. She believed that women, if given the vote, could end the misery of wars.

In 1868, at the suggestion of Judge Krum, a family friend, Phoebe enrolled as the first woman student in the Washington University Law School. Amid much fanfare she received her degree in 1871 and was admitted to the bar of several western states. She never actually practiced law, probably because she did not have adequate finances to open a law office. However, her considerable talents on the lecture podium, plus her elegant femininity, did much to dispel the concern that a woman would become mannish by studying law.

Phoebe was a leader in the national suffrage movement for the next thirty years. She lectured tirelessly for women's rights as well as temperance and other reforms. By the late 1890's Phoebe was often confined to a wheelchair with arthritis, was short on money, and had become bitter that she had not achieved more. She quarrelled with suffrage leaders, causing her to renounce the movement in 1897. She also reversed her stand on temperance, lobbying in Washington for the United Brewer's Association.

Phoebe died in St. Louis in 1913 in abject poverty; her funeral costs were assumed by a childhood friend.

Phoebe's writing is from the closing address she gave before the Senate Committee on Woman Suffrage, March 7, 1884. It is included in Volume IV of History of Woman Suffrage, *edited by Susan B. Anthony and Ida H. Harper, and published in 1902.*

Eliza Brock

Far from home

Sunday, July the 3rd, 1853
Begins with moderate trades and hazy weather steering
South. A long lonesome day is this to spend upon the
dark Ocean far away from home and friends and
Religious Privileges. No sound of the church going bell
is heard, nothing but the wailing of the wind and the
roaring of the sea. Have been employed this morning in
reading and writing letters home. . . . Steering S W,
Latitude 18, 12, longitude 23, 13.

Eliza Brock was born September 9, 1810, on Nantucket Island,
Massachusetts. She married Peter C. Brock, captain of the
whaling ship *Lexington*, and they had four children.

At forty-three Eliza joined her husband on his ship and
sailed from Nantucket across the North Atlantic, around the
Cape of Good Hope and across the Indian Ocean to New
Zealand. She kept a detailed journal of her voyage, even
recording how many whales were caught each day with little
sketches of that number of whales at the top of the page.

*Eliza's journal, written in a
beautiful hand, is in the
Nantucket Historical Society.*

Hannah Webster Foster

Misplaced optimism

1797
You have cut me off from life in the midst of my days.
You have rendered me the reproach of my friends, the
disgrace of my family and a dishonor to virtue and my
sex. But I forgive you, added she. Yes, Sanford, I forgive you, and sincerely pray for your repentance and
reformation. I hope to be the last wretched female
sacrificed by you to the arts of falsehood and seduction.

Hannah Webster Foster was born September 10, 1758, in
Salisbury, Massachusetts. At twenty-six she married the Reverend John Foster. They settled in Brighton, Massachusetts,
where he became minister of the First Unitarian Church for
the next forty-five years.

Hannah took up writing after the birth of her sixth and
last child. She published her first novel, *The Coquette*, in 1797,
and it was an instant success. The plot was loosely based on a

*Hannah's writing is from
The Coquette; or, The
History of Eliza Wharton,
a Novel: Founded on Fact
by a Lady of
Massachusetts, first
published in 1797.*

scandal that had occurred in Connecticut: the elopement, subsequent desertion and ultimate death of a young woman from a prominent family.

The Coquette was reprinted numerous times, enjoying the peak of its popularity between 1824 and 1828. Hannah wrote only one other book during her long life of eighty-one years.

Mary Hanson

1824

The first part of Thanksgiving week is usually employed in preparing to celebrate the great New England festival. Monday is washing day where the family rise very early, and commence their laborious task. Hot water is thrown in every direction. The hearth is covered with kettles. Pails and tubs are seen in every part of the room, and when it is time for the table to be spread for breakfast, what do we see, but a scanty meal, perhaps not enough for a mouthful apiece. Only a hurried dinner is allowed, and at supper, it is barely possible, that you may get something a little better.

Next day baking commences, which continues with various intervals, until Thursday, which brings the long-expected annual family supper and then we are fully compensated for all those scanty meals, which were our portion before. This is a New England Thanksgiving.

Thanksgiving in New Hampshire

Mary Hanson was born September 11, 1808, in Sandwich, New Hampshire.

Mary's father, Elisha Hanson, was the town postmaster. The mail came once a week by horseback from Dover, New Hampshire. A neighbor described Mr. Hanson as "early a man of money, and a farmer of great taste in care of his smooth acres and fine cattle." He saw to it that his children were well-educated. Two of Mary's sisters attended New Hampton Academy, and Mary went to the Wolfeboro and Tuftonboro Academy. Mr. Hanson loved to take his girls travelling, going to Saratoga Springs or to Boston for four and five weeks at a time.

Mr. and Mrs. Hanson died within a few days of each other in 1839. The children continued to live in their parents' house until they were married. Since Mary remained single, she stayed there until her death and was buried with her parents in Little's Pond Cemetery, Sandwich, New Hampshire.

Mary's writing is from one of her school themes, "Thanksgiving," that she wrote in 1824 when she was sixteen. It is among her papers in the Center Sandwich, New Hampshire Historical Society.

Maria Lydig Daly

*B*eneath the surplice

Sep 13 1861

Our church system has had much to do with the annoyances of my life. Our unmarried clergy are a great source of scandal; their egregious vanity is never satisfied, and young women, led away by a sentiment—half-religious, half-sensuous—are doubly intoxicated, confounding the young man with his office and looking upon the surplice as not only an emblem, but the evidence of purity. They seem to think that they may be trusted and allowed greater freedom than other men. The clergy, denied many other gratifications, are seldom holy enough to refuse any such delicate offerings to their vanity. Both of our parish priests have lost my respect from their behavior toward my own sisters; and yet, both are held forth in the world as pattern men. One even dared to try me, but I could never forget that the man was beneath the surplice. Thanks to my sensitiveness, I was always protected from their tender attentions.

Maria Lydig Daly was born September 12, 1824, in New York City, the oldest of ten children. Her father retired from the family business a millionaire, in his early thirties. Thereafter, he spent a great deal of time at home, educating and raising his large family.

Maria was still single at the age of thirty-two when she met Judge Charles Daly at a party. They fell in love instantly. He was the son of poor Irish immigrants; self-reared and self-taught, he had climbed to the top of his profession. He was well-respected in New York as a philanthropist, art patron and Shakespearean scholar. None of this impressed Maria's father, who saw him in regard to his daughter as a gold digger.

Maria and her father fought over her desire to marry Charles for almost a year. Meanwhile, she carried on a correspondence with her sweetheart as their form of courtship. Finally, Maria's mother intervened and wrote a letter to the judge giving permission to marry.

Maria and Charles were married in 1856. Her father gave her a $20,000 dowry and bought them the beautiful townhouse they occupied during their thirty-eight happy years together.

Maria's writing is from a diary she kept during the Civil War describing the effects of the war upon the city of New York and its people. It was published in 1962 as Diary of a Union Lady—1861-1865, *edited by Harold Hammond.*

Ann Eliza Young

1876

To the wives of Brigham Young, . . .

Divergent paths

You have been my companions and my sisters in tribulation. Now our paths diverge. I go on the way that I have chosen alone, while you stay sorrowing together. I wish I had the power to influence you to throw off the fetters which bind you, and to walk triumphantly forth into the glories of a faith, whose foundation is in God the compassionate Father, whose principles are those of a tender mercy, whose ruling spirit is love.

Ann Eliza Young was born September 13, 1844, at the Mormon settlement of Nauvoo, Illinois. Her father was an expert wagon maker who made many of the wagons for the great Mormon migration to the west. He took his second wife when Ann was still a toddler. After their arrival in Utah in 1848, he married three other women, so that Ann saw as a child, through her mother's suffering, the evils of the polygamy system.

The Mormon leader Brigham Young became infatuated with Ann when she was only sixteen, but she refused to be a plural wife. Two years later she married James Dee and had two children, but when the union proved to be an unhappy one, Brigham Young aided her in obtaining a civil divorce. They were married three-and-a-half years later, when he was sixty-eight and she was twenty-four.

Since Ann would not live in the Lion House with his other wives and children, Young built her a separate home. However, she was miserable, feeling lonely and abandoned; in 1873 she filed for a divorce, seeking $200,000 as a settlement and $20,000 for lawyers' fees. After years of court battles, she ultimately received nothing when it was decided the marriage had never been legal in the first place due to its plurality.

Ann's divorce created a scandal in the American press. She began a lecture tour that made her instantly famous. She spoke out against polygamy wherever she went, including to Congress and before President and Mrs. Ulysses S. Grant. The Poland Bill, the first federal anti-polygamy legislation, was passed largely due to her efforts. She continued her highly successful lecture tours until the 1882 Edmunds Bill outlawed polygamy; the Mormon church officially gave up the practice eighteen years later.

Ann's writing is from Wife Number Nineteen, or the Story of a Life in Bondage, Being a Complete Exposé of Mormonism, and Revealing the Sorrows, Sacrifices and Sufferings of Women in Polygamy, *published in 1876.*

Alice Stone Blackwell

Contributing to vice

1918

Women in all countries have objected to the compulsory medical examination of prostitutes, the illusion of security increases vice. . . . When it is announced that all prostitutes are to be frequently examined, and that those who are found diseased will not be allowed to ply their trade, the customer looks upon it as a blanket certificate that any such woman who is at large and is plying her trade has lately been examined and found free from disease . . . women have always objected to such laws because they are never applied impartially to men.

Alice Stone Blackwell was born September 14, 1857, in Orange, New Jersey. Her father was a strong supporter of women's rights, and her mother was the famous suffrage leader Lucy Stone [August 13]. Because both parents were away from home frequently, Alice resented the women's rights movement for taking so much of her mother's time.

Alice attended Boston University in 1881, one of two females in a class of twenty-six males. She graduated at the top of her class as a member of Phi Beta Kappa and class president. By this time she had outgrown her youthful resentment of the women's movement, and "the child of the regiment" joined the force. She began working at her mother's newspaper, the *Woman's Journal*, and for the next thirty-five years was the chief editor as well as a regular contributor.

The suffrage movement lagged due to the rift between the American Woman Suffrage Association and Susan B. Anthony's rival association. In 1890 Alice helped effect a truce, and after the two organizations merged she became the recording secretary, a position she held for twenty years.

Alice lived to be ninety-three and never stopped working for her causes, which included the W.C.T.U., the N.A.A.C.P., the American Peace Society and the Anti-Vivisection Society. After women won the right to vote, she helped start the League of Women Voters in Massachusetts. She became engrossed in the Sacco and Vanzetti case, firmly believing in their innocence and carrying on a lengthy correspondence with Vanzetti during his years in prison. In 1930 she published a biography of her mother which she had been working on for forty years. Lucy's dying words to her daughter were, "Make the world better." Alice spent her life trying to do so.

Alice's writing is from her article, "State Regulation of the Social Evil—A New Policy," in the August 17, 1918, issue of The Woman Citizen, *Volume III, Number 12.*

Mary Sheldon Barnes

1892

The study of history demands most serious work; like mathematics, it involves logic; like language, it demands analysis and fine discrimination of terms; like science, it calls for exact observation; like law, it needs the cool, well-balanced judgment; beyond all these, it requires the highest, fullest use of the sympathetic imagination. In fact, no study is more difficult; none calls more completely on all the mental powers; none affords the mind more generous play. . . . The teacher may be surprised at the small dose of dates, and may wish to add to it but it is the opinion of the author that a few dates thoroughly mastered, may always be kept in mind as nuclei for all historical reading and study.

*T*he study of history

Mary Downing Sheldon Barnes was born September 15, 1850, in Oswego, New York. Her father founded the Oswego State Normal School, for years the leader of Pestalozzian influence on American education.

Mary attended her father's school, and in 1871 entered the University of Michigan, recently opened to women, as a sophomore. She returned to the Normal School to teach "History, Latin, Greek and Botany for one thousand dollars a year and fun."

Mary began teaching history at Wellesley College in 1876 where she pioneered her "source" method of instruction. She used no textbooks, but handed out copies of primary sources each week for discussion in class. Her main aim was not to instill historical facts by rote but to encourage each student to observe, weigh evidence, and come to his or her own conclusions based on critical thought.

In 1885 Mary married Earl Barnes, a former student eleven years her junior. They moved to California in 1891 when he was offered the position of head of the education department at newly founded Stanford University. He applied his wife's source method to his teaching. Mary joined the Stanford history department the following year as an assistant professor.

Mary's writing is from Studies in American History: Teachers' Manual, *published in 1892.*

Anna Webber

A positive attitude

Blue Hill, Kansas
May 9, 1881
Well, here I am at my first school. I really wonder if I'll like it. . . . I have a scholar that is some deaf, and I've "hallooed" and talked today until my throat aches. I am among entire strangers, not knowing before I came here a single person.

. . . The school house is in a little valley, surrounded by hills. It is a small frame house, facing the South-west (or I guess it is, I can't tell one direction from another here). It has three windows and a door. There are no benches, seats, black board or writing desks. I am now sitting on the floor with my paper on "the Teacher's chair," which is as high as my chin (almost). For seats we have two boards placed on rocks. I think if I had more scholars, and things more convenient, I should like teaching very much.
May 10, 1881
Well, school is out. And I'm awful tired, and hungry enough to eat a stewed cat, if it was cooked tender, and I didn't know what it was. I have got along very nicely today. The wind has blown very hard. I have ten scholars.

Anna Webber was born September 16, 1860, in Breckenridge, Kansas. She passed the teacher's exam when she was twenty-one and was hired at the district school in Blue Hill, Center Township, Kansas. At that time schools in rural Kansas were makeshift at best and the terms were only three months long, usually in summer.

Anna's diary from her first teaching position in May through July, 1881, is in the Kansas State Historical Society.

Anna loved her profession and continued teaching for many years in both Kansas and Nebraska. She married Robert H. Gravatt in 1891 and settled in Talmadge, Nebraska, where she lived the rest of her life.

Cora Frances Stoddard

1932

The direct purpose of the instruction in the primary grades is to make the children understand that the use of alcoholic drinks is injurious for children; that it is also a disadvantage for grown men as well as for the general public; that life without alcoholic drinks is beautiful, good and worthwhile. . . .

Without going into the question of hereditary injury, there are plenty of other results of drink in the home to consider: bad housing, insufficient clothes and food, lack of sleep. If the father or mother lose their self-control as a result of alcoholism, the entire environment of the family is demoralizing to the soul of the young child.

Teaching temperance

Cora Frances Stoddard was born September 17, 1872, in Irvington, Nebraska, where her father was making an attempt at farming. They soon returned to New England, settling in East Brookfield, Massachusetts. Both parents were active in the temperance movement, and her mother was president of the local W.C.T.U.

After receiving her A.B. degree from Wellesley College in 1896, Clara became the private secretary to Mary Hunt [June 4], director of the Department of Scientific Temperance Instruction of the National W.C.T.U. Following Mrs. Hunt's death in 1906, Cora joined a small group in founding the Scientific Temperance Foundation to perpetuate Mrs. Hunt's work. She was its executive secretary for the next thirty years, compiling statistics, preparing exhibits, and writing numerous articles on the evils of alcohol.

The interest in school temperance education slackened after Prohibition went into effect in 1920. Cora then diversified her interests, studying the effects of Prohibition and the correlation between Prohibition and rising drug addiction.

Cora's writing is from her article, "Extent and Character of School Temperance Teaching," in the Spring, 1932, issue of Scientific Temperance *Journal.*

Emma E. Bailey

A fitting name

1901

When I was a little girl my father called me "Bird," because he said I seemed so joyous in all my manifestations. I well remember how ecstatic I was, bounding and laughing everywhere, with the birds singing in my soul and the flowers mirroring themselves in my spirit. I was heard to exclaim, "I never walk anywhere; I always run, because I am so happy." When asked my name I would say "Bird," and skip away to show the very spirit of the songsters, whom I adored with all my little being.

As the magnetic influence of the individual fitteth the within, and is a part or continuation of the same, so the name my father had given me seemed to fit my heredity and oncoming life.

Emma Bailey was born September 18, 1844, in Wilmington, Vermont, where her parents were ministers in the Universalist Church. They were sent to a different parish every few years, so her childhood was spent in many different states.

Emma read the entire Bible at the age of ten and at fourteen was sent to the Genesee Wesleyan Seminary. She commenced college, but the deaths of her father and her older sister, and the wounding of her brother in Civil War combat, forced her to return home.

Following the war she moved with her brother to Titusville, Pennsylvania, where he started his career as a Universalist minister. She was very active in his church and accompanied him when he was transferred to Cincinnati. It was there she received the calling to go into the ministry herself. In her autobiography she recalled her mother's story: "During a few months before I was born she had been very much engaged in the female prayer meetings held at parishioners' houses, and this she believes had a great effect upon my heredity."

Emma's writing is from
Happy Day or the
Confessions of a Woman
Minister, *published in 1901.*

Emma preached her first sermon in 1879 in Aurora, Indiana. For more than twenty years she was a minister in various small towns in Ohio, Pennsylvania, New Hampshire and New York.

Annie Wall

1886

Sordello is the history of the development of a soul.

It would seem to be, in some respects, the story of a soul whose complete and harmonious development has been thwarted by the circumstances amid which it finds itself; cut off by a lonely life from the educating influences of the outside world and from that correction of individual views that comes from contact with one's fellows.

Annie Carpenter Wall was born September 19, 1859, in Richland County, Wisconsin.

Due to ill health, Annie was educated at home by her mother. She published her first poems at fourteen and thereafter contributed to all the major literary journals in the United States.

Annie taught school from the age of seventeen until her marriage to Burton Wall of Marion, Indiana, in 1878. They moved to Pueblo, Colorado, in hopes that the climate would improve her fragile health. Burton went into the mercantile business while Annie took care of the home and pursued her literary and artistic interests. She published short stories, novels and several volumes of poetry, all with illustrations she did herself.

A lonely life

Annie's writing is from Sordello's Story Retold in Prose, *published in 1886.*

Elizabeth Smith Miller

1875

THE TABLE.

No silent educator in the household has higher rank than *the table*. Surrounded three times a day by the family, who gather from their various callings and duties, eager for refreshment of body and spirit, its impressions sink deep, and its influences for good or ill form no mean part of the warp and woof of our lives. . . .

An attractive, well-ordered table is an incentive to good manners; and being a place where one is inclined to linger, it tends to control the bad habit of fast eating.

*T*he power of the table

Elizabeth's writing is from her best-selling book of recipes and table etiquette, In the Kitchen, *published in 1875.*

An uninviting, disorderly table gives license to vulgar manners, and encourages that haste which has proved so deleterious to the health of Americans. Should it not, therefore, be one of our highest aims to bring our table to perfection in every particular?

Elizabeth Smith Miller was born September 20, 1822, in Hampton, New York.

Elizabeth, known as "Lizzie," married Charles Miller, a well-known New York lawyer, in 1843.

In 1851, Lizzie devised a simple outfit for comfort and mobility when working in her garden because the customary long skirts of the day were too awkward. She described the costume as a "short dress" with a skirt reaching "some four inches below the knee and Turkish trousers to the ankle." Her cousin, Elizabeth Cady Stanton [November 12], loved the idea and quickly adopted it. Soon Amelia Bloomer [May 27] began writing about it in the woman's reform paper, the *Lily.* Although it was Lizzie's idea, it became known as the Bloomer Costume through the publicity Amelia gave it.

Sophia Peabody Hawthorne

A light burden

Sophia's writing is from a letter she wrote to her husband while visiting her mother. It is included in Memories of Hawthorne *by her daughter Rose Hawthorne Lathrop, published in 1898.*

July, 1848

Every mother is not like me—because not every mother has such a father for her children; so that my cares are forever light. . . . Even in the very centre of simultaneous screams from both darling little throats, I am quite as sensible of my happiness as when the most dulcet sounds are issuing thence. I have suffered only for you, in my babydom. You ought not to be obliged to undergo the wear and tear of the nursery; it is contrary to your nature and your mood. You were born to muse, and through undisturbed dreams to enlighten the world.

Sophia Peabody Hawthorne was born September 21, 1809, in Salem, Massachusetts. She received most of her education at home; as an avid reader she mastered French, German, Italian, Latin, Greek and Hebrew. When she was fifteen she began to study art, but at the same time she developed migraines and began a steady diet of paregoric and opiates. She spent most of her time in her room, until one day Nathaniel Hawthorne, a neighbor, came to call. She went downstairs to meet him and stayed.

Sophie and Nathaniel were married in 1842 after a four-year engagement. She pursued her art, sharing a Boston studio with a woman friend. She illustrated books by Bronson Alcott and her husband, and made a bust of Laura Bridgman [December 21], the famous deaf mute, that was reproduced in plaster for distribution in schools. Since Hawthorne's earnings as an author were not enough to support their family of three children, Sophia painted shades and screens to augment their income. She always encouraged her husband and tried to create an atmosphere that was conducive to his work.

In 1850 the publication of *The Scarlet Letter*, and the critical and financial success that followed, altered their lives. *The House of the Seven Gables* came out the following year and *The Blithedale Romance* the year after that, further increasing their financial well-being. They bought the Wayside in Concord, next door to the Alcotts and down the road from the Emersons.

Margaret Lynn

1914

A delicious moment

Did you ever get a note in school?—from a boy? from a big boy? I suppose there are other experiences in life that are comparable to this, but certainly there is nothing else at that time which combines the same elements, dramatic, embarrassing, gratifying, triumphant, delicious, queer. The contents, I regret to say were insignificant, negligible. It is to be hoped that the big boys learned more about the art in time. But the mere fact of getting such a note, of having the other girls see you get it, all that in addition to the exciting fear that the teacher might see—once she made a girl read a note out loud!—fill the moment with peculiar emotion.

Margaret Lynn was born September 22, 1869, in Atchison County, Missouri. Her father ran the Tarkio Nursery, a large farm of 372 acres. Although she had seven siblings, Maggie spent most of her youth alone, reading. She especially loved poetry, Tennyson being her favorite.

After receiving her B.S. degree from Tarkio College and her Masters from the University of Nebraska, she commenced teaching at the University of Nebraska. She later became an associate professor of English literature at the University of Kansas, as well as the librarian.

Margaret's writing is from A Stepdaughter of the Prairie, *published in 1914.*

Following her death at eighty-nine her personal library, containing many rare books and first editions, was donated to the Tarkio College Library.

Sara Clarke Lippincott ("Grace Greenwood")

A little rural incident

Grace Greenwood's writing is from her book, Records of Five Years, *published in 1867.*

1867

During one of my morning rides, a week or two ago, I was amused, or rather, I will own, touched, by a little rural incident. A fine two-year-old colt made her escape from a farmyard, and went madly galloping down the road before me, evidently exulting in her freedom . . . suddenly catching sight of a somewhat melancholy-looking old bay, ploughing in single harness on the hillside near the road, she paused in mid career, wheeled, and dashed up on to a high, rocky bank. There, with arched neck, dilated nostrils, tail erect and waving like a signal, she saluted with a shrill, joyous neigh the elderly bay, who responded with a mild, motherly whinny. Then it became at once apparent that an incursion into the field was meditated. A farmer rushed to the fence to prevent the threatened leap; and then began an animated contest, which lasted several minutes. I checked my horse, and watched it with eager interest. Again and again the colt reared herself for the leap, now at one point, now at another; again and again was she driven back by the farmer's shouts and blows. Sometimes he made a feint of abandoning the enterprise altogether, but only to return speedily and more gallantly to the attack. At length, when the blows were falling heaviest on head and neck, and barbarous oaths were added to angry shouts, there came again that mild, motherly whinny, and the daring trespasser, gathering up all her energies, strong in young blood and filly-al piety, made one grand, successful vault over the highest portion of the fence, and with a few quick bounds was at the side of her dam. Rubbing her pretty head against the arched maternal neck, she seemed quietly to exult in the success of her bold yet virtuous undertaking, and the two seemed to exchange glad and loving greetings.

The expression in the face of *la mère* would have gone to any mother's heart. It was almost human in its joy, pride and placid content.

Sara Jane Clarke Lippincott, journalist and lecturer, was born September 23, 1823, in Pompey, New York. Local newspapers began publishing her poetry when she was thirteen. She wrote poems and essays under the pen name of Grace Greenwood. Her writing was so popular that the name was a familiar household word and she used it the rest of her life, both professionally and privately.

In 1849 Grace became an assistant editor at *Godey's Lady Book*. However, she also wrote for an anti-slavery magazine which so offended Southern subscribers that she was removed from the staff. She travelled abroad for two years until her marriage to Leander K. Lippincott.

Grace's choice of a husband was not a happy one. He was indicted by a grand jury for making fraudulent Indian land claims and disappeared forever to Europe. Grace continued writing for magazines to support herself and her daughter until her death in 1904.

Eliza Southgate Bowne

1802

A careful choice

... My dearest Mother, I submit myself wholly to the wishes of my father and you, convinced that my happiness is your warmest wish, and to promote it has ever been your study. That I feel deeply interested in Mr. Bowne I candidly acknowledge, and from the knowledge I have of his heart and character I think him better calculated to promote my happiness than any person I have yet seen; he is a firm, steady, serious man, nothing light or trifling in his character, and I have every reason to think he has well weighed his sentiments towards me, nothing rash or premature. I have referred him wholly to you, and you, my dearest Parents, must decide.

Eliza's letter requesting permission from her parents to marry "Mr. Bowne" is included in A Girl's Life Eighty Years Ago—Selections from the Letters of Eliza Southgate Bowne, *published in 1887.*

The third of twelve children, Eliza Southgate was born in Scarborough, Maine, on September 24, 1793. Her parents gave their children the best education available. Eliza went to the village school in Scarborough and at fourteen was sent to boarding school in Boston.

The first boarding school she attended was unsatisfactory. Her father, a doctor, found the situation of crowding two pupils in one bed and four to a room not proper for a growing girl. Eliza was then enrolled in the Young Ladies Academy conducted by Susanna Rowson where she was very happy. She wrote her parents, "I am again placed at school under the tuition of an amiable lady, so mild, so good, no one can help loving her; she treats all her scholars with such a tenderness as would win the affection of the most savage brute."

Eliza Southgate married Walter Bowne in 1803 and died six years later, soon after the birth of her second child.

SEPTEMBER 25　　*Maria Parloa*

A difficult choice

1889

My work—the teaching of cooking—has taken me into many of the States in our great union and given me an opportunity to study many phases of life. . . . Somebody may ask why then so many folks are pleased to live in hotels and boardinghouses. . . . Many couples, particularly those newly married, are deterred from keeping house by two reasons; lack of money to establish themselves as they would like, and secondly, the inexperience of the wife in the discharge of household duties. . . . It may be that there are funds enough, and experience enough, but that the wife and mother is not strong enough to bear the burdens of a housekeeper. It is, therefore, not always by choice that people flock to boardinghouses. Probably a majority of those who patronize them long for homes of their own.

Maria Parloa was born September 25, 1843, in Massachusetts. An orphan, she supported herself by cooking for private families or at New Hampshire resort hotels.

At the age of twenty-eight, Maria enrolled in the two-year teaching program at the Maine Central Institute. After graduation, she took a job in Mandarin, Florida. The local Sunday school was trying to raise money for an organ, so Maria gave a cooking lecture to bring in funds. It was so popular that her friends urged her to open a cooking school, which she did in 1877 in Boston.

Maria's writing is from her article, "Is Housekeeping a Failure?," in the 1889 issue of The North American Review, Volume 148, Number 2.

Maria continued to study cooking herself, travelling to England and France. In 1883 she opened another school in New York City, and she gave free evening classes at city mission schools. She published several cookbooks and cooking textbooks, which went through numerous editions. Maria became a part owner of the *Ladies' Home Journal*, to which she contributed articles regularly until her death at sixty-six.

Julie Schramm

1836

My dearly beloved sisters and brothers-in-law!

I miss you so all the time, my dear sisters! I never before felt so deeply how much I love you, and how very much I depend upon you. The thought of being so widely separated from you was almost unbearable; particularly at the time little Mathilde was on the way, and I didn't yet know where I should be able to get help. But even in the vastest solitudes, God, who is the Father of us all, can send His help and protection. This I have observed very clearly in my own case. I was a little more indisposed than after Nanni's birth; that is to say, very weak. My dear husband had some good wine and beer brought out for me from the city. That gave me back my strength quickly, so that now I am quite well and happy again, along with our little Mathilde.

Johanna Juliana Junghans Schramm (Julie) was born September 26, 1807, in Wilsdruff, Saxony, Southern Germany. In 1831 she became engaged to Jakob Schramm. His father objected to Julie, arguing that she was not from a good enough family for his son.

Jakob and Julie were married. He gave a large sum of money to a friend who was leaving for America with instructions to purchase land for him. Four years later the Schramms, with one daughter, a fourteen-year-old servant girl, and Julie's father, embarked for the United States. Jakob brought an extensive library and four musical instruments, which he later taught his four children to play. Julie brought furniture, and hand-carried coral honeysuckle seeds which she planted on one side of the front porch.

Initially Julie and Jakob thought they would return to

In need of help

Julie's letter, in the The Indiana Historical Society, Indianapolis, was translated by her great-granddaughter, Norma Stone.

Germany after seven or eight years, (all they thought they could endure in the "wilderness"). However, despite illness, hard labor, mosquitoes and bad roads, their farm prospered and they grew to love America. Julie is the great-grandmother of well-known author Kurt Vonnegut, Jr.

Martha Jefferson Randolph

*A*n order for wigs

October 29, 1802

Dear Papa,

We received your letter, and are prepared with all speed to obey its summons. By next Friday I hope we shall be able to fix a day; and probably the shortest time in which the horses can be sent after receiving our letter will determine it, though as yet it is not certain that we can get off so soon. Will you be so good as to send orders to the milliner, Madame Peck, I believe her name is, through Mrs. Madison, who very obligingly offered to execute any little commission for us to Philadelphia, for two wigs of the color of the hair enclosed, and of the most fashionable shapes, that they may be in Washington when we arrive? They are universally worn, and will relieve us as to the necessity of dressing our own hair, a business in which neither of us are adept. . . .

Adieu, dearest father

Martha Jefferson Randolph, eldest child of Thomas Jefferson, was born on their Virginia estate, "Monticello," September 27, 1772. Following her mother's death when she was ten, Martha accompanied her father to Philadelphia for the Continental Congress and then to France on a diplomatic mission. They remained in France five years. She received an excellent education, especially in the arts and classics, spoke fluent French, and attracted a great deal of attention with her cheerful personality.

A few weeks after returning to Virginia, Martha was married to her cousin Thomas Randolph. He and his father were alienated, and as their family grew they became more and more reliant on Jefferson for financial aid. He helped them to acquire "Edgehill," an estate a few miles down the road from Monticello. Martha had twelve children. Following Thomas' retirement in 1809, they spent nearly all their time with him at Monticello.

Martha's letter to her father, responding to his invitation to visit him in Washington, is included in Worthy Women of Our First Century, *edited by Mrs. O.J. Wister and Miss Agnes Irwin, published in 1877.*

Give Her This Day

Martha was in dire financial straits after her father's death in 1826. She was forced to sell Monticello, but fortunately the South Carolina and the Louisiana Legislatures each appropriated her enough money for her remaining years.

Frances Elizabeth Willard

1892

Beloved Comrades of the White-Ribbon Army. . . . . .

I regard the women's temperance movement as without parallel and without peer because it does not expect to win through any sleight-of-hand, it does not expect to surprise the enemy by skirmishes of night attacks, but in the strong day-light of reason, conscience, faith—it does expect to put to rout the armies of the aliens—those aliens of appetite, ignorance and greed which form the only hope of whisky makers and beer politicians.

*T*he White-Ribbon army

Frances Elizabeth Willard was born September 28, 1839, in Churchville, New York. At six the family relocated to the Wisconsin frontier; their farm was so remote that often months would pass without their seeing other people.

Frances taught school for several years following college, then embarked on a two-year tour of Europe. Upon her return she had determined to achieve some good for "the girls of my native land and my times."

When the National Woman's Christian Temperance Union was founded in 1874, Frances was chosen corresponding secretary. Five years later she became president and served as such for the remaining twenty years of her life. She was the originator of the official W.C.T.U. slogan, "For God and Home and Native Land." Frances believed membership for women in the W.C.T.U. could be a first step toward bringing them out of their homes to become more involved in society and its needs.

Frances' writing is from an address she gave before the nineteenth National W.C.T.U. Convention in Atlanta in 1892.

Mary Julia Allyn

*W*yoming squatters

1955

Squatters were required to make improvements on their lots, thus showing their intention of proving up on them. Following a year's residence the lot-holders proved up on their property, paying a fee of $2.50 a lot, after which they became the legal owners and the lots were then subject to tax.

We had two lots staked out south of Main Street. The Monday morning after we arrived I carried a grubbing hoe and a city map and with the girls, went to the location. I worked most of the day grubbing sage-brush, stacking it neatly in a corner of the lot. We carried a load back to the tent for use as fuel in our little stove. Later I discovered that I had dug the sage-brush from Dave Nelson's lots instead of ours. He then hired the grubbing of our lots.

Mary Julia Moore Allyn, Wyoming pioneer, was born September 29, 1875, in Ray, Illinois. Her family moved to Wyoming in 1894. Five years later Mary married Frank Allyn and they settled in Cheyenne.

In 1904-5, Frank and several other surveyors were working on an area of land ceded by the Indians that was to be opened for settlement. He quit his job to register for the drawing. On the big day, "five or six hundred people arrived in sight of their destination, making a great dust. Some were on horseback, others in wagons and buckboards. Many were walking. The lots that had already been staked were soon 'squatted' upon." Frank claimed a good piece of land in the new settlement of "Riverton" and three days later Mary joined him with their two daughters.

When Mary was eighty her daughter prevailed upon her to write a book about what it had been like to be a pioneer.

Mary's writing is from her book, Twentieth Century Pioneering—Our Frontier Days Experience at Riverton, Wyoming, *privately printed in 1956.*

Give Her This Day

Lucinda Hinsdale Stone

1897

I received an invitation to go to Mississippi to teach
in the family of a wealthy planter who lived near
Natchez. . . . In driving from Natchez to my new
residence, we passed through a slave market on a market day. Although I had heard of slavery, I had no idea
of it. A girl stood upon the block. The auctioneer was
showing off her good points, making her open her
mouth to show her teeth, use her limbs in various antics
to test her agility, while he chuckled, wheedled, scolded
and threatened, by turns, to make her do her very best.
It seems strange to me now that I could have lived
through such a scene, but I am not the same person or
being now as then, else I could not have borne it. In
looking back to that time, it seems to me that I must
have been benumbed, or had not the same senses that I
now possess.

Lucinda Hinsdale Stone was born September 30, 1814, in
Hinesburg, Vermont, the youngest of twelve children. She
attended Hinesburg Academy, then took a job for three years
as tutor for a wealthy Mississippi plantation owner's children.
In 1840 she married James Stone, the former principal of
Hinesburg Academy.

Lucinda and James settled in Kalamazoo, Michigan,
where he headed the recently established Kalamazoo College
and she became principal of its "Female Department." She
held regular gatherings for teachers at her home, with interesting speakers such as women's rights leaders, abolitionists
and authors. Local women requested she do the same for
them, so in 1852 she launched the Kalamazoo Ladies' Library
Association.

Lucinda retired from Kalamazoo College in 1863 and
began taking groups of girls to Europe and the Near East to
study history and art. Each trip lasted from twelve to eighteen
months. Between trips she continued to organize women's
clubs, believing them to be the best way to educate adult
women. She wrote a weekly column for Michigan papers entitled "Club Talks," and was known as the "mother of clubs."

Seeing slavery

Lucinda's writing is from
Lucinda Hinsdale Stone,
Her Life Story and
Reminiscences *by Belle Perry*
(President of the Michigan
State Federation of Women's
Clubs), published in 1902.

OCTOBER

Kate Field

1894

I take exception to what Miss Anthony has said, because
I think she has misconstrued my position entirely. I
never have been against woman suffrage. I have been
against universal suffrage of any kind, regardless of sex.
I think that morally woman has exactly as much right to
the suffrage as man. It is a disgrace that such women as
you and I have not the suffrage, but I do think that all
suffrage should be regarded as a privilege and should
not be demanded as a right. It should be the privilege of
education and, if you please—I will not quarrel about
that of a certain property qualification. I have not
changed my opinion, but I did say that I was tired of
waiting for men to have common sense . . . that is my
position . . . I withdraw my former attitude and take my
stand on this platform.

*A*gainst universal suffrage

Kate Field was born October 1, 1838, in St. Louis, Missouri.
She received a good education and enjoyed a carefree childhood until her father's death when she was eighteen. She and
her mother were left with only a small insurance payment, but,
luckily, they were quickly taken in by a very wealthy uncle,
Milton Sanford.

Uncle Milton put Kate through three years of Lasell
Seminary, introduced her to the social scene in Boston and
Newport, and took her abroad for a two-year stay in Florence.
While in Italy, she wrote a column for the Boston paper, the
Transcript, which began her thirty-year career as a journalist.
It was fortunate that she had learned to support herself, as her
outspoken pro-Union views alienated her from her uncle
during the Civil War. He drastically reduced his financial aid
and also greatly reduced her inheritance in his will.

Kate was associated with several major newspapers until
January 1, 1890, when she launched her own weekly review,
"Kate Field's Washington." She wrote most of the articles
herself, covering politics, the arts, reform movements and
society news. However, she was unable to operate in the black,
and was forced to shut down the presses in 1895. She died of
pneumonia the following year in Hawaii, where she had gone
to lecture and relax.

*Kate's excerpt is from a speech
she gave before the 1894
National Woman Suffrage
Convention. It is included in
Volume IV of* History of
Woman Suffrage *(1883-
1900), edited by Susan B.
Anthony and Ida Harper,
published in 1902.*

Mary Pickard Ware

Qualms about marriage

January 30, 1827
Dearest Emma,

    . . . A change has passed over the spirit of my earthly dreams, and instead of the self-dependent, self-governed being you have known me, I have learned to look to another for guidance and happiness; and more than that, have bound myself, by an irrevocable vow, to live for the future in the exercise of the great and responsible duties which such a connection inevitably brings with it. . . . You need no explanation, nor have I time to give any; it would require one of our long nights to trace the rise and progress of the influences that have thus terminated. At present, the idea of the change I am making is so solemn, so appalling, that my faculties are almost paralyzed. . . .

Mary Pickard Ware was born October 2, 1798, in Boston, Massachusetts. She was sent at thirteen to be tutored by the Misses Cushing in Hingham, but soon after her arrival had to return home to nurse her seriously ill mother who died a few months later. For young, sensitive Mary this was the beginning of a life of confinement with the sick and dying.

    Mary attended two more years of school in Hingham until her grandfather died, and she returned to spend two years caring for her grandmother as she had cared for her mother. Following the grandmother's death Mary and her father lived in a Boston boardinghouse until his death in 1823. She wrote to a friend that she thought "trouble was to be her destiny."

    At twenty-nine Mary became engaged to Henry Ware, Jr., a widowed Unitarian minister. She married a man she barely knew and became stepmother to his two children. As fate would have it, even Mary's husband turned out to be sickly. He had to resign his pastorate in Boston due to ill health and a teaching position was arranged for him at Harvard.

    Henry died in 1843 at the age of forty-nine. Mary moved with her four children to Milton, Massachusetts, where she became the governess for a wealthy family until her death six years later.

Mary's writing is from a letter to one of her best friends on the day she became engaged. It is included in Mary's memoir book, compiled by Edward B. Hall and published in 1853.

Jeannette Leonard Gilder

1901

*H*appy girl

Every one said that I was a tomboy; and, being a good
American, I bowed to the verdict of the majority and
was happy. I never quite understood why a girl who
climbed trees, clung to the tail end of carts, and otherwise deported herself as a well-conditioned girl should
not, was called a tomboy. It always seemed to me that,
if she was anything she should not be, it was a tomgirl.
However, tomboy was the accepted name for such girls
as I was, and there was no use in arguing the case. After
all, it made little difference. I did not care what they
called me, so long as they let me alone.

Jeannette Leonard Gilder was born October 3, 1849, in Flush-
ing, New York. The family moved in with relatives in
Bordentown, New Jersey, when Reverend Gilder left to join
the Union army as a chaplain during the Civil War.

    After Jeannette's father died of smallpox during the war,
she took her first job at the age of fifteen to help support the
family. Soon after, she began working at the *Newark Morning
Register* and discovered her true calling as a journalist.

    In 1875, Jeannette moved to New York City to become
literary editor of the *New York Herald*. She was immediately
accepted into the local literary scene and befriended many
well-known authors and artists. She and her brother Joseph
co-founded the *Critic*, a weekly magazine of literary review and
criticism. The magazine had a readership of five thousand and
remained in print for twenty-five years.

Jeannette's writing is from The
Autobiography of a Tomboy,
published in 1901.

Agnes Booth

1900

*L*earning doesn't hurt

When I began, girls had to begin at the very beginning—at the bottom—and climb up. Girls didn't star
the first season or jump into public favor the first year,
as a rule, in those days. We had no schools of acting
then. All a girl could do was to get a chance and work
hard and depend on her ability to bring her fame. I

*Agnes' writing is from an
interview that was included in
her obituary in the January 8,
1910,* New York Dramatic
Mirror.

began by going on in the ballet—not a desirable way, perhaps, but my mother believed it to be the best way. I went on and danced. It never hurts you, you know, to learn anything.

Agnes Booth was born October 4, 1843, in Sydney, Australia. She joined a dance troupe at fourteen and left for San Francisco the following year.

Agnes played various roles in touring theater companies in the west. She married Harry Perry in 1861, but he died the next year. In 1867 she married Junius Brutus Booth, Jr., the elder brother of Edwin and John Wilkes. Agnes had been playing to full houses in Washington, Chicago and Boston. Following her second marriage, she joined Edwin Booth's theater company in New York.

After Junius Brutus' death in 1883, she married for a third time to theater manager John Schoeffel, although she retained her stage name, Agnes Booth. She owned a beautiful home in New York, as well as one in Manchester-by-the-Sea on the Massachusetts coast, where she was known as a gracious and lavish hostess.

OCTOBER 5

Belle Moskowitz

A cloak of love

July 29, 1907
Dearest,
        . . . We have nearly come to four years since we ventured together and sometimes it is like four days— and again, four*teen* years. It is curious to think how each of us has become a vital part of the other and how the four years are just a steady growth of love and confidence. You are an inexpressible something to me that is just as real a necessity as the air I breathe and you always seem to be about me surrounding me with a cloak of love and devotion and "work-for-you" that is too beautiful to be told about. I only hope I am worth it all and that I do in some measure bring you a compensating help.

Belle's letter to her first husband, Charles Israels, is in the Moskowitz Manuscript Collection, Skain Library, Connecticut College Special Collections, New London, Connecticut.

Belle Lindner Israels Moskowitz was born October 5, 1877, to a prominent Polish-Jewish family in New York City. All through high school and her one year at Teachers College of Columbia, she volunteered at the Educational Alliance, an organization which provided recreational and cultural services to the poor immigrants of the East Side.

In 1900 Belle became a full-time member of the Educational Alliance's staff. There she met Charles Israels, an architect. They were married in 1903 but he died eight years later, leaving Belle to raise their three children alone.

Belle became involved in reform politics and befriended Henry Moskowitz during his unsuccessful bid for Congress on the Progressive ticket. They were married in 1914. In 1918 she began working for Alfred E. Smith, Democratic candidate for governor of New York. Women were voting for the first time that year, and she directed a special campaign toward winning their support. Although she held no official position, she was his constant advisor during his eight years as governor and his failed attempts at the presidency. He described Belle as having "the greatest brain I ever knew."

Fanny Appleton Longfellow

May 27, 1844

Love at sunset

Henry took his sunset row on the river. Sat at window and followed the flashing of his oars with my eyes and heart. He rowed round one bend of the river, then another, now under the shadow of the woods and now in the golden sunlight. Longed to be with him and grew impatient for wings he looked so far away. How completely my life is bound up in his love—how broken and incomplete when he is absent a moment; what infinite peace and fullness when he is present. And he loves me to the uttermost desire of my heart. Can any child excite as strong a passion as this we feel for each other?

Frances (Fanny) Appleton Longfellow was born October 6, 1817, in Boston, Massachusetts. Following a long courtship, she became Henry Wadsworth Longfellow's second wife in 1843.

Longfellow was a Harvard professor at the time of their marriage, and they settled in "Craigie Castle" on Brattle Street in Cambridge. Their home was filled with happiness and love. They eventually had two sons and three daughters.

On July 9, 1861, Fanny was heating sealing wax to close a package containing a lock of one of her children's hair. A sleeve of her gossamer dress caught fire, and she was engulfed

Fanny's journal is in her papers in the Longfellow House, Cambridge, Massachusetts. This excerpt was written twelve days before the birth of her son Charles.

in flames. She ran from the library to the front room where Henry was writing. He was able to protect her face and part of her body, but she was badly burned and died the following morning. Longfellow was so seriously burned that he could not attend her funeral.

Martha McChesney Berry

*B*uilding a school

1904

I drove eight miles to Possum Trot Creek, and found an abandoned old house that had been built long before the war. The roof had tumbled in and there were no doors or windows. Once it rained while I was holding my Sunday-school, and my thin muslin dress was wet from the rain dripping through the roof. I would shift the Sunday-school from one corner to the other seeking protection from the rain. I asked the people to put on a new roof. . . . I saw a board tree nearby and told the men that if they would fell it and cut it into boards by a certain date, I would bring up nails and treat the workers to lemonade. Quite a number came and worked very hard. . . . Some were very much amused, and one old man declared that he "never heard of a woman a-bossin' of a house-roofin' before."

Martha McChesney Berry was born October 7, 1866, on a cotton plantation, "Oak Hill," near Rome, Georgia. She was always concerned with the plight of the mountain people whom she encountered on visits to the family hunting lodge on Mt. Berry in the Blue Ridge range. One Sunday in the late 1890's, she was reading at the log-cabin retreat her father had built for her near the lodge. Three local children stopped by and she offered to read them Bible stories. They returned the following week with others, and so commenced her career as an educator.

Martha's father had died several years earlier, leaving her financially comfortable. After discovering the lack of educational opportunities available to the mountain people, she decided to use her inheritance to establish schools. In 1902 she opened the Boys' Industrial School, and seven years later she added the Martha Berry School for Girls. The majority of students were cash-poor, so she worked out a system whereby tuition could be paid off through manual labor.

Martha dreamed that her graduates would return to the

Martha's writing is from her article, "A School in the Woods," from the August 6, 1904, Outlook, *Volume 73.*

Give Her This Day

mountains to educate and inspire others. In 1926 she established Berry College. Following her death in 1941, she was buried on the grounds of the Berry Schools, which are still in operation today with over one hundred buildings spread over thousands of acres.

Caroline Gilman

1837

*R*eason to blush

I am sure of the sympathy of my female readers, who, whatever may be their station in society, have, I doubt not, been over-dressed at least once in their lives. Who can forget the first pang at the suspicion of the fact; the furtive glance around the company, to ascertain some companionship in finery; the earnest gaze at every new-comer, in hope that some extra ribbon or lace may be displayed; and then the settling down into the conviction that one is altogether *out of taste*, while the blush that began on the cheek spreads and deepens, till the forehead glows and the fingers tingle?

Caroline Howard Gilman was born October 8, 1794, in Boston. She began writing poetry when she was eleven, but was ashamed of her talent and did not start publishing regularly until the 1830's.

In 1819, Caroline married Samuel Gilman, a Harvard graduate who wrote the poem "Fair Harvard." They settled in Charleston, South Carolina, where he became a Unitarian minister. After raising seven children, Caroline began publishing *The Rosebud—or Youth's Gazette*, one of the first American children's magazines.

She produced a tremendous variety of work, including novels, short stories, poetry, travel books, children's books, a woman's almanac and a biography of her husband.

Caroline had to flee inland during the Civil War. When she returned to Charleston in November of 1865, she found that her home and most of her possessions, including her personal papers, had been destroyed. She never wrote again.

Caroline's writing is from Recollections of a New England Bride and of a Southern Matron, *published in 1837.*

Harriet Goodhue Hosmer

The artist's assistants

1864

I have heard so much, lately, about artists who do not do their own work, that I feel disposed to raise the veil upon the mysteries of the studio as well as to correct the false, but very general impression, that the artist, beginning with the crude block, and guided by his imagination only, hews out his statue with his own hands. . . .

We women-artists have no objection to its being known that we employ assistants; we merely object to its being supposed that it is a system peculiar to *ourselves*. When Thorwaldsen was called upon to execute his twelve statues of the Apostles, he designed and furnished the small models, and gave them into the hands of his pupils and assistants, by whom, almost exclusively, they were copied in their present colossal dimensions. The great master rarely put his own hand to the clay; yet we never hear them spoken of except as "Thorwaldsen's statues."

Harriet Goodhue Hosmer was born October 9, 1830, in Watertown, Massachusetts.

Harriet was sent to boarding school in her early teens, where her artistic talents were encouraged. She took lessons in sculpting technique in Boston and in 1852 departed for further study in Rome. She became the only pupil of the British sculptor John Gibson.

Harriet's reputation as a sculptor began to spread as she sold pieces abroad. She received a commission for a piece for the St. Louis Mercantile Library, and her sales soared. In 1864, rumors were started that one of her statues was not her work but that of her mentor Gibson. She sued two magazines who had printed the suggestion for libel, and wrote an article for *The Atlantic Monthly* defending herself.

Harriet's writing is from her article, "The Process of Sculpture," in the December, 1864, issue of The Atlantic Monthly, *Volume 14.*

Harriet Newell

February 1812

Accept, my ever dear Sarah, the last tribute of heartfelt affection from your affectionate Harriet, which you will ever receive. The hour of my departure hastens. . . .

I shall bid a last farewell to a beloved widowed mother, brothers and sisters dear, and the circle of Haverhill friends. The stormy ocean must be crossed; and an Indian cottage in a sultry clime must shortly contain all that is Harriet. Perhaps no sympathizing friend will stand near my dying bed, to wipe the falling tear, to administer consolation, or to entomb my worthless ashes when my immortal spirit quits this earthy tabernacle.

My Friend, there is a rest for the weary pilgrim in yonder world—Shall we meet there—"when the long Sabbath of the tomb is Past?"

Sarah—my much loved friend—farewell. Farewell perhaps forever. Though trackless forest separate— though oceans roll between—Oh, forget not.

Harriet

Harriet Atwood Newell was born October 10, 1793, in Haverhill, Massachusetts. As a child she already showed an interest in dedicating herself to a Christian life, telling her teacher at thirteen that "I have one constant companion, the Bible, from which I derive the greatest comfort."

At the age of eighteen, Harriet married Reverend Samuel Newell. They set sail almost immediately on the *Caravan* out of Salem, Massachusetts, to begin their life as missionaries in India. During the long voyage, Harriet began to get to know her husband, who was practically a stranger when they married. Luckily, she found him to be a wonderful man, writing to her mother to "unite with me in praising God, for one of the best husbands . . . he is *all* that I could wish him to be."

Upon arriving in Calcutta, they found the government would not allow them to set up a mission because the English East India Company was violently opposed to missions. They were ordered by the government to return to America immediately, but after a few days they obtained permission from the East India Company to go to the Isle of France (Mauritius).

Harriet gave birth to a daughter during the voyage from

Farewell

Harriet's writing is from A Sermon, preached at Haverhill, Mass., in remembrance of Mrs. Harriet Newell, Wife of the Reverend Samuel Newell, Missionary to India, who died at the Isle of France, November 30, 1812, aged nineteen years, to which are added Memoirs of Her Life, *by Leonard Woods, D.D., published in 1814.*

India to the Isle of France. Sadly, the baby died after five days and was buried at sea. Harriet died seven weeks later of consumption and complications from childbirth.

Harriet Boyd Hawes

Discovery

1901

Two boys were digging in a place which appeared to me quite unpromising; they were new at the work and I did not like to transfer them at once to another spot for fear of discouraging their zeal, which was admirable. The trench they were digging was blocked by a pile of stones jutting in irregular lengths at all angles. Suddenly it was discovered that by removing these stones they had made a window in the side of a "bee-hive" tomb. The tomb remained as it had been left almost three thousand years ago. Looking in, we saw a large pithos, whole, lying upon its side surrounded by vases, with four skeletons stretched out beside it. . . .

Harriet Ann Boyd Hawes was born October 11, 1871, in Boston. Her mother died when she was an infant, and she was raised in a primarily masculine environment. She especially revered one of her brothers, who taught her to share his love of ancient history. In 1892, she graduated from Smith College and went on to do graduate work at the American School of Classical Studies in Athens.

At the end of the nineteenth century, the Turks were finally driven from the island of Crete, and the region was suddenly opened to archaeologists. The English, French and Italians had quickly seized the opportunity, and Harriet was anxious to do the same. Since she received no support from her school, she set off for Crete on her own in 1900, using her own funds and what remained of her fellowship grant.

Harriet began excavating at Kavousi and discovered many Iron Age tomb sites. She described her findings in a thesis for Smith, for which she earned an M.A. degree in 1901.

Harriet taught at Smith from 1900 to 1906, but she was always anxious to return to the field and did so frequently. In 1901 she found an ancient town site, one of the "ninety cities" of Crete described in the *Odyssey*. Harriet directed the excavations in 1901, 1903 and 1904, making her the first archaeologist to find and completely excavate a Minoan town of the Early Bronze Age.

Harriet's writing is from her article, "Excavations at Kavousi in Crete," in the American Journal of Archaeology, *April-June, 1901, Volume V, Number 2.*

1910

Talent is born with us, but the influence of surroundings shapes, develops or subdues it. That sweet sadness,
which for the most part exists in Polish melodies and
poems and which is the outcome of the whole nation's
sufferings, that limitless tenderness and longing,
unconsciously rooted itself in my soul from my very
childhood, in spite of the fiery and stormy temperament
I brought with me into the world—presumably an inheritance from a Hungarian great-grandmother. That
note of tenderness always predominated both in my
nature and my work, in which often flashes of inborn
vivacity and passion were overshadowed by that touch of
Slavonic *Tesknota*, a word quite untranslatable into a
foreign language, which may be best interpreted by the
following verse of Longfellow:

> A feeling of sadness and longing
> That is not akin to pain,
> And resembles sorrow only
> As the mist resembles rain.

*S*weet sadness

Helena Modjeska was born October 12, 1840, in Krakow,
Poland. She attended convent school but yearned to be an
actress, so she dropped out of school to take music and acting
lessons. She made her theatrical debut in 1861.

    Helena married Karol Chlapowski, a Polish aristocrat, in
1868. He took over the reins of her career and guided her to
become the leading actress in Warsaw. Eight years later they
moved to a farm in the Santa Ana Valley of southern California with eight other Polish immigrants. The others were to
start a communal farm, while Helena's goal was to conquer the
American theater.

    Helena studied English for four months, then made her
stage debut in California. She was very successful and went on
to a New York engagement and an eastern tour. In Boston,
fans crowded the street and blocked her carriage to catch a
glimpse of her. For the next twenty years, she travelled the
United States in an elegant private railroad car, playing
opposite America's leading men.

    Madame Modjeska gave her farewell performance at New
York's Metropolitan Opera House on May 2, 1905. She was
given a public testimonial at which all the major figures in the

Helena's writing is from
Memories and Impressions
of Helena Modjeska—An
Autobiography, *published
in 1910.*

American theater paid homage to her. She and her husband, both naturalized citizens, settled at Arden, their estate in the Santiago Canyon of the Santa Ana Range, twenty miles from the site of their original cooperative farm. Following her death, the canyon was renamed Modjeska Canyon.

Mary Barr Clay

Questionable chivalry

1902

We are told that men protect us; that they are generous, even chivalric in their protection. Gentlemen, if your protectors were women, and they took all your property and your children, and paid you half as much for your work, though as well or better done than your own, would you think much of the chivalry which permitted you to sit in street-cars and picked up your pocket-handkerchief?

Mary Barr Clay was born October 13, 1839, in Lexington, Kentucky. Her father was Cassius Clay, the well-known anti-slavery activist. Although they lived in a slave state, she learned at an early age to abhor slavery.

In 1860 Mary married John Herrick, but she divorced him twelve years later. During the late 1860's she heard Lucy Stone speak at a women's rights convention and became a convert. She wrote articles for the local papers and became the first native Kentuckian to take the public platform for woman suffrage.

Mary travelled to St. Louis in 1879 where she introduced herself to Susan B. Anthony, who was holding a convention there. She asked to be admitted as a delegate from Kentucky; Miss Anthony welcomed her and appointed her vice-president for her state.

In later years Mary moved to Ann Arbor, Michigan, for her two sons' education. She immediately organized a suffrage club there, and edited a column in the *Ann Arbor Register* on woman suffrage. She frequently travelled to Washington, D.C., to address the House and Senate Committees for the rights of women.

Mary's writing is included in Volume IV of History of Woman Suffrage *(1883-1900), edited by Susan B. Anthony and Ida Harper, published in 1902.*

Lydia W. Foster

10th Mo., 14th, 1855
This is my birthday. Eighteen years of my life have
sped; I can hardly realize that it is so. How unprofitably
much of my time has been spent!—more in gratifying
selfish desires and pleasures, than endeavoring to serve
the Lord. O Heavenly Father, help me to spend the
future more to thy glory and honor, so that at the
winding up of my earthly career, whether my time be
shorter or longer, I may be found ready to meet the
Bridegroom.

Birthday concerns

Lydia W. Foster was born October 14, 1837, in Hopkinton,
Rhode Island. She was raised in a devout Quaker family,
travelling frequently within the state and to Massachusetts for
meetings.

Lydia suffered all her life from ill health and passed away
a month after her twenty-third birthday. Following her death,
her mother wrote, "She was a kind and dutiful child, being
religiously inclined from early life. The loss of two dear
brothers, in the years 1854 and 1855 tended much to wean her
from the world and to increase her desires that she might
become more devoted to the cause of truth."

*Lydia's writing is from her
diary, published posthumously in
1872.*

Helen Hunt Jackson

1883
The sheep ranches are usually desolate places . . . home
and outbuildings clustered together in a hollow or on a
hillside where there is water; the less human the neighborhood the better . . . for the small sheepmen, the
shepherds, and, above all, the herders, it is a terrible life,
how terrible is shown by the frequency of insanity
among herders.

After learning this fact, it is no longer possible to
see the picturesque side of the effective groups one so
often comes on suddenly in the wildernesses: sheep
peacefully grazing, and the shepherd lying on the
ground watching them, or the whole flock racing in a

A terrible life

*Helen's writing is from the
chapter, "Industries in
Southern California," in her
book* Glimpses of California
and the Missions, *published
in 1883.*

solid, fleecy, billowy scamper up or down a steep hillside, with the dogs leaping and barking on all sides at once. One scans the shepherd's face alone, with pitying fear lest he may be losing his wits.

Helen Maria Fiske Hunt Jackson was born October 15, 1830, in Amherst, Massachusetts. She was orphaned when she was seventeen, and five years later married Lieutenant Edward Hunt, an army engineer. His job forced them to move constantly, causing Helen to refer to the life of an army wife as "scatterdom."

In 1863 Edward was accidentally killed while testing one of his inventions, an underwater projectile launcher. Two years later their last surviving son died of diphtheria. Helen was so grief-stricken that her friends feared she would go insane.

Helen did recover from her grief, and began writing poetry, which was published in the *New York Evening Post* and *The Nation*. By the 1870's, she was regarded as the newest star among contemporary female authors, and Emerson thought she was the best woman poet in America.

In 1873 Helen travelled to Colorado, hoping the dry winter weather would benefit her septic sore throat. While there, she met and married William Jackson, a Quaker banker. She became aware of the poverty of the western Indians and began a personal campaign against the federal government for their negligent conduct in Indian affairs.

Helen turned her crusade for Indian reform into the famous novel *Ramona* which has gone through more than three hundred editions, has been made into three movies, and is the subject of an annual pageant in Hemet, California.

OCTOBER 16

Mary Agnes Brent

A question of
commitment

*Mother Agnes' letter to Bishop
Rosati of St. Louis is from the
archives of the St. Francis de
Sales Library, Academy of the
Visitation, St. Louis, Missouri.*

5 Aug 1833

My Lord and very dear Brother

Deeming it incumbent on me to let you know all that concerns us, I have to inform you that one of our sisters has become quite discontented and has requested me to let her petition to the Mother Superior of Georgetown to recall her: I acceded to her request, but have not sent the letter, wishing to know your opinion on the subject; it is the Lay-Sister, knowing her unquiet disposition, I am not surprised.

Give Her This Day

Rev. Mr. Condamini spoke to me, of a sister of charity wishing to join us, we are willing to receive her, provided she be willing to bear the inconvenience of poverty: for, it is not in vain, that St. Francis de Sales calls us daughters of calvary, we must die daily to ourselves to live only in God and for God, we rely entirely on divine providence for support.

Mother Mary Agnes Brent was born October 16, 1796, in Port Tobacco, Maryland. Her uncle was Bishop, later Archbishop, of Baltimore. She attended convent school and soon after finishing her religious training was put in charge of the new sisters entering the convent. By the age of twenty-five she had become Mother Superior of the convent.

In 1833 Mother Agnes responded to the Bishop of St. Louis' call to go to Illinois to start a school. She and seven Visitation nuns established the Menard Academy in Kaskaskia. In 1843 the town flooded, and the nuns and the pupils had to be rescued from the second floor of the academy. The building was so severely damaged that they moved the school to St. Louis.

In the late 1850's, Mother Agnes borrowed $113,862 from the Archbishop's building fund to erect a new Visitation Academy on a large piece of property that had been donated to her by a wealthy widow. The three-story brick building in the Federal style became a landmark in the northwest section of St. Louis. As the years went on and the school thrived, she was able to pay back the Archbishop's entire loan. Mother Agnes retired from active school duties shortly before her death at eighty-one.

Louisa Yeomans King

1910

It will be as well to say at the outset that my tastes are as far as possible removed from those popularly understood to be Japanese. I almost never regard a flower alone. I can admire a perfect Frau Karl Druschki rose, a fine spray of Countess Spencer sweet pea, but never without thinking of the added beauty sure to be its part if a little sea-lavender were placed next to the sweet pea, or if more of the delicious roses were together. Wherefore it will be seen that my mind is bent wholly

Added beauty

Louisa's writing is from her article, "Companion Crops in the Flower Garden," in the June, 1910, issue of Garden Magazine.

on grouping our masses, and growing companion crops of flowers to that end.

Louisa Boyd Yeomans King was born October 17, 1863, in Washington, New Jersey. She married Francis King when she was twenty-seven. They had three children.

Louisa first became interested in gardening through her mother-in-law, whom she described as "one of the ablest and most devoted gardeners of her generation." She learned a great deal from her, which she put into practice in her first garden in 1902. She tested her theories through correspondence with well-known British horticulturists.

In 1910, Louisa began publishing magazine articles on gardening. Five years later, she published her first book, *The Well-Considered Garden*, which was followed by nine more. She gave lectures throughout the country, and was one of the founders of the Garden Club of America in 1913.

In 1921, Louisa was presented the George White Medal of the Massachusetts Horticultural Society, the highest gardening award in America; she was the first woman ever to receive it. Following her death when she was eighty-four, her ashes were scattered over her cherished garden according to her wishes.

OCTOBER 18

Martha Bishop Moore

*W*est by wagon

May 15, 1859
Sunday 15th. Left camp at 1/4 to 7 and came to a fine spring branch before 8. Crossed Box Elder at 1/2 past 9 and came out on the prairie to noon. One of the largest steers died today of murrain. We are now through the Black Hills having been just a week among them. As I look back they rise with bristling ruggedness as if to shut out forever from my sight the home of my childhood and the friends whom I love so well. . . .
May 29, 1859
Tuesday 29th. Morning cool and cloudy. Of all the nights I ever spent, last night was the worst. The wind rocked my wagon so much there was danger of tilting it over. In vain I wooed the goddess sleep, she would sit lightly on my eyelids for a few minutes when a sudden jerk would make one as wide awake as ever. The day was very unpleasant and we were all glad when

---

Give Her This Day

night came. Camped on a little creek, found gooseber-
ries, also plenty of wood, water and grass. Made 12 miles.
May 31, 1859

Thursday 31st. A rainy day, everything goes wrong,
lost 7 head of sheep. Passed a new made grave. What a
train of sad reflections it awakened on a trip like this. . . .
June 9, 1859

Saturday 9th. A dismal morning, weather cold and
chilly. We concluded to wait for a better time to cross
the Platte. Made part of my dress, found poor Mag
crying to go home. Had rather a pleasant time while
camped there but I can enjoy myself anywhere; what
would make anyone else scold and fret I am content with.

Martha Bishop Moore was born October 18, 1837, in Benton
County, Missouri. Martha and James Preston married in 1858
and started for California the next year.

Martha, whose nickname was "Missouri," kept a detailed
journal of their five-and-a-half-month trip west from their
departure date May 1, 1859, to their arrival in "the Promised
Land." Their journey was complicated by the presence of
five thousand sheep and many cattle and horses that were
driven along with the wagons to stock the ranch at the end of
the trail.

Martha reached California safely in October, 1859. In
her last journal entry she wrote, "The roughest road I ever
came over, I was never so tired of jolting in all my life."

*Martha's journal was hand-
copied by her niece, Frances
Bishop Sweany, in 1934 and
given to the Missouri Historical
Society, St. Louis, Missouri.*

Amanda Theodosia Jones

1906

My parents imagined that a child of three, exceptionally
vigorous, who could name all the letters of the alphabet
after a single telling, was old enough to go to school. . . .

After snowfall they kept me out till the time of
mud. The first abiding affection I had outside of home
was for a man who saw me astray in the middle of the
road on my way to school, and, wading through, pulled
me out of my shoes and carried them and me to the
schoolroom door. As I never asked for help, the older
ones had forgotten me.

An abiding affection

*Amanda's writing is from the
preface to her book,* Poems
1854-1906, *published in 1906.*

Amanda Theodosia Jones was born October 19, 1835, in East Bloomfield, New York. Although the family was not well-to-do, they believed that books were "more necessary than daily bread," so Amanda received an excellent education at home.

Amanda began teaching in a rural school when she was fifteen. Nine years later she put aside her teaching career when her first poem was accepted in the *Ladies' Repository* of Cincinnati. She became a contributor to the magazine for the next ten years.

Amanda became interested in the Spiritual movement following the death of a brother. By 1854 she firmly believed that she was a medium.

In 1872 Amanda embarked on yet another career, one that would occupy her until her death but was never successful. She invented a vacuum process to preserve food for which she took out five patents. She tried to establish a canning factory, which was finally incorporated in 1890 as the Woman's Canning and Preserving Company in Chicago. She attempted to make her business an exclusively feminine organization, including the stockholders, but she could not achieve success and the company was dissolved in 1921.

Amanda resided with her sister and continued her canning experiments until her death at seventy-nine.

OCTOBER 20

Maud Nathan

Consumer power

1926

To my self-imposed query, "Has the Consumers' League reached its peak?" my answer is: The work of the Consumers' League will never be fully accomplished. It is an educational work which, in its very nature, must be progressive. The League must continue to encourage consumers to throw their weight and power constantly on the side of justice and fairness. Consumers must recognize their own power and, through the force of public opinion . . . I feel that it cannot be too strongly emphasized that the rights of consumers are to be respected equally with the rights of capitalists and workers.

Maud Nathan was born October 20, 1862, in New York City to a prominent family descended from the Sephardic Jews. She married her first cousin, Frederick Nathan, a wealthy broker twice her age, when she was seventeen.

Maud's writing is from The Story of an Epoch-Making Movement, *published in 1926.*

Give Her This Day

Soon after her marriage, Maud became concerned with the plight of the poor working girl; in 1890 she co-founded the Consumers' League of New York.

Following the death of her only child in 1895, she worked twice as hard, becoming vice-president of the National Consumers' League. The League tried to involve the public in forcing business to treat labor more fairly. It published a "White List" of stores that acted properly, and allowed acceptable businesses to place a "consumers' label" on their products.

During the time Maud was lobbying for her cause in Albany, no one was paying much attention to voteless women. She joined the struggle for woman suffrage, going across the country on speaking tours with her husband in a flag-draped car.

Anne Gilbert

1901

Beautiful silver

Even when Miss Russell asked me to come to her after the performance that evening, I was simple enough to think it was to be only a little supper at her home. Instead came public speeches at the theatre, and the public presentation of the silver that, to me, stands for the personal affection of many dear friends, old and new. . . .

Miss Russell has made the Lyceum Theatre like home to me, and I am very happy.

One good friend of mine says that if she had such beautiful silver she should give up acting, and simply stay at home and have tea all the time. It sounds attractive, but if I did that, I should have serious doubts as to the supply of tea, to say nothing of the other necessities of life.

Anne Jane Hartley Gilbert was born October 21, 1821, in Rochdale, Lancashire, England. As a child, she studied ballet and became a featured dancer in a London troupe.

When she was twenty-five, Anne married George Gilbert, a fellow dancer and manager. They decided to give up dancing in favor of moving to America to farm. They settled in the Wisconsin frontier, but they were not good farmers and soon returned to the stage.

Anne and George joined a theater company in Chicago. She gradually abandoned dancing for acting and received

Anne's writing is from The Stage Reminiscences of Mrs. Gilbert, *edited by Charlotte M. Martin, published in 1901.*

much acclaim, especially when portraying eccentric old women.

The Gilberts moved to New York City in 1864. George passed away two years later. Anne continued her career, playing a wide variety of roles in both comedy and drama. In 1904, at the age of eighty-three, she began her grand farewell tour. She received standing ovations in New York and Chicago. She died a month into the tour.

Abigail Scott Duniway

Catching a wagon

June 29, 1852

. . . Independence rock is an immense mass covering an area of, I think about ten acres, and is about three hundred feet high. My sisters and I went to the base of the rock with the intention of climbing it but we had only ascended about thirty feet when a heavy hail and wind storm arose obliging us to desist. We then started on after the wagons and before we reached them they had all crossed the river except the last wagon in the train which by hard running we managed to overtake. They had intended to let us wade it (it was waist deep) to learn us not to get so far behind the team;, I would have liked the fun of wading well enough but did not like to get joked about being left.

Abigail Jane Scott Duniway, Oregon pioneer and suffrage leader, was born October 22, 1834, in Groveland, Illinois. The family migrated to Oregon in 1852.

As there were nine children in the family, Mr. Scott gave each child a specific task for the trip, and Abigail's was to keep the daily journal. In later years she used her writings as the basis for two novels.

Abigail married Benjamin Duniway shortly after their arrival in Oregon, and they settled on a farm and had six children. In 1862 they lost the farm when a friend, whose notes Benjamin had endorsed, defaulted. Abigail was incredulous that a man could so jeopardize his family's security without permission from his wife, and thus began her interest in the women's movement. She believed that woman's inequality with man could only be rectified through the vote, and for the next twenty-five years she travelled the country lecturing on woman suffrage.

Abigail's writing is from the journal she kept on her journey across the country. The original manuscript belongs to David C. Duniway of Salem, Oregon.

Oregon granted women the right to vote in 1912, three years before Abigail died at eighty. She was given the major credit for its passing. Despite being confined to a wheelchair, she wrote the suffrage proclamation, which she co-signed with the governor, and became Oregon's first registered woman voter.

Anna Cogdell Howell

January 28, 1861

Jimmie Tillman was here last Tuesday night. He and Felix Hicks went to the Capitol with Jenny & me to hear Bill speak on the political affairs of our falling country. They both came home with us, and stayed until a quarter after twelve! I had a splendid time. Jimmie Tillman is so very intelligent, smart, brilliant, attractive, gentlemanly and *everything* a lady most wishes to see in a gentleman, that I could *almost love* him, if I did not think he loved Jenny, although he knows she is to be married. He went back to Lebanon on Wednesday. I will not see him any more until next summer—if then—I suppose he will forget all about me by that time. Heaven forbid! He has put my ring on with a wish. I will hear what it is the first time he writes to Jenny. I am very anxious indeed to know it. I do most concisely hope he likes me as much as I like him, and more. I wish I could find out what he thinks of me but it is eleven. I must go to bed and seek "tired Nature's sweet restorer—balmy sleep." I hope in my dreams I may see his face and that he may think of me also tonight. I cannot remember his features at all but the color of his eyes, if that may be called a feature—but goodnight again! I hope "pleasant dreams and rosy slumbers." Goodnight! Goodnight!! Goodnight!!! And once again Goodnight! May *he* think of me and I of him. Goodnight.

Anna Cogdell Howell was born on October 23, 1843, in Nashville, Tennessee. She kept a detailed journal from 1861-1862. Her activities consisted of school, voice lessons, visiting friends, reading and sewing. Her daily entries described sewing a gingham dress, mending her hoops, making a square for a silk quilt, and other typical activities of young girls. Also,

Hoping for love

Anna's writing is from her journal, which is part of the Howell Collection at the Tennessee State Library and Archives in Nashville, Tennessee.

much space was devoted to her crushes on boys, and her pinings for Jimmie or Paul could have been written in any era by any young woman learning about love.

Sarah Josepha Hale

Disguise fools

1855

There is an old and quaint verse that I recollect reading when a child, which now frequently recurs to my mind when I witness some ridiculous displays of those who attempt to fill a niche for which nature never designed them.

> The man of wisdom may disguise
> His knowledge, and not seem wise;
> But take it for a constant rule
> There's no disguising of a fool.

There is no disguise for such a one but in silence; and thrice blest are those simpletons who have the gift of silence.

Sarah Josepha Buell Hale was born October 24, 1788, in Newport, New Hampshire. She was educated at home in her early years by her mother and later by her brother. (He attended Dartmouth College and shared with her, on his vacations, what he had learned during the terms).

At twenty-five Sarah married David Hale, a lawyer from a neighboring town. They had five children, but David died four days before the birth of the last child. Sarah was left penniless and turned to writing as a means of support. She published her first novel in 1827 which was written "literally with my baby in my arms." Three years later she published *Poems for Our Children* which contained "Mary Had a Little Lamb," the best-known children's rhyme in the English language.

Sarah was offered the editorship of the *American Ladies' Magazine*, starting with its first issue. In 1837 she moved on to become editor of *Godey's Lady's Book*, a position she held until four months before her death at the age of ninety. She complied with Louis Godey's wishes that the magazine be cheerful. Therefore, no radical ideas, political or economic news, or even the Civil War were ever mentioned.

Sarah's writing is from Woman's Record, Sketches of All Distinguished Women, *published in 1855.*

In addition to her duties at *Godey's*, Sarah found time to start more of our present permanent institutions than any other American. She was responsible for establishing Thanksgiving as a national holiday, she started the first day nursery for working mothers, and she was the first to suggest public playgrounds. She founded the Seaman's Aid, established the first Sailor's Home, sent out the first women medical missionaries, and raised the money to finish Bunker Hill Monument in Boston.

Carolyn Sherwin Bailey

1913

Our emotions, that is, our feelings of anger, joy, sorrow, hatred, jealousy and love are older than we are. They may almost be classed as instinctive, for they manifest themselves so early. . . .

I came across one of my own, old Mother Goose books not long ago with the leaves that held the story of the "Babes in the Wood" *pinned* securely together. It told me as nothing else could have done the emotion caused in a child's mind by this gruesome tale. I was afraid when I read the story. I felt all the terror experienced by the Babes in the Wood. My fear emotion was so unpleasant that I had pinned the story out of my sight.

A fearful story

Carolyn Sherwin Bailey was born October 25, 1875, in Hoosick Falls, New York. Her mother, a teacher and author of children's books, educated her at home until she attended Teachers College at Columbia University. After graduation, she studied at the Montessori School in Rome.

Carolyn returned to America, settling in New York City. At nineteen she began publishing fiction and poetry in children's magazines. She also wrote nonfiction such as *Boys Make-at-Home Things*, which combined instruction and entertainment for children.

Between 1935 and 1944, Carolyn published four books on American arts and handcrafts which many critics considered her finest achievement. She researched "genealogical records, personal letters and diaries, rare village and county records, and. . . old maps" for the series.

Carolyn was awarded the Newbery Award for her most popular book, *Miss Hickory*, about a dour old maid from New England whose head was a hickory nut and body was a twig of applewood.

Carolyn's writing is from For the Story Teller, *published in 1913, in which she wrote about her theory of storytelling for teachers and parents.*

Adelaide Phillipps

A stage triumph

Adelaide's journal entry, describing a concert she gave in Milan, is included in Adelaide Phillipps—A Record, *by Mrs. R. C. Waterston, published in 1883.*

July 21, 1854

At last I was on the stage. They all looked at me. *Not a hand!* I sang the recitativo without any applause; a faint *brava* once or twice, and that they seemed afraid to do. At the end, however, of the recitativo, I had a good round of applause; then several times in the adagio, at the end of which I felt I had the audience with me entirely. The applause was so great I almost forgot that I had any more to sing. During the cabaletta I could scarcely utter a phrase but what they would cry out and applaud me so that I was in a perfect delirium, and sang as I never sang before. I was called out seven times, and was obliged to repeat the cabaletta. It was such a triumph as I did not dream of having, much less hope for. I felt very much like crying.

Adelaide Phillipps was born October 26, 1833, in Bristol, England. The family soon emigrated to America where Adelaide made her stage debut at eight in Boston. She received glowing reviews, being called a "prodigy" by the *Boston Transcript.*

A talented child actress, Adelaide worked in Boston's major stock company for over ten years. The music director took an interest in her vocal talent. With his financial help, and that of others such as the famous singer Jenny Lind, Adelaide was sent to London in 1851 to study with the top singing master.

Adelaide remained abroad for several years, studying in Italy as well as England. Returning to America, she performed light and Italian opera up and down the east coast.

In her thirties, Adelaide had contracted yellow fever, which left her with recurring bouts of illness. She died at forty-eight in Karlsbad, Germany, where she had gone to "take the waters."

Mary Elizabeth Wilson Sherwood

1897

The next day my father took me to Mrs. Webster's reception. The house of the Secretary of State was the great attraction; it was full of brilliant company. Mrs. Webster's nieces and some of the fashionable ladies from New York were there, many of the diplomatic circle, and a number of literary women.

A young Englishman, named Charles Dickens, entered the room. Then my heart stopped beating.

I had read *Pickwick* and several of his novels, and, like all the world, I admired and wondered how a genius looked. I can see him now, overdressed, with billows of green-satin necktie, long hair, a rather handsome face, and hanging on his arm a pretty little fat, rosy-cheeked wife.

I also remember (and I fear no one else does) what I wore on this momentous occasion: a black-velvet tight-fitting jacket with gold buttons down the front, and a skirt of deep blue, heavily flounced. I saw that other ladies wore this tight jacket with tight sleeves, so I knew I was correct. We had bonnets on, and I remember thinking that Mrs. Dickens's bonnet was dowdy. When we got into the carriage I said to my father, "Oh! I am so glad that mother allowed me this pretty dress!"

Whereupon he addressed me severely. "My daughter, I am sorry that after such an afternoon, where you have met so many distinguished people, you should be thinking of your clothes.

Mary Elizabeth Wilson Sherwood, author of etiquette books and novels of manners, was born October 27, 1826, in Keene, New Hampshire.

Mary married John Sherwood, a New York lawyer, in 1851. She led a very social life, giving literary afternoons in her home, organizing society charity events, and travelling abroad. Maintaining their fashionable West 32nd Street residence and Mary's first-class travel to Europe greatly depleted Mr. Sherwood's funds, so she took up writing to augment their income. She contributed stories and articles on manners to the currently popular ladies' magazines, wrote

Among the great

Mary's writing, describing a visit to Washington, D.C., with her father when she was sixteen, is from Volume I of her autobiography, An Epistle to Posterity—Being Rambling Recollections of Many Years of My Life, *published in 1897.*

three novels, one book of poetry and two volumes of her memoirs. Her most popular book was *Manners and Social Usages*, first published in 1884 and reprinted many times.

Anna Elizabeth Dickinson

A low point

Anna's writing, describing her early days on the lecture circuit, is included in Eminent Women of the Age; Being Narratives of The Lives and Deeds of the Most Prominent Women of the Present Generation, *published in 1869.*

1862

No one knows how I felt and suffered that winter, penniless and alone, with a scanty wardrobe, suffering with cold, weariness, and disappointment. I wandered about on the trains day after day, among strangers, seeking employment for an honest living, and failed to find it. I would have gone home, but had not the means. I had borrowed money to commence my journey, promising to remit soon; failing to do so, I could not ask again. Beyond my Concord meeting all was darkness; I had no further plans.

Anna Elizabeth Dickinson was born October 28, 1842, in Philadelphia. Her father died when she was two, leaving the family destitute. Two of her three brothers were sickly, and all three were unable to contribute to the family's support, so Anna began working when she was fifteen.

In 1860, she gave her first speech before the Pennsylvania Anti-Slavery Society and became so successful that by the time she was twenty she was hailed as the "Joan of Arc of the Unionist cause."

Anna toured the country giving rousing anti-slavery lectures throughout the duration of the Civil War. Following the war she joined the lyceum lecture circuit, averaging 150 lectures and twenty thousand dollars per year.

In 1888, the Republican National Committee hired Anna to make several campaign speeches, but she spoke so violently that newspapers questioned her sanity, and she was asked to stop. Three years later she was committed to a hospital for the insane. Upon her release she spent the remaining forty years of her life in anonymity.

Lucy Goodale Thurston

1855

My Dear Daughter Mary:

I have hitherto forborne to write respecting the surgical operation I experienced in September, from an expectation that you would be with us so soon. That is now given up; so I proceed to give a circumstantial account of those days. . . . During the latter part of August they decided on the use of the knife. . . . Meantime, the tumor was rapidly altering. It had nearly approached the surface, exhibiting a dark spot. The doctors met in consultation, and advised an immediate operation. . . . Both doctors advised me not to take chloroform because of my having had the paralysis. I was glad they allowed me the use of my senses.

That night I spent in the house alone for the first time. The family had all retired for the night. In the still hour of darkness, I long walked back and forth in the capacious door-yard. Depraved, diseased, helpless, I yielded myself up entirely to the will, the wisdom, and the strength of the Holy One. At peace with myself, with earth, and with heaven, I calmly laid my head upon my pillow and slept refreshingly. A bright day opened upon us. My feelings were "As the day is, so shall thy strength be.". . .

Dr. Ford looked me full in the face, and with great firmness asked: "Have you made up your mind to have it cut out?"

"Yes, sir."

"Are you ready now?"

"Yes, sir; but let me know when you begin, that I may be able to bear it. Have you your knife in that hand now?"

He opened his hand that I might see it, saying, "I am going to begin now." . . . It was nearly an hour and a half that I was beneath his hand. . . . When the whole work was done, Dr. Brayton came to my side, and taking me by the hand said: "There is not one in a thousand who would have borne it as you have done."

Courage

Lucy's letter to her daughter, describing her mastectomy, is included in Life and Times of Mrs. Lucy G. Thurston, Wife of Reverend Asa Thurston, Pioneer Missionary to the Sandwich Islands, Gathered from Letters and Journals Extended over a Period of more than Fifty Years, Selected and Arranged by Herself, *published in 1882.*

Lucy Goodale Thurston was born October 29, 1795, in Marlborough, Massachusetts. While teaching at a local school, she was introduced by her cousin to the Reverend Asa Thurston, a Congregational minister. They were engaged the following day.

Lucy and the Reverend were married on October 12, 1819, and eleven days later they set sail from Boston for Hawaii. Following a five-and-a-half-month voyage, they landed in Kailua, where King Kamehamaha requested they remain to establish a mission in the King's residence.

Lucy and Asa spent a long, happy life in Hawaii, where they raised five children. At sixty, Lucy developed cancer and had to endure a mastectomy without any anesthesia. She survived the operation and lived another twenty-one years.

At the age of seventy-seven, Lucy Thurston compiled and edited letters she had written during her lifetime into a book for the Woman's Board of Missions for the Pacific Islands. In the preface she wrote: "In the very commencement of missionary life, my husband strongly advised me to preserve a copy of my letters, and gave me a blank book for the purpose."

OCTOBER 30

Elizabeth Leslie Comstock

Warm approval

1874

I took the opportunity of this short session to pay a visit of one hour to the Men's Meeting. . . . It was at the very right time, for just then they were discussing the liquor question, and I blew a blast against the three great sins that have been such curses to Christian lands in this our day, viz., Intemperance, Licentiousness, and War. I spoke thirty-five or forty minutes, and offered a short prayer. Then followed a true, warm-hearted Irish welcome, so much approval with my visit and message as almost overwhelmed me.

Elizabeth's writing is from a temperance address she gave to a Sunday School Conference in Dublin. It is included in The Life and Letters of Elizabeth L. Comstock, *compiled by her sister C. Hare, published in 1895.*

Elizabeth Leslie Rous Comstock was born October 30, 1815, in Maidenhead, Berkshire, England. She married when she was thirty-three, but was widowed three years later.

Elizabeth emigrated to Canada and began her religious and philanthropic activities. In 1858, she married John Comstock and moved to his Michigan farm on a Quaker anti-slavery settlement. With her husband's support, Elizabeth established her Quaker ministry.

Elizabeth's talent for public speaking placed her in high

demand at Quaker meetings. Her topics were abolition, women's rights, temperance and peace. She also did missionary work in growing urban areas, giving money and religious instruction to the poor and to prison and asylum inmates.

Sallie Hester

1850

April 25. We leave next month for San Jose. We are all glad that we are going to have a home somewhere at last. Have met a number of nice young men here— George W. Crane, of Baltimore, a young lawyer, and William Allen, who has been in California for some time. I am too young for beaux, but the young men don't seem to think so.

Sallie Hester was born October 31, 1835, in Bloomington, Indiana. When she was fourteen, her family set forth in a wagon train for California. They called their group "the Missionary Train" because so many members of the fifty wagons were Methodist ministers.

When Sallie was sixteen she became engaged, but she called it off due to her young age. She waited until she was thirty-six to marry James Maddock, an assayer from Eureka, Nevada.

Sallie kept a diary beginning on August 25, 1849, the first day of her westward trip, and ending on October 5, 1871, her wedding day. It was published posthumously in seven serialized episodes of *The Argonaut*, a California weekly periodical.

Maybe later

Sallie's diary entry was published in the September 19, 1925, issue of The Argonaut.

NOVEMBER

Mary Adelaide Nutting

1918

Dearest Isabel

Here it is *July 8th* and you are in the midst of launching our seventh summer session. We had our first in 1911, didn't we? Anyhow, I think this bids fair to be the most useful yet because it has a direct aim, at a vulnerable spot in our work—Teachers, more teachers! You must begin to search the horizon for an assistant, who will help you in improvising the hospital teaching. . . .

You must be freer to do some at least of the other things to be done. Your book on teaching—the History—and who knows what else!

Mary Adelaide Nutting was born November 1, 1858, in Waterloo, Quebec. In addition to her regular schooling, she pursued studies in music and art. During her early twenties, she gave several public concerts and taught music at the Cathedral School for Girls in Newfoundland. However, she felt an increasing need to be more useful to the world. In 1889 she read a newspaper account of the opening of Johns Hopkins Hospital Training School for Nurses in Baltimore. That very day she wrote to inquire about admission. She commenced nursing school at thirty-one, one of seventeen students in the first class.

After graduation, Mary stayed on as a head nurse, working her way up to superintendent of nurses and principal of the training school. She came to believe that nursing schools were merely a way to supply hospitals with a cheap work force, and started her lifelong crusade to bring nursing education into the universities. In 1899, Teachers College at Columbia University launched an experimental program in hospital economics; Mary became the first nurse appointed to a university chair.

Mary co-authored the four-volume standard textbook *History of Nursing* and helped found the *American Journal of Nursing*. When she died at age ninety-nine, she had accomplished more in the development of nursing education than any other person in her time.

For the cause

Mary's letter to her friend and assistant, Isabel Stewart, is included in the Special Collections, Millbank Memorial Teachers College, Columbia University, New York, New York.

Rheta Childe Dorr

Learning to be worldly

1924

I discovered, after coming back to New York, that I occupied a doubtful position with men. As a young girl I had a train of respectfully devoted admirers. As a woman yet young and pretty, but a woman separated from her husband, I had a train of men openly game-hunters. Not all but most of the men with whom I was acquainted, sooner or later became in speech and behavior over-familiar. They told me stories they would never dare tell to a girl. When they took me to dinner they frequently tried to make me drink too much. . . .

The worst of it was—how shall I express it—the worst was that I was young and warm-blooded and sometimes I did not know how to hide the effect of the second cocktail or the too-amusing story. I could protest, I could say sharp and sarcastic things, but I had not yet acquired the armor with which a woman of the world protects her dignity.

Rheta Childe Door was born November 2, 1866, in Omaha, Nebraska. When she was twelve, she disobeyed her father and attended a lecture on women's rights by Elizabeth Cady Stanton and Susan B. Anthony. She became an instant convert and joined the National Woman Suffrage Association.

Rheta attended the University of Nebraska, then moved to New York City to study further and write poetry and fiction. In 1892 she married John Dorr, a conservative businessman. She found he hampered her pursuit of a journalism career, so she left him after six years.

Rheta's first job was at the *New York Evening Post* in 1902, writing a woman's column. Four years later she took her first of nine trips to Europe which provided topics for her free-lance articles. Always concerned with the working woman, she labored as a laundress, seamstress and factory worker to be able to report accurately the sweatshops' conditions. She was the first editor of *Suffragist*, the newspaper of the Congressional Union for Woman Suffrage.

During World War I Rheta was a war correspondent for the *New York Evening Post*, and her column was syndicated in over twenty other papers. An unfortunate accident with a motorcycle in 1919 left her health and memory impaired, putting an end to her career.

Rheta's writing is from her book A Woman of Fifty, *published in 1924.*

Give Her This Day

Isabella Macdonald Alden

1929

Shame and dishonor

The only thing that hung about and troubled her was her own shame. Her part in the terrible drama that had just been played to the finish. Her foolishness and gullibility, her readiness to fall for the handsome eyes of a man of the world, whose flattery had been merely used for his own passing amusement. . . .

And now in the few short minutes the cloak of illusion had been torn from him, and left his shame naked to her view; left him without a charm or virtue; shown his love to be a mere worthless pretense, for how could he possibly love her when he had so deceived her? How could he dare bring her a love so dishonored by his own broken, worse than broken vows? For she was not one of those girls who feel it a fine feather to have won for herself a man who belongs to another.

Isabella Macdonald Alden, author of religious literature, was born November 3, 1841, in Rochester, New York. She started a career as a teacher but a friend secretly entered her novel, *Helen Lester*, in a contest. She won first prize and the book was published in 1866.

Shortly thereafter Isabella married Gustavus Alden, a Presbyterian minister. Her marriage further convinced her that her life's purpose was to "win souls for Jesus Christ," which she felt best qualified to do through her writing. Using the pen name "Pansy," a childhood nickname, she wrote over seventy-five books during the next fifty years. Her standard plot involved a young child or woman who was beset with misery yet overcame life's suffering through strong religious beliefs. Good always triumphed in the end.

Isabella's writing is from her novel, An Interrupted Night, *published in 1929.*

Anita Newcomb McGee

Dec. 21, 1894

No outlet

Women—neurotic or neurasthenic, belong to a certain stage of mental development. Below that stage they are satisfied with manual work, idleness, "society"—as their brains have no further needs. But when they are capable of more—in fact, inherit the ability which carries their brothers through a successful career—and find no outlet for their abilities, but are relegated to a half-idle, half-petty life, their unused energy degenerates and they become neurasthenic.

Anita Newcomb McGee was born November 4, 1864, in Washington, D.C. After graduation from private school she travelled and studied for three years in England and Switzerland. Upon her return in 1888 she married William J. McGee, a geologist and anthropologist. William encouraged his wife to have an identity of her own, and she became a doctor.

Anita's greatest triumph was in establishing the Army Nurse Corps. At the outbreak of the Spanish-American War in 1898 hundreds of women volunteered to nurse injured soldiers. However, the majority of them were untrained. Surgeon General George Sternberg appointed Dr. McGee acting assistant surgeon general after she offered to screen and train nursing applicants. She reviewed five thousand applications and accepted and educated almost one thousand nurses, who were then assigned to duty both at home and abroad.

When Anita died she was buried with full military honors in Arlington National Cemetery.

Anita's writing is from her "idea book," a small leather address book with handwritten notes on different subjects arranged alphabetically. It is part of the Anita Newcomb McGee Collection in the Library of Congress.

Ella Wheeler Wilcox

*P*oetry and figures

1918

My memory treasures golden summer hours when "Dosia" [Theodosia Garrison] sat at one desk and I at another writing poems which we afterward read to each other, each glad of the honest criticism of the listener.

One day she was writing a lyric at the Bungalow, and I was filling an editor's request to write an article on giving daughters an independent income. Undertaking to calculate how many dollars would result for a penny a day for eighteen years, I became confused and appealed to my poet friend. "Dosia," I called, "how much money would a girl have at eighteen if her parents had saved a penny a day from the time she was born?" "Wait a minute," Dosia replied, "and I will tell you." After a few moments she called forth, "I make it about seven thousand dollars." "Well," I said, "I made it six and over so I am safe to say it would be over five thousand." I sent in my little article and the kind and trusting editor used it without blue-penciling. It appeared in an evening paper while my husband was on a trip West. He read it and wrote me, "Great Heavens, Ella, some mathematician! You are safe on verse, my dear, but do go carefully when you approach mathematics." A stranger wrote me a few days later: "Madam, I have considered you a good poet and very much of a philosopher but God knows you are no mathematician. Are you aware that your blushing bride in order to have that amount of money for a *dot* would be ninety-five years old?"

Ella Wheeler Wilcox, poet and journalist, was born November 5, 1850, in Johnstown Center, Wisconsin. Ella wrote an eleven-chapter novel, bound in kitchen wallpaper, when she was nine, and she left school when she was fourteen to write full-time after several of her pieces had been printed in magazines.

Her reputation was made in 1883 when a Chicago firm refused to print a collection of her love poems, calling them immoral. Newspapers across the country carried the story and she was dubbed the "Poetess of Passion."

Ella married Robert M. Wilcox in 1884 and settled in Connecticut. They had one son who died at birth.

When her husband died in 1916, Ella began to decline mentally. After the death of their son they had dabbled in Spiritualism and studied with a Hindu mystic, in an attempt to contact the dead infant. Now she launched a serious effort to communicate with the spirit of her dead husband, and reported her progress in her newspaper columns. She had a nervous breakdown in 1919 and died three months later. After a Spiritualistic service, her ashes were sealed with those of her husband in a granite ledge near their home.

Ella's writing is from her autobiography, The Worlds and I, *published in 1918.*

Ellen Olney Kirk

1897

Mother as model

Whatever her mother had felt or done Kitty expected in her time to feel and do. To Kitty her mother's wit, skill, resource, were inexhaustible. Her manner, her conversation, her dress, although it was always the same, was something to study and find poetry in. To do things as her mother did was an impossible dream of perfection.

Ellen Olney Kirk was born November 6, 1842, in Southington, Connecticut. Her father wrote popular textbooks, most notably *Geography and Atlas*, which was a standard in American schools and went through over one hundred editions. He instilled in his daughter a love of learning, especially reading literature.

Ellen's first novel was published in 1876 after being serialized in *Lippincott's Magazine*. Three years later she married John F. Kirk, editor of *Lippincott's*. Ellen looked upon her writing as a job, working at it daily, and produced one or more novels a year for the next twenty years.

Ellen's writing is from The Revolt of a Daughter, *published in 1897.*

Lotta Crabtree

Mirror of our thoughts

Lotta's writing is from the article, "Theatrical Reminiscences of Lotta Crabtree," in the February 18, 1912, Boston Sunday Globe.

1912

If my own face is younger than that of the average woman of my age, it is because I have tried to raise my thoughts above the storm and stress of daily life. Life is hard, is it not?—a tragedy if we choose to regard it so, but, my dear, it is within our power to make it as sweet and peaceful as the most gladsome dream. When we are able to thus control the workings of our minds, you will see the result mirrored in the face.

Lotta Crabtree was born November 7, 1847, in New York City. Her father developed gold fever when she was four and left for California to search for gold. He never found any, but the family eventually joined him in Grass Valley, in the heart of mining country, where Mrs. Crabtree ran a boardinghouse. One of the guests was the actress Lola Montez, who taught Lotta to sing and dance and nurtured her interest in the theater.

Mrs. Crabtree was a classic stage mother. She pushed eight-year-old Lotta to perform in a saloon theater. Lotta sang and danced and was a big hit with the miners, who threw coins and nuggets on the stage. Lotta expanded her repertoire to include banjo playing as she toured the mining country in the Sacramento and San Joaquin Valleys. In 1856 the family moved to San Francisco, where she played variety halls and soon was billed as "Miss Lotta, the San Francisco Favorite." From that time on she supported her family with her earnings. For the next twenty years she toured the country with her own company, performing plays which showcased her personality.

Lotta retired from the theater at the age of forty-three.

Although financially secure, she led an isolated, lonely life. She left an estate of over four million dollars, bequeathed primarily to charities for aging actors, veterans, convicts and abandoned pets.

Jessie Jack Hooper

1922

*O*nward the struggle

I am thoroughly convinced that women will have to make as hard a struggle for positions in our governing bodies as we did for suffrage. My experience has been most interesting. I have not learned anything about men in politics that I did not know before. I have simply verified my former knowledge. . . . I believe I owe the vote I received to the women of the state. They were honestly and earnestly concerned in having me elected.

Jessie Annette Jack Hooper was born November 8, 1865, in Winneshiek County, Iowa. A sickly child, she was educated at home by a governess. In her late teens she went to Des Moines and Chicago to study art.

Jessie met an attorney, Ben Hooper, while on a visit to her sister in Oshkosh, Wisconsin. They were married on May 30, 1888. While her husband pursued his successful legal career, Jessie took up various civic projects in her new home-town. She established the first kindergarten, the first visiting nurse program and a tuberculosis sanatorium.

Jessie joined the Wisconsin Woman Suffrage Association and went on to become a leader in the national American Woman Suffrage Association. She frequently travelled to Washington to lobby for a federal suffrage amendment. After Congress passed the Nineteenth Amendment, her efforts helped make Wisconsin the first state to ratify it.

In 1922 Jessie ran as a Democrat for the United States Senate. Although she had little chance of defeating the in-cumbent, she felt it was the duty of newly enfranchised women to make the effort to run for public office.

Following World War I, Jessie devoted much of her time to the peace movement. She made hundreds of speeches on behalf of world disarmament. Three years before her death, she joined women from around the world in presenting peace petitions with over eight million signatures to the League of Nations disarmament conference in Geneva.

Jessie's writing, describing her unsuccessful bid to become a United States senator, is from an article in the December 22, 1922, issue of The Woman Citizen.

Nan Britton

Warren Harding's baby

1927
Several mornings after the baby was born Dr. Ackerman came to see me. . . . He informed me that he needed certain data for registering the child's birth. I didn't know exactly what that might mean to Mr. Harding and so I inquired if it was necessary to register the child's birth always. "Unless you want to pay a fine of $100," he replied. . . . I longed to shout the whole truth to the whole world, that my baby was Warren Harding's baby, that we were not married in the eyes of the world, but truly married in the sight of God and that I was proud, proud, proud to be her mother!

Nan Britton was born November 9, 1896, in Claridon, Ohio. During high school Nan had a special relationship with her English teacher, Miss Abigail Harding. In 1910 Abigail's brother, Warren G. Harding, ran for governor as a Republican. From the first time Nan saw his picture she thought he was her "ideal American," and she knew at fourteen that she was in love with him.

When Nan was twenty her girlhood crush on Harding, thirty-one years her senior, developed into a secret love affair that lasted until his death six and a half years later. She was the mother of his only child.

After Harding's death Nan published *The President's Daughter*, the story of their love affair, their child, and her rejection by the Harding family. Her motive for writing it was "the need for legal and social recognition and protection of all children in these United States born out of wedlock." Six policemen and an agent for the Society for the Suppression of Vice tried to stop the book from being printed by seizing the plates and printed sheets; however, a court order allowed the publisher to continue.

Nan's writing is from her book,
The President's Daughter,
published in 1927.

Mabel Loomis Todd

1899

I went over to the little lighthouse and mounted to its summit, —an ideal vantage ground for a spectacle beyond anything else it has ever been my fortune to witness. . . .

A penetrating chill fell across the land, as if a door had been opened into a long-closed vault. It was a moment of appalling suspense; something was being waited for—the very air was portentous. . . .

Absolute silence reigned. No human being spoke. No bird twittered. Even sighing of the surf breathed into utter repose, and not a ripple stirred the leaden sea.

It was as if the hand of Deity had been visibly laid upon space and worlds, to allow one momentary glimpse of the awfulness of creation.

Mabel Loomis Todd was born November 10, 1858, in Cambridge, Massachusetts. Her father, a poet and astronomer, studied with her at home until she was ten. After graduating from the Georgetown Seminary, she completed her education in music and painting in Boston.

In 1879, Mabel married a professor of astronomy and director of the observatory at Amherst, Massachusetts. She became interested in astronomy through her husband and studied it for five years. In 1887, she accompanied Professor Todd to Japan, where she served as his assistant, to observe the total eclipse of the sun. She wrote articles describing the expedition for several American papers and magazines. Two years later, she again helped her husband with a journey to West Africa to observe another total solar eclipse.

Mabel's other major interest was the poet Emily Dickinson. She edited and published two volumes of her poetry and gave drawing-room talks on her life and literary works.

Hand of Deity

Mabel's writing is from Corona and Coronet, being a narrative of the Amherst Eclipse Expedition to Japan, in Mr. James's Schooner-Yacht Coronet, to observe the sun's total obscuration 9th August, 1896, *published in 1899.*

Anne Lynch Botta

Seize the day

1865

My dear Botta,

. . . You know, my dear, that we can die only once; that death is only a swallowing up of our poor individuality in the great ocean of being;

So let us dash on with it, enjoying what we can, bearing what is to be borne, and meeting the close of it all, which at the farthest cannot be far off, with heroism and calmness. . . .

My desire is to live for your sake more than for my own. And while we both are as well as we are now, what is the use of looking forward and fearing something which may never happen?

My dearest one, I could go on preaching through another sheet; but, as you know, I have always to turn the crank to my own organ; so I will stop here. . . .

Anne Charlotte Lynch Botta was born November 11, 1815, in Bennington, Vermont. Her father died at sea when she was four, and the family relocated in Connecticut.

Anne graduated with honors from the Albany Female Academy and commenced teaching. She and her mother moved to Providence, Rhode Island, where she edited *The Rhode Island Book*, an anthology of local prose and poetry. She began hosting evening literary receptions in her home, for which she was to become famous in later years.

When she was forty, Anne married Vincenzo Botta, a New York University professor. She expanded her literary salon, which was attended by the most prominent authors, politicians and artists of the day.

Although Anne was primarily known for her literary receptions, she also wrote poetry and newspaper articles.

Anne's letter to her husband, written while he was travelling abroad, is included in Memoirs of Anne C. L. Botta, *compiled by "Her Friends," published in 1894.*

Elizabeth Cady Stanton

Seneca Falls,
October 14, 1851
Dear Nell,

Dare to be different

You do not wish me to visit you in a short dress! Why, my dear child, I have no other. Now, suppose you and I were taking a long walk in the fields and I had on three long petticoats. Then suppose a bull should take after us. Why, you, with your legs and arms free, could run like a shot; but I, alas! should fall a victim to my graceful flowing drapery.

Like the deer, you remember, in the fable, my glory would be my destruction. My petticoats would be caught by the stumps and the briars, and what could I do at the fences? Then you in your agony, when you saw the bull gaining on me, would say: "Oh! how I wish mother could use her legs as I can." Now why do you wish me to wear what is uncomfortable, inconvenient, and many times dangerous? I'll tell you why. You want me to be like other people. You do not like to have me laughed at. You must learn not to care for what foolish people say.

Elizabeth Cady Stanton was born November 12, 1815, in Johnstown, New York. Following the death of her only brother, her father said, "Oh, my daughter, I wish you were a boy!" She resolved to prove to him that a daughter was just as good as a son.

While attending anti-slavery meetings with her cousin Elizabeth Smith Miller [September 20], she heard the rousing speeches of Henry Stanton, a journalist ten years her senior. They were married soon after their first meeting. Elizabeth had the word "obey" stricken from their wedding ceremony, and asked friends to address her mail to Elizabeth Cady Stanton rather than Mrs. Henry B. Stanton, believing it wrong for women to lose their identity after marriage.

Soon after their wedding, Elizabeth and Henry attended the World's Anti-Slavery Convention in London, to which he was a delegate. At this time, she became friends with Lucretia Mott [January 3]. They discussed plans to organize a women's rights convention upon their return to the United States.

The long-planned-for convention took place in July, 1848, in Elizabeth's hometown of Seneca Falls, New York.

Elizabeth's writing is from a letter to her nine-year-old son, Daniel. It is included in Elizabeth Cady Stanton as Revealed in Her Letters, Diary and Reminiscences, Volume II, edited by Theodore Stanton and Harriot Stanton Baltch, published in 1922.

She drafted the Declaration of Sentiments and submitted a resolution asking for suffrage for women. This was the first time in the United States that a public demand had been made by a woman for the right to vote.

Following the death of her husband in 1887, Elizabeth moved to New York City. She continued lecturing and writing books and articles championing her feminist causes. She died suddenly in 1902 when she was eighty-seven, just after finishing a letter to President Theodore Roosevelt urging him to declare himself for woman suffrage.

NOVEMBER 13

Mary Ringo

A death and a prayer

July 30, 1864, Saturday
And now Oh God comes the saddest record of my life for this day my husband accidentally shot himself and was buried by the wayside and oh, my heart is breaking, if I had no children how gladly would I lay me down with my dead—but now Oh God I pray for strength to raise our precious children and oh—may no one ever suffer the anguish that is breaking my heart, my little children are crying all the time and I—oh what am I to do. Everyone in camp is kind to us but God alone can heal the breaking heart. After burying my darling husband we hitch up and drive some 5 miles. Mr. Davenport drove my mules for me and Oh, the agony of parting from that grave, to go and leave him on that hillside where I shall never see it more but thank God tis only the body lying there and may we only meet in Heaven where there is no more death but only life eternally.

Mary Ringo was born November 13, 1826, in Fort Leavenworth, Kansas. In 1848, she married Martin Ringo, a local farmer, and they moved to Indiana.

The Ringos farmed in Indiana and Missouri. They had five children, two sons and three daughters. In 1864, they decided to move to California to join Mary's sister and her husband, a prosperous cattle breeder. They departed for Liberty, Missouri, on May 18, 1864. Mary was thirty-eight and expecting her sixth child.

Two and a half months into the journey, Martin died in an accident. The family continued on for two months to Austin, Nevada, where Mary delivered a stillborn son. Her daughter Mattie later wrote, "Fortunately it was stillborn for

Mary's diary entry is from Covered Wagon Women— Volume VIII, *edited and compiled by Kenneth Holmes, published in 1989.*

he was terribly disfigured from mother seeing father after he was shot. Even my brother [John] who was fourteen years old noticed it and said he looked just like father did." John grew up to be Johnny Ringo, the notorious cattle rustler whose life inspired songs, movies, T.V. programs and books.

Isabel Bevier

1911

Home economics

I realize that the term home economics is to some a "stone of stumbling," to others "a rock of offense"—that to some it means baking and millinery, to others old wives' tales. But there are people who (while not regarding it as a balm for all the woes of life), see in it a sane and safe program for meeting some of the demands of this industrial age.

Isabel Bevier was born November 14, 1860, on a farm near Plymouth, Ohio, the youngest of nine children. She graduated in 1885 from Wooster College and received her master's degree in Latin and German three years later. That same year her fiancé drowned.

Isabel accepted a professorship of natural sciences at Pennsylvania College for Women to be near friends. She became convinced that women's future in chemistry lay in work with food. She studied agricultural chemistry and calorimetry at Harvard and Wesleyan, and conducted nutrition studies in Pennsylvania and Virginia.

In 1890 Isabel joined the faculty of the University of Illinois. At the time, home economics was being developed as a discipline and was just being introduced as a university subject. Isabel insisted on naming her new department "household science." Over the years she gradually won respect for the department; six hundred and thirty students were graduated during her tenure.

Isabel wrote numerous articles and textbooks on home economics. In 1907 she came up with the idea of using a thermometer in the cooking of meat. She established a laboratory on campus, the first of its kind, to test her theories. She was a vital force in the development of the study of home economics until her retirement when she was seventy.

Isabel's writing is from a talk she gave to the alumnae of Glendale College on February 11, 1911, entitled "College Women and Home Economics." It appeared in The Wooster Quarterly, *published by the College of Wooster, Wooster, Ohio.*

Eliza Leslie

Telling all

1859

In truth, upon most occasions, a married woman is not a safe confidant. She will assuredly tell everything to her husband; and in all probability to his mother and sisters also always, perhaps, under a strict injunction of secrecy.

A man of some humour was to read aloud a deed. He commenced with the words, "Know one woman by these presents." He was interrupted, and asked why he changed the words, which were in the usual form, "Know all men by these presents." "Oh!" said he, "'tis very certain that all men will soon know it, if one woman does."

Eliza Leslie was born November 15, 1787, in Philadelphia. When she was six, the family moved to London, where Eliza was educated at home. After their return to America, the family's finances were greatly diminished, and following Mr. Leslie's death in 1803, she and her mother were forced to open a boardinghouse.

Eliza and her mother moved to West Point in the mid-1820's to live with her brother Thomas. On his suggestion she published a book of recipes, one of the earliest American cookbooks.

Following this success Eliza wrote numerous children's books and articles for women's magazines. Her concern for the lack of manners in the United States prompted her to write an etiquette book, *The Behavior Book*, which went through several editions.

Eliza's writing is from Miss Leslie's Behaviour Book—A Guide and Manual for Ladies, *published in 1853.*

Miss Leslie resided at the United States Hotel in Philadelphia, where she was a colorful institution until her death in 1858.

Mary Peabody Mann

At the start

1882

I probably learnt a good deal more than my pupils did, except in French, which I really think I taught well. I was terrified by the array of pupils, some of whom were older than myself, that whenever I entered the school-

---

room my heart fell to my feet; and after a few days, a young woman of twenty-five, who was the greatest bugbear, gathered up her books, and concluded, as I afterwards heard, "not to go to school to that little girl!"

Mary Tyler Peabody Mann was born November 16, 1806, in Cambridge, Massachusetts. One of her sisters, Sophia [September 21], married Nathaniel Hawthorne, and another was Elizabeth [May 16], the well-known reformer and educator.

Mary received an excellent education, primarily from her mother. She left home at eighteen to replace Elizabeth in a teaching job in Maine, and joined her the following year in Boston where they opened a "dame school" for young children. They lived together in a boardinghouse, where in 1832 they met Horace Mann. He had recently lost his wife; both sisters comforted him and helped him to regain his interest in his work. They both would have liked to marry him, although he regarded them merely as close friends.

Mary began assisting Horace in 1839 with his educational research, copying letters and recording statistics. Finally, when she was thirty-seven years old, he asked her to marry him.

Horace died in 1859, after which Mary left their home at Antioch College in Ohio to return to New England. She bought a house in Cambridge so that her three sons could attend Harvard, and rejoined Elizabeth at her Boston kindergarten. Together they did much to promote the new kindergarten movement. Mary wrote her first novel at the age of eighty, and died the following year.

Mary's writing is from her article, "Reminiscences of School Life and Teaching," in the 1882 American Journal of Education.

Eliza Burhans Farnham

1864

Wedlock and widowhood, births and deaths have enriched and impoverished me. I have lived in the thoughtful solitude of the frontier, and amid the noise and distractions of the crowded mart. Years of severe manual labor have been exacted of me for the support and education of my children—years of travel have thrown me among great varieties of men and women; . . . Each phase of this varied experience has taught me its lesson, each has furnished its test whereby to try the Truth.

Lessons from life

Eliza's writing is from Woman and Her Era, *published in 1864.*

Eliza Wood Burhans Farnham was born November 17, 1815, in Rensselaerville, New York. She married Thomas Farnham, an Illinois lawyer, when she was nineteen.

In 1840, the couple returned to New York State and Eliza turned her experiences in Illinois into her first book, *Life in Prairie Land*. She became interested in prison reform and served as matron in the women's department of Sing Sing for four years.

Thomas died unexpectedly in 1849 while on a trip to California. Eliza decided to go west to settle his estate. She tried to organize a group of unmarried women to accompany her, to establish stability in the disarray of the Gold Rush. However, when she set sail from New York only a few women joined her.

In 1856, Eliza began her most important work, *Woman and Her Era*, which was published eight years later. She presented her case for the superiority of women based on biology, art, literature, history, religion and philosophy. She equated woman's ability to reproduce as a creative power second only to God.

Eliza died prematurely at forty-nine, probably from an illness she contracted the year before while volunteer nursing at Gettysburg.

Rose Knox

A subtle lesson

1921

When my husband was away on one of his business trips, his private secretary died. He had been with the business for years and held a very unusual place there. Because of this fact, I was asked whether the plant should be closed immediately as a mark of honor to an old and trusted employee. I had to decide the matter at once and I said we would not close, except on the day of the funeral. In the meantime, I myself went to the office desk and handled the matters that required attention. When my husband returned, I asked him if he approved. "Yes," he said. "That was all right." What I wanted, of course, was to have him say, "Yes, indeed! You did *exactly* right. Just what I should have done if I had been here. You showed remarkable judgment!" And so on and on. But he did not treat me like an inexperienced outsider who *surprised* him by doing the

Rose's writing was quoted in the article, "How One Man Trained His Wife to Take Care of Herself," by Mary Mullet, published in the October, 1921, issue of American Magazine.

Give Her This Day

correct thing; but as if it were quite natural that I *should* do it, and as if flattery had no place in business.

Rose Markward Knox was born November 18, 1857, in Mansfield, Ohio. In her early twenties, she moved to Gloversville, New York, where she took a job sewing gloves. She met and married Charles Knox, a glove salesman, in 1883.

In 1890, the Knoxes invested their life savings of five thousand dollars in a gelatine business in Johnstown, New York. At the time gelatine was not yet a common food, so Rose accompanied her husband on selling trips to promote the product. She tested recipes at home, publishing them in a booklet, "Dairy Desserts."

Mr. Knox died in 1908 and Rose took over the business; within seven years its value had tripled. She claimed she used common sense in running the company, "but from the first I determined to run it in a woman's way." She shortened the work week from five and a half days to five, and provided two weeks' vacation and sick time. Eighty-five percent of her employees remained with the firm at least twenty-five years.

In 1937, the staff helped Rose celebrate her eightieth birthday. She arrived at the plant daily at 9:30 a.m. until she was eighty-eight, when arthritis forced her to work from her home. At ninety she finally made her son president; she became chairman of the board until her death two years later.

Lizzie Wilson Goodenough

1867

July 7, Monday.

Is not this a lovely morning. It is not quite light yet, wish that my washing was done and I had nothing to do but sit here and write or enjoy myself any other way I chose, but not so, I have got to go to the hot tub instead of the writing desk.

July 15, Sunday.

Another lonesome dreaded week of tiresome housework and drudgery is begun for me. Nothing better was my lot it seems.

August 5, Saturday.

We are baking as usual this forenoon. I have been baking white and graham bread, pies, doughnuts, etc.

*A*n orphan's lot

Lizzie's diary is in the Lizzie A. Wilson Goodenough and Mrs. Henry Wilson Diaries Collection in the American Antiquarian Society, Worcester, Massachusetts.

Mrs. Trip has been baking cake and hard gingerbread.
August 18, Friday.

Still another Friday has come with its work, sweeping is the order of the day this time. Have blistered my hands sweeping this forenoon, should think I had swept enough to draw blisters on a piece of sole leather.

Lizzie Wilson Goodenough was born November 19, 1844, in Brattleboro, Vermont. She became a housekeeper for other people when she was orphaned at sixteen. Lizzie wrote each day in a small leather-bound diary that had just enough room for a few lines on each page. Often she wrote more than once a day, commenting on the weather, her various tasks, and how long they took to complete.

Poor Lizzie was quite miserable as a maid. On her twenty-second birthday she wrote, "Mine is a hard and lonely life, day after day comes and brings its work. It seems that my life is made up of nothing but long long days for nothing but work work and dig for others. . . ."

In 1869 Lizzie married Henry Goodenough, a brick quarry worker. They had two children.

Emily Howland

A daughter's desire

1856
Dear Mother . . .

Can't thee spare me a while to do what I think my portion? I want to do something which seems to me worthy of life, and if all my life is to go on as have the last ten years, I know I shall feel at the end of it as tho' I had lived in vain.

Thee may think other daughters remain at home contentedly why can't I? Because I have inherited such an amount of the desire to work that I cannot. If I am different from the stereotyped kind I can't help it. . . .

With the most despised and forlorn, my heart is; let me go to them and see what good I can do them.

Emily's writing is from The World of Emily Howland— Odyssey of a Humanitarian, *by Judith Breault, published in 1976.*

Emily Howland was born November 20, 1827, in Cayuga County, New York, to a devout Quaker family.

Emily's mother's health was always fragile, so she quit school at sixteen to return home and assume the household chores. This was not a happy period for the intellectually curious Emily, who said, "I am as a bell that cannot ring." She turned to the anti-slavery movement out of a need to do something meaningful.

In 1856, Emily moved to Washington, D.C., to take over as principal of the ailing Myrtilla Miner's [March 4] school for free Negro girls. She remained there for two years. In 1867, she persuaded her father to buy four hundred acres in Heathsville, Virginia, where she began relocating freed slaves. She opened a rural school which she ran for the next fifty years until she turned it over to the state.

When she was ninety-nine Emily received an honorary doctoral degree from the University of the State of New York. She died at her home when she was one hundred and one.

Hetty Green

1908

I saw the situation developing three years ago, and I am on record as predicting it. I said then that the rich were approaching the brink, and that a 'panic' was inevitable. . . .

I saw the handwriting on the wall and began quietly to call in my money, making few new transactions and getting into my hands every available dollar of my fortune against the day I knew was coming. Every real-estate deal which I could possibly close up was converted into cash. . . .

When the crash came I had money, and I was one of the very few who really had it. The others had their 'securities' and their 'values.' I had the cash, and they had to come to me. They did come to me in droves. Some of them I lent money to, and some I didn't. That was my privilege.

Hetty Robinson Green was born November 21, 1834, in New Bedford, Massachusetts. As a child, Hetty read the financial pages to her grandfather and accompanied her father on his business rounds. She later said, "I was forced into business. . . . I was taught from the time I was six years old that I would have to look after my property."

Hetty looked after her property so well that she became the richest woman in America. She shunned speculation in

She had the cash

Hetty's writing is from an interview in 1908 with W. Howard Noble, which was published in the Boston Traveller.

favor of railroad stocks and government bonds. She accumulated over eight thousand pieces of real estate and lent money to other investors.

She married a forty-six-year-old millionaire, Edward Green of Vermont, when she was thirty-two. He was not as conservative as Hetty and went bankrupt through failed investments in 1855. She refused to underwrite his debts and they separated.

Hetty became known as an eccentric, taking the Quaker belief in thrift to the extreme. Although her estate was valued at one hundred million dollars when she died, Hetty lived in shabby boardinghouses, wore old clothes, haggled over pennies, and sought medical treatment from free clinics.

NOVEMBER 22 *Elizabeth Christophers Hobson*

She persevered

1916

On the committee which was formed that day to visit and report on the condition of Bellevue Hospital, I found, to my surprise and dismay, that I was appointed Chairman of the Subcommittee to visit the Surgical Wards for Women. . . .

I had never been in a hospital before. On my first visit the sight of the patients and the loathsome smells sickened me so that I nearly fainted and had to leave, but I persevered. . . .

Elizabeth Christophers Kimball Hobson was born on a farm on Long Island, New York, November 22, 1831. On a visit to San Francisco when she was seventeen she met Joseph Hobson, a wealthy banker. They became engaged after ten days and married in 1850.

After residing in Chile and Peru for many years for business purposes, the Hobsons returned to New York, where Elizabeth became involved in charity work. In 1872, she chaired a committee to investigate the unsanitary conditions and untrained personnel at Bellevue Hospital. Her report led to the creation of the Bellevue Training School for Nurses, the first American school that trained nurses using Florence Nightingale's methods. The school helped reform public hospitals and established a new profession for women in America.

Elizabeth's writing is from her autobiography, Recollections of a Happy Life, *published in 1916.*

Marie Louise Van Vorst

1903

Through the looms I catch sight of Upton's, my land-lord's, little child. She is seven; so small that they have a box for her to stand upon. She is a pretty, frail, little thing, a spooler—"a good spooler, tew!" Through the frames on the other side I can only see her fingers as they clutch at the flying spools; her head is not high enough, even with the box, to be visible. Her hands are fairy hands, fine-boned, well-made, only they are so thin and dirty, and her nails—claws; she would do well to have them cut.

Marie Louise Van Vorst, author and reformer, was born on November 23, 1867, in New York City. She came from a well-to-do family and received her education from private tutors.

Marie and her widowed sister-in-law, Bessie, went to France at the turn of the century to write. They collaborated on one novel and wrote poetry and fiction independently.

Upon returning to the United States, Marie and Bessie became concerned with the plight of the working woman and decided to experience factory life for themselves. Marie, disguised as "Bell Ballard," toiled in a Massachusetts shoe factory and a Southern cotton mill. Bessie assumed the name "Esther Kelly" and worked in a Pittsburgh pickle factory and a Buffalo knitting mill. They lived in dreary rooming houses and did factory work for several years, culminating in their book *The Woman Who Toils: Being the Experiences of Two Ladies as Factory Girls.* They were especially concerned with the poor treatment of children and women who worked in terrible conditions for unscrupulous factory owners.

Marie married Count Gaetano Cagiati of Italy in 1916 in a ceremony at Notre Dame Cathedral in Paris. They adopted a son. She continued to write after her marriage and took up painting, exhibiting at a gallery in New York. She died in Florence, Italy, in 1936.

Little girls at work

Marie's writing about a child worker in a Southern mill is from her part of The Woman Who Toils: Being the Experiences of Two Ladies as Factory Girls, *published in 1903.*

Frances Hodgson Burnett

A special place

1893

In the centre of the Square was a Lamp Post. I write it with capital letters because it was not an ordinary lamp post. It was a very big one, and had a solid base of stone, which all the children thought had been put there for a seat. Four or five little girls could sit on it, and four or five little girls usually did when the day was fine.

Ah! the things which were talked over under the Lamp Post, the secrets that were whispered, and the wrongs that were discussed! In the winter, when the gas was lighted at four o'clock, there could be no more de-lightfully secluded spot for friendly conversation than the stone base of the lamp which cast its yellow light from above.

Frances Hodgson Burnett was born November 24, 1849, in Manchester, England.

The Hodgsons emigrated to America when Frances was sixteen. To help support her family, she taught school, raised chickens, and gave music lessons. When she was nineteen she had her first story accepted by *Godey's Lady Book*.

In 1872 Frances became engaged to Dr. Swan Burnett, and married him a year later. For the next decade she pro-duced highly acclaimed novels. *The Secret Garden* is still pop-ular with today's children.

Despite her success, Frances was nervous, depressed and sickly. She doted on her two sons, dressing them daily in elaborate costumes and curling their long hair. She made them two special outfits of velvet and lace which were later immortalized in her *Little Lord Fauntleroy*.

In 1890, her eldest son Lionel died. She divorced her husband to marry the younger doctor who had administered to Lionel. The marriage lasted only a year as Frances became more and more eccentric, wearing titian-colored wigs and long, flowing gowns of chiffon and lace.

Frances' writing is from The One I Knew the Best of All, *published in 1893.*

Carry Amelia Nation

1908

I shall not in this book speak much of my love affairs,
but they were, nevertheless, an important part of my life.
I was a great lover. I used to think a person never could
love but once in this life, but I often now say, I would not
want a heart that could hold but one love. It was not the
beauty of face or form that was the most attractive to me
in young gentlemen, or ladies, but that of the mind.
Seeing this the case with myself, I tried to acquire knowledge to make my company agreeable. I see young ladies,
and gentlemen, who entertain each other with their silly
jokes and gigglings that are disgusting. When I had
company I always directed the conversation so that my
friend would teach me something, or I would teach him.

Love of the mind

Carry Amelia Nation was born November 25, 1846, in Gerrard
County, Kentucky. Her childhood was an unhappy one: the
Civil War decimated the family's finances, and her mother suffered from severe mental disorders which eventually led to her
being committed to a state mental institution. Carry rushed
into a marriage in 1867 and soon discovered her husband was
an alcoholic. She left him and returned home.

Carry taught school for several years until her second marriage to David Nation, a lawyer and journalist nineteen years
her senior. This marriage was also an unhappy one. Carry said
in later years that she realized God had denied her a happy
home so that she might become a Home Defender for others.

The Nations settled in Medicine Lodge, Kansas, where
she helped found the county chapter of the W.C.T.U. In the
summer of 1899 she entered a saloon, tears streaming down her
face, singing an emotional temperance song, and closed the
place down. Thus began her eleven-year crusade against the
selling of liquor. She developed a militant modus operandi: she
would enter a saloon armed with a hatchet and some bricks,
sing a few hymns, quote Bible verses, and then proceed to break
up the place—smashing bottles, furniture and tawdry pictures
on the walls. Although she was nearly six feet tall and very
strong, she was often beaten, mobbed or jailed for her efforts.

Many people thought Carry was the country's saviour,
while others thought her insane. After being beaten by a
woman saloon owner in 1910, she retired her hatchet and died
the following year.

Carry's writing is from The
Use and Need of the Life of
Carry A. Nation, *published in
1908.*

Sarah Moore Grimké

*O*ut of the kitchen

Sarah's writing is from an address she gave in 1838 before the Boston Female Anti-Slavery Society. It was published later that year in pamphlet form as Letters on the Equality of the Sexes, and the Condition of Woman.

1838

Let no one think, from these remarks, that I regard a knowledge of housewifery as beneath the acquisition of women. Far from it. . . .

All I complain of is, that our education consists so almost exclusively in culinary and other manual operations. I do long to see the time, when it will no longer be necessary for women to expend so many precious hours in furnishing "a well spread table," but that their husbands will forego some of their accustomed indulgences in this way, and encourage their wives to devote some portion of their time to mental cultivation, even at the expense of having to dine sometimes on baked potatoes, or bread and butter.

Sarah Moore Grimké was born November 26, 1792, in Charleston, South Carolina, the sixth of fourteen children. On a trip to Philadelphia with her father in 1819, she was impressed by the simplicity and piety of the Quakers, as well as their hatred of slavery. Two years later she left the family's Episcopal faith, moved to Philadelphia, and became a Quaker.

Eight years later, Sarah's youngest sister Angelina moved to Philadelphia, and the two sisters never again resided in the South. They took up the anti-slavery cause as a vocation. Angelina was most effective as a lecturer, and Sarah wrote abolitionist arguments based on scriptural grounds. Having lived under the slave system and rejected it increased their credence.

Angelina married in 1838, and Sarah made her home with them for the rest of her life. She and her sister retired from actively campaigning against slavery and turned to teaching.

Both Sarah and her sister accomplished much in the anti-slavery movement and helped inspire the feminists of the day to take up the combined fight against the subjugation of Negroes and women.

Elsie Clews Parsons

1914

In the United States to-day a mother sometimes tells her daughter not to speak to any strange man in the street—except a policeman; and it was once thought bad form for a girl to go "buggy-riding" with a man or in town to be seen with one in a cab. Only a few years ago a New York girl told me that having to drive home late in the evening in a "strange" cab and without a chaperone, she required her escort to sit on the box with the driver.

Extreme caution

Elsie Clews Parsons was born November 27, 1875, in New York City. Although her mother would have preferred her to be a society belle, Elsie attended Barnard College and received her A.B., A.M. and Ph.D. degrees, majoring in anthropology and sociology.

In 1900 Elsie married Herbert Parsons, a lawyer. In addition to raising their family of four children she continued to study, teach, and write books.

In 1915 Elsie travelled to the southwest, where she saw Indians in their environment for the first time and decided to make them her focus. The following year she left the younger children in the care of her oldest daughter and departed for a long field trip to the pueblos of Arizona and New Mexico. Thereafter she made annual expeditions to live with and study the Zuni, Hopi, Taos, Tewa and Laguna tribes, which resulted in several books and over one hundred articles.

Elsie's writing is from her book,
Fear and Conventionality, *published in 1914.*

Lucretia Epperson

(Wyoming - near the Green River)
June 30, 1864

. . . camped near a mountain stream, which abounded with fine mountain trout. All hands were soon busy preparing lines and hooks; started out, and soon returned with a supply of fish, enough for supper and breakfast. Found a stranger in camp, who proved to be a Mormon elder, who wished to convert Mr. Epperson.

No sale

Lucretia's journal is included in
The History of Colusa
County, *published in 1880.*

His efforts were in vain. Mr. Epperson told him he was afraid they would want him to take another wife. Told him he could never do that, as his hair was nearly all pulled out by the one he had, and if he were obliged to take two or three more, he would have no head left. The elder looked a moment at Mr. Epperson, then left in disgust.

Lucretia Lawson Epperson was born November 28, 1840, in Hardin County, Illinois. In 1861 she married Brutus Clay Epperson.

Lucretia and Brutus settled on a farm in Etna, Illinois, and had a son. However, Brutus had been to California with his brother nine years earlier and he longed to return. He determined to buy as many good breeding horses as possible, drive them to California, and start a livestock business.

On April 1, 1864, the Eppersons and a business partner set off for the west. Four and a half months later they reached their destination, Colusa County, where they built their ranch and had three more children. Later on they built the "Bartlett Springs and Bear Valley Toll Road" which brought in a large income in addition to their profitable livestock business.

Louisa May Alcott

*D*eciding to go

Louisa's writing is included in Louisa May Alcott: Her Life, Letters, and Journals, *edited by* Ednah D. Cheney [June 27], *published in 1889.*

1862

November.—Thirty years old. Decided to go to Washington as nurse if I could find a place. Help needed, and I love nursing, and *must* let out my pent-up energy in some new way. Winter is always a hard and a dull time, and if I am away there is one less to feed and warm and worry over.

I want new experiences, and am sure to get 'em if I go. So I've sent in my name, and bide my time writing tales, to leave all snug behind me, and mending up my old clothes,—for nurses don't need nice things, thank Heaven!

Louisa May Alcott was born November 29, 1832, in Germantown, Pennsylvania. Her father's last steady job was when she was seven, so the family moved frequently and had very little money. Louisa began her literary career in an effort to

---

improve the family's conditions, and quickly became the breadwinner.

Most readers assumed that the plot and characters in *Little Women* paralleled Louisa's life and family, but this was far from the truth. Her mother was angry and bitter and her father was eccentric and demanding. He believed Louisa was destined for evil because of her hair and skin, and on her tenth birthday gave her nothing but a letter urging her to change her behavior. She never married, and believed that "liberty is a better husband than love to many of us."

Louisa volunteered as an army nurse in 1862. She served in Georgetown, D.C., for a year before being forced to return home with typhoid fever. She recorded her experiences, which were published as *Hospital Sketches*.

Buoyed by the success of that book, she pursued her writing in earnest and produced a variety of popular novels, poetry and children's fiction. Before she died she had published 270 works. *Little Women* alone sold over two million copies and earned her $200,000.

Mary Eliza McDowell

1929

First I visited the Sewage and Garbage plant on the edge of the city [Granblurt, Germany]. It was a surprise to find the buildings of good and attractive architecture in the midst of well-planned landscape gardening. . . . As we entered the sewage plant our American sense of humor was tickled as we saw on the wall a mural painting of the legend of "The Old Woman's Mill." Old creatures were laboriously climbing the hill to the mill where they were made over into new and attractive young women and then they were seen dancing down the slope on the right hand side of the mill. This was the German way of saying to the public, "Science, like the mill, can take ugly stuff and make it over into that which is useful and beautiful."

Mary Eliza McDowell was born November 30, 1854, in Cincinnati, Ohio. She attended local schools, but stated in later years that her education was derived "mostly in being the oldest daughter of a large family with an invalid mother."

Mary's induction into social service came after the Great Chicago Fire of 1871, when she assisted her pastor with the

A use for science

Mary's writing is from Mary McDowell and Municipal Housekeeping, *edited by* Mrs. Caroline Hill, *published in 1929.*

relief forces. She continued working for various charitable organizations until 1894, when she was offered the position of director of the University of Chicago Settlement, a newly opened settlement house that was to serve as a social service laboratory for the university. They chose the treeless region behind the stockyards and meat-packing plants, near the garbage dump and "Bubbly Creek" (a dead branch of the Chicago River which had become an open sewer).

Mary took an apartment in the area amid the Irish, German and Slavic immigrants. She established a day nursery, clubs for adults and children, and classes in music, arts and crafts and English. She organized a summer camp, built a gymnasium and a neighborhood playground, and persuaded the city to build a public library, a municipal bathhouse and a community park.

In 1911 Mary went to Europe to study garbage disposal methods, and upon her return launched a campaign against the city council to force them to stop dumping garbage. Next she tackled the problem of "Bubbly Creek." Eventually the city council constructed a new sewer, filled in the creek, and developed a manufacturing district. She retired as director of the University of Chicago Settlement at the age of seventy-five, and died seven years later.

DECEMBER

Jane Andrews

1873

*T*he best cure

"Poor little Phillis!" she said, "what is the matter?" The sobs stopped for a minute and the black little figure in the bed turned towards the kind voice that spoke to her out of the darkness. Then the sad cry of "Mother!" burst out again. Patty's tears, too, began to flow; in vain she tried to think of anything comforting to say. She could not promise that mother should come soon, could not even say that Phillis could ever go back to her; there was indeed no comfort to offer but sympathy, and the longer Patty thought about it the more sympathetic she grew. Her bare feet were cold upon the floor. Should she go back to her own bed? How could she leave this poor child alone to cry all night for her mother? She hesitated a minute, and then, gently lifting the bed-clothes, crept softly into the bed, and put her arms about the weeping child. After all, that was the best cure. I sometimes think love will cure anything; and, at any rate, the two children were soon sleeping soundly.

Jane Andrews was born December 1, 1833, in Newburyport, Massachusetts. As a teenager she had already begun teaching, giving instruction to cotton-mill workers at a free evening school. She graduated from the State Normal School in 1853 as valedictorian of her class.

While living in the same boardinghouse as Elizabeth Peabody [May 16], she met her brother-in-law, Horace Mann, who encouraged her to enroll in his new college—Antioch—in Ohio. She was the first student to register on its opening day, one of only eight of one hundred fifty applicants who were deemed qualified to enter. However, life in the half-finished college building brought on a neurological illness which forced her to quit before the year was up.

In 1860 Jane opened a small primary school in her home which she operated for the next twenty-five years. Her teaching reflected Horace Mann's belief in the individual's responsibility to society. She introduced innovative teaching techniques and augmented textbook study with field trips, experiments, games, theater and stories.

Jane published her first and most famous book, *Seven Little Sisters Who Live on the Round Ball that Floats in the Air*, in 1861. It was the story of seven happy children who each lived

Jane's writing is from her short story, "Patty's Responsibility," published in the September, 1873, issue of Our Young Folks.

in a different place on earth but were all members of God's family. The book sold a half-million copies and was translated into German, Chinese and Japanese. She wrote five other books in her series, and the six "Andrews Books" were used in elementary schools for sixty years.

Mary Mortimer

*A*utumn's glory

Lima, N.Y.
1855

It is a beautiful Sabbath morning in that most beautiful of summers,—the Indian Summer. I am in a charming place to which I have taken quite a liking, and feel that I should be very grateful for so much beauty,—so much to lead me above the trials of our common life. . . . Does this sunlight fall over the landscape, over the fading foliage, more gorgeous in its decay than in its noontide glory. Among many lessons does it not whisper to us this, that we, too, should increase in glory and excellence as life wanes? Are not the glories which are to be revealed growing nearer? And this light,—O! what unutterable things it says of Him who is its Source.

Mary Mortimer was born December 2, 1816, in Trowbridge, Wiltshire, England. The family emigrated to New York when she was five. Both parents died eight years later, leaving her in the care of an older brother. She asked to use her share of her father's small estate for schooling, but her brother refused.

At the age of twenty-one, Mary inherited her father's money and immediately entered Madame Ricord's Seminary in Geneva, New York. She completed the four-year course in two years, in addition to teaching history, mathematics and metaphysics. However, she developed a partial paralysis of her right hand and foot from which she never recovered.

In 1848 Mary met Catharine Beecher [September 6], who was in the process of establishing non-sectarian girls' high schools in the west. Catharine felt Mary had one of the "original, planning minds" that she had been looking for and invited Mary to join her. In 1851, they opened the Normal Institute and High School of Milwaukee, with Mary as a teacher and head of the faculty. In 1853, the name was changed to Milwaukee Female College. Mary spent fifteen years there, retiring from the principalship in 1874. She died three years later of an "inscrutable malady."

Mary's letter to her sister-in-law is included in A True Teacher: Mary Mortimer in Memory *by Minerve Norton, published in 1894.*

Margaret O'Neale Eaton

1873

Mr. Timberlake was a great sufferer from the asthma through our whole married life. I remember the distressed condition in which I frequently saw him. One night when he was speechless with agony, I was aroused by the touch of his elbow, and springing up and striking a light saw him in such unutterable distress that I hardly knew what to do. In the frenzy of my love and excitement I bound his arm tight with my garter, opened a vein with a penknife, flung a wrapper around myself, rushed across the street, and brought our family physician, old Dr. Simms, who pronounced my hurried treatment as the salvation of the life of my husband under the circumstances, but as having been very perilous.

Margaret O'Neale Eaton was born December 3, 1799, in Washington, D.C. Her father ran a combination tavern and boardinghouse, the Franklin House, which was popular with government officials. Margaret, called "Peggy," was a flirtatious beauty who enjoyed the attentions of the boarders. She was sent to boarding school in New York City at fifteen after an attempted elopement with an army officer. Upon her return, she soon married John Timberlake, a navy purser.

Two years after her marriage, Senator John Eaton took up residence at Franklin House, as did Andrew Jackson a few years later. Eaton took an interest in the family and helped Timberlake to secure commissions at sea. In his absence, Peggy and Eaton were frequent companions, and rumors linked them romantically. Timberlake died in a Mediterranean seaport in 1828.

Andrew Jackson was elected to the presidency the same year, and John Eaton was a likely prospect for a cabinet post. Jackson advised him to "marry Peg forthwith" to put an end to the gossip which was harming his career. They were married in 1829, and two months later he was appointed secretary of war. Scandalous rumors about the couple continued for years. Peggy dictated her autobiography in 1873 as her "contribution to the truth of history." She concluded: "God help the woman who must live in Washington! . . . If the lines have fallen to them by Providence to be natives or residents, they require the sympathy of the civilized world."

John died in 1856, leaving Peggy a large estate. Within three years, she again scandalized Washington by marrying her

First aid

Peggy's writing is from The Autobiography of Peggy Eaton, *published posthumously in 1932.*

grandchildren's nineteen-year-old Italian dancing teacher. After defrauding her of her fortune, he ran off with her youngest granddaughter.

Julia Ditto Young

*H*er dream man

1889

. . . It was impossible to look into Jerome Harvey's deep-set gray eyes without seeing that he was a man who lived in earnest.

He was extremely tall, and carried himself with the unconscious and pardonable pride which is the inevitable component of remarkable stature in a man. He was of a sinewy, athletic build, without an ounce of superfluous flesh on his frame. He had that rarest embellishment of young American men, a fine head of hair, which lay thick, soft brown waves above a broad white forehead. His features were good, and his earnest eyes seemed to grow in beauty and impressiveness with every year of his life. The whole effect of his physiognomy was grave, stern, almost solemn.

Julia Evelyn Ditto Young was born December 4, 1857, in Buffalo, New York. She already showed promise as a writer at an early age, and her talent was nurtured by her parents. She published her first story at fourteen in the Buffalo *Evening Post*. The opening lines: "Shriek upon shriek rent the air, mingled with yells. . ." caused quite a sensation among the local readers.

Julia married Robert Young, a banker, when she was nineteen. She raised two sons while continuing her literary career as a frequent contributor of poetry and short stories to the leading magazines of the day. She also translated French and German poetry into English.

Julia's writing is from her first novel, Adrift: A Story of Niagara, *published in 1889.*

Susan Hale

Matunuck, Rhode Island
September 7, 1907

... You must know that I had been thinking of becoming an example of the Perfect Old Lady, for, like you, I love growing old, and have been in the habit of saying that each age I came to was the most interesting yet. But here comes roaring ears, and knocks me flat. Nobody ever told me about that (perhaps they did, and I paid absolutely no attention. In fact Carry Weld says her dear old mother,—she was a plucky example, used to have awful noises in her ears all the time). But no matter. I am now determined to acquire the art of being a Perfectly Fascinating Old Deaf Person. This resolution of mine furnishes me with ample occupation,— often lacking to the aged, watching out to see that I don't get cross or suspicious or inquisitive, or those things. I was thinking, you know, of becoming bed-ridden as soon as I got bald, but now there's no fun lying in bed with roaring ears. ...

A perfect old lady

Susan Hale, painter and world traveller, was born December 5, 1833, in Boston, Massachusetts. She began teaching in the early 1800's when the family fortune declined due to her father's ill health. After her parents' deaths, Susan and her sister Lucretia [September 2] embarked for Egypt, where brother Charles was consul general for the United States. She started to paint, taking courses abroad and at home.

Susan studied watercolors in Paris in the early 1870's and then returned to New England and taught painting. She then set up a pattern for her life which she followed for the rest of her seventy-six years: summers in Rhode Island painting, swimming, writing and entertaining; and winters travelling to Europe, Africa, Mexico or Jamaica.

Susan's letter to her friend Miss Charlotte Hedge is included in Letters of Susan Hale, *published in 1918. Susan left behind many wonderful letters that reveal her witty and fun-loving personality.*

Jane Grey Swisshelm

An angel's devotion

1880

About ten days after I went to Campbell, I was called at midnight to a death-bed. It was a case of flesh-wound in the thigh, and the whole limb was swollen almost to bursting, so cold as to startle by the touch, and almost as transparent as glass. I knew this was piemia and that for it medical science had no cure; but I wanted to warm that cold limb, to call circulation back to that inert mass. The first thought was warm, wet compresses, hot bricks, hot flannel; but the kitchen was locked, and it was little I could do without fire, except to receive and write down his dying messages to parents, and the girl who was waiting to be his wife.

When the surgeon's morning hour came he still lived; and at my suggestion the warm compresses were applied. He said, "they feel so good," and was quite comforted by them, but died about ten o'clock. I was greatly grieved to think he had suffered from cold the last night of life, but how avoid any number of similar occurrences? There was no artificial heat in any of the wards. A basin of warm water was only to be obtained by special favor of the cooks; but they had been very courteous. The third day of my appearance among them, one looked up over the edge of the tub over which he bent, washing potatoes, and said, as I stood waiting for hot water,

"Do you know what you look like going around here among us fellows?"

"No! but nothing dreadful I hope."

"You just look like an angel, and that's what we all think; we're ever so much better since you came."

The memory of this speech gave me courage to go and lay my trouble before the cooks, who gathered to hear me tell the story of that death, the messages left for the friends who should see him no more, and of my sorrow that I could not drive away the cold on that last, sad night.

They all wiped their eyes on their aprons; head cook went to a cupboard, brought a key and handed it to

Jane's writing is from her memoirs, Half a Century, *published in 1880. The "Campbell" she refers to was an Army Hospital in Washington, D.C., where she served as a volunteer during the Civil War.*

me, saying:

"There, *mother*, is a key of this kitchen; come in here whenever you please. We will always find room on the ranges for your bricks, and I'll have something nice in the cupboard every night for you and the nurses."

This proved to be the key to the situation, and after I received that bit of metal from cook, there was not one death from piemia in any ward where I was free to work, although I have had as many, I think, as sixty men struck with the premonitory chill, in one night. I concluded that "piemia" was French for neglect, and that the antidote was warmth, nourishing food, stimulants, friction, fresh air and cheerfulness, and did not hesitate to say that if death wanted to get a man out of my hands, he must send some other agent than piemia. I do not believe in the medical theory concerning it; do not believe pus ever gets into the veins, or that there is any poison about it, except that of ignorance and indifference on the part of doctors and nurses.

Jane Grey Swisshelm was born December 6, 1815, in Pittsburgh, Pennsylvania. She became a schoolteacher at fourteen to help her widowed mother.

Jane married James Swisshelm, a devout Methodist who, together with his overbearing mother, made Jane's life miserable by trying to repress her independent spirit. With "a breaking heart" she gave up painting and reading to please him.

Jane started her literary career with a series of anonymous newspaper articles condemning capital punishment. In 1848 she began publishing her own anti-slavery magazine in Pittsburgh. For ten years she used it as a forum for her ideas, until her marriage became so unbearable that she gave up her editorship and fled with her only child to her sister's in St. Cloud, Minnesota. She became a familiar figure on the lecture circuit until her death.

Abby Hopper Gibbons

May 6, 1854

*T*he poison weed

My dear Willie,

There is one matter resting upon my mind that I must be relieved from; therefore, I ask of L____ and S____ if they use tobacco in any form. If they do, it is not my business to do more than remonstrate, so far as they are concerned; but I beg of thee, my dear son, to allow no one—not thy dearest friend—to smoke in thy room. I do not wish thee to inhale the poison weed. I speak in all plainness and say that they have rights in their own rooms, and I trust my son will have the manliness to act independently in the matter. You may have your good times on gingerbread and cold water. . . .

Abigail Hopper Gibbons, anti-slavery reformer and Civil War nurse, was born December 7, 1801, in Philadelphia to a strong Quaker family. Abigail married James Gibbons in 1833. He was eight years younger than she was.

The Gibbons made their home in New York City and raised six children. Abby was very active in the Manhattan Anti-Slavery Society. The conservative Quakers disowned her husband and her father in 1842 for their abolitionism, so Abby stood up in meeting and renounced her membership.

During the Civil War Abby and her daughter served as nurses in Washington. Upon her return to New York, she continued to work for various reform and welfare interests. She considered her crowning achievement to be the 1892 passage of a bill to create a woman's reformatory in New York City. Abby had lobbied for years for the measure, making her final appearance before a legislative committee at ninety-one.

Abby's letter to her son at Harvard is included in The Life of Abby Hopper Gibbons Told Chiefly Through Her Correspondence, *edited by her daughter, published in 1897.*

DECEMBER 8

Mother Mary Aloysia Hardey

*E*ducating children

1869

The secret of bringing up children well lies in the knowledge of the human heart, in patience, in influence, in example. An education which does not give self-possession, personal discipline, is an *education manquée*. Remember that children often become like the mistress whom they most love. . . . Some of you are too agitated, always running about. That's time lost. Hold your children through the heart, through their sense of honour, reward them generously, but three or four times a year it is well to come down upon them with the majesty and thunder of the Lord Judgment.

(Mother) Mary Aloysia Hardey was born December 8, 1809, on her grandfather's estate in Piscataway, Maryland. When

Mother Hardey's writing is from an address she gave to her teachers in 1869. It is included in Second Sowing: The Life of Mary Aloysia Hardey *by Sister Margaret Williams, published in 1942.*

Give Her This Day

she was six the family moved to Louisiana, travelling with their slaves and household goods on a flatboat down the Ohio and Mississippi Rivers to Operlousas in the bayou land.

Mary was sent to the Sacred Heart Convent School at the age of thirteen. The Society of the Sacred Heart had been founded in Paris in 1800 to establish schools for well-to-do Catholic girls; it spread to America in 1818.

Following graduation, Mary entered the novitiate and was sent to St. Michael's, Louisiana, to help found a Sacred Heart convent and school there. Although still in her teens, she was placed in charge of the school, and at twenty-seven she was named Mother Superior.

In 1841, Mother Hardey was asked to go to New York City to found the society's first convent and school in the east. During the next twenty-seven years she established sixteen houses and schools of the Sacred Heart in Cuba, Canada, and across the United States.

Elizabeth Buffum Chace

1891

I wore the Quaker costume in its entirety, and had never said "you" to a single person in my life, or given the title of "Mr." or "Mrs." to anybody. I was constant in the attendance of our religious meetings, and firmly believed in the efficacy of our simple, and as we called them, un-ceremonious modes of worship. But, to be an Abolition-ist, put me down among the ostracized. I remember, on one occasion, at the yearly meeting, when an epistle was read by the clerk and presented for approval, which con-tained the usual formula of the declaration of our testi-mony against the enslavement of "Africans," I objected to this designation, as most of the slaves in this country, at that time, were natives of America. Another Anti-Slavery woman seconded my remonstrance, and finally the word was changed. We afterward learned, that a friend present from Philadelphia, inquired *who those young women were*, and expressed her surprise that our protest was heeded.

Elizabeth Buffum Chace was born December 9, 1806, in Providence, Rhode Island. When she was twenty-two she

Young women win

Elizabeth's writing is from her Anti-Slavery Reminiscences, published in 1891.

married Samuel B. Chace, a Quaker merchant from Fall River, Massachusetts.

Elizabeth's family had been active in the anti-slavery movement for several generations. Her grandfather had hidden runaway slaves and her father was a founder of the New England Anti-Slavery Society. After her first five children all died as infants, Elizabeth turned to anti-slavery work to try to assuage her grief. She used her organizational skills to raise funds, write letters and petitions, locate speakers and set up meetings. Her home became a stop on the Underground Railroad where fleeing slaves hid until they could get on the train to Canada.

After the birth of five more children, all of whom lived, Elizabeth's anti-slavery activities were curtailed to her home.

Emily Dickinson

Concealed feelings

Emily's writing is from a letter to her only brother, Austin. It is included in The Life and Letters of Emily Dickinson *by her niece Martha Dickinson Bianchi, published in 1924.*

1851

My Dear Austin,

. . . I miss you very much—I put on my bonnet to-night, opened the gate very desperately, and for a little while the suspense was terrible—I think I was held in check by some invisible agent, for I returned to the house without having done any harm!

If I hadn't been afraid that you would "poke fun" at my feelings, I'd have written a sincere letter, but since "the world is hollow, and dollie's stuffed with sawdust," I really do not think we had better expose our feelings. . . .

Emily Dickinson was born December 10, 1830, in Amherst, Massachusetts. After graduating from Amherst Academy, she spent one year at the Mount Holyoke Female Seminary, but found it too exhausting and returned home.

In the early 1850's, Emily began writing poetry; by 1858 she was sufficiently satisfied with her style to recopy her poems and bind them into neat packets. She wrote to Thomas Higginson of *The Atlantic* in reply to his request for fresh talent, asking, "Are you too deeply occupied to say if my Verse is alive?" He was fascinated by the "half-cracked poetess" from Amherst, and although he advised against publication, he remained her friend and advisor through their correspondence.

Emily always dressed in white, and after her early thirties, never left her family's home and garden. She rarely received visitors. When she did, she would hide upstairs and send down a poem or a note to her guest. She preferred to socialize through her letters and poems.

When Emily died at the age of fifty-five, she left behind 1,775 poems in her bedroom dresser drawer. Considered by many the greatest woman poet in the English language, she had only published seven poems, anonymously, during her lifetime. However, she evidently sensed that success would come to her once her poems were discovered, as she wrote, "I have a horror of death; the dead are so soon forgotten. But when I die, they'll have to remember me."

Annie Jump Cannon

1941

They aren't just streaks to me, each new spectrum is the gateway to a wonderful new world. It is almost as if the distant stars had really acquired speech and were able to tell of their constitution and physical condition.

Gateway

Annie Jump Cannon was born December 11, 1863, in Dover, Delaware. Her mother had taken an astronomy course as a girl, and she passed along her interest to her daughter. Together they built a makeshift observatory in the attic, where Annie spent many hours observing the constellations and recording their positions in the sky.

At sixteen, Annie enrolled in the fifth freshman class at Wellesley College, where she avidly pursued astronomy, physics and spectroscopy. She recalled in later years that as a child she had been fascinated by the pretty spectra cast by prisms hanging off an ornate candelabrum. She cherished the candelabrum as an early omen of her life's work, and kept it prominently displayed in her home.

Following the death of her mother, to whom she had always been extremely close, Annie became a special student in astronomy at Radcliffe. Two years later, she began working as an assistant at the Harvard College Observatory investigating stellar spectra, the study of the characteristics revealed when the light of a star is photographed through a prism.

She received numerous awards and honorary degrees for her work, which she modestly attributed to patience. Annie resigned from Harvard eight months before her death at the age of seventy-seven.

Annie's feelings about spectral data were included in her obituary in the April 14, 1941, Boston Herald.

Lillian Nordica

How to sing

Lillian's writing is from her article, "How to Sing a Ballad" from the March, 1931, Musical Digest.

1931

I remember hearing a woman say she could sing right through and not move her face at all. That was perfectly lovely, wonderful, so refined! Not at all! Rather, you must give the meaning of the song in the expression of your face, and in order to do that you must study before a glass.

Do not be afraid to have plenty of movement of the lips for the vowels. Do not make any motions not required for the interpretation, but make every one necessary to convey to your public all the sentiment contained in the words or the music. If you are singing about flowers and trees, you want to look as if the flowers and trees gave you pleasure. If you are singing about the "joyous, joyous spring," you do not want to look as if you were going to a funeral in autumn.

Lillian Nordica was born December 12, 1857, in Farmington, Maine. She was the youngest of six children in a talented family. In 1871, at the age of fourteen, Lillian began singing lessons at the New England Conservatory of Music.

Lillian graduated from the Conservatory in 1876 and departed for Europe to prepare for the operatic career that was her goal. She studied in London, Paris and Milan, where her voice teacher secured her an operatic debut. Since "Norton" was difficult to say in Italian, he changed her last name to "Nordica." For the next fifteen years Lillian, the "Lily of the North," toured constantly throughout the United States and Europe.

Lillian was not as successful in her private life as she was in her career. She was married and divorced twice, and although she remained with her third husband, she wrote her sisters that she had been "duped, betrayed, deceived and abused" and concluded that she was "just a poor picker of husbands."

Lillian gave a performance on November 25, 1913, in Melbourne, Australia, after which she began the long journey home by boat from Sydney. The ship struck a coral reef in the Torres Strait, and although it was able to reach land after several days, Lillian had developed pneumonia due to exposure. She never recovered, and she died within a few months on the island of Java.

Mary Todd Lincoln

Chicago
July 11, 1865
My Dear Mrs. Lee,

    . . . I am realizing, day by day, hour by hour, how insupportable life is, without, the presence of the One, who loved me and my sons so dearly and in return, was idolized. Tell me, how can, I live, without my Husband, any longer? This is my first awakening thought, each morning and as I watch the waves of the turbulent lake, under our windows, I sometimes feel I should like to go, under them. I receive letters, every day, from the many friends, who in my deep bereavement, appear to me, dearer than ever, yet I hesitate, in many cases, replying to them, for the sadness, of my letters, would only infect their kind spirits.

*H*ow can I live?

Mary Ann Todd Lincoln was born December 13, 1818, in Lexington, Kentucky. Her mother died when she was six, and her father remarried the following year. Her stepmother bore nine children of her own, leaving little time or attention for Mary.

    At twenty-one, Mary went to Springfield, Illinois, to live with her married sister, Mrs. Ninian Edwards. The Edwardses were socially prominent, and Mary became a popular belle. She met Abraham Lincoln, a lawyer and legislator ten years her senior, and they fell in love at first sight. They became engaged, but Ninian and her husband disapproved. Unsure of himself because of his backwoods origins and lack of money, Abe broke off the engagement. He became ill, calling himself "the most miserable man alive," but they were reunited after a year. Mary announced to her sister on November 4, 1842, that she and Lincoln were going to be married. Realizing they could not prevent the wedding, the Edwardses allowed it to occur at their home that evening.

    The Lincolns resided in Springfield, and later Washington, following his election to the presidency. Mary's mental well-being began to unravel due to three of her sons' predeceasing her and Lincoln's shocking assassination as they sat watching a play and holding hands. She spent some time confined in a private sanatorium, after which she travelled abroad for four years, humiliated at having been considered a "lunatic." She died at her sister's home at the age of sixty-four.

Mary's letter to a friend is in the Abraham Lincoln Manuscript Collection, Library of Congress.

Mary Willcox Glenn

More than money

1912

Mrs. Schneider, the widow of a builder had not only what might be called a bourgeois attitude towards labor, but a wrong conception of business obligation. When she came broken in health and fortune to the attention of a charitable society, she and her four intelligent children needed more than mere money—they needed to be trained to have a new outlook on life.

Mary Willcox Brown Glenn was born December 14, 1869, in Baltimore, the eldest daughter in a family of thirteen children. She was educated at home, after which she undertook the education of her younger brothers and sisters. Her family believed in practicing its religion as well as professing it, so she commenced social welfare work at an early age.

In 1902, Mary married John Glenn, a prominent lawyer active in volunteer social work. They spent their honeymoon abroad, studying settlement houses in major European cities. Upon their return, they moved into Baltimore's settlement area, where Mary worked for the Charity Organization Society.

In 1907, John was chosen as executive head of the newly created Russell Sage Foundation in New York, a position he held until 1931. Mary joined the faculty of the New York School of Philanthropy (later the New York School of Social Work of Columbia University). She served for thirty-one years on the central council of the Charity Organization Society of New York, and became the second woman elected to the presidency of the National Conference of Charities and Correction.

Mary's writing is from a paper she delivered before the New York State Conference of Charities and Correction at Syracuse in 1912, which was reprinted in the January 4, 1913, issue of The Survey.

Edith Stratton Kitt

A frontier childhood

1949

I was born in Florence, Arizona Territory, on December 15, 1878. My birth was really an experience for my father since I came while he was scouring the town looking for the only doctor, whom he found later drunk and playing cards in the back room of a saloon. The small house in which I was born had dirt walls, a dirt floor and a dirt roof. There was only one board floor in the village, and that was in the most prosperous saloon. Once in a while the townspeople would clear out the bar and hold their dances in this saloon. All the mothers brought their babies and put them to bed on a long bench. Mother was a New Englander, but she did go to these dances until some man sat on me. After that, she refused to go any more. That may have been the first time I was ever sat upon, but it was far from the last.

Edith Stratton Kitt was born December 15, 1878, in Florence, Arizona Territory. When she was one and a half, the family moved to a remote ranch, the "Pandora Ranch," twelve miles north of Oracle. At first they "lived in a dugout—a dwelling actually dug out of the side of a hill."

Edith's home was "thirty miles from Tucson as the crow flies, but seventy-five as the road crawled." Occasionally, the whole family would make the trip, but not often. She later remembered, "Mother was once on the ranch for eight months without seeing another American woman." Her father made the journey every two to three months for supplies, and the four children were tutored at home.

Edith enjoyed a tomboyish youth: doing chores, riding and hunting. She began riding as a baby in a sling from an old tablecloth knotted around her father's neck and shoulder. She graduated to her own horse, "Little Bill," and was given her first shotgun at ten. She hunted quail, duck, deer and even skunk because "skunk skins were worth fifty cents to a dollar, and in one season I made fifteen dollars this way."

Edith's writing is from Pioneering in Arizona: The Reminiscences of Emerson Oliver Stratton and Edith Stratton Kitt, *edited by John Alexander Carroll and published by the Arizona Pioneers' Historical Society in 1964.*

Josephine Shaw Lowell

March 3, 1889
Dearest Annie:

Today is Mr. Cleveland's last day as President, a real misfortune to this country, I truly believe. He has stood, a firm rock, opposed to the folly and extravagance of Congress and his very last veto [of a bill to pay back to the states an 1861 war tax] is perfectly splendid—so wise and clear and full of principle. He is a great man and a true patriot.

Josephine Shaw Lowell was born December 16, 1843, in West

A great man

Josephine's letter to her long-time friend Annie Haggerty Gould is included in Philanthropic Work of Josephine Shaw Lowell, *collected and arranged by William Rhinelander Stewart, published in 1974.*

Roxbury, Massachusetts. The entire family were radical abolitionists. Her father organized the Freedmen's Bureau to provide aid to newly freed slaves. Her brother, Robert Gould Shaw, led the first Negro regiment from the free states into battle. He is memorialized by a statue across from Boston's State House, and by the movie "Glory." Josephine and her sister Anna made their war effort through the New York Association of Relief.

Josephine married Colonel Charles Lowell of the Second Massachusetts Cavalry in 1862. He was wounded the following year at Cedar Creek, and he died six weeks before Josephine gave birth to their daughter. A widow at twenty, Josephine threw herself into the National Freedman's Relief Association of New York.

In 1875, Josephine was selected to make a study of New York's able-bodied paupers. Governor Samuel Tilden was so impressed with her work that he appointed her as the first woman member of the State Board of Charities. She became one of the most influential women in her generation's charity movement and a leader in preventive social work.

Abbie Bright

*N*o fuss

1871

January 20 . . . We often see a mouse run around the room. Last Monday there were two frozen on the stove hearth. This a.m. I was sitting by Ruth helping her with the arithmetic lesson, when I felt something move between my dress and skirt. I was wise enough not to make a fuss, for I guessed what it was.

I got up quietly—went out the door, shooked my skirts vigorously—and down dropt a mouse.

Another thing to be thankful for—that I am not afraid of mice.

Abbie Bright was born December 17, 1848, near Danville, Pennsylvania. She attended Keystone State Normal School at Kutztown and received her teaching degree. She began teaching at the local Blue's School for sixteen dollars a month.

Abbie's diary was published in two volumes of the 1971 Kansas Historical Quarterly *under the title* Roughing it on her Kansas Claim, the Diary of Abbie Bright, 1870-1, *edited by Joseph Snell.*

During a visit from her brother Hiram and his wife from Indiana, Abbie became interested in going west. She departed for Red Oak Shelter, Indiana, when she was twenty-two, and took a job teaching in a one-room schoolhouse which stood at an isolated crossroads on the prairie. She had nineteen pupils, and her salary was forty dollars per month.

Abbie's brother Phillip had staked a claim near what is presently Clearwater, Kansas. Abbie also took 160 acres as an investment and stayed with him for a year, helping him to get settled. After he was murdered for his money in 1873, Abbie sold off both parcels and never returned to Kansas.

Abbie married William Achenbach, a former math teacher at Keystone Estate, in 1873. They settled in Gladbrook, Iowa, where she remained until her death in 1901.

Josephine White Griffing

Washington
Feb. 10, 1856
Dear Sir,

I hope I shall not be considered intrusive in expressing to you my deep gratitude for and high estimation of your unparalleled speech, made in the Senate Feb. sixth . . . the sayings of great men have lived in the hearts of the people correspondingly as they have touched the fundamental principle of human rights, but you have attached all persons to these rights and thus have banished from the world the very element of war, and have introduced a millennium of peace and a harvest of good will. It is enough.

A millennium

Josephine Sophia White Griffing was born December 18, 1814, in Hebron, Connecticut. At the age of twenty-one Josephine married Charles Griffing, a machinist. They settled in Litchfield, Ohio, and had five daughters, two of whom died in infancy.

After hearing the speeches of the Garrisonian abolitionists who toured the west, Josephine became involved in the anti-slavery movement. She assisted the Underground Railroad, opening her home to fugitive slaves. She became one of the most active women abolitionists, lecturing on behalf of the Western Anti-Slavery Society and contributing articles to the *Anti-Slavery Bugle*.

Following the Civil War, Josephine concerned herself with the plight of the newly freed slaves, particularly the thousands who were descending on Washington. She moved to the capital in 1865 as general agent of the National Freedman's Relief Association of the District of Columbia. She

Josephine's letter to Senator Charles Sumner is in the Charles Sumner Papers, Houghton Library, Harvard University.

operated a resettlement program for Negroes, providing food, fuel and temporary housing in abandoned barracks donated by the War Department at her request. She established an industrial school for training seamstresses and helped hundreds of former slaves find jobs and homes in the North.

Mary Ashton Livermore

*T*he secret chamber

Mary's writing is from her autobiography, The Story of My Life or The Sunshine and Shadow of Seventy Years, *written and published when she was seventy-eight (1898).*

1898

But it requires some courage to write one's biography. Every human soul has its secret chamber, which no one is allowed to invade. Our uncomforted sorrows, our tenderest and most exquisite loves, our remediless disappointments, our highest aspirations, our constantly baffled efforts for higher attainments, are known only to ourselves and God. We never talk of them.

Mary Ashton Rice Livermore was born December 19, 1820, in Boston.

In 1845, Mary married Daniel Livermore, a Universalist minister.

When the Civil War began Mary hired a governess and a maid to take care of her family and volunteered her services to the Chicago Sanitary Commission, where she worked full-time for the duration of the war. She raised money, gave lectures, inspected hospitals, and delivered supplies. In 1863, when Grant's army was threatened with scurvy, she organized donations of fruits and vegetables and shipped one thousand barrels South per week until "a line of vegetables connected Chicago and Vicksburg."

After the war Mary was convinced that women needed the vote to be able to change conditions. She started her own suffrage paper, *The Agitator*, in 1869, and became president of the Illinois Woman Suffrage Association. Lucy Stone invited her to move to Boston to edit the new weekly, *Woman's Journal*, and the Livermores relocated to Melrose, Massachusetts. Mary then took to the lecture circuit in earnest, giving 150 speeches a year for the next twenty-three years. Her topics were varied, but the role of women was a predominant theme.

She became president of the Massachusetts W.C.T.U. and served for ten years, giving anti-liquor talks at camp meetings, churches and suffrage gatherings. Frances Willard, president of the National W.C.T.U., referred to her as "our chief speaker."

Mary retired from lecturing when she was seventy-five

and spent her time working with local charities. Her husband's death in 1899 was a tremendous loss. She died six years later in 1905.

Laura S. Haviland

1881

*T*ime for mischief

I found great relief, one day, while listening to a conversation between father and grandfather, as to what age children were responsible to their Creator. Father gave his opinion that ten years, in the generality of children, is the age that God would call them to an account for sin. Grandfather said that was about the age he thought children were accountable, and all children that die previous to that age are happily saved in heaven. At this great relief to my troubled heart, I ran out to play with my brother Harvey, to tell him how long we would be safe, if we should die, for father and grandfather said children that died before they were ten years old would go to heaven, and I would be safe almost two years, and he would be safe a good while longer (as he was two years and a half younger than myself).

Laura Smith Haviland was born December 20, 1808, in Kitley Township, Ontario, Canada. At seventeen she married Charles Haviland, Jr., a fellow Quaker with a similar concern for aiding humanity.

Laura and Charles moved to the Quaker settlement at Raisin Township, Michigan Territory. They co-founded the first anti-slavery society in the state and opened a small school at their farm. Their school, the River Raisin Institute, was open to all sexes and colors.

In 1845 Laura lost her husband, her parents, a sister and her youngest child to an erysipelas epidemic. She turned to anti-slavery work for solace after her terrible tragedy. For the next twenty years she aided Negroes in the North and the South. She rode the Underground Railroad to help slaves escape, gave speeches, and taught in Negro schools. During the Civil War she worked in army hospitals and prison camps.

Following the Civil War, Laura helped newly freed slaves resettle, mostly in Kansas. She also broadened her concerns to include underprivileged and orphaned children, temperance and woman suffrage.

Laura's writing is from her book, A Woman's Life—Work, *published in 1881.*

Laura Dewey Bridgman

A glorious Sunday

1864

... As Mr. H. took me by the hand crossing the pure water, I felt a thrill of crying for joy, though not one drop of a tear fell in sight from my eyes. I did not have any fear nor trouble in the least, because my trust and hope were in my Redeemer. My dear father and a gentleman aided me up out of the water, and I sat in the chair with the wet clothes, on utterance of another prayer, I went to church and the holy communion. It was a most glorious and pious Sunday, ever more for me to remember.

Laura Dewey Bridgman was born December 21, 1829, in Etna, New Hampshire. At the age of two she contracted scarlet fever; two of her sisters died, and she was left deaf and blind with her senses of taste and smell severely impaired. She received little attention and spent long hours alone, fondling her only toy, an old boot, as if it were a doll. Luckily she had one companion in Asa Tenny, a kind old handyman who communicated with her through a system of signs.

In 1837 Doctor Samuel Howe, of the Perkins Institution in Boston, read an article about Laura by a Dartmouth professor. He was interested in experimenting with teaching a deaf-blind pupil, to disprove the current theory that it was impossible. He brought her to Perkins just shy of her eighth birthday. He taught her the alphabet by touch, then labeled common objects with raised lettering which she was supposed to match up with the appropriate labels. She worked at this for weeks without comprehension until one day her "countenance lighted up with a human expression; it was no longer a dog, or parrot—it was an immortal spirit, eagerly seizing upon a new link of union with other spirits!"

Laura learned to read and write. Reports of her success spread across America and Europe, and people flocked to Perkins to stand behind a barrier to watch her work. At twenty-three she went home, but after so many years away she could not adjust. She returned to Perkins, where she remained her entire life. She paved the way for other handicapped people, making the world aware of an entire group who desperately needed assistance.

Laura's writing, describing her baptism when she was thirty-three, is from a letter she wrote to a friend, and is included in Life and Education of Laura Dewey Bridgman *by Mary Lamson, published in 1879.*

Ann Hasseltine Judson

1821

I was early taught by my mother the importance of abstaining from those vices, to which children are liable—as telling falsehoods, disobeying my parents, taking what was not my own, etc. She also taught me that if I were a good child, I should, at death, escape that dreadful hell, the thought of which sometimes filled me with alarm and terror. I, therefore, made it a matter of conscience to avoid the above-mentioned sins, to say my prayers night and morning, and to abstain from my usual play on the Sabbath, not doubting but that such a course of conduct would ensure my salvation.

Ann Hasseltine Judson was born December 22, 1789, in Bradford, Massachusetts. After several years of teaching school, she met Adoniram Judson when she was twenty-one. They were married on February 5, 1812, he was ordained as a Congregationalist minister the following day, and two weeks later they set sail for India to become missionaries.

   During the five-month voyage, Ann and Adoniram converted to the Baptist faith. This resulted in their separation from their sponsors, the American Board of Commissioners for Foreign Missions.

   The British East India Company was not receptive to the idea of establishing missions in its territory and ordered the Judsons deported to England. However, they managed to escape during the night and made their way via Mauritius to Burma. They settled in Rangoon, a squalid city of forty thousand, and began building their mission. The Burmese were such strong Buddhists that it was four years before they had their first conversion.

   In 1823 the Judsons relocated to Ava, capital of the Burmese empire, three hundred and fifty miles up the Irrawaddy River. After the British captured Rangoon in 1824, the Emperor suspected the American missionaries of being spies and threw Judson in prison. For two years, Ann and her infant daughter lived in a hovel near the prison. She constantly appealed, to no avail, for his release. Finally the Emperor freed him for use as an interpreter. Sadly, Ann died of tropical fever the following year at the age of thirty-six, and her daughter died shortly thereafter.

Ensuring salvation

Ann's writing is from Memoir of Ann H. Judson, Late Missionary to Burma, *by James Knowles, published in 1829.*

Harriet Monroe

A bitter moment

1937

As he advanced to greet me the shock was terrific—my romance collapsed like a house of cards. Not this man for me—this ghostly creature of the curved-in sloping shoulders, the body wasted and shrunken to the width of the molding behind him, and the voice, when he spoke, a thin unvarying dribble of sound, hardly more audible than a whisper. In that stark moment never a thought of his genius, his growing fame, his long heroic fight against disease, of the letters he had magnanimously written from his sickbed to a faraway foolish young girl, never a generous emotion of loving pity at finding my hero so ill; just the tragic shock of finality, of knowing that something beautiful was finished and gone.

For two years I had been informed, by the man himself and others, that he was an invalid; but I never really knew it until his bodily presence gave me this bitter moment of disillusion.

Harriet Monroe was born December 23, 1860, in Chicago. After graduating from the Visitation Convent School and joining the Chicago social scene, she befriended many authors and journalists, including, through a long-distance correspondence, Robert Louis Stevenson.

During the late 1880's Harriet and her sister Lucy spent several winters in New York attending the popular literary salons. In 1888 she published her first sonnet in *Century Magazine*, launching her career as a writer. She was asked by Chicago's city fathers to write a dedicatory cantata for its new auditorium. Three years later, the committee on ceremonies of the Chicago Columbian Exposition chose her to write a "Columbian Ode" for the dedication ceremonies.

Harriet's writing, describing her initial meeting with Robert Louis Stevenson, is from A Poet's Life, Seventy Years in a Changing World, *published in 1938.*

In 1911 Harriet decided to start a magazine for poets; the first issue of *Poetry: A Magazine of Verse* appeared in October, 1912. She edited the magazine for twenty-four years in addition to contributing poems to every issue. She died at seventy-six while climbing the Peruvian Highlands to visit the Inca Ruins at Cuzco. Her magazine continues in print to this day.

Elizabeth Margaret Chandler

1830

Too great a cause

. . . Your cause is a righteous one, and *worth every effort.* There are times when I feel as if I could go unflinching to the stake or the rack, if I might by that means advance it. I never expected to do 'great things' in this cause—I have never indulged in speculations as to the effect of what I attempted to do, yet I sometimes feel as if I had been a mere idle dreamer, as if I had wasted my time in nothingness—so disproportioned does the magnitude of the cause appear to all that I have done; so like a drop in the ocean are my puny efforts.

Elizabeth Margaret Chandler was born December 24, 1807, near Wilmington, Delaware. Her parents both died when she was a child, leaving her to be raised by Quaker relatives in Philadelphia. At the age of eighteen, she won a literary prize with a poem entitled "The Slave Ship" which caught the eye of the anti-slavery leader Benjamin Lundy. He asked her to write for his paper, the *Genius of Universal Emancipation*, which she did until her premature death in 1834.

Elizabeth's essays and poems covered a wide range of reform topics, but her major concern was the immediate abolition of slavery. Many of her poems were set to music and were performed regularly at anti-slavery meetings. In her essays she constantly encouraged women to think for themselves and stand beside men in the fight against slavery as "the only means of avoiding participation in guilt." She supported the free produce movement whereby women would refuse to buy goods produced by slave labor.

Elizabeth's writing is from a letter to her abolitionist friends. It is included in The Political Works of Elizabeth Margaret Chandler, *by Benjamin Lundy, published in 1836.*

Evangeline Cory Booth

1945

The message

As I speak, I think upon the day my mother died. She passed away in a little cottage by the sea.

It was stormy, and the waves, leaping high against the rugged rocks, were like the sorrow that struck our breaking hearts. . . .

Her eyes, shining with the brilliancy of stars to the

last, passed from one child to another, and then became fixed upon my father's face—that face which had been the one face of all the world to her.

It seems that she had had an understanding with my father, that if speech left her before death came, and if she realized that Christ was with her in the valley, she would wave her handkerchief to let her husband and her children know that all was well with her at the last.

Rallying her remaining strength, she raised it— up—up—up! Once—twice—thrice!

For all time that precious finger of my dying mother covered with the little white handkerchief, signalling the triumph of Grace in death—will mean more to my soul's faith than all the theological books and scientific arguments history has ever known.

Evangeline Cory Booth was born December 25, 1865, in London. Her father left the Methodist ministry soon after her birth to start an independent missionary organization. That organization became the Salvation Army.

The lives of the whole Booth family revolved around the Salvation Army. Seven of the eight children grew up to assume leadership positions. Evangeline had her first post at seventeen and quickly earned the nickname "White Angel of the Slums."

In 1904, following the death of her sister Emma, Evangeline took over her position as commander of the rapidly growing United States Salvation Army forces. Under her thirty-year leadership, the Army expanded its social service programs, emergency aid programs and evangelical efforts. Homes for young women working away from their families, called "Evangeline Residences," were opened in twelve major cities.

Evangeline became an American citizen in 1923. In 1934, however, she was elected General, which required her to move to the London headquarters. She retired after five years, the last of the Booth family to head the Salvation Army, and returned to her beloved home in Hartsdale, New York, where she died when she was eighty-five.

Evangeline's writing is from a speech she gave on Mother's Day, 1945. It is included in the Salvation Army National Archives and Research Center, New York City.

Emma D.E.N. Southworth

1872

It was on a dark, cold, rainy night, that a miserable old beggar woman sat crouching in a corner, near one end of London Bridge.

She drew her tattered red shawl closely over her head and shoulders, and cramped herself all up in a heap, to keep out of the way of passengers, and escape being ordered off by the policeman on duty there.

And so she sat and watched through the deep darkness and the driving rain.

And so she had sat through many a night and watched the one who never came, for one whom she longed, yet dreaded to see.

The weather was so dismal, the passengers so few, that there seemed but little chance for the fulfillment of her hope that night. But still she sat in the deep darkness, under the driving rain, and moaned and watched.

Emma Dorothy Eliza Nevitte Southworth was born December 26, 1819, in Washington, D.C. After graduating from her stepfather's academy, she taught school until her marriage to Frederick Southworth.

The Southworths settled in Wisconsin, where Emma resumed teaching and had one son. In 1844, pregnant with her second child, she separated from her husband and returned home. She never discussed her unhappy marriage, but abandoned and mistreated wives were to be a recurring theme in her novels.

Emma's salary of $250 a year as a teacher was not enough to support her family, so she turned to writing. Her first story, published in 1846 in the *Baltimore Sun Visitor*, caught the eye of the editor of Washington's *National Era*. He bought several of her stories and published her first book in 1849 which was very well-received. From then on Emma was able to give up teaching for a full-time writing career.

Emma began her association with Robert Bonner and the *New York Ledger* in 1857. Over the next thirty years, he published thirty of her novels in serial form in his magazine. She often wrote three novels per year, working from morning to midnight. Mrs. E.D.E.N. Southworth became the most popular of all the sentimental American novelists of her day.

A wretched scene

Emma's writing is from her novel, The Lost Heir of Linlithgow, *published in 1872.*

Adèle Cutts Douglas

A little embroidery

Chicago
August 7th 1857
My dearest Mother

I cannot tell you how sadly I felt at parting with Madison—although I know it must be a great pleasure to you to have him with you again. He leaves Monday and I shall feel quite deserted here although I am becoming more reconciled to Chicago. I shall be with you very soon meantime, I leave it with you to choose my carpets of any colour you like best. I should like green and pink in my bed chamber . . . anything you can do in my new house that you think is needed pray do or have done for me dear Mamma. Also dearest Mother have me four pairs of linen sheets made and 6 pairs of handsome pillow cases—I would like them a little embroidered—they do them quite nicely at the benevolent Society on 7th Street. I have only a moment to write as we decided to go this morning. . . . I hope to write you some pleasant descriptions of Minnesota with love from all to you dearest parents.

I am again yours
Addie

Adèle Cutts Douglas was born December 27, 1835 in Washington, D.C. She spent much of her girlhood with her great-aunt Dolly Madison [May 20] and grew up to be a popular Washington society belle, as Dolley had been in her day.

Adèle met Stephen A. Douglas in 1855, just after he had lost the Democratic presidential nomination to James Buchanan. They were married that year, and she assumed her role as hostess in his mansion and stepmother to his two sons.

Adèle was a great comfort to her husband and travelled with him on his frequent political trips. She accompanied him to Illinois to debate Lincoln and through the South in 1860 to warn against secession. She nursed him through his final illness, which took his life the following year.

After several years in seclusion, Adèle married Captain, later General, Robert Williams and spent the next twenty years on remote western army posts raising their six children.

Adèle's letter to her mother is in the Adèle Cutts Douglas Papers Illinois State Historical Library, Springfield, Illinois.

Julia Newberry

Baden Baden, Germany
August, 1871

A rapturous evening

. . . That evening there was to be a ball, and Strauss the magnificent was to lead his own waltzes. The Americans here do not dance at the balls, so we went merely as spectators. We were early and found good seats. . . . When Strauss led it was perfectly magnificent. He inspires the band to such a degree that they play as if under enchantment. . . . We got so excited that Mamie and I nearly screamed and she kept squeezing my hand and "oh Julia it is too beautiful, I must dance, I can't keep still." Even Sister who is so cold-blooded and never gets wrought up by anything of the kind was wildly excited and when the cotillion began and he led the first waltz I thought we should go crazy. I never, never heard anything so beautiful. . . . We went home in a rapturous state after a never-to-be-forgotten evening and my brain played waltz after waltz all night long.

Julia Newberry was born December 28, 1853, in Chicago, Illinois. Her parents were wealthy and influential.

The family travelled frequently to Europe. During one of these trips in October, 1871, they lost their home and all their possessions in the Great Chicago Fire.

Unfortunately both Julia and her sister suffered from fragile health. Mary Louisa died in 1874 and Julia died in Rome two years later at the age of twenty-three.

Julia's diary was discovered in a trunk in 1930 by a distant cousin. It was published in 1933 as Julia Newberry's Diary.

Kate Tannatt Woods

1886

*B*oyhood

Yet she had never, even in her worst imaginings, thought of Dick as running away. She had always connected that with vicious boys and those whose heads were full of something called "trash," written for their snare and delusion.

Now for the first time in her life she was brought

Kate's writing is from That Dreadful Boy—An American Novel, *published in 1886.*

face to face with a new fact, and made to realize that the restless activity of boyhood sometimes seeks outlets un-looked-for by the most cautious parents.

Kate Tannatt Woods was born December 29, 1838, in Peek-skill-on-the-Hudson, New York.

As a teenager Kate began teaching school; often she was the same age or younger than her pupils. While on an extended trip to New York City she met and married George Woods, a lawyer from Minneapolis. She returned with him to his home and began writing poetry and short stories at that time.

George organized the First Minnesota Regiment at the outbreak of the Civil War. Kate, plus two toddlers, followed him to the front, where she became a friend and nurse to the soldiers. George was seriously wounded and suffered from his injuries the rest of his life.

Following her husband's death, Kate returned to his parents' home in Salem, Massachusetts, where she took care of the aged couple in addition to raising her own children. She also found time to pursue her writing career in earnest, publishing one novel a year and contributing poems and stories to magazines. She wrote children's books under the name "Kate True," and became an editor of the *Ladies' Home Journal*.

DECEMBER 30   *Agnes Irwin*

A cherished gift

Radcliffe College
Cambridge, Mass.
October 20th, 1894
My Dear Girls:

. . . It is not possible that the years to come can ever bring me ties so strong as those to you have been. But you have made it easy for me to link the old life to the new, in the way which of all others I should have chosen. What I could not do, you have done for me, and, in my name, for others. The thought sweetens the past and brightens the future for me; and long after I am gone, this generous gift of yours for my sake will "live and act and serve the future hour." I never hoped for such a thing as this; and when I think it has come to me, and come to me through you, I cannot thank you enough; indeed, I cannot thank you at all; I can only

Agnes' letter, written to her former students who had started a scholarship in her name, is included in Miss Irwin's of Philadelphia—A History of the Agnes Irwin School *by Joanne Noel, published in 1969.*

love you, and bless you, and pray for you that God may bless you.

Your friend and teacher,
Agnes Irwin

Agnes Irwin was born December 30, 1841, in Washington, D.C. Her father was a Whig lawyer active in politics, and on her mother's side she was Benjamin Franklin's great-great-granddaughter. In addition to her studies abroad and at a local girls' academy, she read constantly.

In 1862 Agnes began teaching at a private school in New York City. Seven years later she was asked to assume the principalship of the Penn Square Seminary of Philadelphia when its two principals drowned in a boating accident. She remained at the Agnes Irwin School, as it was then called, for the next twenty-five years.

Harvard University began the "Harvard Annex" in 1879 to offer educational opportunities to women. In 1894 it received its charter as Radcliffe College, and Elizabeth Agassiz was made the first president. She soon realized there were too many duties for one person, and a dean was needed. Agnes' name was suggested to the Radcliffe Council and was enthusiastically approved by Mrs. Agassiz and Charles Eliot, president of Harvard. She accepted the appointment in 1894, spent the summer in England studying management techniques at the women's colleges affiliated with Cambridge University, and returned in the fall to assume her new responsibilities.

During her tenure at Radcliffe, Agnes increased the number of courses, initiated a graduate program, and built four dormitories, a gymnasium and a library. She retired in 1909 and died five years later at the age of seventy-two.

Maria Elizabeth Clapp

1857

A brave spirit

The last few weeks, I have been confined to my room with severe illness, unable to see anyone. Now I am slowly recovering and find myself at times almost impatient to be engaged in the active duties of life. Not that I am weary of the sickroom; far from it. I have received every attention—every kindness from earth and heaven. Scarcely a day without some little love-offering from human friends, and not a day without good and perfect gifts from the Father of lights. . . .

And then, too, what a precious time for thought! The past, the present and the future all pass before the mind.

Maria's writing is from the journal she kept for over twenty years. This entry was written a few weeks before she died. Her pastor, Chandler Robbins, D.D., minister of the Second Church in Boston, published her journal in 1859 under the title Portrait of a Christian Life, Drawn from Life: A Memoir of Maria Elizabeth Clapp.

Maria Elizabeth Clapp was born December 31, 1820, in New London, Connecticut. When she was sixteen, her family moved to Boston where she taught school until her death in 1856. She never married, but gave her life instead to her religion and her students.

Maria taught two Sunday school classes in addition to her regular teaching. What leisure time she had she spent visiting the poor and the sick. Her last words, whispered to her father, were "Engrave on my tombstone 'Asleep in Jesus.'" She was buried in Mount Auburn Cemetery, Cambridge, Massachusetts.

Picture credits

Emily Balch	JANUARY 8	Wellesley College Archives
Kate Waller Barrett	JANUARY 24	Schlesinger Library, Radcliffe College
Katharine Lee Bates	AUGUST 12	Wellesley College Archives
Martha McChesney Berry	OCTOBER 7	Library of Congress
Alice Stone Blackwell	SEPTEMBER 14	Library of Congress
Susan Elizabeth Blow	JUNE 7	Missouri Historical Society
Evangeline Cory Booth	DECEMBER 25	Salvation Army National Archives and Research Center
Belle Boyd	MAY 9	Library of Congress
Laura Dewey Bridgman	DECEMBER 21	Richard & Kellie Gutman Collection
Hallie Quinn Brown	MARCH 10	Hallie Q. Brown Memorial Library, Central State University, Wilberforce, OH
Mary Edwards Bryan	MAY 17	Library of Congress
Annie Jump Cannon	DECEMBER 11	Schlesinger Library
Hattie Wyatt Caraway	FEBRUARY 1	Library of Congress
Carrie Chapman Catt	JANUARY 9	Library of Congress
Ednah Dow Cheney	JUNE 27	Sophia Smith Collection, Smith College
Kate Claxton	AUGUST 24	Harvard Theater Collection
Virginia Clay-Clopton	JANUARY 16	Schlesinger Library
Maggie Cline	JANUARY 1	Harvard Theater Collection
Clara Bewick Colby	AUGUST 5	Schlesinger Library
Frances Jane Crosby	MARCH 24	Library of Congress
Charlotte Cushman	JULY 23	Library of Congress
Caroline Healey Dall	JUNE 22	Library of Congress
Katharine Bement Davis	JANUARY 15	Library of Congress
Mary Fenn Davis	JULY 17	Library of Congress
Jane Arminda Delano	MARCH 12	Library of Congress
Adèle Cutts Douglas	DECEMBER 27	Schlesinger Library
Louisa Lane Drew	JANUARY 10	Harvard Theater Collection
Abigail Scott Duniway	OCTOBER 22	Library of Congress
Margaret O'Neale Eaton	DECEMBER 3	Schlesinger Library
Fannie Merritt Farmer	MARCH 23	Schlesinger Library
Martha Farnsworth	APRIL 26	Kansas State Historical Society
Alice Cunningham Fletcher	MARCH 15	Smithsonian Institution
Lucretia Garfield	APRIL 19	Sophia Smith Collection
Anne Gilbert	OCTOBER 21	Harvard Theater Collection
Isabella Marshall Graham	JULY 29	Schlesinger Library
Hetty Green	NOVEMBER 21	Sophia Smith Collection
Sarah Moore Grimké	NOVEMBER 26	Library of Congress
Esther Belle Hanna	JUNE 24	Pacific University
Anna Symmes Harrison	JULY 25	Library of Congress
Constance Cary Harrison	APRIL 25	Library of Congress
Esther Hill Hawks	AUGUST 4	Library of Congress
Grace Raymond Hebard	JULY 2	Wyoming State Archives, Museum and Historical Department

Ellen Martin Henrotin	JULY 6	Library of Congress
Caroline Lee Hentz	JUNE 1	Library of Congress
Hannah Worcester Hicks	JANUARY 29	McFarlin Library, University of Tulsa
Jessie Donaldson Hodder	MARCH 30	Schlesinger Library
Marietta Holley	JULY 16	Schlesinger Library
Isabella Beecher Hooker	FEBRUARY 22	Schlesinger Library
Harriet Goodhue Hosmer	OCTOBER 9	Schlesinger Library
Francesca Janauschek	JULY 20	Harvard Theater Collection
Adelia Smith Johnson	APRIL 20	Eunice K. Halfman, Gilford, NH
Mary Harris Jones (Mother Jones)	MAY 1	Library of Congress
Matilda Sissieretta Jones	JANUARY 5	Harvard Theater Collection
Laura Fish Judd	APRIL 2	Hawaiian Mission Children's Society
Ann Hasseltine Judson	DECEMBER 22	Library of Congress
Caroline Matilda Kirkland	JANUARY 11	Library of Congress
Belle Case LaFollette	APRIL 21	Library of Congress
Octavia Walton Le Vert	AUGUST 11	Georgia Department of Archives and History
Ida Lewis	FEBRUARY 25	Rhode Island Historical Society
Mary Todd Lincoln	DECEMBER 13	Library of Congress
Mary S. Logan	AUGUST 15	Library of Congress
Olive Logan	APRIL 22	Harvard Theater Collection
Fanny Appleton Longfellow	OCTOBER 6	National Park Service, Longfellow National Historic Site, Cambridge, MA
Dorothea Payne Madison	MAY 20	Library of Congress
Julia Marlowe	AUGUST 27	Library of Congress
Mary Eliza McDowell	NOVEMBER 30	Library of Congress
Martha Bishop Moore	OCTOBER 18	Missouri Historical Society
Lucretia Coffin Mott	JANUARY 3	Sophia Smith Collection
Carry Amelia Nation	NOVEMBER 25	Library of Congress
Harriet Newell	OCTOBER 10	Trustees of the Haverhill Public Library, Haverhill, MA
Clarina Nichols	JANUARY 25	Library of Congress
Bethenia Angelina Owens-Adair	FEBRUARY 7	Oregon Historical Society
Alice Freeman Palmer	FEBRUARY 21	Wellesley College Archives
Emily Elizabeth Parsons	MARCH 8	Mount Auburn Hospital, Cambridge, MA
Sara Parton	JULY 9	Library of Congress
Maria Chamberlain Patton	MARCH 19	Hawaiian Mission Children's Society
Josephine Preston Peabody	MAY 30	Wellesley College Archives
Adelaide Phillipps	OCTOBER 26	Harvard Theater Collection
Lydia Estes Pinkham	FEBRUARY 9	Schlesinger Library
Sarah Childress Polk	SEPTEMBER 4	Library of Congress
Martha Jefferson Randolph	SEPTEMBER 27	Library of Congress
Agnes Repplier	APRIL 1	Schlesinger Library

Laura Elizabeth Richards	FEBRUARY 27	Friends of Gardiner's Heritage, Gardiner, ME
Linda Richards	JULY 27	Schlesinger Library
Ernestine Rose	JANUARY 13	Schlesinger Library
Louise Khiele Scovel	AUGUST 31	Carl Scovel, Boston, MA
Elizabeth Cady Stanton	NOVEMBER 12	Sophia Smith Collection
Belle Starr	FEBRUARY 5	The Thomas Gilcrease Institute of American History & Art, Tulsa, OK
Lucy Stone	AUGUST 13	Sophia Smith Collection
Harriet Beecher Stowe	JUNE 14	Library of Congress
Helen Herron Taft	JUNE 2	Library of Congress
Celia Thaxter	JUNE 29	Library of Congress
Martha Carey Thomas	JANUARY 2	Schlesinger Library
Lucy Goodale Thurston	OCTOBER 29	Hawaiian Mission Children's Society
Christiana Holmes Tillson	MARCH 13	Historical Society of Quincy & Adams County, Quincy, IL
Mary Martha Truman	JANUARY 6	Harry S. Truman Library, Independence, MO
Mary Richardson Walker	APRIL 11	H.E. Huntington Library and Art Gallery, San Marino, CA
Henrietta Woodford	AUGUST 29	Kansas State Historical Society

All other photographs are reproduced from books in the public domain.

Reference collections

Grateful acknowledgment is made to the following museums, libraries, historical societies and individuals for courtesy in granting access to their collections:

American Antiquarian Society	Worcester, MA
Center Sandwich Historical Society	Center Sandwich, NH
Chicago Historical Society	Chicago, IL
Connecticut Historical Society	New Haven, CT
Historical Society of Pennsylvania	Philadelphia, PA
Historical Society of York County	York, PA
Illinois State Historical Library	Springfield, IL
Indiana Historical Society	Indianapolis, IN
Kansas State Historical Society	Topeka, KS
Maine Historical Society	Portland, ME
Maryland Historical Society	Baltimore, MD
Nebraska State Historical Society	Lincoln, NE
Minnesota Historical Society	St. Paul, MN
Nantucket Historical Association	Nantucket, MA
Missouri Historical Society	St. Louis, MO

Oregon Historical Society	Portland, OR
South Carolina Historical Library	Charleston, SC
Utah State Historical Society	Salt Lake City, UT
Wyoming State Archives, Museums and Historical Dept.	Cheyenne, WY
National Park Service, Longfellow National Historical Site	Cambridge, MA
Rutherford B. Hayes Presidential Center	Fremont, OH
Harry S. Truman Library	Independence, MO
The Library of Congress	Washington, DC
The Salvation Army National Archives and Research Center	New York, NY
Thomas Gilcrease Institute of American History and Art	Tulsa, OK
Franklin D. Roosevelt Library	Hyde Park, NY
Eugene V. Debs Foundation	Terre Haute, IN
Maine Maritime Museum	Bath, ME
Record of Indian Bureau, National Archives	Washington, DC
Smithsonian Institute, Archives of American Art	Washington, DC
Hallie Quinn Brown Memorial Library	Wilberforce, OH
Hawaiian Mission Children's Society	Honolulu, HI
New York Public Library	New York, NY
Friends Historical Library	Swarthmore, PA
Tennessee State Library and Archives	Nashville, TN
The Boston Athenaeum	Boston, MA
Houghton Library, Harvard University	Cambridge, MA
Schlesinger Library, Radcliffe College	Cambridge, MA
Special Collections, Colby College Library	Waterville, ME
Shain Library, Connecticut College	New London, CT
Wellesley College Archives	Wellesley, MA
Southern Historical Collection, University of North Carolina Library	Chapel Hill, NC
General Library, University of California	Riverside, CA
State College of Washington	Seattle, WA
Harvard Theater Collection	Cambridge, MA
Cornell University Library, Dept. of Manuscripts	Ithaca, NY
Huntington Library	San Marino, CA
Sophia Smith Collection, Smith College	Northampton, MA
Lilly Library, Indiana University	Bloomington, IN
St. Francis de Sales Library, Academy of the Visitation	St. Louis, MO
Millbank Memorial Library, Teachers' College, Columbia University	New York, NY
Baker Texas History Center, The University of Texas at Austin	Austin, TX
David Duniway	Salem, OR
Thomas Miller	Indianapolis, IN
Rev. Carl Scovel	Boston, MA
Verna Payer	Old Mystic, CT
Ann Jeffris Miller	Evergreen, CO
William S. Edgerly	Cambridge, MA
Harriet Moore	Corvallis, OR
Pacific University	Forest Grove, OR

Index

380

Harriet Talcott Buckingham	MARCH 31
Frances Hodgson Burnett	NOVEMBER 24
Theodosia Burr	JUNE 21
Alice Craven Caborn	JANUARY 28
Elizabeth Dwight Cabot	FEBRUARY 13
Annie Jump Cannon	DECEMBER 11
Hattie Wyatt Caraway	FEBRUARY 1
Louise Whitfield Carnegie	MARCH 7
Mary Lovell Carpenter	AUGUST 21
Mary Cassatt	MAY 22
Carrie Chapman Catt	JANUARY 9
Elizabeth Buffum Chace	DECEMBER 9
Elizabeth Margaret Chandler	DECEMBER 24
Ednah Dow Cheney	JUNE 27
Lydia Maria Child	FEBRUARY 11
Maria Elizabeth Clapp	DECEMBER 31
Kate Claxton	AUGUST 24
Mary Barr Clay	OCTOBER 13
Virginia Clay-Clopton	JANUARY 16
Sarah Norcliffe Cleghorn	FEBRUARY 4
Jane Lampton Clemens	JUNE 18
Maggie Cline	JANUARY 1
Florence Nicholson Coates	JULY 1
Rose Coghlan	MARCH 18
Clara Bewick Colby	AUGUST 5
Elizabeth Leslie Comstock	OCTOBER 30
Charlotte Howard Conant	FEBRUARY 3
Susan Fenimore Cooper	APRIL 17
Juliet Corson	JANUARY 14
Phoebe Wilson Couzins	SEPTEMBER 8
Lotta Crabtree	NOVEMBER 7
Mabel Cratty	JUNE 30
Frances Jane Crosby	MARCH 24
Clara Crowninshield	FEBRUARY 8
Charlotte Cushman	JULY 23
Madeleine Vinton Dahlgren	JULY 13
Caroline Healey Dall	JUNE 22
Maria Lydig Daly	SEPTEMBER 12
Margaret Miller Davidson	MARCH 26
Katharine Bement Davis	JANUARY 15
Mary Fenn Davis	JULY 17
Mollie Moore Davis	APRIL 12
Varina Howell Davis	MAY 7
Anna Laurens Dawes	MAY 14
Jane Arminda Delano	MARCH 12
Mary Andrews Denison	MAY 26
Mary Florence Denton	JULY 4
Alice Chipman Dewey	SEPTEMBER 7

Anna Elizabeth Dickinson	OCTOBER 28
Emily Dickinson	DECEMBER 10
Susan Dimock	APRIL 24
Dorothea Dix	APRIL 4
Rheta Childe Dorr	NOVEMBER 2
Adèle Cutts Douglas	DECEMBER 27
Amanda Douglas	JULY 14
Louisa Lane Drew	JANUARY 10
Alice Dunbar-Nelson	JULY 19
Abigail Scott Duniway	OCTOBER 22
Alice Morse Earle	APRIL 27
Margaret O'Neale Eaton	DECEMBER 3
Lucretia Epperson	NOVEMBER 28
Priscilla Merriman Evans	MAY 4
Anne Gorham Everett	MARCH 3
Fannie Merritt Farmer	MARCH 23
Eliza Burhans Farnham	NOVEMBER 17
Martha Farnsworth	APRIL 26
Eliza Rotch Farrar	JULY 12
Rebecca Latimer Felton	JUNE 10
Kate Field	OCTOBER 1
Annie Fields	JUNE 6
Alice Cunningham Fletcher	MARCH 15
Hannah Webster Foster	SEPTEMBER 10
Lydia W. Foster	OCTOBER 14
Jessie Benton Frémont	MAY 31
Margaret Fuller	MAY 23
Matilda Joslyn Gage	MARCH 25
Helen Hamilton Gardener	JANUARY 21
Lucretia Garfield	APRIL 19
Mary Smith Garrett	JUNE 20
Abby Hooper Gibbons	DECEMBER 7
Anne Gilbert	OCTOBER 21
Linda Gilbert	MAY 13
Jeannette Leonard Gilder	OCTOBER 3
Caroline Gilman	OCTOBER 8
Charlotte Perkins Gilman	JULY 3
Mary Willcox Glenn	DECEMBER 14
Anne Wilson Goldthwaite	JUNE 28
Lizzie Wilson Goodenough	NOVEMBER 19
Helen Mar Gougar	JULY 18
Isabella Marshall Graham	JULY 29
Julia Dent Grant	JANUARY 26
Hetty Green	NOVEMBER 21
Mary Greenleaf	JANUARY 31
Josephine White Griffing	DECEMBER 18
Charlotte Forten Grimké	AUGUST 17
Sarah Moore Grimké	NOVEMBER 26

Frances Smith Griswold	APRIL 28
Louise Guiney	JANUARY 7
Alice Gordon Gulick	AUGUST 8
Eliza Gurney	APRIL 6
Lucretia Peabody Hale	SEPTEMBER 2
Sarah Josepha Hale	OCTOBER 24
Susan Hale	DECEMBER 5
Elizabeth Schuyler Hamilton	AUGUST 9
Esther Belle Hanna	JUNE 24
Mary Hanson	SEPTEMBER 11
Lizzie Boynton Harbert	APRIL 15
Mother Mary Aloysia Hardey	DECEMBER 8
Ida Husted Harper	FEBRUARY 18
Anna Symmes Harrison	JULY 25
Constance Cary Harrison	APRIL 25
Mary Dimmick Harrison	APRIL 30
Laura S. Haviland	DECEMBER 20
Harriet Boyd Hawes	OCTOBER 11
Esther Hill Hawks	AUGUST 4
Sophia Peabody Hawthorne	SEPTEMBER 21
Lucy Webb Hayes	AUGUST 28
Grace Raymond Hebard	JULY 2
Ellen Martin Henrotin	JULY 6
Caroline Lee Hentz	JUNE 1
Sallie Hester	OCTOBER 31
Hannah Worcester Hicks	JANUARY 29
Grace Livingston Hill	APRIL 16
Harriet Low Hillard	MAY 18
Elizabeth Christophers Hobson	NOVEMBER 22
Jessie Donaldson Hodder	MARCH 30
Marietta Holley	JULY 16
Mary Austin Holley	AUGUST 30
Sallie Holley	FEBRUARY 17
Leta Stetter Hollingworth	MAY 25
Julia Archibald Holmes	FEBRUARY 15
Mary Jane Holmes	APRIL 5
Isabella Beecher Hooker	FEBRUARY 22
Jessie Jack Hooper	NOVEMBER 8
Harriet Goodhue Hosmer	OCTOBER 9
Anna Cogdell Howell	OCTOBER 23
Emily Howland	NOVEMBER 20
Mary Louisa Hulbert	FEBRUARY 24
Mary Hanchett Hunt	JUNE 4
Susan Mansfield Huntington	JANUARY 27
Addie Hunton	JUNE 11
Agnes Irwin	DECEMBER 30
Helen Hunt Jackson	OCTOBER 15
Alice James	AUGUST 7

Francesca Janauschek	JULY 20
Anna Thomas Jeanes	APRIL 7
Grace Mouat Jeffris	JUNE 12
Sarah Orne Jewett	SEPTEMBER 3
Adelia Smith Johnson	APRIL 20
Helen Kendrick Johnson	JANUARY 4
Annie Fellows Johnston	MAY 15
Amanda Theodosia Jones	OCTOBER 19
Mary Harris Jones (Mother Jones)	MAY 1
Matilda Sissieretta Jones	JANUARY 5
Laura Fish Judd	APRIL 2
Ann Hasseltine Judson	DECEMBER 22
Emily Chubbuck Judson	AUGUST 22
Florence Finch Kelly	MARCH 27
Carrie Burnham Kilgore	JANUARY 20
Louisa Yeomans King	OCTOBER 17
Ellen Olney Kirk	NOVEMBER 6
Caroline Matilda Kirkland	JANUARY 11
Edith Stratton Kitt	DECEMBER 15
Margaret Knight	FEBRUARY 14
Helen Mary Knowlton	AUGUST 16
Rose Knox	NOVEMBER 18
Belle Case LaFollette	APRIL 21
Lucy Larcom	MAY 5
Elizabeth Wormeley Latimer	JULY 26
Emma Lazarus	JULY 22
Octavia Walton Le Vert	AUGUST 11
Eliza Leslie	NOVEMBER 15
Miriam Folline Leslie	JUNE 5
Ida Lewis	FEBRUARY 25
Laura Jean Libbey	MARCH 22
Mary Elizabeth Lightner	APRIL 9
Mary Todd Lincoln	DECEMBER 13
Sara Clarke Lippincott	SEPTEMBER 23
Harriet Livermore	APRIL 14
Mary Ashton Livermore	DECEMBER 19
Mary S. Logan	AUGUST 15
Olive Logan	APRIL 22
Fanny Appleton Longfellow	OCTOBER 6
Alice Higgins Lothrop	MARCH 28
Josephine Shaw Lowell	DECEMBER 16
Maria White Lowell	JULY 8
Margaret Lynn	SEPTEMBER 22
Mary Lyon	FEBRUARY 28
Mary MacLean	MAY 2
Dorothea Payne Madison	MAY 20
Susan Shelby Magoffin	JULY 30
Mary Peabody Mann	NOVEMBER 16

Marie Manning	JANUARY 22
Elizabeth Marbury	JUNE 19
Julia Marlowe	AUGUST 27
Mary Adams Maverick	MARCH 16
Mary McLeod Maybee	MARCH 20
Sarah Edgarton Mayo	MARCH 17
Anne Elizabeth McDowell	JUNE 23
Mary Eliza McDowell	NOVEMBER 30
Anita Newcomb McGee	NOVEMBER 4
Adah Isaacs Menken	JUNE 15
Elizabeth Meriwether	JANUARY 19
Eliza Merrill	JUNE 3
Ynez Mexia	MAY 24
Elizabeth Carr Miller	FEBRUARY 20
Elizabeth Smith Miller	SEPTEMBER 20
Olive Thorne Miller	JUNE 25
Myrtilla Miner	MARCH 4
Maria Mitchell	AUGUST 1
Helena Modjeska	OCTOBER 12
Penina Moïse	APRIL 23
Harriet Monroe	DECEMBER 23
Martha Bishop Moore	OCTOBER 18
Mary Mortimer	DECEMBER 2
Belle Moskowitz	OCTOBER 5
Lucretia Coffin Mott	JANUARY 3
Louise Chandler Moulton	APRIL 10
Sara Maria Mousley	JULY 21
Anna Mowatt	MARCH 5
Maud Nathan	OCTOBER 20
Carry Amelia Nation	NOVEMBER 25
Lizzie Scott Neblett	JANUARY 17
Julia Newberry	DECEMBER 28
Fanny Butterfield Newell	MAY 12
Harriet Newell	OCTOBER 10
Clarina Nichols	JANUARY 25
Eliza Jane Nicholson (Pearl Rivers)	MARCH 11
Lillian Nordica	DECEMBER 12
Mary Adelaide Nutting	NOVEMBER 1
Leonora O'Reilly	FEBRUARY 16
Bethenia Angelina Owens-Adair	FEBRUARY 7
Alice Freeman Palmer	FEBRUARY 21
Emelie Swett Parkhurst	MARCH 9
Maria Parloa	SEPTEMBER 25
Elsie Clews Parsons	NOVEMBER 27
Emily Elizabeth Parsons	MARCH 8
Sara Parton	JULY 9
Adelina Patti	FEBRUARY 10
Maria Chamberlain Patton	MARCH 19

Elizabeth Palmer Peabody	MAY 16
Josephine Preston Peabody	MAY 30
Phoebe Yates Pember	AUGUST 18
Arozina Perkins	MARCH 21
Almira Lincoln Phelps	JULY 15
Mary Phenix	JANUARY 12
Adelaide Phillipps	OCTOBER 26
Susan La Flesche Picotte	JUNE 17
Sarah Pierce	JUNE 26
Lydia Estes Pinkham	FEBRUARY 9
Sarah Childress Polk	SEPTEMBER 4
Maria Louise Pool	AUGUST 20
Elizabeth Allston Pringle	MAY 29
Sara Agnes Pryor	FEBRUARY 19
Alice Whiting Putnam	JANUARY 18
Martha Jefferson Randolph	SEPTEMBER 27
Agnes Repplier	APRIL 1
Laura Elizabeth Richards	FEBRUARY 27
Linda Richards	JULY 27
Mary Ringo	NOVEMBER 13
Sarah Alden Ripley	JULY 31
Amélie Louise Rives	AUGUST 23
Hannah Chandler Ropes	JUNE 13
Ernestine Rose	JANUARY 13
Sarah Royce	MARCH 2
Mary Baptist Russell	APRIL 18
Cordelia Lewis Scales	JULY 10
Julie Schramm	SEPTEMBER 26
Louise Khiele Scovel	AUGUST 31
Mary Elizabeth Wilson Sherwood	OCTOBER 27
Amanda Berry Smith	JANUARY 23
Ann Bryant Smith	AUGUST 25
Luella Dowd Smith	JUNE 16
Emma D.E.N. Southworth	DECEMBER 26
Frances Campbell Sparhawk	JULY 28
Harriet Prescott Spofford	APRIL 3
Elizabeth Cady Stanton	NOVEMBER 12
Phoebe Stanton	MAY 11
Belle Starr	FEBRUARY 5
Florine Stettheimer	AUGUST 19
Cora Frances Stoddard	SEPTEMBER 17
Lucinda Hinsdale Stone	SEPTEMBER 30
Lucy Stone	AUGUST 13
Harriet Beecher Stowe	JUNE 14
Jane Grey Swisshelm	DECEMBER 6
Helen Herron Taft	JUNE 2
Susie King Taylor	AUGUST 6
Celia Thaxter	JUNE 29

Martha Carey Thomas	JANUARY 2
Lucy Goodale Thurston	OCTOBER 29
Christiana Holmes Tillson	MARCH 13
Mabel Loomis Todd	NOVEMBER 10
Mary Martha Truman	JANUARY 6
Mary Palmer Tyler	MARCH 1
Marie Louise Van Vorst	NOVEMBER 23
Catherine Waite	JANUARY 30
Mary Richardson Walker	APRIL 11
Annie Wall	SEPTEMBER 19
Mary Pickard Ware	OCTOBER 2
Susan Bogert Warner	JULY 11
Anna Webber	SEPTEMBER 16
Jean Webster	JULY 24
Charlotte Fowler Wells	AUGUST 14
Lilian Welsh	MARCH 6
Eliza Orne White	AUGUST 2
Narcissa Whitman	MARCH 14
Ella Wheeler Wilcox	NOVEMBER 5
Caroline White Willard	MAY 3
Emma Hart Willard	FEBRUARY 23
Frances Elizabeth Willard	SEPTEMBER 28
Lucia Loraine Williams	APRIL 29
Augusta Evans Wilson	MAY 8
Helen Maria Winslow	APRIL 13
Annie Wittenmyer	AUGUST 26
Henrietta Woodford	AUGUST 29
Kate Tannatt Woods	DECEMBER 29
Ann Eliza Young	SEPTEMBER 13
Julia Ditto Young	DECEMBER 4